Who Believes in Human Rights?
Reflections on the European Convention

Many people believe passionately in human rights. Others – Bentham, Marx, cultural relativists and some feminists amongst them – dismiss the concept of human rights as practically and conceptually inadequate. This book reviews these classical critiques and shows how their insights are reflected in the case law of the European Court of Human Rights. At one level an original, accessible and insightful legal commentary on the European Convention, this book is also a ground-breaking work of theory which challenges human rights orthodoxy. Its novel identification of four human rights schools proposes that we alternatively conceive of these rights as given (natural school), agreed upon (deliberative school), fought for (protest school) and talked about (discourse school). Which of these concepts we adopt is determined by particular ways in which we believe, or do not believe, in human rights.

MARIE-BÉNÉDICTE DEMBOUR is Senior Lecturer in Law at the Sussex Law School, University of Sussex.

The Law in Context Series

Editors: William Twining (University College London) and Christopher McCrudden (Lincoln College, Oxford)

Since 1970 the Law in Context series has been in the forefront of the movement to broaden the study of law. It has been a vehicle for the publication of innovative scholarly books that treat law and legal phenomena critically in their social, political and economic contexts from a variety of perspectives. The series particularly aims to publish scholarly legal writing that brings fresh perspectives to bear on new and existing areas of law taught in universities. A contextual approach involves treating legal subjects broadly, using materials from other social sciences, and from any other discipline that helps to explain the operation in practice of the subject under discussion. It is hoped that this orientation is at once more stimulating and more realistic than the bare exposition of legal rules. The series includes original books that have a different emphasis from traditional legal textbooks, while maintaining the same high standards of scholarship. They are written primarily for undergraduate and graduate students of law and of other disciplines, but most also appeal to a wider readership. In the past, most books in the series have focused on English law, but recent publications include books on European law, globalisation, transnational legal processes, and comparative law.

Books in the Series
Anderson, Schum & Twining: *Analysis of Evidence*
Ashworth: *Sentencing and Criminal Justice*
Barton & Douglas: *Law and Parenthood*
Beecher-Monas: *Evaluating Scientific Evidence: An Interdisciplinary Framework for Intellectual Due Process*
Bell: *French Legal Cultures*
Bercusson: *European Labour Law*
Birkinshaw: *European Public Law*
Birkinshaw: *Freedom of Information: The Law, the Practice and the Ideal*
Cane: *Atiyah's Accidents, Compensation and the Law*
Clarke & Kohler: *Property Law: Commentary and Materials*
Collins: *The Law of Contract*
Davies: *Perspectives on Labour Law*
Dembour: *Who Believes in Human Rights?: The European Convention in Question*
de Sousa Santos: *Toward a New Legal Common Sense*
Diduck: *Law's Families*
Elworthy & Holder: *Environmental Protection: Text and Materials*
Fortin: *Children's Rights and the Developing Law*
Glover-Thomas: *Reconstructing Mental Health Law and Policy*
Gobert & Punch: *Rethinking Corporate Crime*
Harlow & Rawlings: *Law and Administration: Text and Materials*
Harris: *An Introduction to Law*
Harris, Campbell & Halson: *Remedies in Contract and Tort*
Harvey: *Seeking Asylum in the UK: Problems and Prospects*
Hervey & McHale: *Health Law and the European Union*
Lacey & Wells: *Reconstructing Criminal Law*

Lewis: *Choice and the Legal Order: Rising above Politics*
Likosky: *Transnational Legal Processes*
Likosky: *Law, Infrastructure and Human Rights*
Maughan & Webb: *Lawyering Skills and the Legal Process*
McGlynn: Families and the European Union: Law, Politics and Pluralism
Moffat: *Trusts Law: Text and Materials*
Norrie: *Crime, Reason and History*
O'Dair: *Legal Ethics*
Oliver: *Common Values and the Public–Private Divide*
Oliver & Drewry: *The Law and Parliament*
Picciotto: *International Business Taxation*
Reed: *Internet Law: Text and Materials*
Richardson: *Law, Process and Custody*
Roberts & Palmer: *Dispute Processes: ADR and the Primary Forms of Decision-Making*
Scott & Black: *Cranston's Consumers and the Law*
Seneviratne: *Ombudsmen: Public Services and Administrative Justice*
Stapleton: *Product Liability*
Tamanaha: *The Struggle for Law as a Means to an End*
Turpin: *British Government and the Constitution: Text, Cases and Materials*
Twining: *Globalisation and Legal Theory*
Twining: *Rethinking Evidence*
Twining & Miers: *How to Do Things with Rules*
Ward: *A Critical Introduction to European Law*
Ward: *Shakespeare and Legal Imagination*
Zander: *Cases and Materials on the English Legal System*
Zander: *The Law-Making Process*

Who Believes in Human Rights?

Reflections on the European Convention

Marie-Bénédicte Dembour

CAMBRIDGE
UNIVERSITY PRESS

CAMBRIDGE UNIVERSITY PRESS
Cambridge, New York, Melbourne, Madrid, Cape Town, Singapore, São Paulo

Cambridge University Press
The Edinburgh Building, Cambridge CB2 2RU, UK

Published in the United States of America by Cambridge University Press, New York

www.cambridge.org
Information on this title: www.cambridge.org/9780521683074

First published 2006

Printed in the United Kingdom at the University Press, Cambridge

A catalogue record for this publication is available from the British Library

Library of Congress Cataloguing in Publication data

ISBN-13 978-0-521-68307-4 paperback
ISBN-10 0-521-68307-6 paperback

To Bob, again
To Ellis too, of course
To Françoise and all judges and lawyers like her

General table of contents

Detailed table of contents

Acknowledgements

This book has been a long time in gestation. Its academic origin can be traced to my having been asked to teach 'Human and Civil Rights' on my arrival at the University of Sussex in 1991. The personal debts I have accumulated since then are enormous, varied and numerous. The task of remembering all the friends, colleagues and students who have been generous with their help is daunting. I have tried, but must offer my apologies to anyone I may have forgotten at the moment of writing these words.

At Sussex, three people clearly stand out: Jane Cowan (Social Anthropology), Emily Haslam (Law, now Kent) and Neil Stammers (Politics). Jane, my friend since our common induction day in 1991, has been privy to the development of this project through our too infrequent visits to the local pub. Being able to take for granted her emotional support and her intellectual trust has been extremely valuable. Emily has been the first person to read a draft of any passage which can be found in this book. Her unmitigated enthusiasm, her honest reactions and her obvious confidence in the final product always spurred me to continue trying. Neil read the next version after Emily. He enlightened me on many aspects of political theory over necessarily long lunches and saved me from publishing more than one erroneous statement.

I have been helped by many other people at Sussex. Craig Barker (Law), Jo Bridgeman (Law), Elizabeth Craig (Law), Zdenek Kavan (International Relations), Charlotte Skeet (Law), Martin Shaw (International Relations) and Richard Wilson (Social Anthropology, now Connecticut) have read one chapter or another. Students have helped me to identify problems and formulate my positions. Matthias Hinderer (former MA in Human Rights), Mark Jordan (former LLM in International Criminal Law) and Trine Lester (former MA in Migration Studies) have commented on several chapters. My former secretary Amanda Collins, author of a book published by University of Michigan Press, never tired of discussing arguments, structures and titles even after she left Sussex. Cherry Horwill brought the meticulousness of her librarianship skills to the editing of the text. Christopher Gane (former Director of the School of Legal Studies, now Aberdeen) and Malcolm Ross (current Head of the Sussex Law School) must be acknowledged for their full support - as well as, in Christopher's case, for having opened my mind in the early 1990s to the richness of the Strasbourg case law. I have presented individual chapters at various research seminars, especially but not only at Sussex, and have invariably benefited from the reactions of the audiences.

In the course of writing the book, I have called upon a number of scholars whose advice has proved infinitely precious. Bill Bowring (Law, London Metropolitan) has supported the project from beginning to end and has shared with me his ECHR expertise. Louis Wolcher (Law, Washington) took an interest in my project when I first presented it at the Critical Legal Conference of 2001 and has given me invaluable leads whenever I have called upon him. Upendra Baxi (Law, Warwick) became an inestimable correspondent after I met him at a conference in 2003. Right from the start, Gerd Baumann (Anthropology, Amsterdam) encouraged the development of this project. He too became enlisted in reading several chapters. Referring to Wittgenstein's family resemblance concept drew me to call back on Thomas Spitzley (Philosophy, Duisburg), who provided me with punctilious comments on Chapter 8. Serge Gutwirth (Law, Vrije Universiteit Brussel) read some sections of the book. Various people have supplied references and facts, including Kevin Boyle (Law, Essex), Vincent Decroly, Jacqueline Hodgson (Law, Warwick), Heather Keating (Law, Sussex), Philip Leach (Law, London Metropolitan) and Colin Samson (Sociology, Essex). I had the good fortune to be supported at the outset of this project by Brian Simpson (Law, Michigan) and Chris Brown (International Relations, LSE). Towards its end, William Twining (Law, UCL), the editor of the series in which the book is published, sent me penetrating comments, the implications of which I feel I still need to work out. This leads me to stress, more generally, that none of the individuals mentioned in these pages should be held responsible for any error or weakness of judgement or argument from which the book may suffer.

Given my Belgian origin, I had thought it would be a good idea to meet the Belgian judge at the European Court of Human Rights. What I had not been expecting was to be invited to be on *tutoiement* terms immediately (using '*tu*' rather than '*vous*'!), being offered the keys of her flat in her absence and being encouraged to carry on an intellectual exchange. Françoise Tulkens offered both general and specific comments on drafts of virtually the whole book. My thanks go to her for her warmth, generosity and intellectual engagement. Françoise is not the only exceptional person I have met at the Court. I wish to single out Magda Mierzewska, from the Registry, with whom I have had the good fortune to co-author two articles and who also read some chapters. Unfortunately I shall merely list the other people I have met at Strasbourg alphabetically in order to avoid increasingly impossible refinements. In the course of four periods of one week I have spent at Strasbourg between July 2001 and April 2003, I was privileged to meet the following judges: Corneliu Bîrsan (Romanian), Giovanni Bonello (Maltese), Josep Casadevall (Andorran), Jean-Paul Costa (French), Marc Fischbach (Luxembourger), Lech Garlicki (Polish), Hanne Sophie Greve (Norwegian),

Anatoly Kovler (Russian), Wilhelmina Thomassen (Dutch) and Boštjan Zupančič (Slovenian); the following members of the Registry: Anna Austin, Michaele de Salvia, Anne Gillet, Roderick Liddel, Paul Mahoney, Nico Moll, Klaudiusj Ryngielewicz and Wolfgang Strasser; and other individuals from various sections of the Council of Europe, including Andrew Drzemczewski, Pierre-Henri Imbert, Heinrich Klebes, Simon Palmer, Sonia Parayre, Fredrik Sundberg and Tatiana Termacic. I met further people who enlightened me on aspects of the Convention or the Council of Europe not directly relevant to this book and whom I hope to be able to thank in separate publications. Sylvie Ruffenach, Françoise's secretary, has facilitated my research. Nora Binder and Delphine De Angelis, the librarians of the Court's library, have been generous with their time and skills. Laurent Viotti (External Relations) facilitated my first visit to the Court.

Staff at Cambridge University Press, including Finola O'Sullivan, Jane O'Regan and Jayne Aldhouse, have been exemplarily helpful and efficient. Laurence Marsh, who copy-edited the book, suggested the term 'reflections' for the subtitle.

This book would not have been possible without the financial support of a number of institutions. I am grateful to the Leverhulme Trust for a part-time Research Fellowship in 2001–2003 during which the bulk of this book was written, the AHRC for a study leave in the summer of 2004, and the University of Sussex for a study leave in the spring of 2004. My gratitude also goes to the European University Institute, Florence, for a Jean Monnet Fellowship in January–June 1995 during which I started to think about 'The Idea of Human Rights'.

The book owes a lot to my son Ellis, now six, whose arrival led me to devise a research project which would involve relatively little travelling. It also owes much to his father, Bob Morton, my companion of ten years. Bob has been the source of the love and balance without which I could not have worked effectively. He too has read many chapters. He is also the person whom anyone should thank if they find the style accessible and appreciate, amongst other things, the sparse use of 'quotation marks' which, unrestrained, my post-modern self would have put everywhere in the text.

Table of cases, with information on sources

All the cases listed below have been decided by the European Court (or former Commission) of Human Rights. They consist of judgments except when otherwise indicated – as reports of the Commission or decisions of admissibility.

Each reference comprises the name of the case, application number, date of the judgment or decision, location of the official report (when available) and publication in the *European Human Rights Reports* of Sweet and Maxwell (when available). The official reporting was in Series A Nos. 1–338 until 1996 and in the *Reports of Judgments and Decisions* between 1996 and 1998. Since 1999, it takes place in the Reports cited by the Court as ECHR.

Whether reported or not, all judgments and decisions of the Court can be freely accessed on http://www.echr.coe.int/echr by searching the Court's HUDOC database.

List of tables

1

Introduction

This book grew out of my attraction to and discomfort with the idea of human rights. When I led an Amnesty International group as a law undergraduate twenty years ago, the concept of human rights already seemed to me *both* desirable (or even necessary) *and* flawed. Since then I have never been sure which of these two aspects take precedence. If I stress the defects of the concept I immediately want to recall that the concept is important and cannot be dismissed altogether. Conversely, I do not wish to signify my attachment to the concept without highlighting that it is far, very far, from being a panacea. This book represents my attempt to sort out my persistent ambivalence towards human rights. It does so by seeking to answer the following two questions: Can we believe in human rights? Should we believe in human rights? I shall give my personal answer to these questions. I shall also provide an intellectual map of the way I understand current scholarship approaches the concept of human rights.

Human rights as an article of faith

According to a standard definition, human rights are those rights one has by virtue of being human.[1] This definition suggests that human rights belong to every human being in every human society: all human beings have them, equally and in equal measure. Implied in one's humanity, human rights are generally presented as being inalienable and imprescriptible – they cannot be transferred, forfeited, or waived.[2] Many people, especially but not exclusively in the West, believe that human rights exist irrespective of social recognition, although they often acknowledge that the plurality of religious traditions and value systems from which they can be derived make their foundation controversial. For those who believe in human rights, the problem of their source is rarely considered an obstacle to asserting them. From their point of view, what is important is that human rights are evident.

This book starts from the observation that the political hegemony which human rights enjoy through being constantly invoked in contemporary discourse does not lend them, as such, ethical authority. We must differentiate between political dominance and ethical authority.[3] In particular, we should not exclude the possibility that political utopias and/or forms of organization which are outside the human rights logic can be superior to it.[4] This is too easily forgotten in a world where human rights have become, in the words of Elie Wiesel, the secular religion of our time.[5]

Human rights is an article of faith.[6] The fundamental tenet of this credo is that human rights exist and are universal, inalienable and self-evident. I personally do not believe in this, for reasons expounded below. My personal answer to the question 'Can we believe in human rights?' is that it makes no rational sense to believe in human rights because, as far as I can see, reason disproves them.[7] Despite this, I hesitate to answer negatively the question of whether we should believe in human rights. Though an atheist, I may wish to appeal to the value of loving thy neighbour especially in front of a Christian. In the same way, I consider human rights to be the vehicle of useful values in our contemporary world. Though it does not appear to me intellectually tenable to 'believe' in human rights, I am ready to act as if I believed in them in a world where they have become part of the received wisdom – the more so since I almost believe in them, having been socialized in them and being persuaded by some of the values they seek to express. In short, I consider human rights as a potentially useful resource in my world. As far as I am concerned, using them strategically is not hypocritical, but a way to attain moral aims in the absence of a more persuasive language in which to articulate claims for emancipation. This position is not devoid of contradictions, but it is the best formulation of it I can achieve thus far.

The short-sightedness of the universal assertion

My main reason for objecting to the credo of the human rights orthodoxy has to do with their supposed universality – a characteristic so central to their definition, essence and *raison d'être* that it has practically become a trope in human rights discourse.[8] As an anthropologist, I do not see how one can say that human rights exist on a universal plane, nor do I see that human rights are such a good thing that it would be wonderful if they existed on a universal plane. Let me try to explain what I mean through an example.

How would Native Americans have reacted, had they been presented with the concept of human rights before they were colonized and, in many cases, virtually exterminated? Surely they would have objected to its strange, homo-centric ethos.[9] They have indeed asked and continue to ask: what kind of existential dignity prevails when it applies only to human beings, moreover merely those who happen to be in the world of the living?[10] This example is pertinent because 'the Indians' have captivated the contemporary Western imagination for having developed a cosmology which is more respectful of land, water, animals, plants and, arguably, even human beings than Western society. The same conclusion could be drawn in respect of many other societies round the globe.[11]

The idea that human rights are universal flies in the face of societies which are based on social, political and ethical premises completely foreign to the liberal – and possibly market – logic of human rights. In other words, the concept of human rights rests on a peculiarly short-sighted view of humanity. It is sometimes suggested, including by anthropologists, that people who treat one another with respect and compassion actually respect human rights even though they do not use the term 'human rights'. This approach appears to me to suffer from 'occidentalism'.

I use this word as a pendant to 'orientalism'. An example will illuminate my meaning. Upendra Baxi recently talked at a conference of a 'fatwa culture' which encompassed as much President George Bush's as Osama bin Laden's edicts on the so-called war on terror.[12] A member of the audience objected to this terminology, noting that such edicts were not fatwas in the traditional sense of the Islamic term and that Baxi's terminology had the effect of associating bad practice with Islam and/or the East. By contrast, talking of human rights to refer to the 'politics of dignity' puts the West on a pedestal by using the Western word to refer to a good practice or an ideal which can in fact be found across human societies. If we want to talk of the politics of dignity, let us call them that and stress that human rights is only one exemplar of such politics.

Tore Lindholm asserts that to talk of human rights before 1945 is anachronistic.[13] Even if this view be considered too extreme, it remains the case that most scholars locate the origin of the human rights discourse in the seventeenth or eighteenth century, with the French 'Declaration of the Rights of Man and the Citizen' a key moment. The point is that, whether their origin is counted in terms of decades or centuries, human rights are a latecomer in the history of humanity, however much they dominate contemporary political rhetoric. This is enough to make me think that the concept of human rights – when it is presented as a human constant – is not sound.[14] The proposition that human rights exist *irrespective* of social recognition (affecting *all* human beings in *all* human societies across time and space) does not make sense. It suggests that human rights are and have always been somewhere out there – but where? And why?

In my view, the concept of human rights conspicuously lacks 'universal universality' – at the very least their supposed universality does not exist across times and places. There is thus perhaps a sense in which the conclusion to the second question asked in this book is foregone: human rights are not universal, the concept is flawed, we should not believe in it, and that is the end of the matter. For Jack Donnelly among others, however, the 'universality of human rights is a moral claim about the proper way to organise social and political relations in the contemporary world, *not* an historical or anthropological fact'.[15] Rather than stopping the discussion at the fact that human rights is not an empirical constant in humanity, I am willing to examine whether the world *as you and I know it* may well demand something like a framework of human rights.

The shadow of the modern state falls heavily over contemporary society; therefore a counterpart to its power – and, incidentally, the power of any institution as strong as or even stronger than the modern state – is acutely needed. It is therefore interesting to ask whether the concept of human rights is valid as it were on its own ground, defined as the world affected by the modern state and all that comes in its train. This terrain is assuredly wide – it encompasses most if not all of the contemporary world – but it nonetheless ceases to embrace the whole of humanity across time. The question raised by this book can thus be rephrased as follows: in the limited arena of the contemporary world, which problems affect the concept of human rights? Are they such as to make it, even on its own historical terrain, invalid?

Practical and conceptual critiques of human rights

Scepticism regarding human rights has a long pedigree. Classical critiques of human rights thus provide an obvious starting point to contemplate the faults plaguing the concept. This book accordingly contains a series of five 'critical light' chapters which revisit, in turn, the realist, utilitarian, Marxist, particularist (a word I favour over the expression cultural relativist) and feminist critiques of human rights.

At the risk of caricature, the main thrust of each critique can be summarized as follow: realists (among whom I include Jeremy Bentham) intimate that human rights cannot be 'above' or 'beyond' the state but necessarily originate from and are enmeshed within the state; they reject the idea that human rights are natural, existing outside of social recognition. Utilitarians oppose the granting of individual rights regardless of the consequences for the common good; nor do they think it is possible for human rights to be absolute and/or inalienable. Marxists view rights as sustaining the bourgeois order and thus feeding oppression by privileging a particular class to the detriment of the oppressed majority. Particularists object to the idea that moral judgements can be made which hold true across cultures; they call for tolerance of practices which are not comprehensible within the dominant perspective and denounce what they see as the inherent imperialism of human rights which are not universal but the product of the society which has created them. Feminists, finally, attack human rights' pretence of equity and neutrality by observing that rights, which have generally been defined by men, largely bypass the interests and concerns of women; they dispute the idea that human rights are gender-neutral.

None of these critiques is more important than any other, nor does one logically precede another. I have chosen to arrange the five chapters historically, using the date of their 'foundation' text. The realist chapter (Chapter 3) comes first chronologically, with as its starting point the text Jeremy Bentham wrote in reaction to the 1789 French Declaration, where he argued: 'From *real* law come *real* rights; but from *imaginary* laws . . . come *imaginary* rights.' Bentham's prominent place in the utilitarian movement naturally leads to the chapter on utilitarianism, though most of the debates reviewed in Chapter 4 are contemporaneous to us. The Marxist chapter follows: Karl Marx's most direct comment on the French Declaration was written in 1843, in his essay 'On the Jewish Question'. The American Anthropological Association's 'Statement on Human Rights', published a century later in 1947, is widely seen to epitomize the cultural relativist position on human rights and gives a point of departure to Chapter 6, on particularism. The feminist chapter rounds off the series: despite Olympe de Gouges's 'Declaration on the Rights of Woman' of 1790 and the writings of those such as Mary Wollstonecraft, a scholarly feminist critique of human rights has only started to provoke wide academic engagement over the last two or three decades.

In one way or another, each of these critiques points to a gap between the human rights ideal (the promise that every human being enjoys a number of fundamental rights) and the practice (a world where human rights violations abound and where many people are excluded from the enjoyment of human rights).[16] The gap could exist *either* because the practice has, so far, failed to live up to the theory, but without this affecting the validity of the concept of human rights, *or* because human rights cannot be what they are said to be, making the concept invalid. In other words, critiques of human rights can either require human rights to be true to their word or reject them as constructed on unsound premises. In the former case, the problems which are identified are conceived as demanding that a better human rights concept be found (possibly through theoretical input) or that a better practice be elaborated. Crucially, there is no suggestion that the concept is irretrievably defective: it is a matter of 'simply' closing the gap between what the concept promises and what it delivers. In the latter case, the critique points to a concept which is fundamentally flawed, thus advocating a solution which is altogether external to the human rights logic. In the former case, the belief is that human rights must *and* can be improved;[17] in the latter case, the concept of human rights is regarded as ultimately hopeless. These two positions could be called the practical and the conceptual critiques of human rights.

They cut across the classical critiques in that each of the latter comprises elements which in principle accept the concept of human rights but demand that it be better practised or conceptualized (or both) and elements which suggest that the problem of the gap between human rights theory and practice can only be solved by looking outside the human rights logic. Bentham famously described the rights of man as 'Nonsense upon stilts', suggesting his was a conceptual critique of rights; however, many utilitarians have defended theories of rights which correspond closely to modern notions of human rights, thus allowing for the development of a more practical critique of rights. Though this may come as a surprise to some readers, Marx was less scathing than Bentham in his critique of human rights. While he did not regard human rights as a panacea, Marx nonetheless welcomed their introduction as a step towards communism and the emancipation of man. Moreover, a number of Marxist thinkers (including E. P. Thompson and Etienne Balibar) have wholeheartedly approved of the rule of law and the idea of rights. Cultural relativists seem intractably opposed to the idea of human rights; more sophisticated particularists, however, recognize the importance of the aspiration to a universalist position as expressed in the language of human rights even though they do not believe that pure 'universality' is attainable. Many, though not all, feminists work within a human rights agenda: they denounce a practice which is blind to its neglect of women but without objecting to the idea of a human rights agenda *per se*. In summary, each critique – which always encompasses various strands – has a variety of answers on the question of whether the gap between human rights theory and practice is due to a conceptual or a practical failure.

Liberal and non-liberal critiques of human rights

Liberalism and human rights are closely connected,[18] with the polysemic term 'liberalism' probably meaning, in this context, the political philosophy which holds that government should interfere as little as possible in the lives of its citizens.[19] From this perspective, a government is liberal when it strives to provide a forum in which citizens can pursue their own ends, in the absence of the establishment of any collective goal. This liberalism can therefore be characterized as 'procedural' (or 'thin')[20] rather than 'substantive' (or 'thick'). Particularly prominent in the Anglo-American world,[21] it puts great emphasis on the autonomy of the individual, and relies on the idea of giving the individual inalienable rights.[22] Given the intimate connection between this kind of liberalism and human rights, one might wish to ask: is a conceptual critique necessarily opposed to liberalism? Taking it the other way around, is it possible to oppose the *concept* (rather than the practice) of human rights from a liberal perspective?

Before answering these questions, it is worth identifying what the *conceptual* critique of human rights consists of. The critique encompasses at least the following three propositions: (1) the concept of human rights is wrongly presented as universal; (2) it pertains of a logic which focuses on the individual to the neglect of solidarity and other social values; (3) it derives from a reasoning which is far too abstract. The first point has already been touched on above when I noted that human rights lack 'universal universality': the claim that they would be relevant to all human beings across time and space is simply not credible in the light of societies which do not fall within the model of the modern state. The problem of a universal deficit is also noted by Marxists and feminists, though from a different angle. For Marxists, human rights lack universality because they primarily benefit the bourgeois; for feminists, because women are excluded from their definition and implementation. Interestingly the feminist critiques advocate solutions which fall either within or outside liberal parameters. To simplify, liberal feminists believe that the problem of the exclusion of a women's agenda by human rights should be, and can be, solved by including women. Thus they seek a solution to the lack of universality *within* the liberal/human rights logic: the sole requirement – however difficult to implement in practice – is the inclusion of women. Some feminists, however, are not persuaded by this 'internal' solution. Radical feminists (who tend to be influenced by Marxism) argue that it is the liberal/human rights premise itself which needs revision. For good reasons, Marxists have the reputation of locating the solutions they advocate outside of liberalism. Nonetheless, valuable attempts to reconcile Marxism and liberalism make this proposition an unwarranted simplification.[23]

The second problem with which all the critiques reviewed in this book take issue is the individualism inherent in human rights logic. To generalize (which I admit does not do justice to the sophistication and/or multiplicity of the arguments), some realists argue that for the state to ensure its own survival and to protect its own interests is to the benefit of its citizens; utilitarians call for political action to be governed by the principle of the happiness of the greatest number, which may or may not coincide with the protection of individual rights; Marxists ask man to behave as a member of humankind whose individual interest corresponds to the interest of the community; particularists call for the impact of and the reward of socialization to be recognized; feminists, especially those of a 'woman's voice' persuasion, demand that greater value be given to a more typically feminine ethic of care which stresses responsibilities towards others. Only the strand of liberalism which values individual autonomy above anything else does not regard individualism as a false aspiration.[24] To counteract the individualism inherent in human rights logic, realists and utilitarians tend to propose solutions congruent with liberalism – which is why utilitarianism is an acknowledged branch of liberalism in political theory. As noted in the previous paragraph, Marxists and feminists variously call for solutions within or outside liberalism.

All of the critiques are, finally, dissatisfied with the fact that the concept of human rights derives from an excessively abstract definition of man. Utilitarianism subscribes to the idea that the government's duty is to seek the common good – conceived of as a substantive project. In utilitarianism, rights are not Kantian categorical imperatives but, rather, tools to achieve a particular goal, under particular circumstances. The utilitarian perspective thus requires extensive contextualization. Realists, Marxists and feminists all examine (from different angles) whether human rights deliver their promises, and thus tend to assess their performance in practice, rather than to contemplate their theoretical basis. Particularists obviously do not believe, though for different reasons, that rights can be defined in the abstract. Again, it is possible for each of these critiques to seek contextualization within or outside liberalism.

It could be tempting to associate a conceptual critique of human rights with a perspective located outside liberalism, and a practical critique of human rights with a perspective which would be liberal in its inspiration. This would suggest that one could neither defend the concept of human rights without being a liberal nor oppose it on liberal ground. Things are not that simple, however. To give one example, Costas Douzinas defends the concept of human rights from outside liberalism: for him, as for other protest scholars, the concept has been 'hijacked' by liberalism.[25] To give a second example, there are liberal utilitarians, including most famously Bentham, who oppose the concept of human rights.

Are those who find the concept of human rights altogether defective *against* human rights? It would be ridiculous to assume that they are in favour of their supposed binary opposite, namely, violations of human rights. This is because a world devoid of human rights does not necessarily mean a world full of injuries to human dignity.[26] On the contrary, what this type of critique may wish to suggest is that human rights are not the best way to try to implement the ideas of justice, equality and humanity which human rights supposedly stand for, and that better ways have to be found.[27] From some perspectives, the route towards emancipation does not take the form of human rights.[28]

Linking the classical critiques to the Strasbourg human rights case law

This book was planned around the assumption that the five classical critiques of human rights reviewed in it continue to tell us something important about human rights today so that their fundamental theoretical insights, whether they were formulated two hundred or twenty years ago, were bound to be reflected in human rights practice. I have decided to explore how these insights manifest themselves in the case law of the European Court of Human Rights (hereafter 'the Court'). The focus on the European Convention on Human Rights (hereafter 'the Convention') is arbitrary: I could have carried out the same exercise with respect to other human rights sites, for example the Inter-American system of human rights protection, the UN system or a host of non-judicial human rights struggles.

My concern is to effect a direct linkage between theory and practice so that the practice helps to explicate and refine the theory, while at the same time the theory generates more subtle readings of practice. Wishing to render theory and practice mutually responsive to each other, I have avoided the sequential examination of theory and its application, or practice; instead I move between theory and practice in each chapter through a succession of detours and bridges which lay out the premises and implications of both the theoretical arguments and case law.

I have allowed the argument to develop organically, without imposing an overly rigid structure. It is not my aim to test hypotheses in a traditionally 'scientific' manner and to present the reader with A to Z demonstrations which follow a positivist causal logic. Instead I seek to produce an 'essay' where, so to speak, I 'think aloud', provoking in turn my interlocutor to think. Louis Wolcher, struck by the unconventionality of my method, commented that

I was 'musing'. I took this as a compliment; the Muses, offspring of Zeus and Mnemosyne, are traditionally seen as inspiring creativity and learning. 'Musing' also embraces the idea of meditation, perhaps of wasting time but in order better to ponder and reflect.

The selection of a judicial institution as the practical focus of my reflection results in a book which contains far more law than non-lawyers are used to, though less law than lawyers may have wished. I briefly introduce the Convention in Chapter 2 so that the reader can see how the cases I discuss fit within the law of the Convention. Without claiming to offer systematic treatment of the rights guaranteed by the Convention,[29] I have sought to provide an account of how the Convention operates, the rights it covers, the recurrent principles in the Court's legal reasoning and key cases. My primary aim is nonetheless to explore the intricacies of judicial argument in order to expose the reasoning or the processes which reflect traces of the classical critiques of human rights.

The chapters develop the following and somewhat predictable arguments: first, state interests play a major role in the development of human rights law, though the Court can also come down hard on the state; second, the Court endlessly engages in trade-offs and compromise, gauging the potential consequences of its position even while creating the impression that human rights prevail over all other considerations; third, a privileged applicant has far greater chances to be heard by the Court than an underprivileged one, though even the latter can be heard; fourth, the prima facie objective of establishing common standards while acknowledging the need to respect social diversity, means that the Court cannot but pursue a controversial path; fifth, the Convention system remains biased towards men in many respects even if it is, on the face of it, gender-neutral and equally open to women.

The case law I cite *illustrates* these points. In each instance, other cases could have been used to support my argument. Indeed, my view is that the tensions I explore manifest themselves repeatedly in the case law, though in differing forms. Readers acquainted with the Strasbourg system will no doubt think of their own examples as they read my analyses. At times they may wonder why I am not referring to a case or a series of cases which, in their view, demonstrate even better the saliency of the issue under discussion. Given that the book does not aim at comprehensiveness, a selection was necessary. I do not even list further cases in footnotes, as these lists themselves become arbitrary and potentially never-ending.

Separate (generally dissenting, but sometimes concurring) opinions, as they are called, are of special interest to me. In a separate opinion, the judge is free to express himself or herself outside the constraints of a collegiate text. The assumptions underlying his or her logic are more likely to surface, because the coherence of his/her reasoning need not be lost in the process of accommodating the various perspectives of the individual judges who constitute a bench. This book thus makes far greater use of separate opinions than is generally the case in legal commentaries.

A kaleidoscopic reading of the Convention

Given that the cases I discuss in the book are merely illustrative, there is a strong element of fortuity in the way the five 'critical light' chapters are assembled. The image of the kaleidoscope comes to mind in that it points to an infinite number of combinations of either theoretical or empirical elements, or both. In each chapter it is as if I had collected pieces of case law, shaken them, and observed the resulting combination – if not exactly symmetry – in the mirror (or light) of a particular theory. I could have repeated the exercise over and over again, *ad infinitum*, either with the same or with slightly different material (case law) or mirrors (critiques).[30] Each time the result would have been different but, I would argue, no less compelling.

The image of the kaleidoscope draws attention to the way our senses construct patterns which do not 'really' exist except through the artifice of reflection (theory). It could be said that I offer a kaleidoscopic reading of the Convention, i.e. one generating arrangements which are, if not aesthetically pleasing, at least deceptively attractive in their simplicity and (imposed) regularity. A friend who read Chapter 3 was not deceived. She remarked, disapprovingly, that it was as though I were using Bentham as a *tuyau* (trick) to allow me to discuss *my* points and to say what *I* felt about the Convention. I have two responses to the objection: first, there is a sense in which one can read whatever one wishes into the Convention (even if the post-modern ring of this observation may not convince everyone); second my analysis, however much it may be a trick, helps to explore a legitimate discomfort towards what could be labelled the human rights credo and, beyond this, to identify various visions as to what human rights are.

Not one, but several concepts of human rights

I do not immediately address the crucial question: what are human rights? Readers could have expected me to start the book with it, on the ground that it is surely appropriate to delineate a concept before examining the critiques to which it has been subjected. The delay, however, is deliberate. As I have said, I do not believe that human rights exist outside of social recognition; to me, human rights exist only to the extent that they are talked about.[31] It is therefore logically impossible for me to discuss either the real or idealized nature of human rights; the only thing I can do is to investigate the way people use the concept of human rights - what it means to them. This is not a philosophical but an empirical investigation (which I have personally chosen to approach through the examination of European Convention cases).

I thought it would nonetheless be interesting to try to identify and systematize the essential features of the human rights concept by reading closely what scholars said about it. In the course of this exercise I came to the conclusion that there is not one single concept of human rights, but several: human rights are conceived of as 'given', 'agreed', 'fought for', or 'talked about', by those I propose to refer to as – respectively – natural, deliberative, protest and discourse scholars. This conclusion is presented in Chapter 8.

Natural scholars dominate the field. They believe that human rights constitute minimal entitlements originating from an immanent source which, taking a Kantian route, they variously label as Nature, God, Reason, Humanity, etc. These entitlements can and should be provided for in positive law. Natural scholars regard the development of human rights law in the last half-century as 'progress'. Deliberative scholars look at human rights as procedural principles, which reflect the consensus as to how the rules of the political game – and the political game only – should be conducted. To them, human rights do not exist as an immanent idea but as political or legal principles which have been agreed upon. They are influenced by Habermas. Protest scholars constitute a significant minority. They have a 'fiery heart'.[32] In their view, human rights is first and foremost a language of protest. Levinasian, they feel summoned by the suffering of the other and want to respond to unacceptable situations as these arise. They fail to share the hope of natural scholars that positive law could ever put human rights definitions and/or implementation at rest and they regard the enthusiasm of deliberative scholars for setting up conditions of free deliberation through human rights law as fired by a delusion that power is not a major player. In fact, for them, human rights law almost inevitably entails a cost to the human rights ideal. There are, finally, a small number of discourse scholars, among whom I count myself. They believe that human rights have no essential immanence but exist only because they are talked about. For them, human rights law is neither good nor bad as such; it must be judged, each time, by its outcomes. Discourse scholars are heavily influenced by post-modernism.

My contention is that the vast majority of human rights scholars fall within one of these four schools; sometimes squarely, though many waver.[33] The first school could be said to represent the orthodoxy of the human rights credo. The second school appears resolutely secular in the sense that it continually stresses that human rights should not be conceived as a blueprint for a complete way of life and should not be approached like a creed.[34] The word 'evangelical', though slightly too strong, comes to mind in trying to characterize the third school, for there is a sense in which its disciples (if I may be allowed the word)[35] stress the need to interpret human rights by reference to their 'original' inspiration[36] and are 'driven', accepting no rest in the fight for human rights. The fourth school, to draw out the religious analogy, would represent the nihilist position on human rights.

The moral stance of human rights nihilism

For the natural scholar, human rights are simply there, and they are definitely a good thing, part of our moral universe. For the deliberative scholar, human rights are not a thing but they provide good principles (the application whereof leads to results which are acknowledged to be potentially controversial). For the protest scholar, human rights guide human conduct in the fight against injustice and oppression. Only for the discourse scholar is the moral status of human rights open to question. To him or her, human rights are not necessarily good. Such a nihilist position may appear objectionable, especially in the post-9/11 context where human rights are openly denied by those who were amongst the first to declare their existence. This book will conclude that such a position is entirely defensible.

A note on terminology is in order. Agnosticism refers to the view that 'human reason is incapable of providing sufficient rational grounds to justify *either* the belief that God exists *or* the belief that God does not exist'.[37] By contrast, atheism endorses 'positive disbelief rather than mere suspension of belief'.[38] Transposing these two definitions to the 'secular religion' of human rights, I am not merely a human rights agnostic but also a human rights atheist, for I am ready to affirm the non-existence, across the ages, of human rights. Going further, I could even describe myself as a human rights nihilist.

Nihilism is 'principally characterised by a devaluation of morality and moral reasoning'.[39] Contrary to what is popularly assumed, it does not necessarily entail the rejection of all moral principles. Such a common understanding nonetheless made me at first hesitant to refer to myself as a 'nihilist'. But my philosopher friend Louis Wolcher remarked: 'Why steer away from nihilism? Read Nietzsche: "nihilism" means the state of affairs in which Western values de-value themselves. I think that is exactly what you do: you are afraid of the absence of foundations for human rights, so you say we can't believe in them. What is this if not a loss in faith in the "value" of human rights, and hence nihilism in Nietzsche's sense? . . . in truth you are agnostic *because of nihilism* – because nihilism made the foundations for religious belief and human rights questionable and unconvincing'.[40]

One clarification is in order: it is not so much the absence of foundation of the human rights concept which worries me as the fact that the concept appears to me altogether misguided. It appears to me not only empirically wrong but also (and perhaps in direct consequence of this first feature) imperialistic in its deployment. I am a nihilist to the extent that I feel unable to provide anything better, once and for all. I am like Wittgenstein who thought that ethics were 'unsayable' in propositions which 'can express nothing that is "higher" than what is in the world'.[41] Does this stance, which suggests that ethics is very important at the same time that nothing whatsoever sensible can be said about them, prevent me from passing moral judgments on political actions, policies and theories of which I morally disapprove? The short answer is no.

Neither simply for nor against human rights

This may be the point at which to say that if my selection of the European Convention system to 'test' classical critiques of human rights was arbitrary in that I am convinced that any other human rights context would have lent itself to a similar exercise, my choice was not completely random. My original inspiration was my anger towards, and my wish to react against, the self-congratulatory tone of many commentaries on the Convention. Reading these texts, one would think that the system is so flawless and wonderful that the rest of the world need only follow the European example of human rights protection in order for problems magically to disappear.[42] This attitude makes me wince.

As an Africanist whose doctoral research focused on the Belgian Congo, I am acutely aware that Europe's privileged political and economic position (including the guarantee of human rights to its citizens) has much to do with the historic subjugation of other peoples, a subjugation which continues in the so-called post-colonial era. Costas Douzinas expresses my feelings in his characteristically eloquent prose: 'Human rights have become the symbol of superiority of Western states, a kind of mantra, the repetition of which soothes the painful memory of past infamies and the guilt of present injustices.'[43] Even as a European citizen looking inwardly at Europe, I cannot fail to identify a plethora of problems arising from the way human rights are understood and practised at Strasbourg. I have already intimated that the Convention largely bypasses women. I might add that over 90 per cent of individuals who feel they suffer a violation of their human rights and complain at Strasbourg are turned away, their applications declared inadmissible; or that the Convention allows states to derogate from some of its provisions in case of national emergencies. These examples, and many others, are documented in the book.

I started the book on the assumption that the Convention was not worth much more than the paper on which it was written. I would not have been alone in this view. Douzinas writes of the bureaucratization of human rights: 'Official thinking and action on human rights has been entrusted in the hands of triumphalist column writers, bored diplomats and rich international lawyers in New York and Geneva, people whose experience of human rights violations is confined to being served a bad bottle of wine. In the process, human rights have been turned from a discourse of rebellion and dissent into that of state legitimacy.'[44] One suspects that Douzinas may have been ready to mention Strasbourg alongside New York and Geneva. Certainly, many of my 'protest' friends objected to my selection of the European Convention to probe the meaning and significance of the human rights concept, urging me to look at the action of NGOs instead (in line – I now see – with their view that human rights law may well entail a loss of the 'pure' human rights idea).

With the hindsight gained from the research on which this book is based, I no longer wish to offer even the slightest suggestion that human rights law is 'no good' as a matter of principle. My visits to Strasbourg have made me aware that individuals who work at the European Court of Human Rights, either as judges or as members of the Registry, often do not fit Douzinas's description. Many share my misgivings about the problems which plague human rights both as concept and practice. They believe in human rights (far more than I do) and they want to make a difference by carving routes through the law of the Convention which can then be used, notably by applicants. Through persuasion, logic and sometimes, of course, diplomacy, they achieve small victories; but they would not deny that the greater battle continues. The victories need to be acknowledged as forcefully as the failures of the Convention.

In conclusion, it is my view that each reference to human rights needs to be assessed morally on its own merits, by which I principally mean its outcome. This stance prevents me from making sweeping pronouncements on the moral status of either the European Convention or human rights more generally.[45] It none-theless allows me to offer views and doubts, as well as to express admiration. This book is neither unreservedly for nor against human rights. Considering most people around me seem to believe in human rights, this may well make me a heretic: I certainly defy human rights orthodoxy. My nihilism, however, does not mean I reject all values – only that I find it impossible to ground them metaphysically. I shall thus continue to defend the best ideals behind the human rights concept, if not the concept itself, and denounce what we have learnt to call human rights abuse.

Notes

1 See e.g. the opening sentence of Jack Donnelly, *Universal Human Rights in Theory and Practice* (1st edn, Ithaca: Cornell University Press, 1989) at 9.

2 This is a brief paraphrase of: Louis Henkin, *The Age of Rights* (New York: Columbia University Press, 1990) at 2–3. The original reads: 'Human rights are universal: they belong to every human being in every human society. They do not differ with geography or history, culture or ideology, political or economic system, or stage of societal development. To call them "human" implies that all human beings have them, equally and in equal measure, by virtue of their humanity – regardless of sex, race, age; regardless of high or low "birth", social class, national origin, ethnic or tribal affiliation; regardless of wealth or poverty, occupation, talent, merit, religion, ideology, or other commitment. Implied in one's humanity, human rights are inalienable and imprescriptible: they cannot be transferred, forfeited, or waived; they cannot be lost by having been usurped, or by one's failure to exercise or assert them.'

3 Peter Sutch, 'Global Civil Society and International Ethics: Mervyn Frost's Restatement of Constitutive Theory' (2000) *Review of International Studies* 485–9, at 486. In the same article, Sutch remarks, disapprovingly: 'Consent is a classically liberal way of conferring authority' (ibid., at 488). In our field the signature and ratification of human rights instruments across a wide range of states is typically taken to signify both consent and authority.

4 Wendy Brown, '"The Most We Can Hope For . . .": Human Rights and the Politics of Fatalism' (2004) 103 *South Atlantic Quarterly* 451–63.

5 Elie Wiesel, 'A Tribute to Human Rights', in Yael Danieli, Elsa Stamatopoulou and Clarence Dias (eds.), *The Universal Declaration of Human Rights: Fifty Years and Beyond* (Amityville, NY: Baywood, 1999) at 3. See also Luc de Heusch, 'Les droits de

l'homme comme objet de réflexion anthropologique', in *Laïcité et droits de l'homme. Deux siècles de conquête* (Brussels: Université Libre de Bruxelles, 1989) 83–95, at 91.

6 Henkin, *Age of Rights*, at 6; Michael Ignatieff, *Human Rights as Politics and Idolatry* (Princeton: Princeton University Press, 2001) at 77. Henri Pallard, 'Personne, culture et droits: Polyphonie, harmonie et dissonance', in Jacques-Yvan Morin (ed.), *Les droits fondamentaux dans le monde francophone* (Brussels: Bruylant, 1997) 121–35, at 132 and 134.

7 I first had written more laconically: 'we cannot believe in human rights'. I am indebted to Louis Wolcher for pointing out to me that this was in contradiction with my opening statement 'human rights is an article of faith'. Wolcher explains: 'the usual way of interpreting the relation between faith and reason is to say that reason cannot "disprove" faith, that faith (in God) is a gift (Luther) and not an intellectual achievement; it is possible to believe in human rights (as a religion) but only by surrendering reason (personal communication)'. Andrew Fagan also makes the point that: 'Most argue that religious belief is simply not amenable to rational or empirical validation; that it is a different category of "knowledge" altogether': 'Paradoxical Bedfellows: Nihilism and Human Rights' (2005) *Human Rights Review*, 80–101, at 92. Leaving aside that human rights as a religion cannot be rationally validated (i.e. proved right), it appears to me that human rights can be and indeed are rationally invalidated (i.e. proved wrong).

8 Thus, for example, the universality of human rights is the starting point of Jack Donnelly's widely acclaimed *Universal Human Rights*.

9 On the link between human rights and a humanist philosophy which takes man as the ultimate measure of all things, see Fagan, 'Paradoxical Bedfellows', at 11–12.

10 On Native American cosmology and conflicts between European and indigenous concepts of rights, see e.g. Taiaiake Alfred, *Peace, Power, Righteousness: An Indigenous Manifesto* (Don Mills, Ontario: Oxford University Press, 1999); Alfonso Ortiz, 'Indian/White Relations: A View from the Other Side of the "Frontier"', in Frederick Hoxie (ed.), *Indians in American History* (Arlington Heights, Ill.: Harlan Davidson, 1988) 1–18; Colin Samson, 'Rights as the Reward for Simulated Cultural Sameness: The Innu in the Canadian Colonial Context', in Jane K. Cowan, Marie-Bénédicte Dembour and Richard A. Wilson (eds.), *Culture and Rights: Anthropological Perspectives* (Cambridge: Cambridge University Press, 2001) 226–48.

11 But, for a reminder that not all 'folk' traditions aim at preserving the natural environment, see Gordon Woodman, 'The Chthonic Legal Tradition – or Everything That Is Not Something Else' (forthc.) 1 *The Journal of Comparative Law*.

12 Upendra Baxi, 'The Globalization of Fatwas: Legal Pluralism, Violence, and Terror', presented at the Conference on 'Developing Anthropology of Law in a Transnational World' held at Edinburgh on 17–19 June 2004.

13 Tore Lindholm, 'The Plurality of Normative Traditions and the Need for Cross-Cultural Legitimacy of Universal Human Rights' (1998) 1 *Human Rights: Universal or Cultural Specific. North-South Coalition Information Bulletin* 10–46.

14 For a different view from scholars who are as enraged as I am by the pretence of universality found in the liberal account of human rights but who think the universality of human rights derives from the universality of resistance to oppression *all over the world*, see e.g. Upendra Baxi, *The Future of Human Rights* (New Delhi: Oxford University Press, 2002) and Neil Stammers's forthcoming book on human rights and social movements. What these scholars would say – I presume – is that

I mistakenly equate the notion of human rights with the liberal notion of human rights, thus failing to see the real thing beyond what Stammers calls 'the hall of mirrors'. Those I call deliberative scholars still have a different view: they take the universality of human rights less as a given and more as a project which can be achieved through consensus and factual spread.

15 Jack Donnelly, 'The social construction of international human rights', in Tim Dunne and Nicholas J. Wheeler (eds.) *Human Rights in Global Politics* (Cambridge: Cambridge University Press, 1999) 71–102, at 81, emphasis added.

16 This gap is the point of departure of more than one scholarly reflection on human rights. See e.g. Ignatieff, *Human Rights*, at 4; Costas Douzinas, *The End of Human Rights: Critical Legal Thought at the Turn of the Century* (Oxford: Hart, 2000), at 2.

17 Practical (as opposed to conceptual) problems include double standards in the application of human rights; the way institutions as powerful as if not more powerful than the nation-state such as transnational companies remain to this day outside its compass; the relative neglect of social and economic rights; the status of collective rights; bio-ethical issues. Debates on these crucial questions tend to accept the idea of human rights, but try to make the idea work better.

18 So much so that sometimes they are not distinguished but presented as just overlapping each other. See e.g. Ignatieff, *Human Rights*, at 75. For those I call protest scholars, however, the aim is precisely to retrieve human rights from their liberal 'hijacking'.

19 This is not the only possible meaning of liberalism, however. Utilitarianism and social democracy both belong to the liberal tradition and neither advocates a hands-off approach by the government. See Crawford Brough MacPherson, *The Life and Times of Liberal Democracy* (Oxford: Oxford University Press, 1977). Wendy Brown notes that '[i]n the history of *political* thought . . . liberalism signifies an order in which the state exists to secure the freedom of individuals on a formally egalitarian basis': Wendy Brown, 'Neo-Liberalism and the End of Liberal Democracy' (2003) 7 *Theory and Event*, at para. 6, emphasis in the original. Such an order does not have to be 'thin'. For a short introduction on the many different ways in which the term 'liberal' is used, especially in the United States, see Brown, ibid., at paras 6 and 7. Interestingly, for Donnelly, the United States hardly qualifies as a liberal society. This is because Donnelly has very high benchmarks for the liberal society which he sees as being required for human rights to be able to flourish: Donnelly, *Universal Human Rights*, 1st edn, at 68 and 73.

20 The word is from Ignatieff, *Human Rights*, at 75.

21 Charles Taylor, 'The Politics of Recognition', in Amy Gutman (ed.), *Multiculturalism: Examining the Politics of Recognition* (Princeton: Princeton University Press, 1994) 25–74, at 56.

22 Douzinas puts it succinctly: 'A key claim of liberalism is that it does not impose a conception of the good life, but allows people to develop and carry out their own life-plans, through the use of rights': *End of Human Rights*, at 215. It should be stressed yet again, however, that there are more strands to liberalism than this one. 'Communitarian' liberals, such as Will Kimlicka, Joseph Raz, and George Sandel, say they pay attention to individuals as members of groups.

23 See e.g. Robert Fine, *Democracy and the Rule of Law: Marx's Critique of the Legal Form* (Caldwell, NJ: Blackburn, 2002).

24 For a powerful defence of the individualism inherent in human rights, see Ignatieff, *Human Rights*, at 75.

25 To quote him: 'Liberal jurisprudence claims that rights and human rights are historically, structurally and politically indistinguishable. . . But we must resist this equalisation of rights (the building blocks of every positivism) and human rights, which are the promises of a future and the critique of all positive law and system of rights': Douzinas, *End of Human Rights*, at 373–4.

26 Berdal Aral makes this point in an article about Ottoman rule: '[An] obvious difference between Islam and modern human rights doctrine does not imply that societies living under Islamic rule are subject to arbitrary rule or even to oppression': Berdal Aral, 'The Idea of Human Rights as Perceived in the Ottoman Empire' (2004) 26 *Human Rights Quarterly* 454–82, at 461.

27 See e.g. Wendy Brown's article purposely entitled '"The Most We Can Hope For . . .": Human Rights and the Politics of Fatalism'.

28 For example Brown seems interested neither in a liberal nor a human rights perspective; Bentham was a liberal but did not believe in human rights.

29 For excellent legal commentaries on the Convention, see references given in note 1 of Chapter 2.

30 Critiques which are not discussed in the book but would have been highly relevant include communitarianism, critical race theory and strands within the critical legal studies movement.

31 Marie-Bénédicte Dembour, 'Human Rights Talk and Anthropological Ambivalence: The Particular Contexts of Universal Claims', in Olivia Harris (ed.), *Inside and Outside the Law: Anthropological Studies of Authority and Ambiguity* (London: Routledge, 1996) 19–40.

32 To borrow an expression found in Douzinas, *End of Human Rights*, at 4.

33 Thus, to give a few examples, I surmise in Chapter 8 that Jack Donnelly (Politics), Alan Gewirth (Philosophy), Michael Perry (Law) and Michael Freeman (Government) are natural scholars; Michael Ignatieff (History), Conor Gearty (Law) and Richard Wilson (Anthropology) deliberative scholars; Upendra Baxi (Law), Costas Douzinas (Law), Guy Haarscher (Philosophy) and Ken Booth (International Politics) protest scholars; Talal Asad (Anthropology), Wendy Brown (Politics), Makau Mutua (Law) and myself (Law, with a training in Anthropology) discourse scholars. As this brief presentation makes clear, I do not believe that fault-lines in scholarly debates about human rights follow disciplinary boundaries.

34 Thus, Michael Ignatieff qualifies a religious-like approach to human rights as 'idolatry': Ignatieff, *Human Rights*. This secular-like approach to human rights (which does not prevent deliberative scholars from being religious in the primary sense of the term) is also humanist: Fagan, 'Paradoxical Bedfellows'.

35 I think I should be allowed the use of the word 'disciple': Guy Haarscher, whom I classify as a protest scholar in Chapter 8, uses the French word '*dressage*' (literally training, also drilling (of recruits)) for talking of the way human rights are or need to become part of our mental/practical universe.

36 As it were, by removing the liberal 'filter' through which we have looked at human rights in the last two or three centuries.

37 William L. Rowe, 'Agnosticism', in *Concise Routledge Encyclopedia of Philosophy* (London: Routledge, 2000), at 17, emphasis added.

38 William L. Rowe, 'Atheism', in *Concise Routledge Encyclopedia of Philosophy*, at 62.

39 Fagan, 'Paradoxical Bedfellows', at 14.

40 Personal communication.

41 Louis E. Wolcher, 'A Meditation on Wittgenstein's *Lecture on Ethics*', (1998) 9 *Law and Critique* 3–35, at 7 and 15 respectively. In Wittgenstein's words, 'Ethics, if it is anything, is supernatural and our words will only express facts; as a teacup will only hold a teacup of water [even] if I were to pour out a gallon over it': quoted in Wolcher, 'A Meditation', at 17.

42 The current President of the Court declared: '[W]e have become an enormous success story. We are the only institution of this kind and we are an inspiration in other continents': Fred J. Bruinsma and Stephan Parmentier, 'Interview with Mr. Luzius Wildhaber, President of the ECHR' (2003) 21 *Netherlands Quarterly of Human Rights* 185–201, at 193. 'Few would deny that the system of protection of human rights established by the European Convention on Human Rights has been a staggering success', starts Robin White in 'Tackling Political Disputes Through Individual Applications' (1998) 3 *European Human Rights Law Review* 61–74, at 61. Antonio Cassese adopts the description of the Court by a member of the Registry as 'no doubt the most developed and successful international human rights instrument': 'The Impact of the European Convention on Human Rights on the International Criminal Tribunal for the former Yugoslavia', in Paul Mahoney et al. *Protecting Human Rights: The European Perspective. Studies in memory of Rolv Ryssdal* (Köln: Carl Heymanns Verlag, 2000) 213–36, at 213. The chauvinistic flavour of the European elite discourse is not specific to the Strasbourg Court. It is general and can for example be found in European foreign policy, as noted by Andy Storey in a paper on 'Europe and Africa: towards the law of the jungle?' given at the University of Sussex on 9 November 2004.

43 Douzinas, *End of Human Rights*, at 153–4.

44 Ibid., at 7.

45 I am therefore in agreement with Wendy Brown when she talks of 'the impossibility of saying anything generic about the political value of rights. It makes little sense to argue for them or against them independently of an analysis of the historical conditions, social powers, and political discourses with which they converge or which they interdict': Wendy Brown, 'Rights and Identity in Late Modernity: Revisiting the "Jewish Question"', in Austin Sarat and Thomas R. Kearns (eds.), *Identities, Politics and Rights* (Ann Arbor: University of Michigan Press, 1997) 85–130, at 88.

2

The Convention in outline

The next chapters will discuss theoretical critiques of human rights with reference to cases decided by the European Court of Human Rights. This will be done without explaining how these cases have emerged and how they fit into European human rights law. The present chapter offers a 'black-letter law' introduction to the European Convention on Human Rights, especially for the benefit of the reader who is not familiar with it.

In the Anglo-Saxon legal jargon, the expression 'black-letter law' refers to the law which can be read, printed on paper, in legislative, judicial and possibly doctrinal documents. A black-letter study stresses the letter of the law, without paying much attention to its theoretical, political or social significance; its main aim is to investigate what a lawyer can do with the law. Black-letter accounts can be highly sophisticated or thoroughly rudimentary. The introduction offered here is of the latter kind.[1]

The work of the Council of Europe

The European Convention on Human Rights owes its existence to the Council of Europe. This European organization must not be confused with the European Community/Union. It was set up in 1949 as one of a number of initiatives to secure peace and security in Europe. Originally made up of ten states, it now counts forty-six member states, including Turkey (since 1949) to the south and the Russian Federation (since 1996) to the east. In its own words, its main aims are to protect pluralist democracy and human rights; to promote awareness and encourage the development of Europe's cultural identity and diversity; to seek solutions to the problems facing European society (such as xenophobia, environmental protection, AIDS and organized crime); and to help consolidate democratic stability in Europe by backing political, legislative and constitutional reform. The European Convention for the Protection of Human Rights and Fundamental Freedoms, commonly known as the European Convention on Human Rights, signed in 1950 and in force since 1953, is heralded as its major achievement; it is nevertheless wrong to reduce the Council of Europe to the Convention alone.

Alongside the European Court of Human Rights, the Council of Europe comprises three major institutions: the Committee of Ministers, the Secretariat and the Parliamentary Assembly. All these institutions sit at Strasbourg. The Council of Europe produces a constant stream of treaties, declarations, resolutions and recommendations. To date it has adopted close to two hundred conventions and agreements.[2] Apart from the European Convention on Human Rights, its most significant human rights instruments are the Social Charter (1961), the European Convention for the Prevention of Torture and Inhuman and Degrading Treatment (1987) and the Framework Convention for the Protection of National Minorities (1994). The establishment of the European Commission against Racism and Intolerance (1993), the creation of the role of the Commissioner for Human Rights (1999) and the development of monitoring procedures (1990s) also deserve mention.

Such a listing, selective as it is, should make it clear that this book, which draws exclusively on the case law generated under the European Convention on Human Rights, does not pretend to comment on and even less to do justice to the whole of the multi-faceted work undertaken by the Council of Europe in the human rights field.

The rights guaranteed by the Convention

The Universal Declaration of Human Rights was proclaimed by the United Nations in 1948. The European Convention on Human Rights was signed two years later. Unlike the Declaration, the Convention possessed the advantage of creating an international mechanism to enforce the rights it guarantees. Not surprisingly, it did not seek to protect as many rights as the UN Declaration. The European Convention focused on civil and political rights, while the Declaration embraced not only these but also economic, social and cultural rights.[3]

Originally the Convention provided for thirteen rights: the rights to life (Article 2), not to be submitted to torture (Article 3), not to be enslaved (Article 4), to remain free (Article 5), to a fair trial (Article 6), not to be punished without law (Article 7), to privacy and family life (Article 8), to freedom of religion and thought (Article 9), to freedom of expression (Article 10), to freedom of association (Article 11), to marry (Article 12), to a national remedy (Article 13) and not to be discriminated against (Article 14).[4]

Protocols to the Convention have added further rights. Protocol no. 1 (signed in 1952, in force since 1954) deals with rights which had proved too controversial for an agreement on their exact phrasing to be possible when the Convention was negotiated; namely, the rights to peaceful enjoyment of possessions (Article 1),[5] education (Article 2), and free elections (Article 3). Protocol no. 4 (signed in 1963, in force since 1968) provides for the right not to be deprived of liberty because of failure to fulfil a contractual obligation (Article 1), freedom of movement and residence (Article 2), non-deportation of nationals (Article 3), and the prohibition of collective expulsion of aliens (Article 4). Protocol 6 (signed in 1983, in force since 1985) concerns the abolition of the death penalty, especially in peace time. Protocol 7 (signed in 1984, in force since 1988) deals with conditions governing the expulsion of lawfully resident aliens (Article 1), review of criminal conviction and sentence (Article 2), compensation for miscarriages of justice (Article 3), the right not to be tried twice for the same offence (Article 4), and the equality of rights between spouses (Article 5). Protocol 12 (signed in 2000, not yet in force) aims to create a free-standing right to non-discrimination.[6] Protocol 13 (signed in 2002, in force since 2003) goes further than Protocol 6 in that it eliminates the death penalty in all circumstances.

General principles of interpretation

Even a cursory reading of these provisions should leave no one in doubt that their concrete application requires interpretation. Over the years, the Court has identified a number of general principles of interpretation. Particularly important among these are the principle of effectiveness, the recognition that the Convention requires an evolutive interpretation, the acceptance that states enjoy a margin of appreciation in respect of most provisions, and the proportionality principle.

The effectiveness principle has been established on the ground that the Convention is intended to guarantee rights that are 'practical and effective' rather than 'theoretical and illusory'.[7] It looks beyond the letter of the law to assess concretely the position of the individual. For example, the right to a fair trial amounts to nothing if access to a tribunal is denied in the first place. Article 6 does encompass the right of access even though this particular aspect of the right to a fair trial is not specifically mentioned in it.

The principle of evolutive interpretation derives from the fact that the Convention is to be regarded as a 'living instrument' which must be able to adapt to new realities and attitudes rather than providing static standards. To give an example, the identification of illegitimate children and their unfavourable treatment compared to legitimate children were regarded as normal and perfectly acceptable at the time the Convention was drafted; in time, the distinction in legal status between legitimate and illegitimate children was nonetheless found to be contrary to the Convention.[8]

The doctrine of the margin of appreciation has been developed in recognition of the fact that states are in principle better placed than the Court to assess what local circumstances require. It comes into play whenever the Convention provides for rights which can be curtailed – and perhaps also, but not necessarily explicitly, in respect of so-called absolute rights which are intended not to be subject to any exceptions.[9]

The proportionality principle has regard to the fact that the interference by a state with a right provided by the Convention, even when allowed under the Convention, must remain proportionate. It has some affinity with the adage:

'Don't use a sledgehammer to crack a nut'.[10] Proportionality implies the need to strike a proper balance between competing interests, including first and foremost those of the individual and those of the state.[11]

The original mechanism of enforcement

The enforcement mechanism provided by the Convention which was signed in 1950 was a first in international law. Its revolutionary aspect consisted of the possibility of petitions which emanated not only from states but also from individuals, to be adjudicated by an international court. While international law had traditionally been concerned with relations between states, even individuals could see their claims that a government had violated a right guaranteed to them under the Convention examined by an international court. At the time of writing, there have been many thousands of individual applications, but no more than twenty-one state applications (relating to a mere thirteen cases, concerned with seven kinds of situation),[12] in line with the fact that states are generally reluctant to bring each other before an international judicial tribunal.

The enforcement mechanism originally provided by the Convention relied on the establishment of a European Commission of Human Rights (hereafter, 'Commission')[13] and of a European Court of Human Rights (already referred to as the 'Court'). The Commission was established in 1954, the Court in 1959 (with its first judgment being delivered in 1961). The Committee of Ministers, previously created by the Statute of the Council of Europe, also played a role under the Convention.

It should be stressed that the jurisdiction of the Court was not automatic in relation to member states that were party to the Convention. It depended on a declaration by states that they accepted the jurisdiction of the Court. This declaration could 'be made unconditionally or on condition of reciprocity on the part of several or certain other High Contracting Parties or for a specified period'.[14] While the Commission was competent to examine inter-state applications from the start,[15] it could only receive petitions from individuals (and bring them subsequently before the Court) if the defendant state had made a second declaration, which could also be made for a fixed period, that it accepted the right of individual petition.[16]

The Commission consisted in a body of independent experts. There were as many commissioners as there were states party to the Convention (with each state party having one commissioner nominated in its respect, generally but not necessarily one of its nationals). The Commission worked part-time, in two-week sessions taking place eight times a year. It represented the 'obligatory pathway'[17] to the Court and thus constituted the first port of call of a petitioner. Acting as a filtering body, its initial task was to examine the 'admissibility' of the petition.

To be considered admissible a petition had to fulfil six main conditions. These remain unchanged today even though the filtering function is now performed by the Court. First, the applicant must be able to show that he or she can claim the status of victim, i.e. it must be his or her rights – rather than those of a neighbour – which are alleged to have been violated. In other words the Convention does not allow *actio popularis*. Second, he or she must have exhausted national remedies, i.e. have done everything possible to have the complaint resolved at national level before turning to Strasbourg – in respect of the principle of 'subsidiarity'. Third, the application must not be anonymous – though a successful request for confidentiality will lead to the applicant being referred to by his or her initials or even a single letter. Fourth, the case must have been lodged within six months of the final relevant domestic decision. Fifth, it cannot be incompatible with the provisions of the Convention, for example by falling outside the scope of rights covered by the Convention or by referring to events which took place before the Convention was in force in respect of the defendant state. Sixth, it must not be manifestly ill-founded, which means that the applicant must substantiate his or her complaint and demonstrate that the complaint falls within the terms of the Convention. Many an application is rejected on the ground that it is manifestly ill-founded. What 'manifest' means in this context is often open to question given that inadmissibility is not uncommonly pronounced by a majority, after extensive legal argument.[18]

The conditions of admissibility are far from being a mere formality: the great majority of applicants are disappointed at the admissibility stage. Commentators have often observed that no more than 10 per cent of applications are passing the admissibility stage.[19] However low, even this figure appears too optimistic today.[20]

Only cases that are declared admissible can be examined on their merits. The Commission used to be responsible for establishing the facts – through fact-finding missions if necessary – but without ever binding the Court on these findings; for encouraging 'friendly settlements' between the parties once the case had been declared admissible; and in the commonly occurring absence of a friendly settlement, of expressing a reasoned opinion as to whether there had been a breach of the Convention. This report, although not binding, was important and added to the case law of the Convention. It could include separate opinions. It was submitted to the Committee of Ministers.

From the date of this transmission, the Commission had three months to bring the case before the Court.[21] The Court then gave a final and binding judgment. It could still declare the case inadmissible or note that a friendly settlement had been reached. Normally, however, a case brought before the Court ended with a judgment on the merits, i.e. a ruling as to whether there had been a violation of one or more substantive provisions of the Convention – to which could be added a ruling on just satisfaction.

Like the Commission, the Court was a part-time institution with as many judges as Convention member states. Cases were normally decided by Chambers of nine judges, but could be relinquished to the plenary Court (until 1993) or a

Grand Chamber (from 1993), if they were deemed to raise 'serious questions affecting the interpretation of the Convention'. The composition of any one Chamber was effected by drawing lots, except for the President and the national judge (i.e. the judge elected in respect of the defendant state) who both sat *ex officio*. Judgments were often adopted by a majority and could include separate (either dissenting or concurring) opinions.

When a case upon which the Commission had written a report had not been referred to the Court within three months, it was the Committee of Ministers which was responsible for deciding whether a breach of the Convention had occurred.[22] In practice non-referral to the Court generally happened in two instances: first, when the Commission had not found a violation and the case did not seem to raise an important Convention issue; second, when the Commission had found a violation but either the case raised an issue which had already been clearly decided by the Court or the government had indicated that it accepted the Commission's finding and was willing to act upon it. The decisions of the Committee of Ministers taken under Article 32 of the Convention were typically short and sparsely reasoned, in line with the political character of this body.

In addition, the Committee was responsible then, as it is now, for supervising the execution of judgments of the Court.[23] Although a crucial issue, what happens after a verdict of violation by the Court is not discussed in this book. Briefly, the state must pay the applicant any just satisfaction ordered by the Court and amend its law or its practice to bring them in line with the Convention's requirements. What exactly the Convention requires can of course be a controversial question.[24]

The current mechanism of enforcement: Protocol 11

A number of 'procedural' (as opposed to 'substantive') protocols to the Convention were adopted over the years in an effort to improve the enforcement system originally put in place by the Convention. They need not detain us here, as the relatively superficial modifications they introduced have been superseded by the adoption of Protocol 11.

The impetus for the in-depth reform represented by Protocol 11 arose, so to speak, from the fact that the Convention became a 'victim of its own success'. Applications had originally been few; they came in ever greater numbers as the years went by and the Convention became both better known and applicable in a larger territory. Just 404 applications were registered by the Commission in 1981, but 2,037 in 1993.[25] It took longer and longer for a case to be the object of a judgment by the Court: commentators spoke of an average of over five years in 1995.[26] Reform seemed imperative if the backlog problem identified in the 1980s was not to continue to intensify. The idea of a single Court (with obligatory jurisdiction in respect of states party to the Convention)[27] took hold.

Protocol 11 was signed in 1994 and came into force in 1998. It abolished the Commission (after a transitional period of one year) and created a single permanent Court which sits, like its predecessor, at Strasbourg. Every member state has a judge who is elected in its respect, ensuring that all legal systems are represented at the Court. The high number of states (now 46) means that the Court has more than quadrupled its composition since the 1960s. The Court is divided into four sections which are so constituted as to present a geographical and gender balance and are reconstituted every three years. The Court sits in Committees, Chambers and a Grand Chamber.

Committees are made of three judges. They are competent to declare a case inadmissible. Such a decision must be reached unanimously. It leaves no public trace: not reasoned, it is communicated to the applicant by simple letter, with the Strasbourg file of the case being destroyed after a period of one year.[28]

Chambers are constituted of seven judges, normally from the same section. A Chamber necessarily comprises the 'national judge'.[29] The first aspect of a case to be considered by a Chamber is its admissibility. Decisions on admissibility can be adopted by a majority, without the exact pattern of voting then being indicated and without any possibility of including separate opinions. The Court is responsible for the tasks which used to be performed by the Commission in respect of fact-finding and the conclusion of friendly settlements. As before 1998, decisions on the merits are adopted through reasoned judgments to which separate opinions, either dissenting or concurring, can be appended.

The Grand Chamber is constituted by the President of the Court, the Presidents and Vice-Presidents of the sections and another eight judges. It can hear cases which have been relinquished to it by a Chamber; it may also, in exceptional circumstances, rehear a case which has been decided by a Chamber.[30] The Grand Chamber acts very much like a Chamber except that it obviously comprises more judges and carries greater authority.

Like the erstwhile Commission and the former Court, the current Court is supported in its work by the Registry, a body which currently numbers about 500 members of staff.

The future mechanism of enforcement: Protocol 14

Even before Protocol 11 came into force, it was widely felt that the ever-increasing number of applications to Strasbourg, and the impact of the accession to the Convention of Eastern and Central European countries following the collapse of communism, would make a 'reform of the reform' more or less immediately necessary. Work on further reform started in 2001. Protocol 14 was signed in May 2004. It will come into force after ratification by all states party to the Convention.[31] The details of this reform do not affect the material presented in this book. Nonetheless they obviously colour the direction which the Strasbourg system is taking.

A number of NGOs and academics were concerned during its negotiation that the ideas which were being formulated could threaten the right of individual petition.[32] The worst has been avoided, even though a new ground of inadmissibility has been added, namely, that 'the applicant has not suffered a significant disadvantage'.[33] Also worrying is the fact that judges sitting in single formations will be able to declare applications inadmissible.[34] On the positive side, however, is to be mentioned the power of a committee to declare a case admissible and render at the same time a judgment on the merits if the underlying question in the case is already the subject of well-established case law.[35] This is clearly a measure which can be expected to increase the efficiency of the Court without endangering the right of individual petition.

Conclusion

The aim of this chapter has been to provide background information which puts the reader new to the Convention system in a position to understand the legal context for the cases which are used to illustrate the theoretical arguments developed in the book. There is no need to summarize the information which has been given. One remark, however, is appropriate: the need for a black-letter law account points to the 'statist' bias of this book. By this, I mean that my study seems to accept that states are the central actors of this world. After all, only states appear as defendants before the European Court of Human Rights. But the point goes further given that law itself is very much enmeshed in the institution of the state. It must therefore be stressed that the concept of human rights need not be as dependent on the state as this book may seem to assume it is.[36] As I said in the introduction, my focus on the case law of the European Court of Human Rights is 'accidental'; any other human rights site, including a less institutional one, could have been used to explore the concrete manifestation, in practice, of the insights of conceptual critiques of human rights.

Notes

1 For excellent accounts of the law of the Convention, see e.g. in an extensive literature: Karen Reid, *A Practitioner's Guide to the European Convention on Human Rights* (2nd edn, London: Sweet and Maxwell, 2004); Philip Leach, *Taking a Case to the European Court of Human Rights* (2nd edn, Oxford: Oxford University Press, 2004); Richard Clayton and Hugh Tomlinson, *The Law of Human Rights* (Oxford: Oxford University Press, 2000); P. van Dijk and G. J. H. van Hoof, *Theory and Practice of the European Convention on Human Rights* (The Hague: Kluwer, 1998); D. J. Harris, M. O'Boyle and C. Warbrick, *Law of the European Convention on Human Rights* (London: Butterworths, 1995); Louis-Edmond Pettiti, Emmanuel Decaux and Pierre-Henri Imbert (eds.), *La Convention européenne des droits de l'homme: Commentaire article par article* (2nd edn, Paris: Economica, 1999). For shorter and more accessible studies, see e.g. Donna Gomien, *Short Guide to the European Convention on Human Rights* (3rd edn, Strasbourg: Council of Europe, 2005); Philip Leach, *Taking a Case to the European Court of Human Rights* (1st edn, London: Blackstone, 2001); Mark Jordan,

Doing the Rights Thing: The Not So Difficult Guide to the Human Rights Act 1988 and the Law of the European Convention on Human Rights (EOS Education, 2001). For texts which reproduce materials, see Alastair Mowbray, *Cases and Materials on the European Convention on Human Rights* (London: Butterworths, 2001); Mark Janis, Richard Kay and Anthony Bradley, *European Human Rights Law: Text and Materials* (2nd edn, Oxford: Oxford University Press, 2000).

2 To be exact, 198 have been adopted so far, with the last three Conventions, of 16 May 2005, relating to the prevention of terrorism, trafficking in human beings, and money laundering and the financing of terrorism.

3 For an excellent introduction to the variety of international human rights instruments, see Rhona K. M. Smith, *Textbook on International Human Rights* (Oxford: Oxford University Press, 2003).

4 See Appendix 1 for the exact wording of these provisions.

5 Article 1 of Protocol 1 is the only substantive provision inscribed in a protocol which will be discussed in this book. See Appendix 1 for its exact wording.

6 Article 14 of the Convention is not 'free-standing': it can only be used in conjunction with another convention provision.

7 The principle was first identified in *Airey* v. *Ireland*, 9 October 1979, Series A, No. 32, (1979–1980) 2 EHRR 305, discussed in Chapter 7.

8 *Marckx* v. *Belgium*, 13 June 1979, Series A, No. 31, (1970–1980) 2 EHRR 330, cursorily discussed in Chapter 4. The principle was first enunciated by the Court in *Tyrer* v. *United Kingdom*, 25 April 1978, Series A, No. 26, (1979–1980) 2 EHRR 1, discussed in Chapter 6.

9 The doctrine, first endorsed by the Court in *Handyside* v. *United Kingdom*, 7 December 1976, Series A, No. 24, (1979–1980) 1 EHRR 737, is repeatedly discussed in this book, especially in Chapter 3 (on realism) and Chapter 6 (on particularism).

10 Jordan, *Doing the Rights Thing*, at 3.41.

11 The principle is extensively discussed in Chapter 4 (on utilitarianism).

12 Søren C. Prebensen, 'Inter-State Complaints under Treaty Provisions – The Experience under the European Convention on Human Rights' (1999) 20 *Human Rights Law Journal* 446–55.

13 Obviously, this Commission should not be confused with the Commission of the European Communities.

14 Article 46 of the Convention as originally signed. In the late 1950s, governments were generally reluctant to allow themselves to be brought before the Court, as contemporary debates in the United Kingdom and the Netherlands for example indicate: Janis, Kay and Bradley, *Human Rights Law*, at 23–5. France, a member state of the Council of Europe since the beginning of the organization (May 1949) only ratified the Convention in 1974 and then only accepted the jurisdiction of the Court in 1981!

15 Article 24 of the Convention as originally signed.

16 Article 25 of the Convention as originally signed.

17 Harris, O'Boyle and Warbrick, *Law*, at 571.

18 As remarked e.g. in Harris, O'Boyle and Warbrick, *Law*, at 628.

19 22,000 cases had been the object of a decision by the Commission up to 1994, of which 2,027 had been declared admissible: Harris, O'Boyle and Warbrick, *Law*, at 580. In 2001, Leach spoke of 20 per cent: Leach, *Taking a Case* (1st edn), at 62; in 2004, Reid advanced again the figure of 10 per cent: Reid, *Guide*, at 2.

20 In 2004, 19,802 applications were declared inadmissible, mostly by committees of three (420 were declared inadmissible by Chambers). In the same year, 842

applications were declared admissible. (The figures have been collated on the basis of the statistics released by the Court and available on its website: http://www.echr.coe. int). The implications of such mass rejection are discussed in Chapter 5.

21 Other parties who could do so were: the contracting party whose national was alleged to be a victim, the contracting party which referred the case to the Commission, and the contracting party against which the complaint had been made (Article 48 of the Convention as originally signed). Few states availed themselves of these possibilities.

22 Under Article 32 of the Convention as originally signed.

23 Article 54 of the Convention as originally signed and Article 46 of the Convention as amended by Protocol 11.

24 Justin Harman, 'Complementarity of Mechanisms within the Council of Europe / Perspectives of the Committee of Ministers' (2000) 21 *Human Rights Law Journal* 296–7.

25 Harris, O'Boyle and Warbrick, *Law*, at 706. By 1990, there had been close to 5,000 individual applications; more than 25,000 followed in the next decade.

26 Ibid.

27 By the 1990s it was considered an aberration to be party to the Convention without accepting the jurisdiction of the Court and the right of individual petition. It similarly became politically unacceptable to become a member of the Council of Europe without promising to ratify the Convention in the near future: Syméon Karagiannis, 'Le territoire d'application de la Convention européenne des droits de l'homme. *Vaetera et nova*' (2005) 61 *Revue trimestrielle des droits de l'homme* 33–120, at 44.

28 For more details, see Chapter 5.

29 This is generally the judge elected in respect of the defendant state, but it is sometimes an *ad hoc* judge.

30 Article 43 of the Convention as amended by Protocol 11.

31 Seventeen (out of forty-six) states had ratified Protocol 14 as of 3 October 2005.

32 John Wadham, 'What Price the Right of Individual Petition: Report of the Evaluation Group to the Committee of Ministers on the European Court of Human Rights' (2002) *European Human Rights Law Review* 169–74; Marie-Bénédicte Dembour, '"Finishing Off" Cases: The Radical Solution to the Problem of the Expanding ECtHR Caseload' (2002) *European Human Rights Law Review* 604–23; Pierre Lambert, 'Quelle réforme pour la Cour européenne des droits de l'homme?' (2002) 52 *Revue trimestrielle des droits de l'homme* 795–805. For a commentary following the signature of Protocol 14, see Marie-Aude Beernaert, 'Protocol 14 and New Strasbourg Procedures: Towards Greater Efficiency? And at what Price?' (2004) *European Human Rights Law Review* 544–57.

33 Article 12 of Protocol 14, in a phrasing which is due to become Article 35 (3) of the Convention.

34 Articles 6 and 7 of Protocol 14, laying down provisions which are due to become Articles 26 and 27 of the Convention, respectively. It is to be noted that the 'national judge' will not be able to sit in a single judge formation in respect of applications directed against his/her state: new Article 26, para. 3.

35 Article 8 of Protocol 14, laying down a provision due to become Article 28 (1) (b) of the Convention.

36 Echoing Neil Stammers: '[W]hat we have is a debate on human rights that is highly state centric [and] where there is little space for thinking about human rights in any other way. This . . . is tremendously problematic . . . [P]roposed statist solutions to

human rights problems . . . might encourage a passive acceptance of state power. Furthermore, the state centricity of the human rights debate is indicative of a top-down way of thinking about human rights. The state is at the top, human beings at the bottom, and the statism guiding the debates is both a symptom and a cause of such thinking. Not only is this elitist, it is also disabling. It constrains the potential for popular mobilization around human rights issues and points any mobilizations that do occur towards nothing other than the state': 'A Critique of Social Approaches to Human Rights' (1995) 17 *Human Rights Quarterly* 488–508, at 506–7.

3

The Convention in a realist light

> From *real* law come *real* rights; but from *imaginary* laws . . . come *imaginary* rights.
>
> (Bentham)

This chapter takes issue with the claim – at the core of the human rights credo – that human rights are natural or self-evident. It explores how the perceptions of two bodies of theory which oppose this claim could be said to be reflected in the Strasbourg case law.

The first critique on which the chapter focuses is that which was mounted by Jeremy Bentham against the 1789 French Declaration; the second, that which implicitly emanates from international relations (IR) realist scholars. These two unrelated theoretical perspectives are juxtaposed in this chapter because they both reject the idea that there exists a natural law which governs the conduct of the state and which is therefore superior to positive national law (Bentham) or which is fit to regulate the way states interact with each other (IR realism). In its own way, each theory stresses the principle of national sovereignty. Both theories regard the idea of human rights as emanating from above/outside the state/society as nonsense. They thus urge us not to believe in the human rights orthodoxy.

This chapter will give many examples which indicate that it is possible to consider that the Convention and its case law are dominated by realist considerations. This is particularly clear in respect of Article 15 which allows the use of derogation in times of national emergency, suggesting that we cannot believe the words of the provisions which purport to guarantee rights. However, negating altogether the influence on the system of supranational and/or idealistic impulses is not justified; this chapter adopts the view that realism and idealism are in tension with each other, including in the Convention system.

The 'Anarchical Fallacies' denounced by Bentham the 'realist'

Jeremy Bentham is best known as the founder of utilitarianism. What interests me in this chapter, however, is not so much his utilitarianism as what I call his realism, a term I derive from the statement, which I put at the head of this chapter, where he contrasts real rights with imaginary rights.[1] The statement in question comes from his critique of the French Declaration of the Rights of Man and of the Citizen (hereafter 'Declaration'), entitled 'Anarchical Fallacies'.[2] The Declaration was adopted on 26 August 1789.[3] It directly influenced the UN Universal Declaration of 1948,[4] which in turn proved a model for the substantive provisions of the European Convention. Given this lineage, one may expect a critique of the French Declaration to be applicable to the European Convention (even if, two centuries on, the language of natural rights has been abandoned in favour of that of human rights).

Bentham did not think that the French Declaration provided real rights. This leads one to ask: what are real rights? For Bentham, real rights are rights that have a positive source (in government), in contrast to rights which are assumed simply to exist and thus come from nowhere in particular as they are immanent. Bentham did not believe in the existence of natural rights. In his view, natural rights may sound impressive, but they are spurious. Thus, the rights of the French Declaration, if taken literally, mean nothing. To give here only one example, human beings are obviously not born equal, contrary to what the Declaration states. If the rights of the Declaration are not to be taken literally, then they still mean nothing as they will need to be given limits. And who will set these limits? The government. In other words, what has been given with one hand (the Declaration) will immediately be taken away with the other (the government).

The fact that rights are given and limited by the government is not one which would have worried Bentham. On the contrary, as far as he is concerned, this is exactly how things should be. Bentham-the-utilitarian believes that the government is there to promote the common good; he also thinks that the government should be able to make the rules. What Bentham opposes is the view that rights could somehow be above the state, providing superior universal moral norms by which the state must abide. Bentham-the-realist favoured rights – however imperfect – which existed in the positive world over rights which were the product of the imaginations of utopian dreamers. As far as he was concerned, the rights proclaimed in the Declaration were 'nonsense upon stilts',[5] a 'mere effusion of imbecility'.[6]

By entitling his critique 'Anarchical Fallacies' Bentham indicated that the Declaration was in his opinion *conceptually* fallacious: a nonsensical flow of words amounting to nothing more than a bundle of contradictions. 'Look to the letter, you find nonsense – look beyond the letter, you find nothing.'[7] The problem as Bentham saw it, however, was also *practical*. As far as he was concerned, the Declaration invited the perpetual overthrow of current political institutions, thus potentially leading to the 'order of chaos'.[8] The title of his essay was meant literally: the rights provided in the Declaration were meaningless and dangerous.

Bentham's critique is broader than the 'silly-or-pestilential'[9] argument. It anticipates virtually all the themes addressed in this book.[10] Nonetheless, this chapter reviews only what I call the 'realist' aspect of his critique.[11] I see it as consisting of three main aspects: a) the words of the Declaration, taken literally, mean nothing; b) to the extent that it encourages insurrection, this nonsense is dangerous; c) in any event, the Declaration provides imaginary, as opposed to real, rights. These aspects are examined in turn in three subsections which do not assume familiarity with the text and thus include many quotations from the original.

'Look to the letter, you find nonsense'

Article 1 of the French Declaration states: 'Men are born and remain free, and equal in respect of rights.' Bentham observes:

> All men born free? Absurd and miserable nonsense! When the great complaint – a complaint made perhaps by the very same people at the same time, is – [sic] that so many men are born slaves. Oh! but when we acknowledge them to be born slaves, we refer to the laws in being; which laws being void, as being contrary to those laws of nature which are the efficient causes of those rights of man that we are declaring, the men in question are free in one sense, though slaves in another; – slaves and free, at the same time: free in respect of the laws of nature – slaves in respect of the pretended human laws, which, though called laws, are no laws at all, as being contrary to the laws of nature.[12]

Bentham refers to the dichotomy – in which he does not believe – between the 'laws in being' and the 'laws of nature', more commonly referred to today as 'positive law' and 'natural law'. The former is man-made and gives rise to positive rights. The latter supposedly exists independently of human recognition; its source is supposed to be absolute and immanent, consisting of God, nature, the universe or reason (or perhaps Reason with a capital 'R'); its proponents often derive from it natural rights – those very rights asserted in the French Declaration. Bentham clearly believed in the existence of positive law only; for him natural law existed only in the imagination of those who erroneously believed in it.[13]

Bentham sees nonsense and contradiction all through the Declaration, up to its last article, which reads: 'Property being an inviolable and sacred right, no one can be deprived of it, unless it be when public necessity, legally established, evidently requires it and under the conditions of a just and previous indemnity.' He writes:

> Here we have the concluding article in this pile of contradictions; it does not mismatch the rest. By the first article, all men are equal in respect of all sorts of rights, and so are to continue for evermore, spite of everything which can be done by laws. By the second article, property is of the number of those rights. By this seventeenth and last article, no man can be deprived of his property – no, not a single atom of it, without an equal equivalent paid – not when the occasion calls for it, for that would not be soon enough, but beforehand; all men are equal in respect of property, while John has £50,000 a-year, and Peter nothing: all men are to be equal in property, and that for everlasting; at the same time that he who has a thousand times as much as a thousand others put together, is not to be deprived of a single farthing of it, without having first received an exact equivalent.[14]

Bentham sees the drafters of the Declaration as constantly oscillating between a utopian world (where all men would be equal) and the real world (where they clearly are not). This leads them to use words in different ways, and in ambiguous ways, speaking for example of 'can', instead of 'ought'.[15] Thus, Article 17 should have read: 'No one *ought to* be deprived', rather than '*can*' be deprived, of property except in the circumstances described in the Article.

'The order of chaos'

According to Bentham, the problem with the 'perpetual vein of nonsense, flowing from a perpetual abuse of words'[16] which makes up the Declaration is not just conceptual, but also practical, for the Declaration will lead people to be dissatisfied with (man-made) laws and to revolt against them.

Article 5 states: 'The law has no right to forbid any other actions than such as are hurtful to society'. Bentham answers:

> The avowed object of this clause is to preach constant insurrection, to raise up every man in arms against every law which he happens not to approve of. For, take any such action you will, if the law have no right to forbid it, a law forbidding it is null and void, and the attempt to execute it an oppression, and resistance to such attempt, and insurrection in support of such resistance, legal, justifiable, and commendable . . .
>
> A government which should fulfil the expectations here held out, would be a government of absolute perfection. *The instance of a government fulfilling these expectations, never has taken place, nor till men are angels ever can take place.* Against every government which fails in any degree of fulfilling these expectations, then, it is the professed object of this manifesto to excite insurrection: here, as elsewhere, it is therefore its direct object to excite insurrection at all times against every government whatsoever.[17]

For Bentham, whose realist vein is clear in the sentence I have italicised, the way to deal with bad laws is to induce the legislator to change them, not to call for their abandonment in the name of non-existent natural rights. This is the more so since such a call amounts to an anarchical move which is, Bentham fears, insurrectional and murderous. The first passage I have quoted in the previous subsection, in relation to Article 1 of the Declaration, continues:

> For such is the difference . . . between the moderate man and the man of violence. The rational censor, acknowledging the existence of the law he disapproves, proposes to repeal it: the anarchist, setting up his will and fancy for a law before which all mankind are called upon to bow down at the first word – the anarchist, trampling on truth and decency, denies the validity of the law in question, – denies the existence of it in the character of a law, and calls upon all mankind to rise up in a mass, and resist the execution of it.[18]

Bentham remarks in his preliminary observations:

> The revolution, which threw the government into the hands of the penners and adopters of this declaration, having been the effect of insurrection, the grand object

evidently is to justify the cause. But by justifying it, they invite it . . . in justifying the demolition of existing authorities, they undermine all future ones, their own consequently in the number . . . *'People, behold your rights! If a single article of them be violated, insurrection is not your right only, but the most sacred of your duties.'*[19]

'Look beyond the letter, you find nothing'

Bentham is known, not altogether accurately, as the founder of utilitarianism.[20] He devoted his life and intelligence to searching for principles of government which would bring happiness to the greatest number. To achieve this utilitarian aim, he turned to law. The law he had in mind was man-made. He was a positivist. For him, it was clear that natural law did not exist, except as a figment of the imagination of deluded thinkers. The American Constitution spoke of men endowed with rights 'by their Creator' and of 'self-evident truths'. The French Declaration said in its Preamble that it 'acknowledges and declares, in the presence and under the auspices of the Supreme Being' the existence of 'natural, inalienable and sacred' rights. All these phrases *sound* good, which is why they have considerable appeal.[21] In fact they do not mean anything:

> [F]rom *real* laws come real rights; but from *imaginary* laws, from laws of nature, fancied by poets, rhetoricians, and dealers in moral and intellectual poisons, come *imaginary* rights, a bastard brood of monsters, 'gorgons and chimeras dire'.[22]

Bentham repeatedly develops this idea of imaginary rights in his textual analysis of the Articles of the Declaration – each one a 'Pandora box'.[23] Here follow two examples, the first related to Article 7, which states that 'No one can be accused, arrested or detained, but in the cases determined by the law, and according to the forms prescribed by the law':

> The professed object of the whole composition [i.e. the Declaration] is to tie the hands of the law, by declaring pretended rights over which the law is never to have any power, – liberty, the right of enjoying liberty: here this very liberty is left at the mercy and good pleasure of the law.[24]
>
> What is the security worth, which is thus given to the individual as against the encroachments of government? What does the barrier pretended to be set up against government amount to? It is a barrier which government is expressly called upon to set up where it pleases.[25]

Or, to quote yet another passage, this time directed at the whole of the Declaration:

> In regard to the rights thus declared, mention will either be made of the exceptions and modifications that may be made to them by the laws themselves, or there will not. In the former case, the observance of the declaration will be impracticable; nor can the law in its details stir a step without flying in the face of it. In the other case, it fails thereby altogether of its only object, the setting limits to the exercise of the legislative power. Suppose a declaration to this effect – no man's liberty shall be

abridged in any point. This, it is evident, would be an useless extravagance, which must be contradicted by every law that came to be made. Suppose it to say – no man's liberty shall be abridged, but in such points as it shall be abridged in, by the law. *This, we see, is saying nothing: it leaves the law just as free and unfettered as it found it.*[26]

The last sentence deserves our full attention. It encapsulates what constitutes to my mind an enormous problem for current human rights law. To paraphrase Bentham: giving or recognizing supposedly 'natural', 'superior', 'inalienable', 'fundamental' (whichever you choose to call them) rights which can then be defeated through legislation amounts to *nothing*. Could it be said that this is what happens in the European Convention system? To borrow Bentham's words, does the Convention provide real or imaginary rights?

The relative protection of the European Convention and the margin of appreciation

Human rights are based on the idea that there is a core of fundamental rights which originate from outside, and are above, the state (and beyond society altogether). This superiority, derived from metaphysical immanence, is supposedly central to their *raison d'être*. If the rights provided in the Convention are man-made rights, defined in a strictly positivist legal framework, this superiority crumbles.

'Look beyond the letter [of the Declaration], you find nothing', Bentham wrote. He observed that the rights 'guaranteed' in the Declaration could come either with or without exceptions. On the latter hypothesis, the absolute phrasing of the Declaration meant that any action by the government (including legislation) immediately flew in its face. On the former, the Declaration obviously failed in its professed aim of setting up rights which could not be limited by the government. At first sight, Bentham's logic appears impeccable.[27]

Following it, one could say that each of the substantive rights provided in the European Convention is imaginary. Even the right to life contains exceptions which include killing when trying to effect a legal arrest or to quell an insurrection. Bentham-the-realist invites us to ask the question: Is the Convention so full of contradictions that it is useless?

The first hypothesis envisaged by Bentham, namely rights to which no exception is attached, occasionally occurs in the Convention. These rights are deemed to be absolute. This is for example the case of the right to be free from torture, inhuman and degrading treatment and punishment (Article 3).[28] The second hypothesis is far more common. For example Article 5 begins: 'Everyone has the right to liberty and security of person. No one shall be deprived of his liberty save in the following cases and in accordance with a procedure prescribed by law.' The exceptions, which provide for the detention of, inter alia, criminals and persons of unsound mind, follow. Article 10 states: 'Everyone has the right to freedom of expression . . . The exercise of [this right] may be subject to such formalities, conditions, restrictions or penalties as are prescribed by law and are necessary in a democratic society, in the interests of national security . . . for the protection of health and morals [etc.].' The reader is invited to consult Appendix 1 to examine exactly how the exceptions to these and other rights are formulated in the Convention.

Most rights 'guaranteed' under the Convention are recognized not to be absolute; they receive 'relative protection'.[29] How is this relative protection achieved? To put it crudely, the Convention says it gives these rights to the individual, but then it immediately places those rights back in the hands of the government. The Convention thus exactly follows the scenario Bentham predicted would need to be resorted to if the observance of the Declaration, or in this case, Convention were not to be impracticable.

Realistically (I stress the word), governments would never have agreed to be bound by the Convention if such a scenario had not been followed – and without governments' signature and ratification, the Convention would never have come into being. It would therefore be stupid to criticize the drafters of the Convention for having followed the practical path of providing for exceptions, at least if one wanted to have something like the Convention.

Significantly, Bentham was of the view that the trouble with the French Declaration lay not in the details of its phrasing, but in the fact that the enterprise of drafting such a declaration had been conceived at all.[30] Can this be said of the European Convention? To start answering this question (which is discussed in various ways throughout the book), let us tease out further the relationship between rights and exceptions in the Convention.

In one way or another all the exceptions concern 'public order' even though the expression appears only occasionally in the text of the Convention.[31] To simplify: when public order demands a particular course of action, the rights guaranteed by the Convention no longer apply. Bentham had this to say about exceptions governed by public order considerations:

> Disturb the public order? – what does that mean? Louis XIV need not have hesitated about receiving an article thus worded [Article 10 of the French Declaration on freedom of expression and religion] into his code. The public order of things in this behalf was an order in virtue of which the exercise of every religion but the Catholic, according to *his* edition of it, was proscribed.[32]

In this passage Bentham alerts us to the risk of deciding on rights and their exceptions by reference to grand words, which can mean just about anything, and the meaning of which is certain to vary depending on who is empowered to give them meaning. In itself, 'public order' means nothing. The same goes for 'public safety', 'the protection of morals', 'the protection of the rights and freedoms of others' and the other expressions found in the Convention to allow for governments to set legitimate limits to the rights it guarantees. If exceptions are granted in the name of public order and its more specific variants, these expressions should be given a more definite meaning. And the Court should check rigorously how each individual government uses them.

The problem in this respect is that the Court tends to grant states a 'margin of appreciation' as to what local circumstances, and thus 'public order', require. The Court explicitly referred to the doctrine of the margin of appreciation for the first time in its *Handyside* judgment, adopted on 7 December 1976.[33] In this case the Court had to decide whether the conviction of the applicant by the English courts for the publication of a book considered obscene violated Article 10 of the Convention, on freedom of expression.[34] Famously, the Court said in its judgment:

> [I]t is not possible to find in the domestic law of the various Contracting States a uniform European conception of morals . . . By reason of their direct and continuous contact with the vital forces of their countries, State authorities are in principle in a better position than the international judge to give an opinion on the exact content of [the local requirements of morals] as well as on the 'necessity' of a 'restriction' or 'penalty' intended to meet them . . . Nevertheless, Article 10 para 2 does not give the Contracting States an unlimited power of appreciation . . . The domestic margin of appreciation thus goes hand in hand with a European supervision.[35]

The last sentence suggests that the doctrine of the margin of appreciation leaves intact the supervisory function of the European Court. This is the theory, which has since been repeatedly reaffirmed by the Court. However, not all commentators are convinced that the promised international supervision takes place in practice. If they were right, it would be difficult not to conclude in the wake of Bentham that the Convention rights (at least those diluted by the application of the doctrine of the margin of appreciation) are illusory. For what is the good of proclaiming, say, the right to liberty and security if an individual can be detained when the government deems it necessary – or merely appropriate? The same question arises in respect of the other rights listed in the Convention.

Negating the Convention system? Derogations under Article 15

The problem is not just that exceptions are very often attached to the rights provided in the Convention; it is also that these rights can sometimes simply be 'erased'. Article 15 of the Convention provides that: 'In time of war or other public emergency threatening the life of the nation any High Contracting Party may take measures derogating from its obligations under this Convention to the extent strictly required by the exigencies of the situation.'[36]

Article 15 often comes as a surprise to students: what is the good of having a Convention, they ask, if the guarantee of the protection of fundamental rights it supposedly provides can be annihilated through derogations? The basic answer is: without a provision of this kind, governments would never have been willing to be bound by the Convention.[37] At the same time, the drafters of the Convention were very well aware that the point of the Convention was precisely to limit state power.[38] Obviously the right to derogate had to be limited if it was not to be abused. The solution of the drafters was to circumscribe the use of derogation in Article 15, which provides that:

- the measures taken must (1) be necessitated by 'war or another public emergency threatening the life of the nation' and (2) be 'strictly required' by the situation (beginning of paragraph 1, quoted above);
- the derogation must not violate other obligations undertaken in international law (end of paragraph 1);
- some articles of the Convention cannot be the subject of a derogation (paragraph 2);
- Strasbourg must be notified of the derogation (paragraph 3).

Paragraph 2 of Article 15 provides which Convention provisions cannot be the subject of a derogation. They are:

- Article 2 guaranteeing the right to life;
- Article 3 guaranteeing the right not to be tortured or subjected to cruel or inhuman treatment or punishment;
- Article 4, paragraph 1, guaranteeing the right to be free from slavery;
- Article 7 guaranteeing the right not to be tried under retroactive criminal laws.

This formulation suggests that the other provisions of the Convention are 'derogable' (if the conditions set in Article 15 are met).

In practice, governments have not entered derogations – or discussed their application – in respect of provisions which come with readily available 'escape clauses' in the Convention, such as Articles 8 to 11, concerned with the right to privacy and the freedoms of religion, expression and association, respectively. In other words, resort to these 'normal' escape clauses, devised with 'normal' times in mind, also takes place in the case of an emergency which leads a government to adopt extreme measures. Referring to Article 15 would have the advantage, from the perspective of the protection of fundamental freedoms, of publicizing the government's action (as notification must occur) and of making it clear that the derogation is meant to have a temporary character (as emergencies are not supposed to last forever).[39] The fact that one may regret the absence of the filing of derogations in respect of Articles 8 to 11 of the Convention speaks for itself: Article 15 is not necessarily as bad as some students spontaneously believe. From a realist perspective, it provides, or at least should provide, limits to governmental impulses to do away with the Convention. This statement, however, immediately needs to be qualified. As Harris and his co-authors have seen, '[o]nce the necessity for derogation is conceded, it becomes difficult to control abusive recourse to the power of suspending rights that [Article 15] permits'.[40] The problem is compounded by the fact that Article 15 is an area of the Convention where the Strasbourg institutions have granted states a wide margin of appreciation.

Although Article 15 has given rise to a limited number of decisions, its significance cannot be overestimated, for it provides for a mechanism which has the potential to destroy the entire edifice of the Convention by making it possible to remove supposedly fundamental guarantees at the heart of the democratic process. Of course, when this occurs, the removal is supposed to constitute a response to real dangers, including terrorism, which, to use the words of Article 15, 'threaten the life of the nation'. Perhaps there is no problem with Article 15 as such. Even if this controversial point is conceded, it remains the case that the approach adopted by the Court when facing Article 15 claims is extremely problematic.

Article 15 is rarely mentioned in the early chapters of legal commentaries on the Convention, if only because these tend to follow the structure of the Convention and start with Article 2 on the right to life, Article 3 on the prohibition of torture, etc. This book is highly unusual in giving it extensive treatment in its first substantive chapter. Given the overall aim of the study, namely, examining the extent to which classical challenges to the human rights orthodoxy hold, granting Article 15 such prominence makes perfect sense. This is because no other provision negates so entirely the idealism and supra-nationality of the rights supposedly, but perhaps not really (this is the whole question), guaranteed by the Convention. No less than three further sections of this chapter are devoted to it. Before continuing the examination of Article 15, however, it is useful to discuss further what can be meant by 'realism'.

Realism in international relations: Virtuous or vicious *raison d'état*?

Realism is a word which is often heard in international relations. In fact, this may be an understatement as realism is often acknowledged as the dominant IR theory.[41] In this context, the name emerged in reaction to the 'idealist' thinking which had prevailed during the interwar period of 1919–39.[42] The theory has a much longer pedigree, however, going back as far as Thucydides' account of the Peloponnesian War (c. 400 BC). Perhaps its most famous proponent is Niccolò Machiavelli, who wrote *The Prince* in 1532.

In a nutshell, the theory holds that the state is the key actor on the international scene – not religion, economic giants, international organizations, civil society or other arguably influential actors. It is essentially pessimistic in that it does not believe that progress is possible in international politics.[43] Phrased in simple words, the theory has it that the state will always follow its own interests; it will do whatever is required (as long as it can afford to do it) to ensure its survival; it will not be guided by a supposedly universal morality; it will tend to rely on itself whenever possible given that cooperation is inadvisable as other states, by definition, also follow their own interests and cannot be trusted; state sovereignty is a chief concern. Tim Dunne and Brian Schmidt encapsulate the theory in 'three Ss': statism, survival and self-help.[44]

The classical theorists of realism developed the idea of a dual moral standard. Accordingly, one morality exists for the private sphere; another and very different one for the public sphere. Machiavelli, for example, stated:

> A prince . . . cannot observe all those things for which men are considered good, for in order to maintain the state he is often obliged to act against his promise, against charity, against humanity, and against religion. And therefore, it is necessary that he have a mind ready to turn itself according to the way the winds of fortune and the changeability of [political] affairs require . . . [A]s long as it is possible, he should not stray from the good, but he should know how to enter into evil when necessity commands.[45]

The idea of *raison d'état* (literally, reason of state) has been taken up by Hans J. Morgenthau in the twentieth century. Morgenthau, like E. H. Carr before him, was highly critical of American President Woodrow Wilson and rejected the idea that political ethics should be brought into line with private ethics. As far as he was concerned, this was 'not only ill-advised but also irresponsible . . . not only mistaken intellectually but also fundamentally wrong morally'.[46] In Morgenthau's view, 'universal moral principles cannot be applied to the actions of states in their abstract universal formulation, but . . . must be filtered through the concrete circumstances of time and place. The individual may say for himself: "*fiat justitia, pereat mundus* (Let justice be done even if the world perish)", but the state has no right to say so in the name of those who are in its care.'[47] The last words are crucial: as Machiavelli intimated, the state leader has a responsibility towards his citizens; he must seek to ensure that the public sphere is such that private morality is allowed to flourish within it.[48] He should let himself be governed by *raison d'état*.

Raison d'état, however, can all too easily become a pretext for 'vicious' actions which have nothing to do with a 'virtuous' necessity, even one existing on a different, public, plane. It becomes synonymous with *realpolitik*, a disparaging term which implies foul play. In common parlance, the three terms *raison d'état*, *realpolitik* and realism are often used interchangeably.[49] They are associated not so much with a different kind of morality existing for statesmanship as with the idea that morality is altogether put aside by statesmen. Realism, as antithesis of morality, comes to be seen as a fact of life which corresponds to the egoistic nature of man and points to the structuring effect of power in international relations. Realism, from this perspective, is not a vision but an inescapable fact. Realists of this second, behaviouralist, persuasion merely observe that states are unwilling to act in ways which restrict their power. In their view, states simply cling to power as much and as long as they can; they act in apparently immoral ways because it is in their interest to do so, not because they follow a public morality different from the one governing relations between individuals.

Comparing Bentham and IR realism

The shift in the theoretical grounding of this chapter from Bentham to IR realism may appear incongruous since these two bodies of theory are not generally regarded as complementary to each other.[50] Bentham was principally interested in the internal conduct of a government; as its name indicates, international relations is interested in international matters. Bentham was infused with optimism, and wanted to establish positive guidelines for government to follow. He believed that progress was possible. By contrast, international relations takes a pessimistic view of human nature; it seeks to discover how states should or do interact without thinking that progress is really possible. Bentham was a liberal;[51] IR realism emerged in opposition to liberalism.[52]

Nonetheless connections between the two strands of 'realism' can easily be established. As the anti-insurrectional leitmotif of 'Anarchical Fallacies' indicates, Bentham highly valued state survival. He wanted to avoid internal (as opposed to international) chaos by seeking to achieve the happiness of the greatest number. The utilitarian in him would have been attracted by the idea of *raison d'état*. Conversely, it is not uncommon to see IR realist arguments phrased in utilitarian fashion, such as in the affirmation that it is sometimes 'necessary to trample on human rights for the sake of the national interest: during war, for example'.[53] Bentham and Machiavelli are not as far apart as a cursory reading of their work would lead one to suppose.

While the 'realist' critiques which Bentham and international relations provide on human rights start from different perspectives, both suggest that human rights law cannot *really* be above the state.[54] They do so for different reasons. In Bentham's view it is because the state is the source of rights; in international relations theory, it is because the state follows its own interests in power games which never amount to a complete surrender of its sovereignty. There is a sense in which these two reasons feed on, rather than oppose, each other. The next two sections explore how realist ideas can be seen to be reflected in Strasbourg early practice.

The creation of the doctrine of the margin of appreciation in the *First Cyprus Case*

Although the doctrine of the margin of appreciation was first referred to by the Court in a judgment of 1976 (*Handyside*, as we have seen), the doctrine was invented almost twenty years before by the Commission, in the *First Cyprus Case*.[55] This case is worth reviewing at some length, not only because it is the first which had involved a derogation by a state under Article 15 but also because of the in-depth study which the historian Brian Simpson has made of it.[56] This study makes apparent a series of twists in the development of the case, typically obscured in legal commentaries but indicating clearly the 'realist' mindsets of the actors involved.

The case concerned the handling by the United Kingdom of the insurrection that developed in the 1950s in its (then) colony of Cyprus. Faced with an increasingly violent movement which sought a union with Greece, the Governor had introduced repressive legislation and emergency powers, including a Detention of Persons Law in July 1955. Aware that this legislative act was plainly in violation of Article 5 of the Convention, on liberty and the security of the person, the British had sent a notice of derogation to Strasbourg in October. The violence on the island deepened in the following months; the colonial government responded with executive detentions, rough (or worse) treatments, executions, curfews, censorship, the closing of schools, the destruction of tree plantations, etc. After a months-long debate, it also deported in March 1956 Archbishop Makarios, a national figure, to another colony (namely, the Seychelles). Two months later, the British Government found itself, much to its surprise and consternation, the object of an application at Strasbourg. This was not an individual application, which was not possible since the United Kingdom was not to sign the relevant optional clause until 1966 (when, having lost most of its colonies, the application of the Convention in these territories had ceased to be deeply problematic). The application was lodged by the Greek Government. It was the first inter-state application to be brought at Strasbourg.[57]

Greece alleged that the United Kingdom was violating nearly all the substantive provisions of the Convention in Cyprus. The British did not doubt that the application was motivated by a political plan which aimed at the incorporation into a Greater Greece of the island (where lived a substantial Turkish minority). But this did not constitute a legal response to the case.[58] Denouncing the Convention, though briefly considered by some members of the British Government, was not a viable option either. The Government was badly caught. It decided to have the most objectionable measures revoked (against the wishes of the island's Governor); for the rest, it tried to convince the members of the Commission that the difficult circumstances existing on the island had compelled it to act in the way it had.[59] A substantial part of the case turned around the legality of its derogation.[60]

The derogation filed by the United Kingdom in respect of Cyprus in October 1955 had been deliberately laconic. Simpson has summarized the argument of the Government before the Commission at the second hearing of the case, held in March 1957, as follows:

A notice of derogation did not have to specify which articles were involved (which could be difficult to determine). Article 6 [on fair trial] was merely ancillary to Article 5 [on liberty]; if Article 5 went Article 6 sank with it . . . [T]he drift of the argument here was that the Commission had no legitimate role in deciding, once it was admitted that there was a public emergency threatening the life of the nation, what measures were strictly required by the exigencies of the situation. The force of this argument was that the executive had to respond to an emergency when it arose, and ought not be inhibited by the possibility that the Commission, whose members had no responsibility for the maintenance of law and order, and no direct experience of the situation, might with hindsight rule that the action which had been taken was unnecessary.[61]

The United Kingdom basically won this argument as the Commission developed, on its own initiative, the doctrine of the margin of appreciation. As Simpson explains, the doctrine was unnecessary to the Commission's decision, for the majority believed that the colonial authorities had acted correctly, as the circumstances demanded.[62] Nevertheless the commissioners were uneasy about 'being cast in a role which might require them to pass judgment on the decisions taken by the government of Cyprus'.[63] Simpson quotes the views expressed by various commissioners in the course of the debates that preceded the adoption of the Commission's report. Clearly the doctrine emerged as a way of addressing the uncertainties they were grappling with.

The Report of the Commission, dated 26 September 1958 (but released only in 1997),[64] gave its opinion on the existence of an emergency that threatened the life of the nation (i.e. the colonial existence of Cyprus):

> ... [the incidents which form the background to the derogation] emanated from a fast growing and militant organisation which, according to its own statements, aimed at obtaining self-determination for Cyprus by all possible means, including force and violence. These two factors together make it at least plausible to assume that there ... existed ... a public danger threatening the life of the nation. The assessment whether or not a public danger existed is a question of appreciation. The United Kingdom Government made such an assessment of the situation prevailing at that time and concluded that there existed a public danger threatening the life of the nation.[65]

On the question of whether the measures adopted had been strictly required, the report took a similar view and articulated the position that the state which exercised the derogation power enjoyed 'a certain discretion'.[66]

The irony of the position of the Commission was not lost on the Greek commissioner, Mr Eustathiades, who wrote that the view of the majority was

> tantamount to conferring on the colonial authorities the means of inordinately consolidating their powers at the expense of the most fundamental individual rights and freedoms, or at any rate of strengthening them to a much greater degree than is permitted by the Convention.[67]

Indeed the Commission adopted a position which was more illiberal than that of the British Colonial Office.[68] It did not attempt to respond to the Greek argument according to which the level of violence attained in the island in 1956 had been the direct result of the British overreaction and emergency powers.[69] On the specific issue of arrest and detention, three dissenting commissioners stressed the critical importance of Articles 5 and 6 in the Convention and argued that the detention law had proved ineffective, concluding that 'the removal of the danger and the pacification of the island can be effected only by political means'.[70] In other words, the last thing the island needed in their view was the type of measure which had led the British Government to file an Article 15 derogation.

Underlying political games: The *Second Cyprus Case*

In the *First Cyprus Case*, Greece had agreed to withdraw allegations of torture but had reserved her right to raise this type of claim in a subsequent application. She lodged a second application which raised forty-nine such cases in July 1957, giving rise to the *Second Cyprus Case*.[71] The meticulous study of this case by Simpson brings back to life the power games which realists expect or know states play before the European Court of Human Rights – but which are unlikely to be played overtly and tend to become lost anyway in the texts of judgments that articulate 'neat' legal arguments.

When Greece lodged her second application, the British Government reacted by trying to have the whole of the second application declared inadmissible. When this failed, it nonetheless persuaded the Commission to declare twenty cases inadmissible after the first hearing. These included cases where the British knew that unjustifiable violence had occurred. For example, in case 1, a doctor had confirmed that the applicant had come out of detention with broken ribs.[72] The initial declarations of inadmissibility raised Britain's hope that there would not be an enquiry on the spot. The British legal team worked to have further cases declared inadmissible. It also sought to delay the proceedings while endeavouring to put the blame for these delays on the Greeks. As it turned out, the British greatly benefited from these delaying tactics: the awareness by the Commission that contact had taken place between the Foreign Ministries of Greece and Turkey in the United Nations in December 1958 persuaded it to put the outstanding Cyprus application on the 'back burner'.[73] In February 1959, a political settlement for the island was discussed at Zurich and formalized in London. This led the agents for both the British and the Greek governments to request in May that the proceedings should be terminated without an examination of the substance of the application. The Commission reported to this effect in July 1959, accepting that 'some friction might be engendered by the continuance of an investigation into as yet unproved allegations'.[74]

This outcome led the Solicitor-General, head of the British legal team, to comment: 'It prompts some reflections upon the cynicism of the Greeks. The alleged victims of the alleged atrocities have been left wholly without remedy once the political value of their complaints is no more'.[75] Undeniably so. We can ask, however, whether the British attitude was any more commendable. A few months before, the Solicitor-General had recommended that it be argued that the Commission's requests were unreasonable.[76] This had the advantage of making it possible not to cooperate without saying so, while a flat refusal would have constituted a breach of the Convention and would have had adverse political consequences, not least in terms of the 'reputation [of the United Kingdom] as one of the principal guardians of Human Rights'.[77] As for the attitude of the Commission, its decision to close the matter without commenting on its substance was motivated by 'realist' considerations, which had nothing to do with the defence of individuals who had suffered grave violations of their right to physical integrity. The 'as yet unproved allegations' mentioned in the Commission's report were, in fact, often reasonably well documented in the Greek submissions.

Simpson's study of the *Second Cyprus Case* reveals that none of the actors involved acted at Strasbourg in a way devoid of realist motives. If this happened half a century ago, recent case law suggests that realist considerations continue to play a role today.[78] Given this, optimistic assessments of the Convention may appear somewhat unwarranted.

Realism and the Convention: Forsythe versus Allott and Imbert

David Forsythe must be credited with having anchored the study of human rights in international relations. His book with that title[79] examines whether realists are right to think that human rights policy is subordinated, not to the liberal aim of ensuring respect for the individual, but to state interests and state power. He documents many examples of devious policy, not least by the United States. Nonetheless his conclusion is optimistic in respect of the Council of Europe where he finds realism 'largely irrelevant'.[80] He thus shares the view of those who believe that progress can be achieved in international relations. The Council of Europe, resting as it does on state cooperation and on each state relinquishing at least some of its national sovereignty in favour of agreed superior political moral standards, could be testimony to the fact that realism can be defeated. Forsythe argues: 'Global international relations would be much improved if it approximated the regional international law of western Europe with its interlocking human rights standards as specified by the European Court of Human Rights and European Court of Justice.'[81]

Realists may wish to retort that the most a regional system can do is to change the face of realism, not its intrinsic nature. They may argue that *each* state calculates what is in its best interests – joining or not joining, ratifying or not ratifying, presenting this or that argument to the Court, etc. To give a more concrete example, they are unlikely to believe that the accession of the central and eastern European states to the Council of Europe following the end of the Cold War occurred with the primary aim of fostering human rights. Instead they may see the adherence to the Convention system as a move undertaken to facilitate accession to the European Union, and thus ultimately motivated by the pursuit of economic and political advantages. To give another example, the refusal by France to accept the right of individual petition until 1981 is certainly to be explained by reference to realist considerations, having to do, in particular, with the status of France as a colonial power. Realists would be wary of taking rhetorical incantations of human rights at face value. For them the international rhetoric does not signal the defeat of statism, but its continuation by other means.[82]

More generally, Philip Allott has remarked:

> [T]he installation of human rights in the international constitution after 1945 has been paradoxical. The idea of human rights quickly became perverted by the self-misconceiving of international society. Human rights were quickly appropriated by governments, embodied in treaties, made part of the stuff of primitive international relations, swept up into the maw of an international bureaucracy. The reality of the idea of human rights has been degraded. From being a source of ultimate anxiety for usurping holders of public social power, they were turned into bureaucratic small-change. Human rights, a reservoir of unlimited power in all the self-creating of society, became a plaything of government and lawyers. The game of human rights has been played in international statal organizations by diplomats and bureaucrats, and their appointees, in the setting and ethos of traditional international relations.[83]

Allott does not mince his words: 'perverted', 'degraded', 'small-change', 'plaything', 'game'. Admittedly these words are not specifically directed at either judicial members or the European Convention system, though some would certainly be ready to apply them to the Strasbourg Court.[84]

One person one might not expect to share Allott's damning assessment is the Director of Human Rights at the Council of Europe. But Pierre-Henri Imbert adopted what can only be characterized as a realist view of the Convention system. He remarked in a contribution about the relationship between human rights and international law that he did not believe that human rights have fundamentally affected international relations.[85] He further noted that inter-state applications are still regarded as hostile acts and that states responsible for serious violations are rarely put on the stand at Strasbourg. He finally observed how 'Human Rights Europe' watched powerlessly when events of the scale that had led to its creation *so that precisely these kinds of events would never happen again* unfolded before its eyes in Bosnia and Chechnya. If Human Rights Europe could not react, Imbert asked, is it because it does not exist? Or at least because it does not exist beyond, and thus must be reduced to, the procedural system put in place at Strasbourg? Imbert doubted that the Strasbourg system could be given credit for democracy in Europe. For him, human rights were instruments that allow states to pursue politics that have nothing to do with the aim of safeguarding the dignity of the individual. This led him to coin the term *realethik*.

Until his recent departure, Imbert devoted his life, energy and intellect to building human rights at Strasbourg. He was well placed to criticize the Council of Europe since he was not only knowledgeable but also enjoyed the authority of someone whose aim is obviously not to destroy the institution for which he works. This would nonetheless probably not have led him to disagree with me that the complacency of Forsythe's argument must be resisted.

The position of the Court in cases involving Article 15

Bentham was concerned that the utopianism of the French Declaration or its progeny would open the doors to perpetual insurrection and anarchy. Clearly, he need not have worried. As far as the European Convention system is concerned, both the Commission and the Court have proved strong allies of government and order right from the beginning. We have seen above how the Commission created the doctrine of the margin of appreciation in the *First Cyprus Case*. The present section explains how the Court soon followed in the steps of the Commission concerning the approach to be adopted in cases involving Article 15.

There was no judgment by the Court on the *First Cyprus Case* for the simple reason that at the time the United Kingdom had not yet accepted the jurisdiction of the Court. However, it so happens that the first case to come before the Court, *Lawless* v. *Ireland*, decided on 1 July 1961,[86] also concerned Article 15. In this case the Court had to decide whether the six-month detention of an IRA member or sympathiser, in a military camp in the Republic of Ireland, without any trial, violated Article 5. The Irish government had derogated from the Convention in 1957.

The President of the Commission, Sir Humphrey Waldock, explained in his submissions to the Court:

> The concept of the margin of appreciation is that a Government's discharge of these responsibilities [maintaining law and order in a time of emergency] is essentially a delicate problem of appreciating complex factors and of balancing conflicting considerations of the public interest; and that, once the Commission or the Court is satisfied that the Government's appreciation is at least on the margin of the powers conferred by Article 15, then *the interest which the public itself has in effective Government and in the maintenance of order* justifies and requires a decision in favour of the legality of the government's appreciation.[87]

The Court did not specifically refer to the margin of appreciation in its judgment. Nonetheless it unanimously accepted *both* that there had been a 'public emergency threatening the life of the nation' and that the use of the power of detention was 'strictly required by the exigencies of the situation'. Simpson comments:

> The [judgment] could be read as indicating that governments had little to fear from Strasbourg over the handling of emergencies, more particularly since the claim that there was at the time, in the Republic of Ireland, an emergency threatening the life of the nation was utterly ludicrous; [it] reflected a determination to back the authorities, come what may, as over Cyprus in the earlier case.[88]

As far as Simpson is concerned, the doctrine, though not specifically mentioned, allowed the Court 'to cover the decision with a cloak of legality'.[89] It soon became the 'common staple of judicial rulings on matters involving Article 15'.[90] Its first full articulation in an Article 15 case occurred in *Ireland* v. *United Kingdom*, decided on 18 January 1978.[91] There the Court said:

> [I]t falls in the first place to each Contracting State, with its responsibility for 'the life of [its] nation', to determine whether that life is threatened by a 'public emergency' and, if so, how far it is necessary to go in attempting to overcome the emergency. By the reasons of their direct and continuous contact with the pressing need of the moment, the national authorities are in principle in a better position than the international judge to decide both on the presence of such an emergency and on the nature and scope of the derogations necessary to avert it. In this matter article 15 paragraph 1 leaves the authorities a wide margin of appreciation. Nevertheless, the States do not enjoy an unlimited power in this respect . . . the domestic margin of appreciation is thus accompanied by a European supervision.[92]

Satisfied that there existed in Northern Ireland at the relevant time a public emergency threatening the life of the nation, the Court found no violation of Article 5 or Article 6 in this case. (However, it found the United Kingdom guilty of having violated the non-derogable Article 3 of the Convention through its recourse to the following five interrogation techniques leading to disorientation and sensory deprivation: wall-standing; hooding; subjection to noise; sleep deprivation; denial of food and drink.)

The doctrine was again applied on 26 May 1993 in the *Brannigan and McBride* case, where the Court found that the executive detention of the two applicants under the United Kingdom Prevention of Terrorism (Temporary Provisions) Act 1984, which had lasted for more than four and six days respectively, did not violate the Convention. This judgment was a particular disappointment for civil liberties lawyers for it came after a verdict of violation in what appeared similar circumstances. In the *Brogan and Others* case, decided on 29 November 1988,[93] the Court had found that administrative detentions lasting between four and seven days violated Article 5 of the Convention, even though it had specifically recognized that the investigation of terrorist offences presented the British authorities with special problems. However, legally, there was a significant difference between the two cases. The '*Brogan* detentions' had taken place at a time when the United Kingdom had withdrawn its derogation notice. The United Kingdom reintroduced a derogation a few months after the *Brogan* verdict. The applicants in *Brannigan* tried to argue that the derogation was an attempt by the Government to circumvent its obligations under the Convention. The Court was not persuaded. It accepted the defence of the Government to the effect that, until the 1988 *Brogan* verdict, it had thought that executive detention under the Prevention of Terrorism Act did not violate the Convention.

The granting to states of a wide margin of appreciation in respect of Article 15 has meant that the Court has refrained in practice from undertaking a factually close and theoretically strict analysis of the situation. This, however, would have been the only way it could confidently and persuasively assert (1) that an emergency situation does indeed exist and (2) that the derogating measures adopted by the respondent state (namely, the United Kingdom and Ireland)[94] are strictly required – and, ideally, open the prospect of seeing democracy and Convention rights shortly restored.

Historically one can understand that the Commission and the Court may have been reluctant to supervise closely Western powers – especially those of the stature of the United Kingdom and especially when the Strasbourg controlling institutions were still in their infancy. At the same time, it remains the case that the human rights rationale would have demanded that the Court insist on exercising very strict control in a case where the system of the Convention is, as it were, under attack. Instead of this, the Court has confirmed time and time again that Article 15 is an area where states enjoy a wide margin of appreciation. This approach is difficult, if not impossible, to justify from a human rights perspective. Not surprisingly it has been repeatedly criticized by commentators who cherish the idea of human rights.[95] Interestingly, however, the position of the Court could also be said to be thoroughly predictable. From a 'realist' perspective, it makes perfect sense, explaining why other commentators have accepted it.[96]

Aksoy: Both a realist and a supranational decision

With the exception of *Lawless* v. *Ireland*, the early case law on Article 15 had seen the United Kingdom in the position of defendant. In recent years, the Court's case law on Article 15 consists of four judgments against Turkey.[97] Here again the decisions of the Court are directly based on an application of the doctrine of the margin of appreciation. The Court has repeatedly accepted, with hardly any discussion, that there exists a 'public emergency threatening the life of the nation' in south-east Turkey, a region where Kurdish terrorists operate. However the Court has decided that such an emergency does not justify executive detentions which are inordinately long (fourteen days,[98] twenty-three and sixteen days,[99] and eleven days[100]) or take place in another part of the country.[101]

The first Turkish case that involved an Article 15 claim is *Aksoy*. It was lodged by the applicant on 20 May 1993 and decided by the Court on 26 November 1996. On 16 April 1994 Mr Aksoy was shot and killed (leaving his father to continue the case). The facts were in dispute. The applicant alleged that during a detention which had lasted sixteen days in the winter of 1992, he had been stripped naked and subjected to 'Palestinian hanging' – hands tied behind the back and strung up by the arms – during which he had been electrocuted on his genitals. The treatment, he said, had left his upper limbs paralysed. The applicant's side further reported that he had received death threats directly connected to his application at Strasbourg, which were carried out in April 1994. In reply to these claims, the Government recognized that Mr Aksoy had been in detention for fourteen days without access to a judge. But it argued that this kind of detention was necessary for pursuing the fight against PKK terrorists in south-east Turkey, which its annual derogation under Article 15 made legal under the Convention. It denied that torture had occurred. It said the applicant's death resulted from a settling of scores between quarrelling PKK factions.

The Commission went on a fact-finding mission. It established that the applicant had been medically diagnosed with bilateral radial paralysis on his release in December 1992. This condition was consistent with 'Palestinian hanging'. Given that Mr Aksoy had not been suffering from a disability prior to his arrest and that the Government was not offering an alternative explanation for his injuries, first the Commission and then the Court found that torture had occurred in violation of Article 3. In Article 15 cases against the United Kingdom, Amnesty International had repeatedly observed that executive detention produced circumstances which could easily lead to breaches of Article 3. What was the Court going to say in respect of the detention of Mr Aksoy? Would it be contrary to Article 5, thus invalidating the derogation under Article 15, once Turkey was the defendant state?

The Court followed the broad lines of its earlier decisions. It granted Turkey a wide margin of appreciation in the matter. It dealt in a single paragraph with the issue of the existence of a public emergency threatening the life of the nation. It considered 'in the light of all the material before it, that the particular extent and impact of PKK terrorist activity in South-East Turkey had undoubtedly created, in the region concerned, [such a situation]'.[102] (Incidentally this phrasing proves Judge De Meyer and Simpson right: given that the Court accepts that the emergency does in fact exist, the doctrine of the margin of appreciation is superfluous to its reasoning. It may be that the doctrine is nevertheless used by the Court as a pretext for not explaining on what evidence it relies to form its judgment on the actual existence of the threat. If so, the excuse does not hold: granting the state a margin of appreciation should not, in principle, exempt the Court from examining the details of the situation.) As for the measures required in the circumstances, the Court found the period of – at least – fourteen days 'exceptionally long'.[103] It observed that 'the Government have not adduced any detailed reasons before the Court as to why the fight against terrorism in South-East Turkey rendered judicial intervention impracticable'. The Court found a violation of Article 5, paragraph 3 of the Convention.

One heaves a sigh of relief at the verdict of violation. But the judgment is not unproblematic. First it raises the question of whether the Court applies unspoken double standards. The readiness by the Court to question the necessity of excluding the judiciary from the detention process must be approved. However the finding in this case leaves open the question of why the issue was not addressed by the Court in the previous cases against the United Kingdom. Judge Wald had observed in his dissenting opinion in *Brannigan*:

[T]here is no evidence that the operation of the courts in either Northern Ireland or Great Britain has been restricted by 'the war or public emergency' in Northern

Ireland. It is the United Kingdom which wishes to restrict the operation of the courts by being unwilling to allow arrested persons to be brought before a judge as prescribed by Article 5 para. 3 of the Convention . . . In my opinion the Government has not convincingly shown, in a situation where the courts operate normally, why an arrested person cannot be treated in accordance with [this provision].[104]

The principle of access to the judiciary is important in all countries. Why, then, was the Court more lenient towards the United Kingdom than towards Turkey?

There are different ways of answering this question. On the one hand, it can be pointed out that the detention in *Brannigan* had been under seven days and had not given rise to allegations of torture. On the other hand, it could be retorted that the Court was perhaps too easily swayed by the generally good reputation of the United Kingdom which enjoys a supposedly firm democratic legacy.[105] One should not forget that the United Kingdom has been found in violation of Article 3 in other cases (including most notably *Ireland v United Kingdom*, decided on 18 January 1978). Gross miscarriages of justice (in cases not brought at Strasbourg) have also shown that the state is able to dispense with individual human rights in a wholly illegitimate way. It is wrong for the European Court to trust a government blindly, even one as powerful and with as good a reputation as the British one.

Interestingly, even the generally progressive Judge Martens voted with the majority in *Brannigan*, although 'only after considerable hesitations'.[106] The Dutch judge was not happy that the Court, to grant the United Kingdom a wide margin of appreciation, merely referred to its fifteen-year-old precedent in *Ireland v United Kingdom*. Martens observed that the 1978 decision 'was, presumably, influenced by the view that the majority of the then member States of the Council of Europe might be assumed to be societies which . . . had been democracies for a long time'.[107] He made it clear that continuing to grant a wide margin of appreciation was problematic after newcomers from eastern and central Europe had joined the Strasbourg 'club' – thus endorsing a perhaps too facile conception of western Europe having achieved adequate standards and eastern Europe having to be in the position of the pupil.[108]

In short, it cannot be ruled out that realist factors, including either awareness of differences in power between states or misplaced faith in the credentials of 'long-lived' democracies, may have led the Court, perhaps unconsciously, to be more lenient towards the United Kingdom than towards Turkey. In this respect, it can be noted that the regression, observed in recent UK cases, of an 'earlier, more expansive interpretation of Article 13 in the Turkish cases' is puzzling.[109] This particular case law concerns the obligation for the state to conduct a thorough and effective investigation and prosecution in cases of suspected violations of the right to life. From a supranational perspective, this development cannot but raise cause for concern.[110]

A second problematic aspect of the judgment is the victory of Turkey on two points. The Government had made a preliminary objection with regard to the admissibility of the complaint, arguing that the applicant had failed to exhaust domestic remedies. Mr Aksoy had gone 'directly' to Strasbourg without pursuing the case through domestic criminal, civil or administrative proceedings. He justified this move by saying that, although formally part of the Turkish legal system, such proceedings were in practice illusory given that 'torture and the denial of effective remedies were carried out as a matter of administrative practice'.[111] The Court accepted that 'special circumstances . . . absolved the applicant from his obligation to exhaust domestic remedies', but found it unnecessary to examine the claim about the existence of an administrative practice.[112] The Court's persistent reticence in assessing the existence of an administrative practice is to the advantage of Turkey. The Turkish government may lose particular cases, such as *Aksoy*, but its future position before the Court is formally intact. The finding of an administrative practice would have enabled subsequent applicants immediately to benefit from the implications of the situation which would have been established. In the absence of such a finding, applicants who go directly to Strasbourg must produce evidence which demonstrates to the Court why national remedies were illusory in their particular circumstances.

Turkey must also have been relieved by the finding of the Court concerning Article 25, about the obligation for states not to hinder the right of individual petition. I have mentioned that the applicant died during the Strasbourg proceedings; he was shot dead. His father argued that the killing was at the hands of the Turkish authorities, the culmination of their threats following his son's application to Strasbourg. The applicant was not the first Kurd to report such intimidation to the Court. Invariably in such cases the Turkish Government denies being the author of these threats. The matter is generally left undecided by the Court for lack of evidence: no violation is found because no violation can be established. Typically it is when serious violations are alleged that facts are in dispute between the parties; hence they cannot be established with certainty; hence it is difficult to establish a violation of the Convention. In a sense, the more serious a violation is, the more likely it is that the government will escape judicial condemnation.[113] Perhaps this conclusion is not ironic from a realist perspective.

The Court did not deem *Aksoy* sufficiently important or difficult to transfer it to a Grand Chamber. The verdicts of violation (in respect of Articles 3, 5 para. 3 and 13) were reached by eight votes to one. Only the Turkish judge dissented, on the ground that the case should have been declared inadmissible for failure to exhaust national remedies. In his dissenting opinion, Judge Gölcüklü stated with slight irritation: 'Despite the existence of [national] remedies . . . the applicant . . . only complained to the Commission *via London*'.[114] These two words seem to point to an illegitimate interference in national issues. Of course such interference constitutes, from one perspective, the whole point of human rights. The support of lawyers in the United Kingdom and the development of the London-based Kurdish Human Rights Project have been directly instrumental in enabling applicants such as Mr Aksoy to put their claims to Strasbourg.[115] Having said this, the loss of sovereignty which Strasbourg entails can be hard for national states and their representatives to bear; they may therefore be inclined to reason along 'realist' statist lines.[116]

In conclusion, is *Aksoy* primarily a statist (and thus realist) or a supranational decision? The doctrine of the margin of appreciation in respect of Article 15 points to a realist reasoning, but the Court nonetheless asserted its supervisory role as it applied the doctrine and found Turkey in breach of Article 5 paragraph 3, pointing to an application of supranational principles. But this analysis needs to be taken further. The last point must be assessed in the light of the verdicts on non-violation in previous Article 15 cases involving the United Kingdom. Did the Court take these latter decisions because it did not have the strength or because it did not feel it appropriate to decide against a state which is significant in Europe? If so, is its readiness to decide against Turkey not tainted by realist motives rather than being the expression of a 'pure' supranationalism? Supranational and statist considerations intermingle further in the case. Although Turkey was found in breach of Articles 3 and 13 ('supranationalism'), the Court did not find a violation of Article 25 ('realism'). And while the preliminary objection of the defendant state was rejected by the Court – the irritation of the Turkish judge that the applicant addressed Strasbourg 'via London' obviously cutting no ice with his colleagues ('supranationalism') – the Court nonetheless left the claim of the applicant that an administrative practice exists unexamined ('realism'). These mixed results indicate that *Aksoy* is primarily neither a realist/statist nor a supranational decision. It is both at the same time. This conclusion can probably be applied to most cases.

No realism without idealism, and vice versa

Idealism is generally opposed to realism; utopia to reality. However, these are trends, and they rarely exist in an undiluted form. Moreover, which label is warranted often depends on the perspective which is adopted. Let me take an example. I have presented Bentham in this chapter as a 'realist', a classification which I based on his legal positivism and rejection of natural law. Interestingly, what struck E. H. Carr about Bentham was precisely his lack of realism, namely, the utilitarian 'belief in the sufficiency of reason to promote right conduct' and 'the infallibility of public opinion'.[117] For Carr, Bentham had replaced the natural law of the previous centuries with his own natural law: one which regarded the happiness of the greatest number as the absolute ethical standard.[118]

A second example is provided by Carr himself. Carr is widely considered to have been at the origin of the development, especially in the United States, of IR realism. It would be a mistake, however, to take him for a realist and nothing else: Carr specifically said that he did not wish to be 'a consistent and thorough-going realist'. He considered that consistent realism excluded 'four things which appear to be essential ingredients of all effective political thinking: a finite goal, an emotional appeal, a right of moral judgment and a ground for action'.[119] A realism which was not nourished by idealism was of no interest to Carr. To quote him: 'Every realist, whatever his profession, is ultimately compelled to believe not only that there is something which man ought to think and do, but that there is something which he can think and do, and that his thought and action are neither mechanical nor meaningless . . . [A]ny sound political thought must be based on elements of both utopia and reality.'[120]

This is no doubt a conclusion which Joseph Carens would also be ready to reach. Carens is best known for having defended the idealistic view that states should open their borders so as to lift immigration control, which he regards as immoral from a humanistic perspective.[121] In a subsequent article entitled 'Realistic and Idealistic Approaches to Migration',[122] however, Carens argued that '[w]e have to act responsibly and effectively in the world in which we actually live. [This is because] it is as idle to reflect upon how we ought to act in different circumstances or in a different world as it would be to speculate about the morality of angels or aliens from another planet.'[123] In his observation that an approach capable of acting as a guide to action is likely to pay attention to factors at play in the real world, such as the principle of national sovereignty, Carens the idealist was leaning towards realism.[124] In fact, he saw idealism and realism as ideal types, with actual discussions of ethics normally including elements of both.[125] This conclusion, made with the ethics of migration in mind, can be extended to the whole ethical field, including that of human rights.

Benhebba: The statism of the French judge versus the idealism of other judges

There are areas where we can expect human rights law to feel particularly strongly the tension between realism and idealism. One is the politically sensitive area of national security, public emergency and terrorism, which involves the case law on Article 15;[126] another has to do with the immigration field.[127] I have examined in detail elsewhere what I call the 'quasi-national' case law.[128] There the tension manifests itself in the insistence by the state apparatus on relying on a statist definition of membership, while the human rights idea could be expected to wish to focus on the human being *as such* and thus to dispense with the concept of the national altogether. Not wholly surprisingly therefore this is an area where the statist and idealist perspectives of individual judges within the Court emerge particularly clearly.

By the term 'quasi-nationals', I refer to 'second-generation immigrants' who have not acquired the nationality of their host state. The Court has dealt with a number of cases where quasi-nationals were expelled, following criminal conviction, from the state (most often France) in which they had spent most of their life. The applicants alleged that their deportation violated Article 8, which protects private and family life. Some won, some lost. *Benhebba* v. *France* of 10 July 2003 and *Mokrani* v. *France* of 15 July 2003 are two recent decisions.[129] In the latter case the Court unanimously decided that the deportation of the applicant involved a violation of the Convention, but in the former case the Court adopted by five votes to two a verdict of non-violation, thus reversing what had been its most recent decision on the matter, namely, *Ezzouhdi* v. *France*.[130] The unanimous verdict of violation reached on 13 February 2001 in *Ezzouhdi* had itself put an end to the series of violation decisions that the Court had reached since 1996. In turn, this series of decisions had followed a wave of verdicts of violation in the early 1990s.

The separate opinions in *Benhebba*, though very short, deserve attention. In this case, Judge Costa voted with the majority for non-violation. Such a vote appears incongruous given that in *Baghli* v. *France*, decided on 30 November 1999,[131] the French judge had voted against the majority who had found no violation. There he had said (with Judge Tulkens):

> Mr Baghli is a second-generation immigrant, virtually a French national, the vast majority of whose family, social, occupational and cultural ties were in France . . . [T]hat consideration ought under ordinary circumstances to incite the host country to treat Mr Baghli in the same way as it would treat nationals.[132]

In his concurring opinion in *Benhebba*, Costa made it clear that he remained opposed to the principle of 'double sanction', so called because the second-generation immigrant receives first the sanction of criminal punishment and then, additionally, the sanction of administrative expulsion. Costa even called on the French legislature to change French law. And yet, he decided to vote with the majority that the Convention had not been violated. He gave two reasons for this: judicial discipline, presumably within the Strasbourg system, and consistency with the defendant state's case law on the expulsion of aliens.[133] The first reason demonstrates attachment to the judicial system, an apparatus which is directly linked to the state; the second implicitly identifies the state as a central actor which must be respected. Judge Costa can be said to be statist in his inclination.

By contrast Judges Cabral Barreto and Kūris seemed to follow a line of reasoning directly opposed to a statist logic when they justified their vote against the majority in *Benhebba* by reference to the fact that the applicant was a quasi-national. Legal logic has it that either one is a national of a particular state, or one is not.[134] It does not question how one becomes a national but instead takes nationality rules as a given rather than as a social construction which amounts to a myth. The reference to 'quasi-national' defies this logic and suggests awareness that national classification can justify, on seemingly natural grounds, unjustifiable discrimination between human beings.

Three comments about these separate opinions come to mind. First, this chapter has often talked of 'the state' or 'the Court' as if it were possible to personify these institutions. It is important to stress that these institutions are composed of people who hold a variety of views and who do not necessarily agree with each other. Second, it is worth repeating that realism and idealism are in tension and thus present in various degrees in ethical perspectives. Individuals will favour one or the other, not always in the same measure. In turn, it is virtually impossible for an observer to detect the variety of individual resolutions of the tension between idealism and realism at work in the midst of institutions. Third, while one suspects the presence of statist or realist considerations, one does not necessarily expect them to be as explicitly acknowledged as they were by Judge Costa in *Benhebba*. This honesty suggests that Costa is not embarrassed by realism. This must be because, in the wake of Morgenthau and other classical realists, he does not hold realism to be immoral, but rather to require a different morality than the one generally advocated by civil society. In his view, then, realism would have a positive role to play in human rights law.

In its current composition, the Court includes a number of professors of international law.[135] Added to this, four judges used to represent their governments before the Court until they joined its benches.[136] This explains why it is sometimes said in the corridors of Strasbourg that *raison d'état* is well represented at the Court.[137] I have heard the remark meant as a criticism. What I have said above shows that not all will see it that way.

A Court ready to stand up to the state: The remarkable examples of *McCann* and *Selmouni*

Human rights law is enmeshed in statism and imbued with realism rather than being strictly above the state and seeking to remain true to an idealist conception. From the case law not only on Article 15, but also on freedom of expression, freedom of association, and basically the whole of the Convention, it would be possible to create the image of a Court that is constantly deferring to the states, almost to the point of subservience. Such a picture, however, would be partial; it would miss all the cases where the Court has decided against the state. It is time for me to make it clear that the Court can be, and has been, hard on states.

Considering what I have said above about the Court having been lenient towards the United Kingdom, it is fitting for my first example to consist of a decision against that particular country: *McCann and Others* v. *United Kingdom*, decided on 27 September 1995.[138] The case was brought by the relatives of three suspected IRA terrorists who had been killed by members of the Special Air Service (SAS) in Gibraltar. The four soldiers who shot the two men and one woman had been told that the Provisional IRA was planning a 'spectacular' attack in Gibraltar, which would probably involve a car bomb to be detonated by remote control – it was not known when. The three suspects were identified and were all followed by soldiers when they crossed the border from Spain, one by car, the other two on foot. The behaviour they adopted near the car of the first suspect suddenly appeared highly suspicious to the soldiers who, thinking the terrorists were about to detonate the bomb, shot them. An inspection of the car revealed it contained no bomb, although a bomb was later found in Spain in another car which had been hired by them. The Court exonerated the soldiers: given what they had been told and honestly believed, their action was understandable.[139] However, the Court questioned why the three suspects had not been arrested at the border immediately on their arrival in Gibraltar, considering that the security services had identified them and had their names, aliases and photographs. Moreover, the conduct of the terrorist operation had been represented to the soldiers by the authorities in terms of certainty rather than speculation and hypothesis, thus rendering the use of force almost unavoidable. For the majority of the Court, force had not been 'no more than absolutely necessary in defence of [persons] from unlawful violence' as required by Article 2.

This was the very first time a violation of Article 2 was found by the Court. That this happened in a case where a government was fighting terrorism is also significant. The fact that the judgment was adopted by ten votes to nine and that the Commission had not found a violation shows how controversial the issues were. This is of secondary importance for our present purpose. What stands out is that a verdict of violation was reached against the United Kingdom, in respect of Article 2, in a case that involved terrorism. This is a resounding example of a case which goes against the state. The judgment so much infuriated the British Government that it threatened to withdraw from the Convention system, a threat that was widely publicised in the British media of the time but of course not executed.[140]

The second case I want to discuss is *Selmouni* v. *France*, decided by the new Court on 28 July 1999,[141] less than one year after its coming into existence. The applicant, of Moroccan origin, had been arrested by the French police in connection with the investigation of heroin trafficking from the Netherlands. He alleged that he was systematically beaten and raped in police custody. Medical record made at the time of his release pointed to injuries to his head, left eye (the vision of which the applicant eventually lost), face, torso and legs, for which the defendant state could not provide a plausible explanation. The applicant submitted to the Court that 'it was well known that such police practices existed [in France], and that they required preparation, training and deliberate intent'. According to him, 'the severity and cruelty of the suffering inflicted on him justified classifying the acts as torture within the meaning of Article 3 of the Convention'.[142] Although rape was not proved, the Court accepted that 'all the [other] injuries recorded in the various medical certificates . . . establish the existence of physical and . . . mental pain or suffering'.[143] The acts by the authorities had been 'heinous and humiliating'.[144] They were to be regarded as 'acts of torture for the purposes of Article 3 of the Convention'.[145]

This momentous judgment was adopted, by a Grand Chamber, and unanimously. It signalled a 'sea change' in the attitude of the Court towards violations of Article 3.[146] Until then the only country which had been found guilty of torture had been Turkey. Even in as compelling a case as *Ireland* v. *United Kingdom*, the Court had refrained from accepting a finding of torture, deciding instead that the treatment inflicted on the internees breached the Convention because it was 'merely' inhuman and degrading. The stigma of having been found guilty of torture now attached to a country as prominent as France. The Government had tried to object that the case should be declared inadmissible on the grounds of failure to exhaust national remedies, given that the case against the policemen involved was still going through the French process, albeit slowly, at the time of the Strasbourg proceedings. This line of defence was of no avail. The Court obviously wanted to make a point, irrespective of the *raison d'état* which would have dictated avoiding 'the damage that such a case has to the reputation and public trust in the public officials concerned'.[147]

Idealists could express disappointment at the Court's refusal in *McCann* to grant the applicants compensation 'having regard to the fact that the three terrorist suspects who were killed had been intending to plant a bomb in Gibraltar',[148] as if this made the loss of their life less unacceptable. They could also take issue with a case law on Article 3 which is not always as forceful as *Selmouni* seems to promise. Even so the two cases prove that the Court is well able to rise above realist considerations. They are only illustrations of a much wider trend. If I do not document further how the Court *continually* finds against the state, it is because I think the point is not difficult to grasp. To some extent, Forsythe is right: the very existence of the Court encroaches, by its nature, on the power of states which would otherwise decide, in more or less absolute sovereignty, how to conduct their affairs in their own best interests, irrespective of universal moral standards.

If I were asked whether the Court finds, overall, for or against the state, I would not know what my answer should be. The Court does both. Does it do each in equal measure? I have no idea. My lengthy discussion of *Aksoy*, but also the lack of compensation in *McCann* and the presence of separate opinions which point in different directions in *Benhebba* indicate that it may well be impossible to quantify such matters.[149] What is important, I think, is to realize that the Court does not, and indeed could not, sustain a position which would be completely above realist considerations, at the same time that it succeeds in rising above precisely such considerations.

The image of the sandbag comes to mind.[150] A sandbag does not ensure perfect protection against flooding, but nonetheless holds back the bulk of the water, at least if the tide is not too strong. In the same way, the Convention of course does not provide 'ideal' rights. Within the realism in which it is inscribed, it nonetheless allows for major shows of arbitrariness to be kept at bay, at least if the current towards the abolition of the rights it provides is not too strong.[151] In short, it offers 'relative protection'.

Conclusion

Do we have real or imaginary rights under the Convention? One suspects that Bentham would have responded that the rights of the Convention are real only to the extent that they have been enshrined in positive law. He would no doubt have thought that we delude ourselves if we believe the rights of the Convention to be the expression of natural, self-evident rights. The construction of the Convention, containing justiciable rights inscribed within a system where complaints are heard in a very legalistic way, may vindicate this view.

One point on which Bentham was wrong was to fear that a document such as the French Declaration would lead to 'perpetual insurrection'. However, this may well be because he was correct to deny that rights could be above the state. The doctrine of the margin of appreciation and the possibility of derogating from the Convention under Article 15 both indicate that statist considerations assume a position of choice under the Convention. Indeed, some commentators would argue that human rights law does not make it possible for the authority of the state to be sufficiently questioned.

This would come as no surprise to IR realists. Those among them who think that the state should not abandon its own interests in favour of a universal morality may even welcome such a conclusion. Others would simply point out that state interests and power play a role which must be acknowledged rather than ignored in international affairs, including human rights international law. The Strasbourg case law offers ample evidence in support of this argument, as has been illustrated in this chapter.

Realism, however, should not be examined on its own. It is more useful to consider how realism and idealism, statism and supranationalism, are in tension with each other. Indeed, in the case law, the Court can be seen both to concur with and to stand up to the state. In conclusion, the Convention offers neither 'real' nor 'imaginary' rights, but what could be referred to as the relative protection of the sandbag.

Notes

1 This is not to deny that the utilitarian and realist aspects of his thought are directly related but to separate them for didactic purposes. For a utilitarian reading of the Convention, see Chapter 4.

2 Bentham produced, in French, his response to the 1789 French Declaration in the years which immediately followed its proclamation. The English version of the pamphlet was first published in 1843, posthumously, under the title 'Anarchical Fallacies'. The 1843 English version has recently been re-edited in numerous publications, including a volume prepared by Ross Harrisson: Jeremy Bentham, 'Anarchical Fallacies. An Examination of the Declaration of the Rights of the Man and the Citizen Decreed by the Constituent Assembly in France', in Jeremy Bentham, *Selected Writings on Utilitarianism* (Ware, Hertfordshire: Wordsworth, 2000) 381–459. References to the pamphlet in this chapter are to this text. The statement at the head of this chapter appears at 458.

3 The 1789 17-article-long Declaration was incorporated into the French Constitution of 1791. However the proclamation of the Republic in September 1792 rendered the

1791 Constitution null and void. Another Declaration, appended to another Constitution, was signed in 1793 or Year 1, but never came into force. Nevertheless, this second, 35-article-long, Declaration, became a significant reference point for democratic aspirations in the nineteenth and twentieth centuries: Danièle Lochak, *Les droits de l'homme* (Paris: La Découverte, 2002), at 23–7.

4 Stephen P. Marks, 'From the "Single Confused Page" to the "Decalogue for Six Billion Persons": The Roots of the Universal Declaration of Human Rights in the French Revolution' (1998) 20 *Human Rights Quarterly* 459–514.

5 Bentham, 'Anarchical Fallacies', at 405.

6 Ibid., at 441.

7 Ibid., at 397.

8 Ibid., at 456.

9 Ibid., at 450.

10 Bentham was not a little irritated by the claim of the French to have identified rules of universal applicability (ibid. at 396, 406, 409, 414, 433, 450), giving us a foretaste of the contemporary so-called cultural relativist critique (on which, see Chapter 6). He also pointed to the difficulty of speaking of the generic man and of the nation. These notions seem to encompass women ('For if women and children are not part of the nation, what are they? Cattle?', ibid. at 415); but this would have the effect of making women equal to men, an idea which he resisted (as hinted ibid. at 400 and 420). In a very strange way, by having seen the difficult relationship between man and woman in natural rights, he could be said to have anticipated the feminist critique of human rights (see Chapter 7). Predictably he can easily be seen to have laid the foundations for the utilitarian critique of human rights (see Chapter 4). Finally, through its acute awareness that power governs what natural rights will mean in practice (ibid. at 407), he could be said to anticipate somewhat the Marxist critique of human rights (see Chapter 5), although the central role he gives to government and laws in the running of society admittedly makes this claim slightly far-fetched. This quick *tour d'horizon* should make it clear that Bentham's critique is extremely rich and well worth reading.

11 For a more comprehensive review of Bentham's arguments, see William Twining, 'The Contemporary Significance of Bentham's *Anarchical Fallacies*' (1975) XLI *Archiv fur Rechts- und Sozialphilosophie* 315.

12 Bentham, 'Anarchical Fallacies', at 398–9.

13 Ibid., at 404, 405.

14 Ibid., at 452.

15 Ibid., at 402, also at 393.

16 Ibid., at 397.

17 Ibid., at 417, emphasis added.

18 Ibid., at 399.

19 Ibid., at 395, emphasis in the original.

20 He is not so much the founder of utilitarianism as one of its most articulate proponents.

21 Bentham, 'Anarchical Fallacies', at 421.

22 Ibid., at 458, emphases in the original.

23 Ibid., at 397.

24 Ibid., at 426.

25 Ibid., at 439.

26 Ibid., at 387, emphasis added.

27 Though it suffers from phrasing the alternatives in black and white and does not allow for 'in-between' results, encapsulated in the metaphor of the sandbag described below.

28 But I shall dispute in Chapter 6 the claim that Article 3 provides for an absolute *right*.

29 To use an expression used by Mireille Delmas-Marty: Mireille Delmas-Marty, 'Restraining or Legitimating the Reason of State?', in M. Delmas-Marty (ed.), *The European Convention for the Protection of Human Rights: International Protection Versus National Restrictions* (Dordrecht: Nijhoff, 1992) 1–14, at 1.

30 Bentham, 'Anarchical Fallacies', at 435.

31 In Article 6 on the right to a fair trial and Article 9 on freedom of religion. But see Articles 2, 4, 5 and 8 to 11 for implicit references.

32 Bentham, 'Anarchical Fallacies', at 435, my emphasis.

33 *Handyside* v. *United Kingdom*, 7 December 1976, Series A, No. 24, (1979–1980) 1 EHRR 737. Chronologically, this was the seventeenth judgment of the European Court of Human Rights.

34 For further details and a longer discussion of this case, see Chapter 6.

35 Paras 48 and 40 of the judgment.

36 For the full phrasing of Article 15, see Appendix 1.

37 As the historian A. W. Brian Simpson persuasively explains in *Human Rights and the End of Empire: Britain and the Genesis of the European Convention* (Oxford: Oxford University Press, 2001).

38 Ibid., at 874.

39 See dissenting opinion of Judge Makarczyk in *Brannigan and McBride* v. *United Kingdom*, 26 May 1993, Series A, No. 258-B, (1994) 17 EHRR 539: 'The main point that, in my opinion, the United Kingdom Government should attempt to prove before the Court is that [the emergency measure] does in fact contribute to eliminate the reasons for which [it] needed to be introduced – in other words the prevention and combating of terrorism' (para. 3). However as Susan Marks remarks in the best contribution on the subject: 'If emergency measures pretend to aim at the achievement of future normality, they often in fact become a way of deferring normality. Or rather, they often *become* normality. Emergencies seem apt to tranform themselves from the exception into the rule, from the extraordinary into the ordinary, indefinitely existing, state of things': Susan Marks, 'Civil Liberties at the Margin: The UK Derogation and the European Court of Human Rights' (1995) 15 *Oxford Journal of Legal Studies* 69–95, at 86.

40 D. J. Harris, M. O'Boyle and C. Warbrick, *Law of the European Convention on Human Rights* (London: Butterworths, 1995), at 490.

41 Tim Dunne and Brian C. Schmidt, 'Realism', in John Baylis and Steve Smith (eds.), *The Globalization of World Politics: An Introduction to International Relations* (Oxford: Oxford University Press, 2001) 141–61, at 141; Robert Jackson and Georg Sørensen, *Introduction to International Relations* (Oxford: Oxford University Press, 1999), at 96. It is to be noted, however, that 'the British School' is cosmopolitan in its outlook. *The Anarchical Society: A Study of Order in World Politics* by Hedley Bull (Basingstoke: Macmillan, 1977) is the foundation text of this school. Martin Shaw has talked of a welcome escape from realism in IR in Britain: 'The Unfinished Global Revolution: Intellectuals and the New Politics of International Relations' (2001) 27 *Review of International Studies* 627–47, at 640.

42 And which had been denounced by E. H. Carr in *The Twenty Years' Crisis*, which rapidly became a classic: E. H. Carr, *The Twenty Years' Crisis, 1919–1939: An Introduction to the Study of International Relations*, with a new introduction by Michael Cox (Basingstoke: Palgrave, 2001).

43 Jackson and Sørensen, *Introduction*, at 68.

44 Dunne and Schmidt, 'Realism', at 150.

45 Quoted by Jackson and Sørensen, *Introduction*, at 70.

46 Jackson and Sørensen, *Introduction*, at 77.

47 Hans J. Morgenthau, *Politics Among Nations: The Struggle for Power and Peace*, revised by Kenneth W. Thompson (Boston: McGraw Hill, 1993), at 12.

48 Jackson and Sørensen, *Introduction*, at 84.

49 Dunne and Schmidt, 'Realism', at 160.

50 *The Twenty Years' Crisis* by E. H. Carr, first published in 1939 and commonly presented as marking the development of the profoundly realist discipline of international relations in the United States, can be read as an attack on liberalism, especially in its Benthamite variant: Michael Cox, 'Introduction' to *The Twenty Years' Crisis*, at ix-lix. At the same time, it is interesting that the statement from Bentham I put at the head of this chapter is not dissimilar to that from Bacon which Carr had put at the start of his book, namely, 'Philosophers make imaginary laws for imaginary commonwealths, and their discourses are as the stars which give little light because they are so high' (ibid., at ci).

51 For Morgenthau, Bentham was 'the prototype of the liberal philosopher', who conceived of legislation as 'the technique by which the findings of liberal "science" are translated into social facts': Hans J. Morgenthau, *Scientific Man vs. Power Politics* (London: Latimer House, 1947), at 110 and 103, respectively.

52 Dunne and Schmidt, 'Realism'.

53 Jackson and Sørensen, *Introduction*, at 77–8.

54 Or, to make the point broader, outside social relations (of which the state is a part).

55 *Greece* v. *United Kingdom* (Application 175/56), report of 26 September 1958.

56 Simpson, *Human Rights*, Chapters 17–19.

57 Few have followed. To date there have been only twenty-one inter-state applications. They have generally involved two states between which there is a serious territorial or political dispute (as in Cyprus under British rule, Northern Ireland and Northern Cyprus). See Robin C. A. White, 'Tackling Political Disputes Through Individual Applications' (1998) 3 *European Human Rights Law Review* 61–72, at 62–4.

58 But see memorandum of 23 April 1958 submitted by the United Kingdom in the *Second Cyprus Case*, quoted by Simpson, *Human Rights*, at 1041. On this case, see below.

59 Simpson, *Human Rights*, Chapter 18.

60 By contrast, the *Second Cyprus Case*, lodged by Greece on 17 July 1957, was concerned with specific allegations of torture. This kind of allegation had been consensually excluded from the *First Case*: Simpson, *Human Rights*, 1020.

61 Ibid., at 970–1. Susan Marks identifies four arguments in favour of granting a wide margin of appreciation to the state with respect to an Article 15 claim. They are: the retrospective character of any judicial examination; the political character of the issues; the nature of government responsibility; and the need to maintain the support of states: Marks, 'Civil Liberties', at 74–5 and 91. The first three arguments were clearly present in the British submissions.

62 Judge de Meyer, who expressed his opposition to the doctrine of the margin of appreciation in numerous separate opinions, no doubt would have agreed. In *Demir and Others* v. *Turkey*, 23 September 1998, ECHR 1998-VI, (2001) 33 EHRR 43, he pointed to the inanity of the concept of the margin of appreciation when it came to claims made under Article 15. He added: 'Where human rights are concerned, States may permit themselves only what the Court considers permissible.' This last remark is consonant with the fact that he very much held a natural law position on human rights, which can be contrasted with Bentham's view of rights as necessarily having a governmental origin.

63 Simpson, *Human Rights*, at 1002.

64 Following a request by the British Foreign Office triggered by none other than Simpson (ibid. at 1049). The Report was immediately published in (1997) 18 *Human Rights Law Journal* 348.

65 Quoted by Simpson, *Human Rights*, at 1004.

66 Ibid., at 1006.

67 Quoted by Simpson, ibid. at 1005.

68 Ibid., at 1005.

69 Ibid., at 1002.

70 Ibid., at 1012–13.

71 *Greece* v. *United Kingdom* (Application 299/57), report of 8 July 1959.

72 Simpson, *Human Rights*, at 1034.

73 Ibid., at 1047.

74 Ibid., at 1052.

75 Quoted by Simpson, ibid. at 1052.

76 Ibid., at 1045.

77 Ibid., at 1046.

78 As the following study, for example, demonstrates: Alexander Orakhelashvili, 'Restrictive Interpretation of Human Rights Treaties in the Recent Jurisprudence of the European Court of Human Rights' (2003) 14 *European Journal of International Law* 529–68. See also Syméon Karagiannis, 'Le territoire d'application de la Convention européenne des droits de l'homme. *Vaetera et nova*' (2005) 61 *Revue trimestrielle des droits de l'homme* 33–120.

79 David Forsythe, *Human Rights in International Relations* (Cambridge: Cambridge University Press, 2000).

80 Ibid., at 233; see also 57.

81 Ibid., at 13.

82 In a paraphrase of Dunne and Schmidt, 'Realism', at 159.

83 Philip Allott, *Eunomia: New Order for a New World* (Oxford: Oxford University Press, 2001), at 287–8.

84 This is what Alexander Orakhelashvili does when he quotes exactly this passage of Allott's book in the conclusion of his enlightening study of the *Al-Adsani* and *Bankovic* judgments: Orakhelashvili, 'Restrictive Interpretation', at 567. *Bankovic* v. *Belgium and Others* (Application 52207/00), decision of 12 December 2001, concerned the application by relatives of the victims of the NATO bombing of the RTS broadcasting centre in Belgrade during the Kosovo conflict. This military action has been considered by many experts as illegal under international law. The applicants at Strasbourg argued that NATO states party to the Convention had violated the Convention, including Article 2. The Court, sitting in a Grand Chamber, declared

the application inadmissible, reasoning that the applicants had not been under the jurisdiction of the defendant states. It remains to be seen whether this decision, which has proved highly controversial, will be followed in other cases involving military action outside the territory of the Council of Europe, including, of course, in Iraq. For a wide-ranging and unusually frank analysis which insists on the absence of neutrality in *Bankovic*, see Karagiannis, 'Le territoire d'application', esp. at 103–20.

85 Pierre-Henri Imbert, 'L'utilisation des droits de l'homme dans les relations inter-nationales', in Société française pour le droit international, *La protection des droits de l'homme et l'évolution du droit international* (Paris: Pedone, 1998) 282–5.

86 *Lawless* v. *Ireland*, 1 July 1961, Series A, No. 3, (1979–1980) 1 EHRR 15.

87 *Lawless* v. *Ireland* [Commission], 1 Eur. Ct. H. R. (ser. B), at 408 (Verbatim Report of the Public Hearing Held by the Chamber of the Court on 7, 8, 10 and 11 April 1961), quoted in Oren Gross and Fionnuala Ní Aoláin, 'From Discretion to Scrutiny: Revisiting the Application of the Margin of Appreciation Doctrine in the Context of Article 15 of the European Convention on Human Rights' (2001) 23 *Human Rights Quarterly* 625–49, at 631, my emphasis.

88 Simpson, *Human Rights*, at 1088.

89 Ibid.

90 Gross and Ní Aoláin, 'From Discretion', at 631.

91 *Ireland* v. *United Kingdom*, 18 January 1978, Series A, No. 25, (1979–1980) 2 EHRR 25. This was the eighteenth judgment of the Court.

92 Para. 207 of the judgment.

93 *Brogan and Others* v. *United Kingdom*, 29 November 1988, Series A, No. 145-B, (1989) 11 EHRR 117.

94 The Turkish case law, discussed in the next section, is slightly different.

95 See e.g. Simpson, *Human Rights* at 1003 and 1019; Gross and Ní Aoláin, 'From Discretion'; Noel Whitty, Thérèse Murphy and Stephen Livingstone, *Civil Liberties Law: The Human Rights Act Era* (London: Butterworths, 2001), at 160; S. Peers, 'National Security and European Law', *Yearbook of European Law 1996* (Oxford: Clarendon Press, 1997) 363–404, at 364 and 403; Marks, 'Civil Liberties', at 94. See also concurring opinion of Judge Martens in *Brannigan and McBride*, para. 4.

96 Harris, O'Boyle and Warbrick, *Law*, Chapter 16. For an insightful and balanced account of the risks of, and reaction to, the terrorist threat in the UK, see Whitty, Murphy and Livingstone, *Civil Liberties*, Chapter 3. Michele De Salvia, 'Contrôle européen et principe de subsidiarité: faut-il encore (et toujours) émarger à la marge d'appréciation', in Paul Mahoney, Franz Matscher, Herbert Petzold and Luzius Wild-haber (eds.), *Protecting Human Rights: The European Perspective. Studies in Memory of Rolv Ryssdal* (Koln: Carl Heymanns Verlag, 2000) 373–85, at 385.

97 For a time, one might have thought that the 'Belmarsh' case would have constituted the next case against the United Kingdom involving Article 15 to reach Strasbourg. The unexpected but welcome ruling by the House of Lords of the United Kingdom in December 2004 makes an application to Strasbourg currently unnecessary: *A. and Others* v. *Secretary of State for the Home Department*, House of Lords, [2004] UKHL 56, [2005] 3 All ER 169, 16 December 2004. The case concerned the administrative detention of non-nationals suspected of terrorism who could not be removed with-out infringing the (non-derogable) Article 3 of the European Convention. This led the British government to enter a derogation from Article 5 (which provides for detention to be judicially reviewed) under Article 15. The House of Lords found the

derogation contrary to the Convention in that the measures were not 'necessary' and unjustifiably discriminated between nationals and aliens.

98 *Aksoy* v. *Turkey*, 26 November 1996, RJD. 1996–VI, (1997) 23 EHHR 553.

99 *Demir and Others* v. *Turkey*, 23 September 1998, ECHR 1998–VI, (2001) 33 EHRR 43.

100 *Nuray Sen* v. *Turkey* (Application 41478/98), 17 June 2003.

101 *Sakik and Others* v. *Turkey*, 26 November 1997, RJD. 1997–VII 58, (1998) 26 EHRR 662.

102 Para. 70 of the judgment.

103 Para. 78 of the judgment.

104 Paras. 3 and 11 of his dissenting opinion.

105 In a dissenting opinion in *Bowman* v. *United Kingdom*, 19 February 1998, RJD 1998 I–175, (1998) 26 EHRR 1 (discussed in Chapter 7), Judge Valticos remarked: 'There is something slightly ridiculous in seeking to give the British Government lessons in how to hold elections and run a democracy.' Forty years before, Henri Rolin had opened the speech for the Greek Government before the Commission in the *First Cyprus Case* with the words: 'I am the first to admit the paradox – and personally I regret it – that by a chance of fate the first government to be brought to the bar by another government is the United Kingdom, which governs a country which surely, more than any other in Europe, has always shown concern for human rights': quoted in Simpson, *Human Rights*, at 322.

106 Concurring opinion of Judge Martens, para. 1. See generally W. E. Haak, G. J. M. Corstens and M. I. Veldt, *Martens Dissenting. The Separate Opinions of a European Human Rights Judge* (Deventer: W. E. J. Tjeenk Willink, 2000).

107 Para. 3 of the concurring opinion of Judge Martens.

108 Dissenting, Judge Makarczyk also referred in *Brannigan* to 'the new Contracting Parties', but to a different effect. He felt a derogation was unlikely from these countries who regarded the Convention 'as a privilege . . . not to be disposed of lightly'. So far Makarczyk has been proved right. In the last decade, the 'trouble' of having to deal with a derogation has not arisen from states who joined the Council of Europe after the fall of communism. It has come instead from Turkey, a country with admittedly dubious democratic credentials, but certainly not a newcomer. Turkey ratified the Convention as early as 1954, before the Netherlands, Belgium and Italy amongst others – a reminder that the system put in place by the Convention is completely separate from the European Community/Union. On the politics of condescension between western and eastern Europe, see Marie-Bénédicte Dembour and Magda Krzyżanowska-Mierzewska, 'Ten Years On: The Voluminous and Interesting Polish Case Law' (2004) *European Human Rights Law Review* 517–44, at 541–2.

109 Raquel Aldana-Pindell, 'An Emerging Universality of Justiciable Victims' Rights in the Criminal Process to Curtail Impunity for State-Sponsored Crimes' (2004) 26 *Human Rights Quarterly* 605–86, at 643.

110 Of *Loizidou* v. *Turkey*, decided on 18 December 1996 (merits) and 28 July 1998 (pecuniary damage), Robin White has written that 'those who can be heard criticising the Court for being overly accommodating to the Contracting States may find it difficult to show how the *Loizidou* case fits into that characterisation', above n. 57, at 72. One may wish to ask, however, whether the identity of the defendant state is not relevant.

111 Para. 46 of the judgment.

112 Para. 57 of the judgment.

113 On the difficulty for the Court to deal with the most serious violations of human rights, see Aisling Reidy, Françoise Hampson and Kevin Boyle, 'Gross Violations of Human Rights: Invoking the European Convention on Human Rights in the Case of Turkey' (1997) 15 *Netherlands Quarterly of Human Rights* 161–73.

114 Para. 8 of his dissenting opinion, emphasis added.

115 On this point, see also Chapter 5. On the aims and work of this NGO, see their website at: http://www.khrp.org/homeenglish.htm

116 Even so a scholarly study has shown that national judges do not, on the whole, follow the lines most propitious for their national governments: Fred J. Bruinsma and Matthijs de Blois, 'Rules of Law from Westport to Wladiwostok: Separate Opinions in the European Court of Human Rights' (1997) 15 *Netherlands Quarterly of Human Rights* 175–86.

117 Carr, *Twenty Years' Crisis*, at 28.

118 Ibid., at 26.

119 Ibid., at 84.

120 Ibid., at 87.

121 Joseph Carens, 'Aliens and Citizens: The Case for Open Borders' (1987) 49 *The Review of Politics* 251–73.

122 Joseph Carens, 'Realistic and Idealistic Approaches to Migration' (1996) 30 *International Migration Review* 156–69.

123 Ibid., at 164.

124 Ibid., at 160.

125 Ibid., at 156.

126 It must nonetheless be clear that the case law on national security goes far beyond Article 15. For a comprehensive discussion of the case law outside Article 15, see Iain Cameron, *National Security and the European Convention on Human Rights* (The Hague: Kluwer, 2000). For an earlier intelligent discussion of the Strasbourg case law in light of *raison d'état*, see Delmas-Marty (ed.), *The European Convention.*

127 This was of course precisely the field which interested Carens.

128 Marie-Bénédicte Dembour, 'Human Rights Law and National Sovereignty in Collusion: The Plight of Quasi-Nationals at Strasbourg' (2003) 21 *Netherlands Quarterly of Human Rights* 63–98; 'Etrangers ou quasi-nationaux? Le choix des droits de l'homme [Observations sous l'arrêt *Ezzouhdi*]' (2002) 52 *Revue trimestrielle des droits de l'homme* 959–82.

129 *Benhebba* v. *France* (Application 53441/99), 10 July 2003; *Mokrani* v. *France*, 15 July 2003, (2005) 40 EHRR 5.

130 *Ezzouhdi* v. *France* (Application 41760/99), 13 February 2001.

131 *Baghli* v. *France*, 30 November 1999, ECHR 1999–VIII.

132 Dissenting opinion.

133 'Par discipline contentieuse et pour que l'arrêt soit cohérent avec la jurisprudence relative aux mesures d'éloignement forcé d'étrangers du territoire de l'état défendeur, j'ai voté avec la majorité.'

134 On the way binary oppositions allow inclusion and exclusion, see Stuart Hall, 'The spectacle of the "Other"', in S. Hall (ed.), *Representation. Cultural Representations and Signifying Practices: Culture, Media and Identities* (Milton Keynes: Open University Press, 1997) 225–79, at 234–7.

135 Though Jean-François Flauss observes that this has become recently less so. He regrets this trend at a time when the Court increasingly faces difficult questions of public international law: 'Brèves observations sur le second renouvellement triennal de la Cour européenne des droits de l'homme' (2005) *Revue trimestrielle des droits de l'homme* 5–32, at 8.

136 Judge Bratza (UK), Judge Türmen (Turkey), Judge Ferrari Bravo (San Marin) and Judge Borrego-Borrego (Spain). For a critique of this practice, see Jean-François Flauss, 'Retour sur l'élection des juges à la Cour européenne des droits de l'homme' (2003) 55 *Revue trimestrielle des droits de l'homme* 1114–19, at 1118; Flauss, 'Brèves observations', at 16–17.

137 See also P. van Dijk and G. J. H. van Hoof, *Theory and Practice of the European Convention on Human Rights* (Kluwer, 1990), at 605.

138 *McCann and Others* v. *United Kingdom*, 27 September 1995, Series A, No. 324, (1996) 21 EHRR 97.

139 Para. 200 of the judgment.

140 This has not been the only case to prompt this kind of reaction. See e.g. Mark Janis, Richard Kay and Anthony Bradley, *European Human Rights Law: Text and Materials* (Oxford: Oxford University Press, 2000), at 80–3 (about the *Sunday Times* case, reviewed in this book in Chapter 5). The decision by the House of Lords in the Belmarsh case has recently attracted similar comments. See e.g. Bruce Anderson's article entitled 'The Law Lords have usurped the right of the British people to defend themselves', published in *The Independent*, Monday 20 December 2004, at 25. It includes the statement: 'If we want to restore our ability to make our own laws, we need to get rid of the ECHR, root and branch'. (The branch presumably refers to the incorporation of the Convention in UK law through the Human Rights Act 1998).

141 *Selmouni* v. *France*, 28 July 1999, ECHR 1999–V, (2000) 29 EHRR 403.

142 Para. 91 of the judgment.

143 Para. 98 of the judgment.

144 Para. 103 of the judgment.

145 Para. 105 of the judgment.

146 Mark Jordan, *Doing the Rights Thing: The Not So Difficult Guide to the Human Rights Act 1988 and the Law of the European Convention on Human Rights* (Haywards Heath: EOS Education, 2001), at 4.33.

147 Ibid.

148 Para. 219 of the judgment.

149 And it is certainly not a matter of such things happening or not. In the eloquent image of Edward Said, which can be transposed to our subject, 'notions [such] as modernity, enlightment, and democracy are by no means simple and agreed-upon concepts that one either does or does not find like Easter eggs in the living-room': Edward Said, 'A window on the world', *The Guardian Review*, 2 August 2003, 4–6, at 4.

150 I am grateful to Neil Stammers for suggesting it to me.

151 On the effect of the so-called War on Terror on a human rights culture which we may too readily have come to regard as entrenched, see Richard Wilson (ed.), *Human Rights in an Age of Terrorism* (Cambridge: Cambridge University Press, forthc.).

4

The Convention in a utilitarian light

[Utilitarianism remains] open to the very serious objection that, because it is solely concerned with consequences in terms of the production of beneficence, it obliterates some important elements in our moral and political vocabulary, namely equality, justice and rights. (Barry)

Bentham's critique of the French Declaration was not primarily utilitarian in inspiration. As we have seen in the previous chapter, 'Anarchical Fallacies' denounced three aspects of the Declaration: its meaninglessness, the risk of insurrection it allegedly generated, and the emptiness of its promises. A text directly derived from utilitarianism (rather than merely compatible with it) would have been chiefly concerned firstly with opposing an absolutist reasoning and secondly with stressing the need to pursue the general interest. Why this is so will become clear below.

I cannot think of a classical text which presents a utilitarian critique of human rights. By contrast, the literature is replete with critiques of utilitarianism which lament its antagonism to the idea of individual human rights, as in the statement at the head of this chapter.[1] In response, utilitarians often defend their political philosophy by saying that they are not opposed to rights, to which their detractors reply that they (the utilitarians) can never truly believe in rights. This debate, which is directly relevant to this part of the human rights credo which asserts that human rights are 'fundamental' and 'inalienable',[2] provides the starting-point of this chapter.

Human rights orthodoxy and utilitarianism are commonly regarded as incompatible with each other. The European Convention system, presumably a child of human rights orthodoxy, is nonetheless replete with utilitarian considerations. This chapter shows that major Strasbourg jurisprudential concepts, such as proportionality and positive obligations, can only be understood by reference to a logic which is at least consequentialist and perhaps even utilitarian in its inspiration.

The previous chapter concluded that the Convention system offers, like a sandbag, relative protection. It did so after having demonstrated that state interests are an important consideration of human rights law. The present chapter expands on this idea of relative rights, but links it to the political inappropriate-ness, and indeed impossibility, of giving the individual absolute rights. It takes issue with the idea that there exists or should exist a core of human rights. Most importantly it argues that an absolutist reasoning is not necessarily superior.

To affirm or not to affirm rights: Utilitarianism and its liberal detractors

Utilitarianism is the ethical philosophy which posits that an action must be morally judged by reference to the well-being (utility) it produces. It holds that the good act is the one that maximizes happiness. It is thus a consequentialist philosophy, i.e. one which judges actions – and omissions – by reference to their consequences.

One of its hallmarks is that it never holds a priori that 'there are some goods so precious that they should not be sacrificed for any amount of some other good'.[3] Trade-offs are always possible under utilitarianism.

According to its liberal detractors,[4] utilitarianism leads inexorably to unaccep-table solutions because it justifies or even demands acts which are obviously immoral. This type of argument is typically supported by examples of sacrifices of the individual to the collective interest, such as: the killing of one healthy person in order to provide healthy organs to a number of people in need of them; the imprisonment of one innocent person who is publicly recognized as the culprit to facilitate a return to peace and order in a riot-torn situation;[5] the subjection to torture of a terrorist in order to defeat terrorist plans and save lives.[6]

Significantly, these examples are invariably produced by thinkers who oppose utilitarianism. Self-declared utilitarians rarely accept them. They point out that the hypothetical scenarios are unlikely to present themselves in reality in the clear-cut form abstractly imagined by utilitarianism's detractors:[7] to take the last example, for the police to know everything, including that this person has the necessary information, except for the last crucial piece – where the bomb is – is not a very convincing scenario. They also commonly observe that the crude sacrifice of the individual would, in time, lead to a substantial decrease in general happiness because of the sense of insecurity it would foster across the population.[8]

The ever-present possibility of sacrificing one good to another good has been presented as the central embarrassment of utilitarianism.[9] I fail to detect this embarrassment. It is nonetheless clear that utilitarianism and rights-based liberal-ism seem to work at cross-purposes. Utilitarianism is concerned with pursuing the collective interest, this kind of liberalism with pursuing the interest of the individual. Utilitarianism must logically neglect principled respect for individual rights when their application can be expected to run counter to the maximization of happiness; the foundation of rights-based liberalism is the protection of these very rights, irrespective of the consequences for the public good. In terms of method, utilitarianism is deductive and context-oriented; liberalism, in this variant, inductive and abstract-oriented.

In this scheme, one would probably expect human rights orthodoxy to be on the side of anti-utilitarian liberalism. Things are more complex than that, however. The next two sections introduce the idea that trade-offs are extremely common in the Convention system.

The balance of interests in the Convention and the proportionality test applied by the Court

The Convention was drafted in the wake of the Second World War with the aim of reasserting the importance of the individual against the state and/or against society.[10] Even so, it repeatedly calls for balancing acts to be performed between the interests of the individual and the interests of 'the community' – to use an alternative, and by now favourite term.[11] Except for Article 3 on the prohibition of torture and inhuman and degrading treatment, the trade-offs of utilitarian logic are not shunned in the Convention.

This is particularly striking in respect of Articles 8 to 11 of the Convention which provide in their second paragraphs for restrictions to the rights enunciated in the first paragraphs, respectively related to privacy and family life, and to freedom of religion, of expression and of association. These restrictions, based on the public interest, are expressed in various terms, including 'public safety', 'public order', 'protection of health and morals' and also 'the protection of the rights and freedoms of others'. That Convention rights are limited by the general interest is also clear in respect of Article 5, which seeks to regulate when the state can deprive an individual of his or her liberty. Even a provision as important as Article 2 provides that life can sometimes be taken by the state for a superior interest, immediately indicating a trade-off. Admittedly the bar for this particular trade-off is placed at a high level since only 'the use of [lethal] force which is no more than absolutely necessary' is permitted under Article 2.

When the Court weighs various interests, it normally refers to 'proportionality', a doctrine which originates from nineteenth-century German law and which was first mentioned by the Commission in 1960.[12] The doctrine insists that a reasonable relationship must exist between a particular objective to be achieved and the means used to achieve that objective.[13] It can be used to test a measure in respect of its a) legitimacy, b) suitability, c) necessity and d) proportionality in the narrow sense. In other words it asks whether the measure a) pursues a legitimate aim, b) contributes to fulfilling the aim it purports to serve, c) represents the least restrictive way of achieving this aim, and d) achieves a means/end fit such that, overall, the ends do justify the means.[14] Proportionality has been shown to pervade the whole of the Court's case law.[15]

The margin of appreciation and the proportionality test: *Dudgeon* versus *James and Others*

The proportionality test is intended to assist the Court in deciding whether, *on balance*, a particular restriction of a right is justified, given that the rights provided by the Convention are rarely meant to be absolute, with most explicitly subject to limitations and exceptions. The previous chapter has noted that the Court is ready to grant the state a margin of appreciation as to what local situations require. The wider this margin, the more likely it is that the proportionality test will be found to be satisfied (with the applicant failing to convince the Court that the state acted disproportionately).[16] Conversely, the narrower the margin, the more exacting the proportionality test will be (with this time the state finding it difficult to convince the Court that it has acted in a proportionate manner). *James and Others* on the one hand and *Dudgeon* on the other respectively illustrate these two trends.

To take them in reverse order, in *Dudgeon* v. *United Kingdom*, decided on 22 October 1981,[17] the applicant complained that he was liable to criminal prosecution on account of his homosexuality under the law in force in Northern Ireland, in violation of Article 8 of the Convention guaranteeing privacy. The Court accepted that:

> There can be no denial that some degree of regulation of male homosexual conduct, as indeed of other forms of sexual conduct, by means of the criminal law can be justified as 'necessary in a democratic society'.[18]

It specifically granted a margin of appreciation to the state.[19] However, it observed that:

> The present case concerns a most intimate aspect of private life. Accordingly, there must exist *particularly serious* reasons before interferences on the part of the public authorities can be legitimate for the purposes of paragraph 2 of Article 8.[20]

It continued:

> As compared with the era when that legislation was enacted, there is now a better understanding, and in consequence an increased tolerance, of homosexual behaviour to the extent that in the great majority of the member States of the Council of Europe it is no longer considered to be necessary or appropriate to treat homosexual practices of the kind now in question as in themselves a matter to which the sanctions of the criminal law should apply . . . It cannot be maintained that . . . there is a 'pressing social need' to make such acts criminal offences, there being no sufficient justification provided by the risk of harm to vulnerable sections of society requiring protection or by the effects on the public. On the issue of proportionality, the Court considers that such justifications as there are for retaining the law in force unamended are outweighed by the detrimental effects which the very existence of the

legislative provisions in question can have on the life of a person of homosexual orientation like the applicant.[21]

The Court found a breach of Article 8 (by nine votes to one).

James and Others v. *United Kingdom*, decided on 21 January 1986,[22] concerned the estate of the Duke of Westminster's family (known as the Grosvenor Estate) in the highly desirable area of Belgravia and Mayfair in Central London. The Leasehold Reform Act 1967 had made it possible in England and Wales, under certain circumstances, for tenants to acquire the properties in which they had held a long-term interest. The applicants, trustees of the Grosvenor Estate, complained that the resulting compulsory transfer of some of their properties contravened, inter alia, Article 1 of Protocol 1. On the legitimacy of the aim of the contested legislation, the Court ruled:

> ... the notion of 'public interest' is necessarily extensive. In particular ... the decision to enact laws expropriating property will commonly involve consideration of political, economic and social issues on which opinion within a democratic society may reasonably differ widely. The Court, finding it natural that the margin of appreciation available to the legislature in implementing social and economic policies should be a wide one, will respect the legislature's judgment as to what is 'in the public interest' unless that judgment be manifestly without reasonable foundation[23] ... The applicants ... disputed the existence of any problem justifying the legislation ... The Government conceded that the convictions on which the 1967 Act was based were by no means universally shared ... [T]he justice or injustice of the leasehold system and the respective 'moral entitlements' of tenants and landlords are matters of judgment on which there is clearly room for legitimate conflict of opinions. The Court ... agrees with the Commission's conclusion: the United Kingdom Parliament's belief in the existence of a social injustice was not such as could be characterised as manifestly unreasonable.[24]

The Court's assessment of the means chosen to achieve the aim of the legislation was also favourable to the state. To the applicants who argued that the Act failed to consider their own situation, namely a contractual relationship with well-off, middle-class tenants who hardly needed special protection, the Court answered:

> Expropriation legislation of wide sweep, in particular if it implements a programme of social and economic reform, is hardly capable of doing justice in the diverse circumstances of the very large number of different individuals concerned.[25]

The utilitarian ring of the formulation could not be clearer: some individuals may lose for the benefit of the greatest number.

As Lord Mackay of Clashfern has noted, Article 1 of Protocol 1 is one area (in his view far too isolated) where the Court has generally struck the balance between the individual and society in favour of the latter, as testified by the rare occasions where the Court has found a state in violation of Article 1 of Protocol 1.[26] This could be explained by the not-so-fundamental character of the right of

property amongst the other human rights protected by the Convention system.[27] However, another noticeable area where the wide margin of appreciation granted to the state makes it difficult for the Court to conclude that a
violation has occurred is Article 15 of the Convention about derogation in
times of emergency, examined in the previous chapter.[28] It is difficult to argue
that derogation from the Convention is not liable to affect rights, such as
liberty, which are considered fundamental. Trade-offs between individual rights
and public or community interests are rife in the Convention system.

'Rights as Trumps': The absolutism of Dworkin

The last two sections have established that utilitarian considerations are far from
being absent from the Convention system. The question arises: are they at least
sometimes absent? The present section identifies what a non-utilitarian logic
would require by reference to Ronald Dworkin's rights-as-trumps argument.

Dworkin's argument is informed by the philosophy of Immanuel Kant, who held
that individuals should have autonomy to determine their own ends.[29] Free choice
is central to the Kantian philosophy, premised upon 'the separateness and the
individuality of human beings rather than on their part in an aggregate or collective'.[30] Following Kant, Ronald Dworkin does not associate human dignity with any
particular conception of the common good. He defends the view that a liberal
theory of justice should take no position as to what constitutes a good life. This
leads Dworkin to be primarily interested in procedural rather than in substantive
principles. He demands that individuals be treated fairly, that their dignity as
human agents capable of deciding their own ends be protected. Accordingly the
state must treat its individual citizens with 'equal respect and concern', while
remaining neutral as to competing visions of what the good entails.

Dworkin holds that individual rights (which allow the *process* of democracy to
take place) must trump substantive notions of the good. He opens his essay
'Rights as Trumps' with the following words:

> Rights are best understood as trumps over some background justification for political
> decisions that states a goal for the community as a whole. If someone has a right to
> publish pornography, this means that it is for some reason wrong for officials to act in
> violation of that right, even if they (correctly) believe that the community as a whole
> would be better off if they did.[31]

The 'correctly' which is in parentheses is of crucial importance to Dworkin's
thinking. Dworkin is not saying that, in a conflict between individual right and
collective good, the right must be paramount when the vision of what is good for
the community is mistaken, or at least possibly mistaken. In his view, the right *is*
paramount in such a conflict, full stop. That the right may well run counter to the
benefit of the community is irrelevant; the communal interest must give way,
whatever the consequences. To repeat, Dworkin's view is that 'if someone has a

right to something then it is wrong for the government to deny it to him even though it would be in the general interest to do so'.[32]

This does not mean that Dworkin rejects utilitarian logic altogether. He suggests that not all the things we call rights are or should act as trumps, i.e. deserve to be called rights in his understanding of the term. Dworkin says that he is 'anxious to show how rights fit into different packages' and that he wants to see 'which rights should be accepted as trumps over utility', presumably distinguishing these from others which should not.[33] He specifically accepts that 'an informal kind of utilitarianism . . . has supplied, for example, the working justification of most of the constraints on our liberty through law that we accept as proper'.[34] He does not object to this form of utilitarianism.

Nonetheless, for him, a right, correctly understood, is a trump that does not allow any trade-off with the general interest. As James Griffin observes, if *A* trumps *B*, it means that '*any* amount of *A*, no matter how small, is more valuable than *any* amount of *B*, no matter how large'.[35] In Dworkin's words:

> We need rights, as a distinct element in political theory, . . . when some decision that injures some people nevertheless finds prima-facie support in the claim that it will make the community as a whole better off on some plausible account of where the community's general welfare lies . . . [T]he most natural source of any objection we might have to such a decision is that . . . [it] pays insufficient attention to its impact on the minority . . . We want to say that the decision is wrong, *in spite of its apparent merit*, because it does not take the damage it causes to some into account in the right way and therefore does not treat these people as equals entitled to the same concern as others.[36]

Instead of 'in spite of its apparent merit', someone more inclined towards utilitarian logic might have written: 'in spite of its evident merit'. For Dworkin, however, the evident merit would only be apparent since the kind of liberalism he puts forward is based on the idea that no quantity of benefit resulting from the violation of a trumping right is ever capable of justifying the violation. In his view, the violation of a trumping right can *never* be allowed.[37] By contrast, a utilitarian for whom no trade-off is excluded once and for all can judge as evident the merit of a violation of even a fundamental right.

Dworkin asserts the trumping power of rights. A right is a trump when a calculation as to what could supersede its respect is ruled out.[38] With such a right there is no weighing of interests to be done, no proportionality test to be applied, no balance between competing interests to be struck. Does the Convention provide for any trumping rights?

Article 3 lays down a negative absolute obligation: *Selmouni*'s reiteration

The most obvious contender for this status is Article 3 on torture and inhuman and degrading treatment. That Article 3 lays down an absolute prohibition is often the very first thing which is said about it in commentaries on the Conven-tion.[39] This claim is in line with the affirmations of the Court since its inception. Thus, in *Selmouni* v. *France*,[40] already discussed in the previous chapter, the Court expectedly reiterated that:

> Article 3 enshrines one of the most fundamental values of democratic societies. Even in the most difficult circumstances, such as the fight against terrorism and organised crime, the Convention prohibits in absolute terms torture and inhuman or degrading treatment or punishment. Unlike most of the substantive clauses of the Convention and of Protocols Nos. 1 and 4, Article 3 makes no provision for exceptions and no derogation from it is permissible under Article 15 §2 even in the event of a public emergency threatening the life of the nation.[41]

It follows from the fact that Article 3 is said to lay down an absolute negative obligation that, in response to an allegation of torture, the Court can only discuss whether the act complained of a) has happened and b) amounts to torture.

The substantive issues discussed in *Selmouni* conform to this pattern.[42] On the one hand, the Court found no violation of Article 3 in respect of the alleged rape because rape had not been proven to have taken place. On the other hand, the Court was satisfied that the violence (blows, threats and humiliating actions) which had been inflicted on the applicant by the police with the aim of extorting a confession from him 'must be regarded as acts of torture for the purposes of Article 3 of the Convention'.[43]

One will recall that, twenty years before, in *Ireland* v. *United Kingdom*,[44] the Court had said that the acts of sensory deprivation complained of did not amount to torture. This assessment was bitterly criticized, including by Amnesty Interna-tional.[45] In *Selmouni*, the Court found a violation of Article 3 after having observed that 'certain acts which were classified in the past as "inhuman and degrading treatment" as opposed to "torture" could be *classified* differently in future [having regard to] the increasingly high standard being required in the area of the protection of human rights and fundamental liberties'.[46] The reference to the idea of classification indicates that the matter at issue concerned the very *nature* of the acts complained of. Why this is important will become clear when we discuss, below, other cases (*Pretty* and *Soering*) which also concern Article 3, but where the Court departed from what could be called a negative-obligation reasoning.

Relative or absolute protection under Article 8? The Court's majority versus Judge De Meyer in *Z* v. *Finland*

For the moment, let us remain with our search for places where utilitarian logic might be absent from the Convention. Apart from Article 3, one might think of Article 8, given the firmness of the control which the Court announced – in *Dudgeon* – would apply to the protection of the privacy of the most intimate aspects of personality. But this would be wrong: a close reading of the judgment indicates that the Court never intended the privacy of even these aspects to be absolute.

Dudgeon only said that particularly serious reasons would need to be present for interferences with the most intimate aspects of private life to be legitimate for the purposes of paragraph 2 of Article 8.[47] Granted, the Court did not find such reasons to be present in the case; nonetheless it did not rule out, *once and for all*, a weighting exercise in respect of intimate matters. In fact the Court did balance competing interests in this case; it found that the supposed general interest in prosecuting private homosexual acts between consenting adults did not weigh much at all. It is *because of this* that the Court ruled for the applicant. The Court's finding of violation was not based on the reasoning that – say – the essence of Article 8 had been touched. Such a reasoning would have been in line with the Dworkinian articulation of 'rights as trumps'. Instead, the Court remained on utilitarian ground.

The Court confirmed the relative character of its protection in this area in its subsequent case law, notably *Z* v. *Finland*, decided on 25 February 1997.[48] This case is interesting to review because there one judge (De Meyer) adopted, by contrast to the majority, an absolutist position. In other words, it illustrates how the Court verges towards utilitarianism, but by doing so generates dissent from one of its judges who thinks the Court should make a trump of the right to privacy – without, however, either side using these terms.

Z v. *Finland* was brought by a Finnish national whose husband X (of African origin)[49] was the object of criminal proceedings in Finland for rapes which could amount to manslaughter if X had known he was HIV positive at the time of the assaults. The authorities therefore wanted to establish when X had known he was HIV positive. To do this, they wanted to establish when his wife Z had known she was HIV positive. Z refused to disclose this information. The authorities ordered her doctors to give evidence in court about her medical history – which the doctors did reluctantly. Z's medical records were seized and included in X's investigation file. X was eventually convicted of five counts of attempted manslaughter. In its judgment, the Finnish Court of Appeal released Z's name even though it was legally possible to keep it confidential. It ordered Z's medical data to be kept confidential for ten years – instead of the thirty Z requested.

There had obviously been an interference with Z's rights under Article 8 of the Convention. Had it been 'necessary in a democratic society'? The Court said:

> . . . the protection of personal data, not least medical data, is of fundamental importance to a person's enjoyment of his or her right to respect for private and family life . . . It is crucial not only to respect the sense of privacy of a patient but also to preserve his or her confidence in the medical profession and in the health services in general . . . The disclosure of [HIV status] may dramatically affect [an individual's] private and family life, as well as social and employment situation, by exposing him

or her to opprobrium and the risk of ostracism. For this reason it may also discourage persons from seeking diagnosis or treatment and thus undermine any preventive efforts by the community to contain the pandemic . . . The interests in protecting the confidentiality of such information will therefore *weigh heavily in the balance* in determining whether such interference was proportionate to the legitimate aim pursued. Such interference cannot be compatible with Article 8 of the Convention unless it is justified by an overriding requirement in the public interest.[50]

As in *Dudgeon*, the Court refused to rule out a balancing act between the interest of the individual (which is, however, as the Court recognized, also the interest of the community) and the interest (or, rather, another interest) of the community. The Court 'accept[ed] that the interests of a patient and the community as a whole in protecting the confidentiality of medical data may be *outweighed* by the interest in investigation and prosecution of crime and in the publicity of court proceedings'.[51] It did not think it would be fitting for it to substitute its view for those of the national authorities[52] and thus

recognise[d] that a margin of appreciation should be left to the competent national authorities in striking a fair balance between the interest of publicity of court proceedings, on the one hand, and the interests of a party or a third person in maintaining the confidentiality of such data, on the other hand.[53]

On the facts of the case, the Court had no difficulty finding that the order to maintain the medical data confidential for only ten years and the publication of the applicant's identity in the Court of Appeal's judgment constituted disproportionate interferences with Article 8. This finding was reached unanimously.[54] Eight of the nine judges were also of the opinion that the orders for medical advisors to give evidence and the seizure of the applicant's medical records and inclusion in the investigation file corresponded to an 'overriding' requirement and satisfied the proportionality test.[55] Judge De Meyer, however, strongly disagreed.

The Belgian judge stated in his dissenting opinion:

In my opinion, *whatever* the requirements of criminal proceedings may be, considerations of that order do not justify disclosing confidential information arising out of the doctor/patient relationship or the documents related to it.[56]

As had become his habit, he once again proceeded to castigate the Court for referring to the margin of appreciation. He urged it to recant the relativism it implied and argued:

where human rights are concerned, there is no room for a margin of appreciation which would enable the States to decide what is acceptable and what is not. On that subject the boundary not to be overstepped must be as clear and precise as possible.[57]

In effect what De Meyer called for was an absolute (and well-delimited) prohibition. He aligned himself with a trump-as-rights logic; antithesis of the balancing utilitarian logic, which the Court, by contrast, implicitly followed. It is worth spelling out further how these two logics differ.

Consequentialism versus absolutism, and the law of double effect

Absolutism is a categorical (or deontological) theory: it considers certain kinds of acts to be intrinsically wrong.[58] Holding that some things have intrinsic (non-consequential) value,[59] it requires that some acts be avoided at all costs.[60] By contrast, a consequentialist (or teleological) theory evaluates the morality of an action by reference to its consequences. It does not ask, 'Is this wrong?' but, 'Is this *causing* wrong?' For consequentialism (including utilitarianism),[61] nothing has intrinsic value.

Is bringing about someone's death deliberately the same as bringing it about through the unintended but predictable result of one's actions? For consequentialism, yes. Absolutism, however, which forbids '*doing* certain things to people, rather than bringing about certain *results*',[62] does not think so. It distinguishes between deliberate and indirect killing without, however, necessarily condoning the latter.

Catholic moral theology has developed the law of double effect precisely to make it possible to say that all that is not specifically forbidden should not be considered allowed. Acts have double effect when they have a good intended effect and a bad unintended effect. They are allowed under the law of double effect 'only if the bad effect is unintended, not disproportionate to the intended good effect, and unavoidable if the good effect is to be achieved'.[63] The law of double effect is thus a corrective to the categorism of absolutism: it makes it possible for the negative consequences of an act which is not prohibited as such to be taken into account to reach the conclusion that it is, after all, prohibited.

The law of double effect makes no sense under utilitarianism, for two reasons. Firstly utilitarianism does not recognize a category of acts that are, as such, forbidden. Secondly utilitarianism finds the distinction, upon which the law of double effect rests, between intended and unintended effects neither useful nor convincing.[64] Utilitarianism considers an act to be wrong because of the adverse consequences it produces, full stop.

The recognition of positive obligations by the Court: Utilitarian logic or application of the law of double effect?

The development of human rights law is commonly talked of in terms of three generations and of a progressive recognition of positive obligations. This section argues that these terms must be understood by reference to the prominence of an absolutist logic which allows (implicit) applications of the law of double effect.

The three generations of human rights would consist of, respectively, civil and political rights, economic and social rights, and collective or solidarity rights.[65]

Considering the philosophical basis of the human rights orthodoxy,[66] it is hardly surprising that the so-called first generation imposes on the state duties which are regarded as embodying negative obligations, of *refraining from* violating the enunciated political and civil rights. The second generation has long been controversial, not least because economic and social rights undoubtedly require for their respect positive action on the part of the state – *to provide* education, health services, etc. Some have argued that these rights could not possibly be human rights.[67] This view is rarely found in the literature today.[68] Even though economic and social rights are not given the same attention in practice as political and civil rights, the leitmotif has now become that human rights are 'indivisible, interdependent and interrelated'.[69]

It has also become widely accepted that the state is not able to respect even the first generation of human rights simply by doing nothing. To avoid torture, for example, the state must do something, starting with the training of its police force. I would personally go so far as to say that human rights cannot ever consist of purely negative obligations. Many theorists, if pushed, would probably agree with me. Despite this, the distinction between negative and positive obligations continues to occupy a central place in human rights debates. This is not surprising, given the Kantian premises of much human rights theory.

With regard to the Strasbourg system, the dominant view is that the drafters of the Convention originally laid down negative obligations but that the Court progressively found that the Convention also embodied positive obligations.[70] This development is generally praised for having ensured an effective rather than illusory protection by the Convention system. What is important for the present discussion is that the recognition of the existence of positive obligations happens late, as it were peripherally, by contrast to the obvious (and in this sense original) existence of negative obligations, which are taken to represent the norm.[71] Many commentators have traced the development of positive obligations in the case law of the Court.[72] The exercise has not been carried out in respect of negative obligations presumably because, as a constant (though in my view non-existent) category, they do not appear to require elaboration.

The Court first referred to 'positive obligations' in *Marckx* v. *Belgium*, decided on 13 June 1979.[73] The applicants in this case were a single mother (a journalist by profession) and her 'illegitimate' child. Under the Belgian law then in force, the first applicant had had to adopt the second applicant to become her legal mother. She was prevented from disposing of her property in favour of her child to the extent she would have been able to do if the child had been 'legitimate'. The applicants complained of a number of violations, especially of Article 8, both taken alone and together with Article 14 of the Convention. They mostly won.

In its judgment, the Court endorsed the distinction between negative and positive obligations, qualifying the former with the term 'primarily' and thus signalling that it considered the latter to be secondary:

By proclaiming in paragraph 1 the right to respect for family life, Article 8 signifies firstly that the State cannot interfere with the exercise of the right otherwise than in accordance with the strict conditions set out in paragraph 2. As the Court [has already had occasion to state previously], the object of the Article is *essentially* that of protecting the individual against arbitrary interference by the public authorities . . . Nevertheless it does not merely compel the State to abstain from such interference: in addition to this primarily negative undertaking, there may be positive obligations inherent in an effective 'respect' for family life.[74]

The Court continued:

This means, amongst other things, that when the State determines in its domestic legal system the regime applicable to certain family ties such as those between an unmarried mother and her child, it must act in a manner *calculated* to allow those concerned to lead a normal life. As envisaged by Article 8, respect for family life implies, in particular, in the Court's view, the existence in domestic law of legal safeguards that render possible as from the moment of birth the child's integration in his family. In this connection, the State has a *choice* of means, but a law that fails to satisfy this requirement violates [the Convention].[75]

In effect, what the Court is asking the state to do is to weigh – calculate, says the Court – the implications of the legislative course it chooses to adopt. Once this step towards measuring as opposed to 'simply' avoiding a clear prohibition is taken, one leaves the supposedly black-and-white area of respect versus violation to enter a grey area of relative respect/violation.[76] There are choices to be made – rather than absolute prohibitions to be followed.[77] A weighing exercise is called for. Something akin to proportionality is in sight.

At first sight the injunction given by the Court to the state to *weigh* is at odds with an absolutist position, given that absolutist injunctions are expected to be of a *refrain* kind. The ever-growing positive obligations recognized by the Court – not just in relation to Article 8, but in relation to all sectors of the Convention[78] – could seem to have utilitarian overtones.[79] However, it could also be seen as the practical pendant at Strasbourg to the absolutist theory of the law of double effect. To repeat: this law has it that a double effect action is permitted 'only if the bad effect is unintended, not disproportionate to the intended good effect, and unavoidable if the good effect is to be achieved'.[80] This definition fits the proportionality test operated by the Court rather well. The measure adopted by the authority and contested by the applicant could be the action with double effect. Its intended good effect would consist of the results it is expected to yield in terms of the legitimate aim for which it was adopted; its unintended bad effect would consist of the interference with a Convention right. In what can be seen as amounting to an application of the law of double effect, the Court will accept the measure if its bad effect is not disproportionate and is unavoidable, i.e., in the language of the Court, if it is 'necessary in a democratic society'.

To sum up this section, the implicit acceptance of the central place of negative obligations in the Convention is directly in line with an absolutist view of human rights, which one expects would lay down absolute prohibitions as to what the state *cannot do*. By contrast, positive obligations inevitably require the states, and the Court that controls them, to weigh the consequences of their action. In turn, the balancing exercise inevitably rules out absolutism and entails some kind of relativism. This does not necessarily mean, however, that the consequentialism of positive obligations must be regarded as incompatible with absolutism, given the law of double effect.

Absolutism: Possibly utilitarian up to the point of transgression

Nothing prevents absolutists from being utilitarians as long as this does not lead them to transgress an absolute prohibition. In Thomas Nagel's useful formulation, absolutism 'operates as a limitation on utilitarian reasoning, not as a substitute for it'.[81] Thus, an 'absolutist can be expected to try to maximize good and minimize evil, so long as this does not require him to transgress an absolute prohibition like that against murder'.[82] Phrasing it in simple words, an absolutist can be a utilitarian up to the point of transgression. For an example, we can turn to Dworkin, who despite being the author of the rights-as-trumps argument, readily admits – without finding this problematic – that most legal restrictions on liberty are justified by 'an informal kind of utilitarianism'.[83]

Lest some readers should wonder why I am examining these theoretical subtleties, let me reassure them that the exercise is useful. An understanding of the concepts of negative obligation, positive obligation and law of double effect makes it possible to identify inconsistencies in the Court's reasoning, as I do in the next section in relation to *Pretty*. Most importantly, it lays the ground for assessing the moral value of absolutism (and thus the human rights orthodoxy) and consequentialism. To anticipate, my own position is that absolutism refuses to take on board the demands of particular situations and is thus open to lead to morally dubious decisions, without even feeling bound to ponder the consequences of its edicts.

Pretty: A mixture of absolutist and consequentialist logics

Absolutism and consequentialism follow different logics. This section illustrates how the two can become inadvertently intermingled through an analysis of *Pretty v. United Kingdom*, decided on 29 April 2002.[84] The case concerned assisted suicide. One might have thought that the Court would have been reluctant to abandon a Kantian perspective on a life-and-death matter. A close, theoretically informed, analysis of the judgment nonetheless shows that it did.

Mrs Pretty was a 43-year-old woman who was suffering from a degenerative and incurable illness. She was paralysed to such an extent that she could no longer commit suicide alone. She wanted her husband of twenty-five years to help her to die, sparing her the suffering and indignity of the final stages of the disease. The Director of Public Prosecutions refused to grant her husband immunity from prosecution if he assisted her in committing suicide in contravention of domestic law. Mrs Pretty argued before the Court that this decision infringed her rights under Articles 2, 3, 8, 9 and 14 of the Convention. The Court unanimously found no violation of the Convention. For the purpose of this discussion, I shall pay attention to the reasoning of the Court in respect of Articles 3, 8 and 2.

The applicant had argued that 'there was no room under Article 3 of the Convention for striking a balance between her right to be protected from degrading treatment and any competing interest of the community, as the right was an absolute one'.[85] But even if the Court were not to accept this, the applicant argued that 'the balance struck was disproportionate as English law imposed a blanket ban on assisting suicide regardless of the individual circumstances of the case'.[86] Amongst these, the applicant mentioned 'that her intellect and capacity to make decisions were unimpaired by the disease, that she was neither vulnerable nor in need of protection, that her imminent death could not be avoided, that if the disease ran its course she would endure terrible suffering and indignity and that no one else was affected by her wish for her husband to assist her save for him and their family who were wholly supportive of her decision'.[87]

The contested measure was the refusal by the authorities to give an undertaking that they would not prosecute Mrs Pretty's husband.[88] Was Mrs Pretty asking the Government to act or to refrain from acting? At first sight one could say that the applicant was asking the authorities to *refrain from* doing something, namely, to refrain from prosecuting her husband and thus interfering with the course chosen by her and him. As Mrs and Mr Pretty were asking to be left alone, this could look as if they were claiming a negative obligation under the Convention. It cannot be so, however, for a prosecution would not have inflicted, *as such*, the inhuman and degrading treatment complained of by the applicants. It was the *consequence* of the attitude adopted by the Government, rather than what it did (or, indeed, did not do), which was likely to produce the treatment which the applicant claimed was prohibited under Article 3: the refusal to give the undertaking could cause Mr Pretty not to assist his wife in the taking of her life, thus condemning her to a distressing death. If in contravention of Article 3, the action (or rather omission) by the Government was certainly not in contravention of the negative obligation it contains.[89] Within a logic which asserts that obligations are either of the negative or the positive kind, the failure to give the undertaking, if in violation of Article 3, had to be in contravention of an implied positive obligation.

The Court noted that it was 'beyond dispute that the respondent Government [had] not, themselves [sic], inflicted any ill-treatment on the applicant'.[90] It thus proceeded to classify, rightly in terms of the logic it followed, the undertaking by the authorities not to prosecute as a potentially positive obligation.[91] Having done this, it laconically concluded:

[The applicant's request] would require that the State sanction actions intended to terminate life, an obligation that cannot be derived from Article 3 of the Convention.[92]

This statement constituted a response which would have been more appropriate to a claim that the Government was violating a negative obligation.

In human rights law, negative obligations are the only ones which can be said to be absolute.[93] An absolute prohibition operates on a strictly binary mode: it is either respected or it is not – there is no grey area. In the context of the Convention, either the state has refrained from doing what is prohibited or it has done it – there is no proportionality test to be applied. By contrast, positive obligations are not as clear-cut as negative obligations. It is difficult to define their boundaries and they are not absolute.[94] Proportionality tests are necessary to their application because they appear in shades of grey rather than in black and white.

In its laconic statement the Court spoke of 'sanction' rather than 'lack of interference' and of an obligation being 'derived from' rather than 'found in' Article 3. Nonetheless there is no sense of any measuring or probing. The reasoning is more suited to the discussion of a negative obligation. In respect of the latter, there is only one way to find no violation of the Convention when the state has acted in a way that *seems* to be contrary to the negative obligation laid down in the Convention: it is to consider that, in fact, the action of the state is not covered by the negative obligation.

It would have been more in tune with a discussion of the domain of a positive obligation under Article 3 for the Court to rule that the British Government had acted within its margin of appreciation when it had considered that, *all things considered*, the criminalization of assisting suicide contributed to ensure that individuals would die in a way that was not inhuman and degrading – if only because non-criminalization could be expected negatively to affect vulnerable people who would be pushed towards suicide. Presumably, however, the Court was not ready to follow the logic of weighing the pros and cons of various possible measures which must be associated with positive obligations. It preferred to adopt a black-and-white, on-or-off, within-or-outside-Article-3 reasoning in line with clear religious injunctions which condemn suicide – an approach better suited to the discussion of negative obligations.

I suspect that the main reason why Mrs Pretty lost her case is that her request contravened Christian ideas of respect for the sanctity of life. I suspect that a subsidiary reason, utilitarian in character, also motivated the judges. Not surprisingly, the Court does not mention this utilitarian motivation in its reasoning about Article 3, which is normally presented as being absolute. However, it let it appear in its reasoning about Article 8, on privacy, which everyone agrees is not absolute in character.

Turning to Mrs Pretty's claim under Article 8, the Court said that it was 'not ready to exclude that [the applicant's prevention by law from exercising her choice to avoid an undignified death constitutes] an interference with her right to respect for private life'.[95] In other words, there may be an interference.[96] Paragraph 2 of the Article thus applies. One of the grounds under which a government can legitimately interfere with the rights that Article 8 provides is 'the protection of the rights and freedoms of others'. The Court reasoned:

> [T]he Court finds . . . that States are entitled to regulate through the operation of the general criminal law activities that are detrimental to the life and safety of other individuals . . . The law in issue . . . was designed to safeguard life by protecting the weak and vulnerable and especially those who are not in a condition to take informed decisions against acts intended to end life or to assist in ending life. Doubtless the condition of terminally ill individuals will vary. But many will be vulnerable and it is the vulnerability of the class which provides the rationale for the law in question. It is primarily for States to assess the risk and the likely incidence of abuse if the general prohibition on assisted suicides were relaxed or if exceptions were to be created. Clear risks of abuse do exist, notwithstanding arguments as to the possibility of safeguards and protective procedures.[97]

For the Court, there had been no violation of Article 8 as the interference in this case could be justified as 'necessary in a democratic society'. The right of Mrs Pretty had be set aside for the sake of other individuals, more vulnerable – and more numerous – than her.

In *Pretty*, the utilitarian trade-off explicitly took place in respect of Article 8. It does not seem to intrude on the reasoning of the Court in respect of Article 3, at least if this reasoning can be taken at face value. In the part of the judgment which deals with Article 3, the Court departs from any utilitarian consideration by stating that no positive obligation arises under Article 3 which would require the Government to act in the way requested by the applicant. As for the claim of Mrs Pretty under Article 2, the Court simply notes that it 'is not persuaded that "the right to life" guaranteed in Article 2 can be interpreted as involving a negative aspect'[98] – and that is the end of the matter (dealt with in a – so to speak – on-off Kantian manner).

Formally, these different strands of reasoning are separate from each other. But they may not be as compartmentalized as their legal formulation suggests. Had the Court reached a different conclusion on Article 3, its reasoning on Article 2 would also have been different. This would not have been legally difficult, as what a particular provision contains and does not contain is open to interpretation. The Court could then have ruled on Article 8 by saying that the Government, through its *absolute* ban on assisted suicide, had failed to act proportionately. I personally would have preferred this solution, but this is not my present point.[99] What I wish to suggest is that the various reasons which led the judges to reject Mrs Pretty's claim may be more combined in their minds and hearts than their judicial presentation indicates. It has been remarked that 'the *force* of both the absolutist and the utilitarian types of reasoning can be felt very strongly'.[100]

A utilitarian trade-off may well have influenced the Court's reasoning on Article 3, although it was more convenient – because legally more acceptable – for it not to be mentioned at that particular point in the judgment.

Soering: Going beyond the absolute obligation contained in Article 3

The received wisdom is that Article 3 lays down a negative obligation which is absolute. This did not prevent the Court from speaking of a positive obligation in *Pretty*. The attendant verdict of non-violation was not based on the fact that Article 3 *only* entailed a negative obligation, a conclusion which would have directly contradicted the leading judgment of *Soering* v. *United Kingdom*, adopted on 7 July 1989.[101] In *Soering*, the Court did not use the vocabulary of positive obligations. Nonetheless, its reasoning in terms of the *consequences* of the action of the defendant state signalled a move away from the ground of Article 3's negative obligation. One part of the doctrine heavily criticized this departure, while another acclaimed it for opening the field in a most useful way. This section reviews the decision. The next one explains in what sense its underlying reasoning could appear threatening to human rights orthodoxy.

Let us start with the facts of the case. At eighteen, Mr Soering had killed the parents of his girlfriend who, in an episode of *folie à deux*, had convinced him that this double murder was the only chance for them to survive as a couple. The crime had taken place in Virginia, USA. When Mr Soering, a German national, found himself in the United Kingdom, the US authorities requested his extradition. He argued at Strasbourg that he risked being condemned to death in Virginia and thus being subjected to the 'death-row phenomenon' in contravention of Article 3 of the Convention. By six votes to five, the Commission did not find a breach of this provision. The Court, however, found that a decision by the United Kingdom to extradite the applicant to the United States would entail a violation of Article 3.

The applicant had implicitly based his claim on a negative-obligation foundation by arguing that Article 3

> embodies an . . . obligation *not to put* a person in a position where he will or may suffer [inhuman or degrading] treatment or punishment at the hands of other States.[102]

In a response entirely suitable to the negative-obligation logic, the British Government had observed that

> it would be straining the language of Article 3 intolerably to hold that by surrendering a fugitive criminal the extraditing State has 'subjected' him to any treatment or punishment that he will receive following conviction and sentence in the receiving State.[103]

The reasoning adopted by the Court followed the logic neither of the applicant nor of the state. It consisted in a straightforward (if implicit) application of the law of double effect:

[N]o right not to be extradited is as such protected by the Convention. Nevertheless, in so far as a measure of extradition has *consequences* adversely affecting the enjoyment of a Convention right, it may, assuming that the consequences are not too remote, attract the obligations of a Contracting State under the relevant Convention guarantee.[104]

To the consternation of many a commentator,[105] the Court seemed to move away from absolutism and to embrace the relativism of consequentialism when it declared:

What amounts to 'inhuman or degrading treatment or punishment' *depends on all the circumstances of the case* . . . Furthermore, inherent in the whole of the Convention is a search for a fair *balance between the demands of the general interest of the community and the requirements of the protection of the individual's fundamental rights.*[106]

The Court went on to discuss a number of factors which had to be taken into consideration, namely, the average length of detention prior to execution in Virginia, the conditions on death row, the applicant's age and mental state and the fact that he could be extradited for trial in the Federal Republic of Germany. In the opinion of the Court, *all things considered,* extradition to the US of Mr Soering would have been in breach of Article 3. The verdict of the eighteen judges of the plenary Court was unanimous.

Judge De Meyer appended a concurring opinion. He objected mainly to the failure by the Court to find a violation, under Article 2, of Mr Soering's right to life. He incidentally remarked that the appreciation by the Court of all the circumstances of the case '[left] too much room for unacceptable infringements of the fundamental rights of persons whose extradition is sought'. These two points are in line with his tendency to consider that human rights lay down absolute obligations, already noted above in relation to *Z* v. *Finland.*

It would assuredly have been possible for the judgment to be phrased in absolute terms. The Court only needed to follow the lead of the United Nations Convention against Torture, which provides in its Article 3: 'no State party shall . . . extradite a person where there are substantial grounds for believing that he would be in danger of being subjected to torture'. The Court could have extended the terms of this absolute negative obligation to inhuman and degrading treatment.

I shall not be amongst those who deplore the explicit relativity of the Court's reasoning. My own view is that things are *always* relative, whether we like it or not, whether we recognize it or not. Surely what is important is that *Soering* has allowed amazing results to be reached. Until then it was felt that a state could be responsible only for actions – sometimes omissions[107] – which were directly within its jurisdiction. *Soering* changed that: an act which was happening, strictly speaking, outside the jurisdiction of a state party to the Convention could still be attributed to that state if the state could be shown to have been instrumental in allowing the infringement to take place. The case law adopted in the wake of

Soering has not uncommonly offered refugees, asylum seekers and other non-nationals who would have been at risk of torture if deported, a protection superior to that provided by the 1951 UN Convention on the Refugee (which is not to deny that the case law also contains disappointing decisions).[108]

It is not surprising, however, that *Soering* attracted the ire of a substantive number of commentators. The deployment of explicitly relativist language on the 'sacred' terrain of Article 3, recognized as embodying the least controversial of the absolute obligations which would be incurred by states in human rights law,[109] was bound to displease those who favour an absolute reasoning. Moreover, as the next section argues, unease in the orthodoxy must also have been fuelled by the fact that the decision undermined, barely perceptibly but ineluctably, the belief in the existence of a core of human rights.

From negative to positive obligations: The loss of the human rights core

The Kantian, categorical philosophy on which human rights orthodoxy rests logically demands for a core of human rights to be identified. This is because it posits the existence of absolute negative obligations. One obviously needs to know what these negative obligations are; the boundaries of what is not allowed must be circumscribed.[110] It is therefore not surprising that human rights scholars of what I call the natural law persuasion repeatedly produce lists, presumably exhaustive and definitive, of fundamental human rights. These lists are an attempt to define the human rights core. That they are invariably controversial does not affect the fact that the existence of a human rights core is taken for granted by those who compile them.

By contrast to negative obligations, positive obligations are not clear-cut. It is impossible to draw clear boundaries around them. This is because they derive from a consequentialist philosophy which does not hold that an action is good or bad in itself but which assesses the moral status of an action by reference to the circumstances prevailing at the time. Under such a philosophy, as circumstances change, so do the demands of morality. Rights can thus be added to or taken away from any list of rights which exists at a given moment. The idea of a core of rights dissolves. It suddenly makes sense that *Soering*, which implicitly relied on a view of human rights made of positive obligations, would have been widely criticized in the human rights doctrine. *Soering* introduces, as it were, a slippery slope while a firm ground is what the most orthodox of the human rights orthodoxy seeks.

'It all depends': From Bentham's felicific calculus to the proportionality test of the Court

Something like the proportionality test is necessary to the delineation of positive obligations. However, the proportionality test, as operated by the Court, follows a nebulous logic. This section argues that it is parallel to, and no more satisfactory than, the 'felicific calculus' developed by Bentham.

Starting from the premise that pain and pleasure govern mankind, and aiming at the happiness of the greatest number, Bentham identified seven circumstances of pleasure and pain which he thought could be computed – either as units or as multiples or fractions. These circumstances were the 'intensity' of pleasure and pain, their 'duration', 'certainty' and 'propinquity', as well as their 'fecundity', 'purity' and 'extent'. The felicific calculus could be reached through applying the following formula (summarized by a later scholar):

> The unit of intensity is the faintest sensation that can be distinguished to be pleasure or pain; the unit of duration is a moment of time. Degrees of intensity and duration are to be counted in whole numbers, as multiples of these units. Certainty and propinquity are reckoned as fractions whose limit is immediate actual sensation; from this limit the fractions fall away. In applying the calculus, one begins with the first distinguishable pleasure or pain which appears to be produced by an act, multiplies the number of its intensity units by the number of durations units, and then multiplies this product by the two fractions expressing certainty and proximity. To bring in fecundity one computes by the preceding method the value of each pleasure or each pain which appears to be produced after the first one; the resulting values are to be added to the value previously obtained. To bring in purity one computes the values of all pains that attend a given series of pleasures, or of pleasures that attend a given series of pains; these values are to be subtracted from the preceding sums. That is, pleasure is a positive, pain a negative quantity. Since the unit of extent is an individual, one completes the computation by multiplying the net resultant pain or pleasure ascertained as above by the number of individuals affected. Usually however this last step is more complicated: not all people affected are affected in the same way. In that case one does not multiply by the number of individuals, but makes a separate computation for each individual and then strikes the algebraic sum of the resultants.[111]

The idea that it is possible to allocate precise, objective numbers to states of happiness and suffering appears ludicrous today.[112] Even the very premise that pain and pleasure are direct, straightforward opposites no longer appears convincing. Bentham's faith in the possibility of apprehending the world – including its happiness and suffering – in objective, neutral, *quantifiable* terms reveals a positivism which goes to an extent from which even the most fervent positivists would probably wish to dissociate themselves today.[113]

This is not to say that Bentham was unaware of the difficulties that run through his felicific calculus. Wesley Mitchell, who summarized the formula of the calculus quoted above, observed that Bentham knew that intensity of feelings could not be measured, that increased happiness had different incremental effects depending on whether one was happy to start with or not, or that attempts to compare feelings of different men involved an assumption contrary to fact.[114] Bentham had written:

'Tis in vain to talk of adding quantities which after the addition will continue distinct as they were before, one man's happiness will never be another man's happiness: a gain to one man is no gain to another: you might as well pretend to add 20 apples to 20 pears . . . This addibility of the happiness of different subjects, however when considered rigorously it may appear fictitious, is a postulatum without the allowance of which all political reasoning is at a stand.[115]

Significantly, Mitchell says, neither Bentham nor any of his followers came up with precise numbers: 'No man could apply Bentham's calculus in sober earnest, because no man could tell how many intensity units were included in any one of his pleasures – to go no further.'[116] Mitchell argued that Bentham did not use the calculus as an instrument of calculation, but rather as a basis of classification:

[The calculus] pointed out to him what elements should be considered in a given situation, and among these elements *seriatim* he was often able to make comparisons in terms of greater and less.[117]

Thus, what Bentham tried to achieve was to compare different 'lots'[118] of pleasure and pain. He was doing so not through precise calculation but by classification that served to allocate these lots more and less value.

My contention is that this is exactly what happens with the Strasbourg proportionality test. While the Court – explicitly – talks of '*weighing*' different interests, it merely considers them and – implicitly – *classifies* them as either important or not so important.

The incommensurability – literally, lack of common measure – of the factors that enter either Bentham's calculus or the Court's proportionality test means that strictly speaking the calculus is not a calculating method. It can only be 'calculating' in broad, approximate terms.[119] While this is unavoidable, it is also problematic. The impossibility of assigning a precise value to any of the considered elements makes the method highly susceptible to a lack of transparency. In turn this lack allows the method to be made to yield almost any result without having to provide a justification in precise terms. Mitchell saw it. He said of Bentham that: '[His] felicific calculus turned out to be a singularly versatile instrument. Men could make it prove what they liked by choosing certain assumptions concerning the relative importance of various imponderable factors.'[120]

This conclusion can be applied to the Strasbourg case law. In my analysis of the 'quasi-national' case law, I have shown that the Court has variously found the Convention to have or not to have been violated by reference to factual circumstances which are admittedly listed but unfortunately not compared in any systematic manner.[121] The Court does not necessarily refer to the same factors across apparently similar cases.[122] When it does, it does not always attribute to a given factor the weight it seems to have given it in previous cases. The Court never explains which factor is important and why. It obviously, and regrettably, does not feel that it needs to explain the way it achieves its balancing exercise – its calculus.

Instead it *lists* factual circumstances, and having done so, it concludes without any further explanation – 'somewhat abruptly'[123] – that either the public or the applicant's interest is weightier than the other. The Court's method is as vague and unsatisfactory as Bentham's felicific calculus.

The here and now of the casuistic approach of the Court: Van Drooghenbroeck's critique

Few would contest that Bentham's felicific calculus was simplistic to the point of being fallacious. Interestingly, the shortcomings of the proportionality test operated by the Court have not been the subject of a wide and systematic critique.[124] By contrast with the controversial theory of the margin of appreciation, proportionality is generally regarded as a neutral or even a good tool. In the midst of this tacit approval, Van Drooghenbroeck has constructed a well-informed and persuasive critique.

He argues that the pervasiveness of the recourse to the proportionality so-called 'test' leads the Court to adopt a casuistic (case-by-case) approach, which prevents it from enunciating a norm that is valid beyond the particular facts of the case it has just decided. He draws the apparently logical conclusion that the Court only ever works in the present – its enunciations are neither for the past nor, even more damagingly, for the future.[125] This is because there is and there can be no norm. Legal certainty is lost.[126] The only possible motto is '*On verra*'[127] – literally 'We'll see' but equally translatable as 'It depends'. Against this Van Drooghenbroeck calls for the identification of fixed reference points. He argues that the answer to the subjectivism inherent in the proportionality test – as there is no objective *tertium comparationis*[128] – is for the Court to reaffirm the absolute character of the non-derogable rights and to protect the substance of every fundamental right.[129]

Van Drooghenbroeck calls for the establishment of norms which are meant to be applied again and again, across cases and, thus, over time. This is clearly diametrically opposed to Bentham's position, as ironically expressed in his critique of the French Declaration of the Rights of the Man and the Citizen:

> What . . . was [its drafters'] object in declaring the existence of imprescriptible rights [?] . . . In us [the French] is the perfection of virtue and wisdom: in all mankind besides, the extremity of wickedness and folly. Our will shall consequently reign without control, and for ever: reign now we are living – reign after we are dead. . . . Future governments will not have honesty enough to be trusted with the determination of what rights shall be maintained, what abrogated – what laws kept in force, what repealed.[130]

Bentham's ire against French arrogance and imperialism[131] went hand-in-hand with an important theoretical point: laws are never to be enunciated for all time. From the proponent of the Code, it may be a surprising lesson. Such a lesson, however, is directly in line with methodological features of utilitarianism, such as the constant attention to context and the commitment to deduction rather than induction. To quote Bentham on these two features:

> To know whether it would be more for the advantage of society that this or that right should be maintained or abolished, *the time* at which the question about maintaining or abolishing is proposed, must be given, *and the circumstances* under which it is proposed to maintain or abolish it . . .[132]
>
> If a collection of general propositions [such as is found in the French Declaration] were capable of being so worded and put together as to be of use, it could only be on the condition of their being *deduced* in the way of abridgment from an already formed and existing assemblage of less general propositions . . . the general and introductory part, though placed first, *must have been constructed last*, - though first in the order of communication, it should have been last in the order of composition.[133]

By contrast the absolutist-inclined Van Drooghenbroeck is attracted by a priori starting points. He talks of 'the constitution of norms that are sufficiently precise and compelling to be able to claim truly *to institute* the real while sufficiently general to be able to be reiterated from one case to the next'.[134] Admittedly, Van Drooghenbroeck concedes that normative changes must occur when the norm reveals itself to be inadequate, i.e. unable to order the reality it is supposed to regulate.[135] His emphasis, however, is on continuity. Moreover his reasoning is inductive rather than deductive. These two features inscribe him in a natural law tradition which takes the counterpoint of Bentham's teaching and utilitarianism more generally.

As far as I am concerned, Van Drooghenbroeck's solution to the legal uncertainty inherent in the casuistic approach of the Court is far too essentialist (categorical) to be realistic. I do not believe that one can draw the limits of an essential core of human rights – which is what the absolutist approach requires, as we have seen. I would argue that the solution to the problem of legal uncertainty does not lie in a rejection of the utilitarian logic but in striving to achieve more transparency in the operation of a utilitarian calculus – which is what the proportionality test is.

Ever-changing context or permanent rules? The practical resolution of the dilemma

The utilitarian method is deductive and seeks to develop a response which fits the circumstances of the case but will need to be adapted as soon as new circumstances arise; the absolutist method is inductive and claims to have discovered a solution which should resist the assault of time and changed circumstances. Utilitarianism runs the risk of losing any permanence and coherence; absolutism of being completely out of touch with reality. The two positions appear theoretically irremediably opposed. In practice, however, they are not necessarily far apart in the results they deliver.

On the one hand utilitarianism cannot afford to take a new look at the world every day or every minute: it needs to seek a minimum stability, for example, through laws that provide, until they are changed, the rules which govern action. This is why Bentham was a proponent of the Code. On the other hand absolutism is not as absolute as it may think it is: it needs to react to the facts of life which disturb its assumptions and to accept that it must be adaptable. Utilitarians abide by rule-utilitarianism; absolutists pay attention to context.

In practice utilitarians and absolutists not infrequently share a common ground. As Nagel has observed: 'Few of us are completely immune to either of [the absolutist and utilitarian] types of moral intuition, though in some people, either naturally or for doctrinal reason, one type will be dominant and the other suppressed or weak.'[136] While Judge De Meyer may represent the prototype of the natural law, absolutist judge at the Strasbourg Court, most judges can be presumed to be happy to resort to a utilitarian logic as long as an absolute prohibition is not at stake, which is most of the time. The Convention and human rights law draw on utilitarian considerations far more than is generally recognized.

The moral limitation of the absolutist position: The example of torture

It would be wrong, however, to conclude this chapter on a happy resolution between utilitarianism and human rights orthodoxy and to suggest that the two philosophies amount to the same thing in practice. There is a point where they cannot be reconciled: human rights orthodoxy takes for granted the absoluteness of some obligations including first of all that of not inflicting torture, while utilitarianism does not. Each philosophy considers itself morally superior to the other on this point.

Human rights orthodoxy declares the prohibition of torture to be absolute. Accordingly, whatever the circumstances, torture is never justified; there is no place for arguing that the present situation is so utterly exceptional that, in this very particular case, and this case only, torture is warranted. The whole point of absolutism is precisely to render this type of reasoning impossible. By contrast, utilitarianism can condone torture. Bentham, for one, was not opposed to torture in all cases – even though he put forward no less than fourteen rules to govern its use.[137]

Samuel Scheffler is squarely in the absolutist camp. A vocal detractor of utilitarianism, he writes:

> Suppose that your country is waging a just war, and that an enemy agent you have captured tells you that he has planted a bomb in an area crowded with civilians and that, unless defused, it will soon go off, killing many people. Suppose that there is not

enough time to conduct a general search for the bomb, and that all your attempts to get the agent to reveal its location are unsuccessful. Suppose, however, that you have captured him with his family, and that by torturing his small child in front of him you could eventually destroy his resolve and get him to give you the information. Utilitarianism seems to imply not only that you may but that you *must* torture the child. These implications and others like them strike many people as entirely unacceptable.[138]

Scheffler's argument is in line with the human rights credo. Is it entirely convincing? Even if all the 'ifs' of the scenario were to become realities, the conclusion is not necessarily foreordained. In the situation envisaged, I would say that it is wrong *both* to torture the child *and* to refrain from doing so.

Lincoln Allison, aware of torture's profoundly corrupting effect, says he is less optimistic than Bentham about the possible benefits of torture. As a utilitarian, he nonetheless suggests that the question of whether particular acts of torture can produce benefits which outweigh the harm they do cannot be dismissed entirely. He writes: 'It would be morally attractive, and convenient, if [it could]. But [it cannot].'[139]

Utilitarianism has the potential to draw out the acute moral dilemma found in hypothetical situations such as the one described by Scheffler. Echoing Allison, Thomas Nagel points that it is 'naïve to suppose that there is a solution to every moral problem with which the world can face us'.[140] He observes: 'We must face the pessimistic [possibility that] the world can present us with situations in which there is no honourable or moral course for a man to take, no course free of guilt and responsibility for evil.'[141] By contrast, Scheffler's categorical conclusion rejects the moral necessity of dilemmas, at least with respect to torture. Blind to the utilitarian intuition that it is wrong not to weigh consequences, his absolutism will strike consequentialists as embodying an impoverished vision of morality.

The next section illustrates this very last point through a discussion of *A. v. United Kingdom*, a case where the absolutism of the Court led – in my view – to unacceptable consequences. The rejection of absolutism, implicitly called for in my text, may appear to some to open the doors to any kind of relativism. This need not be the case, however, as the subsequent section argues by showing how one can oppose, on utilitarian grounds, the erosion of civil liberties in the fight against the so-called War on Terror.

A v. United Kingdom: The devastating consequences of an absolute privilege

The advantage of a clear law is that it provides certainty. Its disadvantage is that if it is too clear – categorical – it provides too much certainty and no flexibility. Some lawyers believe the advantage outweighs the drawback.[142] *A v. United Kingdom*, decided on 17 December 2002,[143] can be used to illustrate the strength of the opposite position.

The case concerned parliamentary privilege. During a debate on municipal housing, the Member of Parliament (MP) for a constituency in Bristol referred to a tenant of a housing association living in his constituency, Ms A, as a 'neighbour from hell'. Giving her name and address, he suggested that she and members of her family were involved in acts of vandalism, joyriding, drugs, burglary, etc. The media reported his speech. A hate campaign ensued against the applicant and her family, of such ferocity that they had to be rehoused for their own safety as a matter of urgency. One letter Ms A received for example read: 'You silly black bitch, I am just trying to let you know that if you do not stop your black nigger wogs nuisance, I will personally sort you and your smelly jungle bunny kids out.' The MP had never met the applicant. Ms A stated that none of his allegations were substantiated, having originated from neighbours motivated by racism. The MP did not seek to contact Ms A or to verify the accuracy of his comments after she complained to him. She found she had no judicial recourse against the MP as his remarks, pronounced in the Chamber of the House of Commons, were protected by absolute parliamentary privilege. She complained at Strasbourg of a violation of – inter alia – Article 6 on fair trial, a notion which the Court understands as comprising the right to have access to a tribunal.

The stakes were sufficiently high in relation to the organisation of 'the modern state' for eight states party to the Convention to choose to make third-party interventions about the way in which their national laws provided for parliamentary immunity. The Belgian Government concluded that in respect of this issue, '[p]rivate rights have to be regarded as ceding to the overriding public interest'.[144] The Irish Government argued that 'the importance of the legitimate objectives pursued by parliamentary immunity was difficult to overstate and that it was for the national authorities to seek to balance the right of individual citizens to a good name with the right of free parliamentary expression' – requesting the Court not to interfere.[145] Some governments reported their own ways of dealing with insulting behaviour by Members of Parliament; the Norwegian for example mentioned exclusion from the right to speak for the rest of the day.[146]

The Court noted that '[a]bsolute privilege was designed not to protect individual members, but Parliament as a whole'.[147] It 'pursued the legitimate aims of protecting free speech in Parliament and maintaining the separation of powers between the legislature and the judiciary'.[148] The Court thought that the contested rule, which was in line with the laws of many signatory states, could not 'in principle be regarded as imposing a disproportionate restriction on the right of access to court'.[149] It found no violation of the Convention, by six votes to one.

The judgment is absolutist and categorical in both its reasoning and result. To detect a consequentialist reasoning in this case, one must turn to the dissenting opinion of Judge Loucaides.[150] The Cypriot judge recognized that uninhibited debate on public issues should be encouraged. He accepted that absolute privilege served a legitimate aim. He nonetheless found absolute parliamentary privilege disproportionate and contrary to the Convention.

The consequentialism of his approach surfaces in at least three different ways. First, he contemplates the social repercussions, for the common good, of the protection of the individual. To quote him: '[T]he suppression of untrue defamatory statements, apart from protecting the dignity of individuals, discourages false speech and improves the overall quality of public debate through a chilling effect on irresponsible parliamentarians.' Second, he pays attention to context rather than thinking in abstract terms. Thus, he notes that the general absolute privilege of parliamentarians 'was established about 400 years ago when the legal protection of the personality of the individual was in its infancy' and that this protection has since then been enhanced, implicitly suggesting that the change in circumstances calls for a different outlook – a more appropriate term than 'solution' which has a more categorical overtone. Third, Loucaides specifically refers to *competing* Convention rights.[151] For him competing interests need to be balanced by reference to 'the individual facts of particular cases'. He lists six factual elements in the *A.* case (including the severity of the defamatory allegations, their foreseeably harsh consequences for the applicant and her family, and the lack of reaction by the MP to her complaint) which lead him to conclude that absolute immunity is a disproportionate restriction of the right to access to a court. He concludes, however, by saying that 'even without regard to the facts of the case, the immunity is . . . disproportionate . . . *because of its absolute nature, which precludes the balancing of competing interests*'.[152]

Admittedly *A* v. *United Kingdom* is unusual in that absolutism is deployed in this case to protect the general interest. It nonetheless shows the excesses to which absolutism can lead and the way absolutism refuses to consider how the 'solutions' it proposes may be very problematic.

What the general interest does not require: The erosion of civil liberties during the War on Terror

The previous section did not illustrate the excesses to which an absolute prohibition *not to do harm* could lead. The discussion of *A* v. *United Kingdom* it contains is admittedly unlikely to convince detractors of utilitarianism that an absolutist logic should be abandoned in human rights law. Especially in the post-9/11 climate where the idea of human rights is under attack, the orthodoxy is bound to wish to reaffirm the value of having a core of human rights. The question must indeed be asked: is it morally responsible to remain consequentialist in current times?

Recent judicial history exhibits worrying trends. Decisions have been adopted across the world which would have been barely imaginable before September 2001. For example, on 11 January 2002, the Supreme Court of Canada ruled that the principle that a state could not expel a refugee to a place where he would be put at risk of torture was not absolute.[153] In the United Kingdom, on 11 August 2004, the Court of Appeal ruled that evidence possibly obtained under torture in a foreign jurisdiction need not be inadmissible.[154] Two years before, the same court had found indefinite detention of aliens suspected of terrorism without trial permissible under the Convention.[155] While comfort can be drawn from the overruling of both these decisions by the House of Lords on 16 December 2004 in respect of the latter[156] and on 8 December 2005 in respect of the former, it remains the case that the War on Terror has signalled attacks on civil liberties which had been thought by many to be firmly entrenched in Western democracies.

Some will no doubt be tempted to point the finger at utilitarianism as the culprit of this dramatic erosion of civil liberties. To justify the measures they have adopted since 9/11, the American and British governments have repeatedly said that they sought to safeguard the nation and to protect the general interest. Civil liberties groups have trumpeted in response the rights of the individual. The debate has thus been conducted as if the general and the individual interests were pitted against each other. I want to argue that things are more complicated than this.

In a short and beautifully argued piece, David Lublan insists that the question we confront in times of danger is *not* one of difficult trade-offs between national security and civil liberties.[157] He stresses that a decrease in liberty does not result in an increase in security. Although he writes from a liberal, rights-based, perspective, his argument could be rephrased along utilitarian lines: contrary to what the American (and British) governments argue, the general interest does not demand that the rights of individuals, especially foreigners, be curtailed.

What exactly the general interest encompasses is open to all kinds of inter-pretation. Therefore we should *never* trust anyone, especially not a government, to have discovered it. The realization that where the general interest lies in any particular situation is a political and controversial question, susceptible to fierce debate, may not be comforting. It may lead some to wish to shun the concept of the general interest altogether and to embrace an absolutist stance which appar-ently provides sure and reliable safeguards.[158] Absolutism, however, should not be considered entirely reassuring either.

Firstly, what is allowed under absolutism and what is not is never as clear as the theory has it: absolutism allegedly provides indisputable limits, but it does not. The recognition by the Court in *Selmouni* that perceptions as to what constitute torture change over time illustrates this point.[159] Secondly, absolutism does not provide absolute rights – only absolute prohibitions. Thus the decisions of the Canadian Supreme Court and the British Court of Appeal mentioned above do not, strictly speaking, contradict the absolute injunction to governments not to inflict torture. This is not to deny that other decisions could – and in my opinion, should – have been reached (indeed the House of Lords has now twice overruled the Court of Appeal), but to note the limits of the protection that absolutism extends. Once one enters the arena of positive obligations, relativity cannot but set in. Thirdly, absolutism's refusal to weigh the demands of particular circumstances, *whatever* these demands are, leads it to shy away from confronting, head-on, difficult but real moral dilemmas, as discussed in the previous two sections.

Chassagnou: Where is the general interest?

This whole chapter is underpinned by the question: what is the general interest and where do we find it? This section seeks to problematize it by introducing the idea that the dichotomy with which the Court and its commentators generally work – the individual v. the state/society/community – is a simplistic shortcut. It does this through a discussion of *Chassagnou and Others* v. *France*, decided on 29 April 1999.[160]

The case concerned the so-called Loi Verdeille of 1964 which organized hunting in France. The Loi Verdeille provided for the establishment of approved municipal hunters' associations ('ACCAs') in administrative units (*départements*) made up of holdings deemed to be too small for hunting to be feasible without the creation of these associations. Subdivision of landholdings had typically occurred in southern France. Under the Loi Verdeille, the ten applicants, from Dordogne, Creuse and Gironde, had become automatic members of ACCAs. They argued at Strasbourg that they had been deprived of the right to use their property as they saw fit, in contravention of Article 1 of Protocol 1. They also maintained that automatic membership of ACCAs was in breach of their right to freedom of association under Article 11 of the Convention. Six of them being specifically opposed to hunting on ethical grounds,[161] they finally complained that their right to freedom of conscience under Article 9 had been infringed.[162] The Court had to decide whether the interferences with the rights of the applicants were proportionate. To do so, the aim or aims of the law first needed to be identified.

Generally applicants and defendant states do not spend much time discussing the aim of a contested law. In this case, however, the aim of the Loi Verdeille was in dispute. According to the French Parliament, the object of ACCAs was 'to encourage, on their hunting grounds, an increase in game stocks, the destruction of vermin and the prevention of poaching, to instruct their members in how to hunt without interfering with property rights or crops and in general to improve the technical organisation of hunting so that the sport can be practised in a more satisfactory manner'.[163] According to Judge Costa, before the Loi Verdeille had started to regulate hunting in southern France, 'hunting . . . had become almost a free-for-all', with a 'bad effect on game, crops and, in the final analysis, the whole ecosystem'. Costa argued that 'the Loi Verdeille pursue[d] a real general-interest objective, namely mitigating the effects of the subdivision of landholdings and preventing poaching, while encouraging the destruction of vermin and making possible the establishment of game reserves'.[164] A further aim of the law was identified as follows: 'to regulate a leisure activity which, if left unregulated, would present a real danger [and] to democratise hunting'.[165] As the French Government explained, '[b]y providing for the pooling of small plots of land

and requiring their owners to join an ACCA the Loi Verdeille sought to ensure democratic participation in hunting in order to give as many people as possible access to a leisure activity which would otherwise have been bound to remain the exclusive prerogative of the owners of large estates'.[166]

The applicants, however, suggested that the declared aim of the law could not be taken at face value. This was especially so given the strength of the hunters' lobby in France. The applicants estimated that the hunters' lobby could claim to represent only 3 per cent of the population. Despite this, they said, it managed to force through rules in breach of European Union law and international law, such as the permission to shoot migratory birds in the month of February.[167] According to the applicants, the Loi Verdeille 'had not been enacted in the general interest but only for the benefit of a specific category of people, namely hunters'.[168]

If the applicants wanted to suggest that the general interest should be identified by reference to the number of citizens it served, the Court refused to follow them on this 'majoritarianism' route.[169] It stated that 'in view of the aims which the Loi Verdeille assigns to the ACCAs . . . it is undoubtedly in the general interest to avoid unregulated hunting and encourage the rational management of game stocks'.[170] On the facts, it nonetheless found, by twelve votes to five, that the interference complained of under Article 1 of Protocol 1 was not 'proportionate'. With the same majority, it reached a similar conclusion in respect of Article 11 of the Convention.[171]

The Court did so through a reasoning that referred to individual fundamental rights. To quote:

> Although individual interests must on occasion be subordinated to those of a group, democracy does not simply mean that the views of the majority must always prevail: a balance must be achieved which ensures *the fair and proper treatment of minorities* and avoids any abuse of a dominant position . . . In the present case the only aim invoked by the Government to justify the interference complained of was 'protection of the rights and freedoms of others'. Where these 'rights and freedoms' are themselves among those guaranteed by the Convention or its Protocols, it must be accepted that the need to protect them may lead States to restrict other rights or freedoms likewise set forth in the Convention. It is precisely this constant search for a *balance between the fundamental rights of each individual* which constitutes the foundation of a 'democratic society'.[172]

By contrast, in his dissenting opinion, Judge Costa stressed the balance which needs to be achieved between the general and individual interests (rather than the balance between the fundamental rights of each individual). This may not be surprising considering his 'statist' inclination and given that the state is supposed to act in the general interest.[173] The French judge observed:

> One can be wholly in favour of freedom and the rule of law – as the framers of the Convention were – without necessarily making individual freedom an absolute or excluding the general interest from the rule of law – which was manifestly not the intention of those who drafted the Convention. With regard to hunting, an area where

each State should have a wide margin of appreciation, and where many European States have laws which restrict the right of private property in order to implement a hunting policy, it seems to me that the Court's judgment goes in a very individualist direction, which will make this type of policy very difficult to conduct.[174]

Over and over again, the dissenting judges indicated that it was clear to them that the Loi Verdeille enacted a general interest. To quote Costa once more,

> The Loi Verdeille implies that the landowners belonging to ACCAS, even those who do not hunt themselves and even those who are opposed to hunting, agree, *nolentes volentes*, to permit hunters to come onto their land to hunt, not, I repeat, merely to take part in a sport, but in order to participate in *a true general-interest task* (even though the conduct of certain individual hunters may unfortunately make us lose sight of this).[175]

Judge Zupančič, also dissenting, echoed Costa when he wrote: 'it is not obvious to me that hunting as such has no identifiable social purpose or utility'.[176]

Judge Fischbach took the exactly opposite stance. Dissenting, he found a violation of Article 9 of the Convention by reasoning that 'to oblige an individual to take part in *an activity which serves essentially private interests*', in total contradiction to most deeply held beliefs, manifestly breaches Article 9.[177]

Going further than Fischbach, one could argue that the applicants' stance embodied a superior form of ethics and as such served a general interest which could or should be imposed on everyone. This argument, which could not have been put before the Court with any chance of success,[178] highlights the fact that hunting has become contested and has acquired an unclear cultural status.[179] In *Chassagnou*, was the general interest better represented in the Loi Verdeille or in the stance of the applicants? Let us imagine just for a moment that a decidedly anti-hunting position becomes the norm in the future. The possibility of imagining such a scenario, however unlikely at the moment, makes it clear that where the general interest lies can appear to be, but rarely is, a question that calls for a straightforward answer.

Jersild: 'The individual versus the state' as a fallacious dichotomy

The general interest does not necessarily lie where it is normally taken to lie. For example, in *Chassagnou*, it is arguable – if controversial – that it was the applicants rather than the defendant state who were on the side of the general interest. The interaction between the applicant's individual right and the general interest is also apparent in *Z* v. *Finland*, discussed above. To repeat a passage which I have already quoted:

> [The Court] accepts that the interests of a patient *and the community as a whole* in protecting the confidentiality of medical data may be outweighed by the interest in investigation and prosecution of crime and in the publicity of court proceedings.[180]

That Z did not win her claim under Article 8 is irrelevant to the point that her individual right was inseparable from a communal interest.[181]

Conversely, it would be wrong to dissociate the second branch of the dichotomy – i.e. the state, the community or the general interest – from individual rights. There will be cases where individual rights are best championed through a state action in the name of the general interest. *Jersild* v. *Denmark*, decided on 23 September 1994,[182] comes to mind.

The applicant in this case was a journalist who had prepared a film relaying the extremely racist views of a group of young, economically deprived people involved in crime who called themselves 'the Greenjackets'. The film had been broadcast on a television programme with a reputation for serious journalism. It was only a few minutes long and mostly consisted of statements by the interviewees. The Court included a word-for-word transcript in its judgment. A passage will give the flavour of the film:

(G) The Ku Klux Klan, that's something that comes from the States in the old days during – you know – the civil war and things like that, because the Northern States wanted that the niggers should be free human beings, man, they are not human beings, they are animals, right, it's completely wrong, man, the things that happened. People should be allowed to keep slaves, I think so anyway.

(A) Because blacks are not human beings?

(G) No, you can also see that from their body structure, man, big flat noses, with cauliflower ears, etc. man. Broad heads and very broad bodies, man, hairy, you are looking at a gorilla and compare it with an ape, man, then it is the same [behaviour], man, it's the same movements, long arms, man, long fingers etc., long feet.

(A) A lot of people are saying something different. They are a lot of people who say, but . . .

(G) Just take a picture of a gorilla, man, and then look at a nigger, it's the same body structure and everything, man, flat forehead and all kinds of things.

(A) There are many blacks, for example in the USA, who have important jobs.

(G) Of course, there is always someone who wants to show off, as if they are better than the white man, but in the long run, it's the white man who is better.[183]

Following the broadcast, the Public Prosecutor instituted criminal proceedings against the three youths interviewed by the applicant for the racist statements they had made;[184] the applicant was charged with aiding and abetting the youths. A Danish tribunal sentenced him to pay day-fines (or, alternatively, to five day's imprisonment).[185] This judgment was upheld by the national superior courts.

The applicant had argued before the national courts that his conduct 'could in no way be compared to that of the other three defendants, with whose views [he] did not sympathise' and that he 'sought merely to provide a realistic picture of a social problem'.[186] He complained at Strasbourg that his conviction occurred in contravention of Article 10 of the Convention, guaranteeing freedom of expression. There he elaborated on the argument he had put before the national courts and explained that his intention had been to ridicule the youths and thus to counter, rather than disseminate, their racist opinions.[187]

The Court agreed with the applicant that 'taken as a whole, the filmed portrait surely conveyed the meaning that the racist statements were part of a generally anti-social attitude of the Greenjackets' – who were clearly shown in the short film to be involved in crime.[188] By twelve votes to seven, it concluded that the interference with the applicant's freedom of expression had gone too far, i.e., in legal jargon, that it had not been 'necessary in a democratic society'.[189]

In its reasoning, the Court reiterated – as it had said many times before – that 'freedom of expression constitutes one of the essential foundations of a democratic society'. It added also the leitmotif that '[n]ot only does the press have the task of imparting . . . information and ideas [of public interest]: the public also has a right to receive them'. This statement indicates that, for the Court, there were other interests to take into account beyond those of the applicant: those of every citizen in Denmark to be informed and, thus, beyond those, that of the general interest.

Conversely, the judges who dissented also saw individuals beyond the defendant state. In the words of four of them, 'the majority attributes much more weight to the freedom of the journalist than to the protection of those who have to suffer from racist hatred . . . And what must be the feelings of those whose human dignity has been attacked, or even denied, by the Greenjackets? Can they get the impression that seen in context the television broadcast contributes to their protection? A journalist's good intentions are not enough in such a situation.'[190] These judges did not exclude 'that certain parts of the public found in the television spot support for their racist prejudices'.[191]

When I first read the *Jersild* judgment, I found the reasoning of the majority persuasive – the more so perhaps that it included Judges Martens and Palm whom I greatly respected for their firm pro-integration and anti-expulsion stance on the 'quasi-national' case law.[192] Many commentators, however, were fiercely critical.[193] A visit to Denmark in 2000 persuaded me that these commentators were right. I was told that Denmark had seen a resurgence of racist comments being expressed in the media since *Jersild*, that the attitude towards the expression of racism had become one of virtually complete impunity. With hindsight, this is not wholly surprising given that the judgment, which could not help but lend legitimacy to TV programmes, was given in respect of a country which is far from inclined towards openness to foreigners.[194]

This negative effect would obviously not have been intended by the judges who formed the majority. The *Jersild* judgment nonetheless shows that what counts as a victory in unsophisticated liberal terms – the individual has won against the state – is not necessarily a victory when put in a broader context. Statements implying that verdicts of violation demonstrate the usefulness and progressiveness of the Court are too simplistic. Surely, the picture must be more complex than broad generalizations, based on the fallacious dichotomy of individual versus state, suggest. Behind the individual, there is the community; behind the state, there are individuals. As such, the fact that an individual has won against the state does not tell us whether this victory should be celebrated or not.[195]

Conclusion

There is a sense in which this chapter has concerned itself with the obvious when it has demonstrated that utilitarian considerations enter the reasoning of the Court. The Court itself has asserted repeatedly that it must continually balance the interest of the individual with that of the community.[196] This formulation suggests typically utilitarian trade-offs. It is therefore not surprising that sophisticated theorists of the human rights orthodoxy avoid saying that human rights are absolute; they instead refer to them as fundamental.

Though constantly observed, the intrusion of utilitarian considerations into human rights law may nonetheless appear paradoxical. After all, Bentham declared human rights to be 'nonsense upon stilts' and utilitarianism is perceived as a political and ethical philosophy which runs counter to the logic of individual rights.[197] The paradox is resolved once it is understood that human rights orthodoxy, despite the numerous incursions into utilitarianism which it allows itself, believes there are absolute prohibitions, while utilitarianism does not.

In other words, there is an enormous difference in the way the human rights orthodoxy and utilitarianism envisage political morality. Even though the former can reason on utilitarian grounds, it must cease to do so when this would involve the transgression of what it regards as an absolute prohibition. Under utilitarianism, there is no absolute prohibition, not even in relation to the infliction of torture – which is not to say that utilitarianism easily condones torture.

A priori reasoning is central to human rights orthodoxy. By contrast, a utilitarian could not regard decisions in the human rights field as 'given'; she must conceive of them as political – and thus controversial.[198] Should such an idea be rejected as irresponsible in the post-9/11 era when the American and British governments would wish to forget about human rights? Not in my opinion, for a utilitarian conception need not lead to support for governmental dicta as to where the general interest lies. Indeed this last question is one which is always and must remain open to debate.

It might be retorted that saying the question is open-ended is mere wishful thinking in a world where some have the power to impose their views on others. Admittedly, the improbability of the notion that the Court would negate the affirmation that Article 3 of the Convention lays down a negative absolute is reassuring even for a consequentialist like me! On a theoretical plane, however, I remain unconvinced by the human rights credo, even though it suits some of my political interests.

Thus, to turn to a more particular application, while I regret that the proportionality test is no more convincing than Bentham's infamous felicific calculus, I do not think the defect of the test should be redressed by a return to the 'simplicity' of absolutism. This view is obviously not shared by the human rights orthodoxy which can sense that a consequentialist logic dissolves the firm ground supposedly offered by a core of human rights.

Notes

1 By Norman P. Barry: *An Introduction to Modern Political Theory* (London: Macmillan, 1981), at 101.
2 See e.g. Louis Henkin, *The Age of Rights* (New York: Columbia University Press, 1990), at 2. See also Paul Sieghart, *The Lawful Rights of Mankind: An Introduction to the International Legal Code of Human Rights* (Oxford: Oxford University Press, 1985), at 28: '[It finally became recognized that human rights must be] regarded as "inhering" in all human individuals in virtue of their humanity alone, and as "inalienable" – that is, as universal rights and freedoms which it lay in no one's power either to give or to take away.'
3 Amy Gutman and Dennis Thompson, *Democracy and Disagreement* (Cambridge, Mass.: Harvard University Press, 1996), at 179.
4 Liberalism's chief characteristic is the identification of the pursuit of liberty as the overriding aim. Such an open definition ensures that liberalism can mean many things and take many forms. Utilitarianism is recognized to have developed as part of the liberal tradition. (Hans Morgenthau presented Bentham as the prototype of the liberal philosopher in *Scientific Man vs. Power Politics* (London: Latimer House, 1947), at 110). Today, however, many liberals oppose utilitarianism. Norman Barry classifies John Stuart Mill, Bentham's closest disciple and the 'most famous utilitarian', as a liberal, but only just, because, in Barry's words, Mill expressed a commitment to personal freedom such that it 'qualifies him for admission to the broader liberal tradition': Barry, *Political Theory*, at 101 and 102. Jeremy Waldron defines liberalism as the political philosophy which holds that 'political organizations are justified by the contribution they make to the interests of individuals', with freedom, toleration and individual rights among its core principles: 'Liberalism', *Concise Routledge Encyclopedia of Philosophy* (London: Routledge, 2000), at 486. Costas Douzinas puts it thus: 'Liberalism [is] the political philosophy which treats rights as the fundamental political act and eventually identifies the function of the state with their protection': *The End of Human Rights* (Oxford: Hart, 2000), at 78. Such accounts of liberalism hardly encompass utilitarianism. At the same time utilitarianism continues to assert itself as liberal. See e.g. Matti Häyri, *Liberal Utilitarianism and Applied Ethics* (London: Routledge, 1994), esp. Chapter 3.
5 H. J. McCloskey, 'A note on utilitarian punishment' (1963) 72 *Mind* at 599, cited in Häyri, *Liberal Utilitarianism*, at 79; Lincoln Allison, 'The Utilitarian ethics of punishment and torture', in Lincoln Allison (ed.), *The Utilitarian Response: The Contemporary Viability of Utilitarian Political Philosophy* (London: Sage, 1990) 9–29, at 16. See also John Rawls, 'Classical utilitarianism', in Samuel Scheffler (ed.), *Consequentialism and its Critics* (Oxford: Oxford University Press, 1988) 14–119, at 17.

6 Samuel Scheffler, 'Introduction', in Scheffler (ed.), *Consequentialism* 1–13, at 3.

7 Häyri, *Liberal Utilitarianism*, at 80.

8 Ibid., at 79; Allan Gibbard, 'Utilitarianism and human rights' in Ellen Frankel Paul, Fred D. Miller Jr. and Jeffrey Paul (eds.), *Human Rights* (Oxford: Blackwell, 1984) 92–102.

9 J. L. Mackie, 'Can there be a right-based moral theory?', in Jeremy Waldron (ed.), *Theories of Rights* (Oxford: Oxford University Press, 1984) 168–81, at 171–2.

10 Lord Mackay of Clashfern, 'The margin of appreciation and the need for balance', in Paul Mahoney, Franz Matscher, Herbert Petzold and Luzius Wildhaber (eds.), *Protection des droits de l'homme: La perspective européenne/Protecting Human Rights: The European Perspective. Mélanges à la mémoire de/Studies in memory of Rolv Ryssdal* (Köln: Carl Heymans Verlag, 2000) 837–43, at 837.

11 Phrasing the debate in terms of a balance of interests between the individual and the community has become a standard formulation. To quote Judge Ryssdal, former President of the Court: 'The theme that runs through the Convention and its case-law is the need to strike a balance between the general interest of the community and the protection of individual rights' (cited in Mackay, 'Margin of appreciation', at 839).

12 In its report on the *De Becker* v. *Belgium* case, dated 28 April 1960: *De Becker* v. *Belgium*, judgment of 27 March 1962, Series A, No. 4, (1962) 1 EHRR 43.

13 Richard Clayton and Hugh Tomlinson, *The Law of Human Rights* (Oxford: Oxford University Press, 2000), at 278.

14 Michael Fordham and Thomas de la Mare, 'Identifying the principles of proportionality', in Jeffrey Jowell and Jonathan Cooper (eds.), *Understanding Human Rights Principles* (Oxford: Hart, 2001) 27–90, at 28.

15 This is not widely recognized but is persuasively argued by Sébastien Van Drooghenbroeck in his comprehensive and insightful analysis of the Strasbourg case law: Sébastien Van Drooghenbroeck, *La proportionnalité dans le droit de la Convention européenne des droits de l'homme. Prendre l'idée simple au sérieux* (Bruxelles: Bruylant, 2001), Chapter 2.

16 Although the proportionality test is commonly seen as a counterbalance to the doctrine of the margin of appreciation, Van Drooghenbroeck observes that the test works both for and against the applicant, depending on how it is used. In the case of a wide margin, the state sees its burden of proof substantially lifted: ibid., at 346, 485 and 510.

17 *Dudgeon* v. *United Kingdom*, 22 October 1981, Series A, No. 45, (1983) 5 EHRR 573.

18 Para. 49 of the judgment.

19 Para. 52 of the judgment.

20 Para. 52 of the judgment, emphasis added.

21 Para. 60 of the judgment.

22 *James and Others* v. *United Kingdom*, 21 February 1986, Series A, No. 98, (1986) 8 EHRR 123.

23 Para. 46 of the judgment.

24 Para. 49 of the judgment.

25 Para. 68 of the judgment.

26 Mackay, 'Margin of appreciation', at 840. But this observation should be qualified in view of the recent case law on Article 1, Protocol 1 relating to Eastern European countries.

27 Silvio Marcus-Helmons, 'Le droit de propriété est-il un droit fondamental au sens de la Convention européenne des droits de l'homme?', Union des Avocats Européens (UAE) (ed.), *Les nouveaux droits de l'homme en Europe* (Brussels: Bruylant, 1999) 193–208.

28 Interestingly Michele de Salvia, former Jurisconsult of the Court, was of the opinion that the doctrine of the margin of appreciation only made sense in respect of Article 15 of the Convention and Article 1 of Protocol 1, two areas where 'the strictly political aspect of the measures adopted by the national authorities is paramount': Michele de Salvia, 'Contrôle européen et principe de subsidiarité: Faut-il encore (et toujours) émarger à la *marge d'appréciation*?', in Mahoney, Matscher, Petzold and Wildhaber, *Ryssdal*, 373–85, at 385 (my translation).

29 This paragraph is heavily based on Maleiha Malik, 'Communal goods as human rights', in Conor Gearty and Adam Tomkins (eds.), *Understanding Human Rights* (London: Pinter, 1996) 138–69, at 143–4.

30 Lincoln Allison, 'Utilitarianism: What is it and why should it respond', in Allison (ed.), *Utilitarian Response* 1–8, at 5–6.

31 Ronald Dworkin, 'Rights as trumps', in Waldron (ed.), *Theories* 152–67, at 152.

32 Ronald Dworkin, *Taking Rights Seriously* (London: Duckworth, 1978), at 269.

33 Dworkin, 'Rights as trumps', at 165.

34 Ibid.

35 James Griffin, *Well-Being. Its Meaning, Measurement, and Moral Importance* (Oxford: Clarendon Press, 1986), at 83.

36 Dworkin, 'Rights as trumps', at 166, emphasis added.

37 The last two sentences are a paraphrase of Thomas Nagel, 'War and Massacre', in Scheffler (ed.), *Consequentialism*, 51–73, at 72.

38 Ibid., at 66.

39 See e.g. Clare Ovey and Robin C. A. White, *Jacobs and White, The European Convention on Human Rights* (Oxford: Oxford University Press, 2002), at 58; Philip Leach, *Taking a Case to the European Court of Human Rights* (1st edn, London: Blackstone, 2001), at 113; (2nd edn, 2005), at 201; D. J. Harris, M. O'Boyle and C. Warbrick, *Law of the European Convention on Human Rights* (London: Butterworths, 1995), at 55.

40 *Selmouni* v. *France*, 28 July 1999, ECHR 1999–V, (2000) 29 EHRR 403.

41 Para. 95 of the judgment, references omitted.

42 The case also raised important admissibility issues.

43 Para. 105 of the judgment.

44 *Ireland* v. *United Kingdom*, 18 January 1978, Series A, No. 25, (1979–1980) 2 EHRR 25.

45 Martin Robertson and Amnesty International, *Torture in the Eighties: An Amnesty International Report* (London: Amnesty International Publications, 1984).

46 Para. 101 of the judgment, emphasis added.

47 Para. 52 of the judgment.

48 *Z* v. *Finland*, 25 February 1997, RJD 1997-I, (1997) 25 EHRR 371.

49 The applicant raised two issues of racial and sexual discrimination, but too late in the proceedings for them to be declared admissible. On the way the Strasbourg case law fails to tackle racism, see Chapter 5.

50 Paras. 95 and 96 of the judgment, emphasis added.

51 Para. 97 of the judgment.

52 Para. 98 of the judgment.

53 Para. 99 of the judgment.

54 In *Enhorn* v. *Sweden*, 25 January 2005, (2005) 41 EHRR 30, the Court found by unanimity that Article 5 (1) of the Convention had been violated: the HIV-positive applicant had been hospitalized and isolated against his will without the authorities having considered less severe measures to safeguard the public interest.

55 See esp. paras. 105 and 110 of the judgment.

56 Partly Dissenting Opinion of Judge De Meyer, point I, emphasis added. Judge Greve followed a similar, though less absolutist reasoning, in her concurring opinion in *Odièvre* v. *France*, 13 February 2003, ECHR 2003-III, (2004) 38 EHRR 43, when she stated: 'Basic medical assistance is, when available, in itself a human right not to be revoked by society to achieve some unrelated other social goal.'

57 Ibid., point III.

58 David McNaughton, 'Deontological ethics' in *Concise Routledge Encyclopedia of Philosophy*, 202.

59 Bernard Williams, 'Consequentialism and integrity', in Scheffler (ed.), *Consequentialism*, 21–50, at 21.

60 Nagel, 'War', at 60.

61 Thus, Samuel Scheffler's books, *Consequentialism and its Critics* (ed.) and *The Rejection of Consequentialism* (Oxford; Oxford University Press, 1982) are ostensibly about consequentialism but in fact (mainly) about utilitarianism.

62 Nagel, 'War', at 58, emphasis in the original.

63 Suzanne Uniacke, 'Double effect, principle of' in *Concise Routledge Encyclopedia of Philosophy*, 216.

64 Jonathan Glover, *Causing Death and Saving Lives* (London: Penguin, 1990), Chapter 6.

65 For a critique of the concept of generations in human rights theory: Neil Stammers, 'The emergence of human rights in the North: towards historical re-evaluation', in N. Kabeer (ed.), *Inclusive Citizenship: Meanings and Expressions* (London: Zed Books, 2005) 50–68, at 53–4.

66 Jerome J. Shestak, 'The philosophical foundations of human rights', in Janusz Symonides (ed.), *Human Rights: Concept and Standards* (Dartmouth: Ashgate, 2000) 31, at 43–4.

67 Most famously Maurice Cranston in *What are Human Rights?* (New York: Basic Books, 1962).

68 Though there are remnants of it. See e.g. J.-M. Larralde, 'La Convention européenne des droits de l'homme et la protection de groupes particuliers' (2003) 56 *Revue trimestrielle des droits de l'homme* 1247–74, at 1248: 'Il est donc évident qu'une distinction doit être opérée entre les droits de l'homme proprement dits et les autres droits [tels les droits de nature économique et sociale].'

69 See e.g. Article 4 of the Vienna Declaration and Programme of Action adopted by the UN World Conference on Human Rights in 1993.

70 Van Drooghenbroeck, *La proportionnalité*, at 136.

71 Whether they remain central is sometimes disputed. In respect of Article 2, there is arguably a danger that the procedural positive obligation comes to dominate the substantive negative one.

72 Alastair Mowbray, *The Development of Positive Obligations under the European Convention on Human Rights by the European Court of Human Rights* (Oxford: Hart, 2004); Frédéric Sudre, 'Les "obligations positives" dans la jurisprudence européenne des droits de l'homme', (1995) *Revue trimestrielle des droits de l'homme* 363–84.

73 *Marckx* v. *Belgium*, 13 June 1979, Series A, No. 31, (1970–1980) 2 EHRR 330. The Commission had used the expression three months before in its report on *Van Oosterwijck* v. *Belgium* of 1 March 1979: *Van Oosterwijck* v. *Belgium*, judgment of 6 November 1980, Series A, No. 40, (1981) 3 EHRR 357. *Marckx* was the twenty-fourth judgment of the Court.

74 Para. 31 of the judgment, emphasis added.

75 Para. 31 of the judgment, emphasis added.

76 As noted by Van Drooghenbroeck, *La proportionnalité*.

77 According to Fordham and de la Mare, this is why the 'Strasbourg Court treats these positive obligations with a much lighter hand': Fordham and de la Mare, 'Identifying', at 58.

78 Van Drooghenbroeck, *La proportionnalité*, at 137, n. 172.

79 As laconically but perceptively suggested by Martti Koskenniemi in 'The Effect of Rights on Political Culture', in Philip Alston (ed.), *The EU and Human Rights* (Oxford: Oxford University Press, 1999) 99–116, at 111.

80 Uniacke, 'Double effect', at 216.

81 Nagel, 'War' at 56.

82 Ibid.

83 Dworkin, 'Rights as Trumps', at 165.

84 *Pretty* v. *United Kingdom*, 29 April 2002, ECHR 2002-III, (2002) 35 EHRR 1.

85 Para. 45 of the judgment. The statement should be ruled incorrect in human rights orthodoxy: under absolutism, it is a prohibition – not a right – which is susceptible to being absolute. This is perceptively observed by Steven Greer in a sharp if 'orthodox' analysis of the different kinds of rights contained in the Convention: Steven Greer, 'Constitutionalizing adjudication under the European Convention on Human Rights' (2003) 23 *Oxford Journal of Legal Studies* 405–33, at 416.

86 Ibid.

87 Ibid.

88 Or to provide a lawful opportunity for any other form of assisted suicide.

89 The decision not to prosecute could, however, be classified as a negative obligation under Article 8, which guarantees privacy – though the Court did not follow this reasoning.

90 Para. 53 of the judgment.

91 Para. 55 of the judgment.

92 Para. 55 of the judgment.

93 Van Drooghenbroeck, *La proportionnalité*, e.g. at 158, n. 432.

94 Ibid., at 158.

95 Para. 67 of the judgment.

96 Interestingly, the Court is now using the term 'interference'. As we have seen, under Article 3, it considered the issue to be not one of 'interference' by the State, but of the applicant wanting the State to do something.

97 Para. 74 of the judgment.

98 Para. 39 of the judgment.

99 See also Dan Morris, 'Assisted suicide under the European Convention on Human Rights: a critique' (2003) *European Human Rights Law Review* 65–91.

100 Nagel, 'War', at 53.

101 *Soering* v. *United Kingdom*, 7 July 1989, Series A, No. 161, (1989) 11 EHRR 439.

102 As summarized by the Court, para. 82 of the judgment, emphasis added.

103 Para. 83 of the judgment.

104 Para. 85 of the judgment, emphasis added.

105 As recalled by Van Drooghenbroeck, *La proportionnalité*, at 127, n. 160.

106 Para. 89 of the judgment, emphasis added. The first part of that statement was a simple reiteration of *Ireland* v. *United Kingdom*, where the Court had already affirmed, in para. 162 of the judgment: 'ill treatment must attain a minimum level of severity if it is to fall within the scope of Article 3. The assessment of this minimum is, in the nature of things, relative; it depends on all the circumstances of the case.'

107 For a case where a state had been found in violation of the Convention for an omission, see *X and Y* v. *the Netherlands*, 16 March 1985, Series A, No. 91, (1986) 8 EHRR 235, discussed from a feminist point of view in Chapter 7. By definition, an omission cannot be found to violate a negative obligation. Wrongful omissions immediately suggest the presence of positive obligations. For example, two scholars have recently read Joseph Conrad's *Heart of Darkness* by reference to the choice of the narrator, in this well-known story, of not speaking out about the atrocities he had witnessed in the Congo, which they interpret as moral failure: Birgit Maier-Katkin and Daniel Maier-Katkin, 'At the Heart of Darkness: Crimes against humanity and the banality of evil' (2004) 26 *Human Rights Quarterly* 584–604.

108 Compare e.g. the verdicts of violation in *Chahal* v. *United Kingdom*, 15 November 1996, RJD 1996-V 1831, (1997) 23 EHRR 413, *Ahmed* v. *Austria*, 17 December 1996, RJD 1996-VI 2195, (1997) 24 EHRR 278 and *Jabari* v. *Turkey*, 11 July 2000, ECHR 2000-VIII, with the verdicts of non-violation in *Vilvarajah and Others* v. *United Kingdom*, 30 September 1991, Series A, No. 215, (1992) 14 EHRR 248 and *HLR* v. *France*, 29 April 1997, RJD 1997-III, (1998) 26 EHRR 29.

109 Other obligations laid down in human rights law can be regarded as providing for absolute obligations, but they are more controversial. Judge De Meyer, for example, thought the prohibition against disclosure of confidential medical information for the requirements of criminal proceedings to be absolute (see his dissenting opinion in *Z* v. *Finland*). He was, however, the only judge on the bench which decided *Z* to express this opinion.

110 To recall the words (quoted above) of Judge De Meyer in *Z* v. *Finland*: 'where human rights are concerned, there is no room for a margin of appreciation which would enable the States to decide what is acceptable and what is not. On that subject the boundary not to be overstepped must be as clear and precise as possible.' See also Van Drooghenbroeck, *La proportionnalité*, at 419 and Chapter IV.

111 Wesley C. Mitchell, 'Bentham's Felicific Calculus' (1918) 33 *Political Science Quarterly*, reproduced in Bhikhu Parekh (ed.), *Jeremy Bentham: Ten Critical Essays* (London: Frank Cass, 1974) 168–86, at 168–9.

112 The reliance on interpersonal comparisons of utility is also problematic, not to mention the almost totalitarian logic of classical utilitarianism: Barry, *Introduction*, at 99–100.

113 Though attempts to quantify human rights respect and violation exist. I am not the only one to find exercises which rank states by reference to a precise numerical human rights performance unconvincing: R. L. Barsh, 'Measuring human rights: Problems of methodology and purpose' (1993) 15 *Human Rights Quarterly* 87–121.

114 Mitchell, 'Calculus', at 175.

115 In a manuscript quoted by Halévy and quoted in turn by Mitchell, 'Calculus', at 172.

116 Ibid., at 182.

117 Ibid.

118 This is Mitchell's word, e.g. ibid., at 170.

119 This explains why even though Bentham remarked that one could not add 20 pears to 20 apples, nothing is deemed incommensurable under utilitarianism: Gutman and Thompson, *Democracy*, at 179.

120 Mitchell, 'Calculus', at 180.

121 Marie-Bénédicte Dembour, 'Etrangers ou quasi-nationaux? Le choix des droits de l'homme [Observations sous l'arrêt *Ezzouhdi*]' (2002) 52 *Revue trimestrielle des droits de l'homme* 959–82.

122 Moreover Van Drooghenbroeck notes that it is not even the same aspect of proportionality which is examined from one case to the next: Van Drooghenbroeck, *La proportionnalité*.

123 P. van Dijk and G. H. J. van Hoof, *Theory and Practice of the European Convention on Human Rights* (The Hague: Kluwer, 1990), at 604. See also Greer, 'Constitutionalizing,' at 407.

124 For example, Dan Morris writes that 'though the ECHR might not compute proportionality by any algorithmic method, it certainly does not allow its deliberations to descend to the arbitrary'. Somewhat contradictorily, he later states: 'There are . . . no established formulae according to which the Strasbourg Court conducts such enquiries [related to proportionality]. At best, it seems, what the Court does is to "pick and mix" from amongst the various factors, applying them as it sees fit given the nature of the case in question': Morris, 'Assisted Suicide', at 80 and 89 respectively.

125 Van Drooghenbroeck, *La proportionnalité*, esp. Chapter VII, section IV.

126 Ibid., e.g. at 16–17.

127 Ibid., at 17.

128 Ibid., e.g. at 15.

129 Ibid., esp. Chapter 4. Reached through slightly different concepts and logically equally seductive, Greer's conclusion is conterminous with Van Drooghenbroek's. See Greer, 'Constitutionalizing'.

130 Jeremy Bentham, 'Anarchical Fallacies. An Examination of the Declaration of the Rights of the Man and the Citizen Decreed by the Constituent Assembly in France', in Jeremy Bentham, *Selected Writings on Utilitarianism* (Ware, Hertfordshire: Wordsworth, 2000) 381–459, at 406.

131 'Hark! ye citizens of the other side of the water! Can you tell us what rights you have belonging to you? No, that you can't. It's *we* [the French] that understand rights: not our own only, but yours into the bargain; while you, poor simple souls! know nothing about the matter': ibid., at 396.

132 Ibid., at 406, emphases added.

133 Ibid., at 455, emphases added.

134 Van Drooghenbroeck, *La proportionnalité*, at 715, my translation and emphasis.

135 See e.g. ibid: '[Les normes juridiques] seraient cependant sujettes au changement, lorsqu'il se révèle *a posteriori* qu'elles sont foncièrement *inadaptées* à la réalité qu'elle [sic] prétendent régir, et, à ce titre, incapables de l'ordonner' (emphasis in the original).

136 Nagel, 'War', at 52–3.

137 Allison, 'Utilitarian Ethics', at 24. See also the dissenting opinions of Judge Fitz-maurice in *Tyrer* v. *United Kingdom*, 25 April 1978, Series A, No. 26, (1979–1980) 2 EHRR 1 and *Ireland* v. *United Kingdom*: 'Cases of this kind also show that the gloss that has to be placed upon the literal effect of [Article 3 also] relates . . . to what may in certain circumstances justify its infliction, such as encompassing the greater good of saving the life of the recipient; or, in certain types of cases, the saving of a great many other lives. This last matter is one of much difficulty and delicacy on which it is all too easy to go wrong. I touched upon it . . . in my Separate Opinion in the Irish case': *Tyrer*, Separate Opinion of Judge Sir Gerald Fitzmaurice, point 5. The direct expression of utilitarian reasoning in relation to inhuman and degrading treatment and torture by a judge of the European Court of Human Rights is exceptional.

138 Scheffler (ed.), *Consequentialism*, at 3, emphasis in the original.

139 Allison, 'Utilitarian Ethics', at 24. See also his response to the McCloskey scenario, ibid. at 16–17.

140 Nagel, 'War', at 73.

141 Ibid., at 72.

142 Norbert Foulquier, 'De la protection des droits . . . à l'insécurité juridique. Ou la remise en cause par la Cour européenne des droits de l'homme des fins de non-recevoir et des exceptions d'irrecevabilité consacrées par la procédure juridiction-nelle française', (2003) 56 *Revue trimestrielle des droits de l'homme* 1203–20.

143 *A* v. *United Kingdom*, 17 December 2002, ECHR 2002-X, (2002) 36 EHRR 917.

144 Para. 40 of the judgment.

145 Para. 53 of the judgment.

146 Para. 58 of the judgment.

147 Para. 66 of the judgment.

148 Para. 77 of the judgment.

149 Para. 83 of the judgment.

150 Judge Costa appended a concurring opinion. It indicated that he was uncomfor-table with the result of *A* v. *United Kingdom*, but felt that it was for the legislature, not the judiciary, to settle this matter in a more satisfactory way. He can thus yet again be seen as displaying a 'statist' approach, here in the sense that he respects the principle of the separation of powers upon which the modern state is built.

151 By contrast the Court does not refer to Article 10 of the Convention, on freedom of expression, in its reasoning. Its 'mixture' of two articles of the Convention, for example of Article 10 and Article 9 in *Otto Preminger Institute* v. *Austria*, 20 September 1994, Series A, No. 295-A, (1995) 19 EHRR 34, was heavily criticized by commentators at the time. Such a critique is in line with a categorical reasoning. It arose as the Court had not yet come to realize that rights can be in competition with each other. It is only in the 1990s that the Court started to face this fact: Van Drooghenbroeck, *La proportionnalité*, at 109. For a recent example where a conflict between different rights clearly arises, see e.g. *Odièvre* v. *France*, judgment of 13 February 2003, discussed in Chapter 7.

152 Emphasis added.

153 *Manickavasagam Suresh* v. *Canada (Minister of Citizenship and Immigration) and the Attorney General of Canada*, 11 January 2002, Supreme Court of Canada (SCC) 1. For a commentary, see Stephane Bourgon, 'The Impact of Terrorism on the Principle of '*Non-Refoulement*' of Refugees: The *Suresh* Case before the Supreme Court of Canada' (2003) 1 *Journal of International Criminal Justice* 169–85.

154 *A and Others* v. *Secretary of State for the Home Department*, Court of Appeal (Civil Division), [2004] EWCA Civ 1123, [2004] All ER (D) 62 (Aug), (Approved Judgment), 11 August 2004.

155 *A and Others* v. *Secretary of State for the Home Department*, Court of Appeal (Civil Division), [2002] EWCA Civ 1502, [2003] 1 All ER 816, 25 October 2002.

156 *A and Others* v. *Secretary of State for the Home Department*, House of Lords, [2004] UKHL 56, [2005] 3 All ER 169, 16 December 2004.

157 David Luban, 'Eight fallacies about liberty and security', in Richard A. Wilson (ed.), *Human Rights in the 'War on Terror'* (Cambridge: Cambridge University Press, 2005), at 242–57.

158 Charles Taylor suggests that this is precisely the reason why a human rights discourse arose during the Enlightenment. He speaks of 'the eighteenth-century notion that human beings are endowed with a moral sense, an intuitive feeling for what is right and wrong' and explains that the 'original point of this doctrine was to combat a rival view, that knowing right and wrong was a matter of calculating consequences . . . The idea was that understanding right and wrong was not a matter of dry calculation, but was anchored in our feelings. Morality has, in a sense, a voice within': Charles Taylor, 'The politics of recognition', in Amy Gutmann (ed.), *Multiculturalism: Examining the Politics of Recognition* (Princeton: Princeton University Press, 1994) 25–74, at 28.

159 Para. 101 of the judgment, quoted above, text to n. 46.

160 *Chassagnou and Others* v. *France*, 29 April 1999, ECHR 1999-III, (2000) 29 EHRR 615.

161 Para. 23 of the judgment.

162 They also complained of a discrimination contrary to Article 14 taken in conjunction with Articles 9 and 11 of the Convention and of Article 1 of Protocol 1.

163 Quoted in para. 21 of the judgment.

164 Dissenting opinion of Judge Costa, para. 3.

165 Dissenting opinion of Judge Caflisch joined by Judge Pantîru.

166 Para. 106 of the judgment.

167 Para. 77 of the judgment.

168 Para. 76 of the judgment. The applicants thus raised the question of who benefits from the law, a question which has a Marxist ring. For a Marxist analysis of the Convention, see Chapter 5.

169 Aileen McHarg, 'Reconciling human rights and the public interest: Conceptual problems and doctrinal uncertainty in the jurisprudence of the European Court of Human Rights' (1999) 62 *Modern Law Review* 671–96.

170 Para. 79 of the judgment.

171 The Court also found a discrimination contrary to Article 14 both in respect to Article 11 (by sixteen votes to one) and in respect to Article 1 of Protocol 1 (by fourteen votes to three). It found it unnecessary to examine separately the complaint under Article 9 of the Convention (by sixteen votes to one).

172 Paras. 112 and 113 of the judgment, emphasis added.

173 See Chapter 3; also above n. 150.

174 Dissenting opinion of Judge Costa. The last remark seems yet again to point to the statism of the French judge, who is concerned to make it possible for the state to function by implementing the policies on which it has decided, presumably with the general interest in mind.

175 Para. 8 of his dissenting opinion, last italics my emphasis.

176 Section III of his dissenting opinion.

177 Dissenting opinion of Judge Fischbach, emphasis added.

178 On the contrary, 'the applicants did not contest the right of hunters to enjoy and take part in hunting' simply objecting that 'it was not for Parliament to impose on those who were opposed to it the obligation to join hunters' associations of whose aims and policies they viscerally disapproved': para. 107 of the judgment.

179 Though the French Government observed that hunting was an activity 'with very firm roots in French rural tradition': para. 78 of the judgment. This could suggest that hunting has to be allowed in France, as a 'cultural matter', which would make it possible to submit *Chassagnou* to a cultural relativist reading (on which, see Chapter 6).

180 Para. 97 of the judgment, emphasis added.

181 Also: 'The disclosure of [HIV status] may dramatically affect [an individual's] private and family life, as well as social and employment situation, by exposing him or her to opprobrium and the risk of ostracism. For this reason it may also discourage persons from seeking diagnosis or treatment and thus *undermine any preventive efforts by the community to contain the pandemic*': para. 96 of the judgment, emphasis added.

182 *Jersild* v. *Denmark*, 23 September 1994, Series A, No. 298, (1995) 19 EHRR 1.

183 Para. 11 of the judgment.

184 Under Article 266 (b) of the Danish Penal Code, which provided: 'Any person who, publicly or with the intention of disseminating it to a wide circle of people, makes a statement, or other communication, threatening, insulting or degrading a group of persons on account of their race, colour, national or ethnic origin or belief shall be liable to a fine or to simple detention or to imprisonment for a term not exceeding two years': cited in para. 19 of the judgment.

185 Para. 14 of the judgment.

186 Para. 13 of the judgment.

187 Para. 28 of the judgment.

188 Para. 34 of the judgment.

189 Para. 37 of the judgment.

190 Joint Dissenting Opinion of Judges Ryssdal, Bernhardt, Spielmann and Loizou, points 2 and 3.

191 Ibid., point 3. See also Joint Dissenting Opinion of Judges Gölcüklü, Russo and Valticos: 'It has been sought to defend the broadcast on the ground that it would provoke a healthy reaction of rejection among the viewers. That is to display an optimism, which to say the least, is belied by experience.'

192 Moreover, the applicant was represented by Kevin Boyle, one of the founders of the Kurdish Human Rights Project (on which see Chapter 5).

193 See e.g. Caroline Picheral, 'Discrimination raciale et Convention européenne des droits de l'homme (L'apport de la jurisprudence)' (2001) 46 *Revue trimestrielle des droits de l'homme* 517–39, at 537–8. However, for a recent ringing endorsement, see Conor Gearty, 'Civil liberties and human rights', in Nicholas Bamforth and Peter Leyland (eds.), *Public Law in a Multi-Layered Constitution* (Oxford: Hart, 2003) 371–90, at 382: 'The *Jersild* decision is rightly celebrated for the depth and maturity of its commitment to media freedom.'

194 As their strict laws on nationality for example demonstrate.

195 Two remarks are in order. First, the formulation of the Human Rights Act in terms of minimum standards which can be given higher protection assumes that – to put it colloquially – more is better. It thus singularly fails to address the issue of conflicting rights and interests. Second, the conclusion reached in this section is pertinent when assessing whether the Strasbourg Court is right to censure legislation adopted after much debate by democratically constituted national Parliaments, at least when they have seriously considered the pros and cons of the particular course of action on which they have decided.

196 See also the discussion of *raison d'état* in the previous chapter.

197 See e.g. James Fishkin. 'Utilitarianism versus human rights', in Ellen Frankel Paul, Fred D. Miller Jr. and Jeffrey Paul (eds.), *Human Rights* (Oxford: Blackwell, 1984) 103–7.

198 This point is beautifully made by Martti Koskenniemi in an article which could have been entitled 'Rights are policies, not trumps': Koskenniemi, 'Effect'.

5

The Convention in a Marxist light

[T]he so-called rights of man, the rights of man distinct from the rights of the citizen are nothing but the rights of the member of civil society, i.e. egoistic man, man separated from other men and the community.   (Marx)

There is something presumptuous in writing a chapter which purports to read the European Convention in a Marxist light when one is versed, like me, neither in Marx's voluminous work nor in the many commentaries and theories it has generated. Still, this chapter could not have been omitted: first, because 'the young' Marx touched directly upon the 'rights of man' in an essay which has become very famous and, second, because the main idea of this text remains extremely pertinent today.

As the statement at the head of the chapter makes clear, Marx felt that the rights of man comforted man (he did not think much about women) in his egoism; as such the rights of man were not destined to have a place in the truly communal society which he did not doubt would one day emerge. Though Marx was not a fan of what we now call human rights, there is nonetheless a sense in which he was less scathing of them than Bentham: for Marx, human rights were not nonsense but a step in the right direction in the long march of humanity's history.

The human rights credo would have us believe that human rights are for every human being. Marxism alerts us that this is not so. This chapter explores the idea that the European Convention may serve the capitalist interests of the bourgeoisie and the ruling class; it questions whether human rights provide promising terms in which to formulate a utopian vision capable of guiding humanity's conduct. To illustrate these themes, procedural issues are discussed which raise the question of who can, in concrete terms, turn to Strasbourg and in order to make what kind of claim.

'On the Jewish Question': The denunciation of bourgeois rights

The essay which provides the obvious point of entry into Marx's thinking about human rights is entitled 'On the Jewish Question'.[1] This section summarizes it without placing it in a broader Marxian perspective – an exercise which will be attempted later.

The essay was published in 1843, when Marx was barely twenty-five. 'The Jewish question' must have been close to his heart, for Marx was born in the German town of Trier in 1818 into a Jewish family which had included many rabbis.[2] Located in the province of Rhineland-Westphalia, Trier had been annexed to France from 1795 to 1814, before being reattached to the Prussian Crown in 1815. Under French rule, Jews had enjoyed nominal equality. Under Prussian rule, they were said to enjoy rights which were equal to those of Christians but they were in fact treated unequally. For example, they required an exemption from the king to hold positions in the service of the state. This directly affected Marx's father, a deist influenced by the ideas of the French Enlightenment. In 1817, he chose formally to renounce Judaism and to convert to the German Protestant Church in order to obtain a judicial position. This and other experiences cannot but have marked his son Karl who agreed, in 1842, to present a petition to the Rhineland Diet in favour of the Jews.

The young Marx wrote 'On the Jewish Question' – an essay which is incidentally not devoid of anti-Semitic sentiments[3] – in order to explain his position on how to address the continuing discrimination against Jews in the 'Germany' of the mid-nineteenth century in which he lived.[4] He did so by responding to an argument which had been put forward by Bruno Bauer, a Young Hegelian with whom he often argued in his early writings.[5] The Young Hegelians believed that the philosophy of Hegel (1770–1831) implicitly pointed to the fact that Reason could and should exist within the world; they thought that the critique of religion could in itself produce human emancipation. Though Marx initially associated himself with them, he soon became dissatisfied with this central assumption.[6]

'On the Jewish Question' starts by recalling Bauer's critique of the campaign which had developed in Germany in favour of religious freedom for the Jews. Bauer thought that this campaign was wrong-headed because it did not aim to replace the paradigm of the religious state. He argued that the ruler of a religious state is by definition alien to the people, 'since he is God-given and arrived at without their own co-operation'.[7] He further noted that politics cannot but amount to anything other than religion in a religious state. This led him to conclude that this state is not a real state.[8] Bauer called for the establishment of a truly political state emancipated from religion. In his view, Jews in Germany should have been asking for *both* Christians and Jews to be recognized as citizens.[9]

Like Bauer, Marx was opposed to the religious state; unlike him, he did not find the idea of the political state thoroughly attractive. This is because he thought that the political state did not lead to emancipation from religion, a crucial point in his scheme given that he held that 'the existence of religion is the existence of a defect'.[10] He observed that religion not only survives in the political state, but that it can positively thrive, as demonstrated by extensive religious practice in the so-called free states of mid-nineteenth century North America, which all inscribed the right to be religious amongst the rights of man.[11] This observation logically led him to assert: 'the state can be a free state without man himself being free'.[12] In other words, he wished to distinguish between political and human emancipation.[13]

Central to 'On the Jewish Question' is the idea that the political state induces a split in the individual between his 'citizen' and his 'bourgeois' parts.[14] The citizen part of man is the one that corresponds to the public self and belongs to the political state; this is the part where man regards himself as a communal being. By contrast, the bourgeois part of man corresponds to the private self and belongs to civil society; this is the part where man acts as a private individual and leads an egoistic life. Marx argues that the citizen and bourgeois elements of man contradict each other in the political state, where man is thus condemned to lead a double life and where he is alienated from his true self.

Marx sees this lack of fit between the man and the citizen reflected in the 1791 French Declaration, which is entitled 'Declaration of the Rights of Man and of the Citizen', a formulation which corresponds to the split between the citizen and the bourgeois parts of man characteristic of the political state: the rights of the citizen allow for participation in the community; the rights of man are the rights of the private individual and are exercised in civil society.

Marx is highly critical of the rights of man which 'are nothing but the rights of the member of civil society, i.e. egoistic man, man separated from other men and the community'.[15] The right to liberty, he argues, is the right to do anything which does not harm others, i.e. the liberty of man 'as an isolated monad [who is] withdrawn into himself'; the right to private property is the right to enjoy and dispose of one's possessions 'arbitrarily, without regard for other men, independently from society, the right of selfishness'; the right to equality represents nothing else but access to liberty as described above; the right to security provides the guarantee of egoism.[16] He concludes:

> Thus none of the so-called rights of man goes beyond egoistic man, man as he is in civil society, namely an individual withdrawn behind his private interests and whims and separated from the community. Far from the rights of man conceiving of man as a species-being, species-life itself, society, appears as a framework exterior to individuals . . . The only bond that holds them together is natural necessity, need and private interest, the conservation of their property and egoistic person.[17]

For Marx, it is no small paradox that the sphere in which man behaves as a communal being is degraded below the sphere in which he behaves as a private being: in the political state, the political sphere is at the service of the civil sphere, rather than the other way around.[18] He notes that 'it is not man as a citizen but man as a bourgeois [i.e. a member of civil society pursuing his selfish interests][19] who is called the real and true man' in the French Declaration.[20]

Does the Convention serve selfish man? *Casado Coca* versus *Janowski*

Following Marx, could it be said that the European Convention provides rights for the selfish man? There are certainly plenty of cases in the Strasbourg case law which seem to support such an assertion. Given that the Convention rules out *actio popularis* and requires an individual applicant to be able to claim the status of 'victim' for the case to be admissible,[21] it would be surprising for a sense of selfishness not to underlie most if not all the cases which are brought at Strasbourg.[22] This does not mean, however, that applicants are never motivated by considerations which go beyond their personal interests. *Casado Coca* v. *Spain*[23] and *Janowski* v. *Poland*[24] are tentatively used in this section to illustrate, respectively, selfish and more communal motives on the part of the individual applicant. The tentativeness of the exercise must be stressed: on the one hand, individual motives are rarely straightforward, but normally include a variety of factors, which are moreover not always conscious; on the other hand, what one understands by 'selfishness' and 'communal cause' is bound to depend on the perspective and the values one adopts. Most importantly, it must be recalled that Marx is not interested in selfishness as a characteristic of individuals but as a feature which arises in particular social conditions. In Wendy Brown's useful formulation, Marx criticizes bourgeois rights because (amongst other factors) they naturalize the egoism of capitalist society, 'reifying "the frenzied movement of the material elements" of this society as the nature of man, thereby masking social power and mistaking its effects – atomistic individuals – for its wellspring and agents'.[25]

With these provisos, the two selected cases can be reviewed. The applicant in *Casado Coca* was a practising lawyer who was repeatedly fined for advertising his services in contravention of Spanish law. He argued at Strasbourg that these disciplinary sanctions were against Article 10 of the Convention, guaranteeing freedom of expression. He appears to have been trying to make money, acting upon what a Marxist might call 'the fragmented interests of the petty bourgeoisie'.[26] If this analysis is not completely wrong, it is highly interesting that the case was neither immediately nor unanimously found to be without merit at Strasbourg. The case was declared admissible, and the Commission proceeded to find a violation of Article 10 – though only just, by a majority of nine votes against nine, the President using his casting vote. Subsequently the Court concluded in a judgment of 24 February 1994 adopted by seven votes to two that the Convention had not been violated.

Why did the case receive detailed attention from both the Commission and the Court whilst, in one view of human rights at least, it did not raise a human rights issue? An answer to this question can be sought by reference to Marx's contention that the non-communist (liberal and capitalist) society sets up a public sphere which deals not with public matters, but with the private claims of individuals acting out of selfishness. From this perspective, the eventual dismissal of Mr Casado Coca's claim is irrelevant; the important point is that the Strasbourg apparatus was in place to hear the claims of the bourgeois, understood as the private man motivated by selfishness rather than by a concern for the community.

Some, including perhaps the nine commissioners and the two judges who found a violation of the Convention, might object to my interpretation of *Casado Coca* as a case lacking a communal dimension. Admittedly, had Mr Casado Coca won, other lawyers would have been able to rely on his victory to pursue similar claims; his victory would presumably have led to the Spanish economy and state being run on more liberal, in the sense of *laissez-faire*, lines. From a *laissez-faire* perspective, this would undoubtedly have represented a positive step for society to take and, as such, a collective as well as a strictly individual gain. We can expect, however, that Marx would not have shared this perspective.

For a case where the applicant seemed to be motivated by less immediately recognizable selfish considerations, we can turn to *Janowski* v. *Poland*, delivered on 24 February 1999. Mr Janowski, a retired journalist, was walking through his town when he noticed two municipal guards ordering street vendors to leave. He intervened and pointed out to the guards, rightly as it turned out, that their actions had no legal basis and infringed the laws guaranteeing freedom in the economic field. An altercation followed. Mr Janowski ended up addressing the municipal guards as 'oafs' and 'dumb'. He was charged and convicted of having verbally insulted two municipal guards. The suspended prison sentence was quashed but the fine was upheld on appeal. Mr Janowski complained at Strasbourg of a violation of Article 10. The Commission expressed by eight votes to seven the opinion that Article 10 had been breached. By contrast, the Court found no breach of the Convention by twelve votes to five.

Judge Bonello, dissenting, argued that a 'regime which considers the verbal impertinence of an individual more reprehensible than illicit excesses by public officers is one that has . . . pulled the scale of values inside out'. In my view, this consideration should have led the Court to find Poland in violation of Article 10, the more so since criticizing the authorities openly could hardly be expected to have become entrenched in a society which was just emerging from years of communist subjugation.[27]

The important point for the present discussion, however, is that the applicant had been defending, in the words of dissenting Judge Wildhaber, 'a position . . . in which he had no immediate personal interest'. That there is a difference in the degrees of 'selfishness' and 'communal sense' as between the claims of Mr Casado Coca and of Mr Janowski seems to me unquestionable. The former had not consciously tried to act as a citizen; the latter had. It so happens that Mr Janowski was neither more nor less successful than Mr Casado Coca in his claim that Article 10 had been violated. It would not be excessively difficult to create pairs of cases where the claims of a respectively 'selfish' and 'communally-oriented' applicant are both either declared inadmissible or found by the Court to point to violations of the Convention.

Asking whether the Convention can serve the selfish man created by capitalist society does not promise to be particularly illuminating – it obviously can. A more interesting question might be: do applicants like Mr Janowski invalidate the thrust of Marx's critique in 'On the Jewish Question'? Such a conclusion would be in accordance with the thesis of some scholars, including those reviewed in the next section.

Balibar and Lefort: The man is the citizen

Marx saw the French Declaration of the Rights of Man and the Citizen as based upon a distinction between the rights of man and the rights of the citizen, with the former unfortunately *founding* the latter. The French philosopher Etienne Balibar, former student of Louis Althusser and therefore not lacking in Marxist credentials, has criticized this distinction. As far as Balibar is concerned there is no difference between the rights of man and the rights of the citizen: 'they are *exactly the same*'.[28] In his words:

> The *Declaration* does not posit any 'human nature' *before* society and the political order . . . Instead it integrally identifies the rights of man with political rights and . . . identifies man, whether individual or collective, with the member of political society . . . Man in the *Declaration* is not a 'private individual' in opposition to the citizen who would be the member of the state. He is precisely the citizen . . .[29]

Claude Lefort, another French thinker of the Left, makes a similar observation.[30] Without suggesting that Marx has no point, he nonetheless deplores the fact that his critique of the French Declaration neglects important Articles, such as those on freedom of opinion and on communication. Lefort writes:

> Was Marx so obsessed by his schema of the bourgeois revolution that he could not see that freedom of opinion is a freedom of relationships . . . [The article on freedom of communication of thoughts and opinions] clearly implies that it is man's right, one of his most precious rights, to step out of himself and to make contact with others, through speech, writing and thought.[31]

Lefort thus intimates that Marx was wrong to see every right in the Declaration as 'merely the sign of a fiction which converts man into a monad'.[32]

Balibar and Lefort's arguments are elegantly put. I nonetheless find them a poor rebuttal of Marx's main thesis, as a discussion of a leading case about Article 10 and of *Janowski* will illustrate.

Sunday Times and *Janowski*: Which interests are being pursued?

Sunday Times v. United Kingdom, adopted on 26 April 1979,[33] remains the leading case on freedom of the press in European human rights law.[34] At first sight the judgment looks admirable. The case arose after the Sunday Times decided to run a series of articles about the plight of the children who had been severely deformed by the drug thalidomide, taken by their mothers during pregnancy. A first article, entitled 'Our Thalidomide Children: A Cause for National Shame', was published. It criticized the low level of compensation which had been offered to the parents of the children by the maker of the drug, Distillers. Distillers obtained an injunction preventing the paper from publishing the second article it had announced in the first on the ground that publication could prejudice the ongoing legal proceedings. The Strasbourg Court held that there had been a violation of Article 10: the right of the newspaper to publish articles on matters of public interest outweighed the need to protect the integrity of the legal proceedings.

The great importance in which the Court holds this freedom seems to support Balibar's argument that, before the Court, man is the citizen. This conclusion, however, should not be reached too hastily. First of all, if this was the right decision, then it is disturbing that it was adopted by a very close majority of eleven to nine. More importantly, it should be stressed that the Court does not extend the same level of protection to all areas of social life. For example, it has legitimized severe restrictions on freedom of expression by the authorities in the artistic field.[35] Finally, one should be aware that the press is not interested just in encouraging public debate; more often than not, it is driven by strong financial interests.[36]

Let us return to *Janowski*. At first sight, the case could be taken to illustrate Balibar and Lefort's thesis: Mr Janowski was not defending his own 'little' interest, but was taking a stand, as a citizen, against an abusive demand *on others* by the authorities. This is a somewhat superficial analysis, however, and it can easily be made to fall apart. It must surely be problematic for the thesis in question that the Court failed to find a violation of Article 10. Legally, its verdict of non-violation can be explained by reference to the fact that the statements of the applicant had been witnessed only by a few bystanders, barring them from being considered, in a direct reference to *Sunday Times*, as 'part of an open discussion of matters of public concern',[37] and thus justifying – so the argument would run – a lesser level of protection under Article 10.

From a Marxist perspective, however, it may not even be the verdict of non-violation which appears problematic. An Althusserian might conclude that the self-righteous Mr Janowski, who was relying on freedom in the economic field, had been acting as a transmitter in the cause of the disembodied interest of global capital. The applicant's apparently disinterested pursuit might thus have been serving – and masking – the strategic interests of the ruling capitalist classes. Far from having been a responsible citizen, he might have altogether failed in realizing his autonomy and giving his action a 'communal' dimension, in a Marxist sense of the term.

This argument would of course not be restricted to Mr Janowski: whether we like it or not, we are all enmeshed in the system in which we find ourselves, wittingly or unwittingly, living and thus participating. But problems of false consciousness and deep structures against which we can hardly do anything at an individual level should not be ignored just because they make us uncomfortable. This is to say that I find Balibar and Lefort's arguments too theoretical and too sweeping. These two thinkers suggest that the French Declaration of the Rights of Man and of the Citizen was more beautiful than Marx had conceded. Against this, my contention is that Marx's critique cannot be swept under the carpet. All kinds of problems arise as soon as one goes beyond the summary of the leading cases that are taken to have entrenched fundamental freedoms in Europe. To put it simply: law, including European human rights law, smells bad.

'On the Jewish Question' as a Marxian text

Marx would no doubt have nodded in approval at this last suggestion. To understand why, it is useful to place his essay 'On the Jewish Question' in the context of his whole work, thus introducing, albeit briefly, his general epistemological and ethical perspective.

'On the Jewish Question' belongs to Marx's so-called 'early writings'. Since Marx wrote it when he was in his mid-twenties, this can hardly be an inappropriate description. There is far more than a matter of age in the label, however. A division between the early and the mature Marx has often been posited, with *The Theses on Feuerbach*, written a mere two years after 'On the Jewish Question', presented as the pivotal piece.[38] In his early work, Marx grappled with philosophy and was explicitly interested in discussing the nature of man. In his mature work, he abandoned philosophy and devoted himself instead to the 'scientific'[39] study of material conditions. This led him to elaborate a theory of history as a progress through stages conditioned by the society's attained level of productivity and the requirements of increase. He identified the 'laws of motion' of capitalism, leading him to predict that capitalism would give way to socialism.[40]

Some commentators, most notably Louis Althusser, have paid no attention to Marx's early writings, which they describe as 'pre-scientific'. Others, including Erik Fromm, have developed a humanist interpretation of Marxism that has relied on these early works to denounce the claims of 'scientific Marxism', especially as they were propounded in the USSR. David Walker adopts a middle position. For him, there is no epistemological break between the 'early' and the 'mature' works: the early works represent 'steps in the development of Marx's thought, important in their own right and necessary to an understanding of Marx's later work'.[41] Walker sees the early philosophising as the necessary counterpart of the later 'scientific' work, as the philosophy of Marx's science which is not at odds with it and to which he (Marx) does indeed refer later.[42]

Taking a view of Marx's works as continuous, 'On the Jewish Question' appears recognisably Marxian on at least four counts: (a) it is consonant with (historical) *materialism*; (b) it unmasks human rights as *ideology*; (c) it denounces human *alienation*; (d) it calls for the development of *communism*, away from religion, private property and the state.

At the heart of all of Marx's works lies a *materialist approach*. According to this approach, the material base is primary, ideas secondary. Instead 'of setting out from what men say, imagine, conceive', Marx sets out 'on the basis of [men's] real life-process'.[43] Matter is independent of mind, and everything depends on matter.[44] In his mature works, Marx investigates social production because he sees it as the key to understanding reality.[45] He holds a 'materialist conception of history'[46] in that he puts forward an explanatory thesis in terms of social production. This allows him to demystify history and politics.[47] Saying that the means of production – tools, techniques, productive organization – are primary to institutions, including laws, is the same as saying that the superstructure consists of ideas which derive from the material base.[48] The superstructure functions as an *ideology*. In capitalist ideology, man is presented as free while the reality is that capitalist society *alienates* him.[49] Ideology prevents him from seeing this, leading to false consciousness. Capitalism is synonymous with exploitation, and exploitation leads to class struggle. *Communism* is the dialectical counterpoint of capitalism. In communist society, economic exploitation vanishes. Likewise, the 'opium' of religion, the self-centred institution of private property and the state as public guarantor of private interests have no role to play; no longer required, these institutions wither away. Man's individual interest corresponds to everyone else's interest.

In the context of these tenets, one can see the main point of 'On the Jewish Question' to be an analysis of human rights as an ideology which masks reality,[50] even though the term 'ideology' does not appear in the text (neither does 'exploitation' nor 'class struggle'). Marx says: 'Man is not free in the free state'. Transpose: Rights are supposed to endow man with freedoms; in fact, they alienate him. Although Marx was indignant at this fact, he did not blame the member of civil society for pursuing his selfish interest; he did not judge the individual who happened to be a bourgeois; he 'simply' regretted that the organization of society was such that man was driven to pursue his private, selfish interests.[51] This was a deep regret. It rested on his profoundly – or naïvely – optimistic view of human nature[52] which made him believe that man could become a species-being. It also rested on the adoption of a materialist analysis which made it possible for him to see the 'real' ('material') circumstances of men who supposedly enjoyed equality and freedom, but in fact did not.

The rich more equal than the poor at Strasbourg? Morvai's account

More than one hundred and fifty years on, Marx's essay 'On the Jewish Question' continues to invite us to be attentive to the ideological function which human rights may serve: is there a gap between what human rights say they do and what they actually do? This section is the first in a series of three which explore this question by reference to access to the protection the Strasbourg Convention offers. The proceedings at Strasbourg are free, making it in theory possible for *anyone* who claims to be a victim of a violation of the Convention by a state party to institute them. In practice, is this 'anyone' really anyone? Krisztina Morvai's bitter account of the way applications by poor people were turned down at Strasbourg when she worked there suggests, to paraphrase Orwell, that some people are more equal than others before the European Court of Human Rights.[53]

Morvai says that she had experienced 'the Law of Rule as opposed to the Rule of Law' in the communist Hungary in which she had grown up, but that she had always sensed that democracy, human rights and the rule of law prevailed in the 'Real' Europe, across the Iron Curtain. She enthusiastically embraced all these notions, which Western professors came and lectured Eastern Europeans about, after the collapse of communism. She arrived at Strasbourg in 1994 to work at the heart of the Europe of her dreams as a lawyer in the Registry of the European Commission of Human Rights. She was soon disappointed – and her probation ended. It is probably faithful to her view to say that she came to see human rights Europe as a varnish which was attractive only on the surface. Deep down, ugly things were taking place. Central among these was the fact that thousands of applications were dismissed without receiving the attention they deserved.

The Commission was in charge of filtering the applications to Strasbourg until 1998. On receipt of a letter sent by a person new to the system, its Registry opened a provisional file and sent what was called a P0, consisting of an application form and general comments on the Convention system. A large proportion of correspondents were deterred at this stage; they never made contact with the Commission again and the provisional file was destroyed without a decision having been made upon it. The Registry registered the case if and when it received a completed application form from the applicant. It then sometimes entered into a dialogue with the applicant as to the chances of success of the application being declared admissible. This took the form of so-called warning letters or P2. After registration a decision by the Commission was required regarding the case. It could take one of four forms: a declaration of inadmissibility; a decision to strike the case off the list; a friendly settlement; or a report on the admissibility and merits of the case. Once it had adopted a report on the merits, the Commission could bring the case before the Court for a judgment.

Morvai notes that whether applicants 'came back' after the so-called warning letters largely depended upon what the bureaucrats wrote in their letters. She suggests these letters were generally very discouraging. To quote an example she gives:

> An old woman from a village, with difficult handwriting, describes in detail how she has been hurt and harassed by her neighbour for many years. Finally, the neighbour destroyed the fence adjoining their properties and moved it two metres into her land. She went to court, without a lawyer. She claimed that the judge never wanted to listen to her or her witnesses. The neighbour's lawyer talked incessantly in all proceedings before the domestic courts. She lost her case. I wrote a brief summary for my

superior, arguing that the dispute involved a property rights issue combined with due process complaints, and suggesting that I should request the necessary court documents and register the case.

My superior instructed me to send a P8 form letter, stating that 'no public authority can be held responsible for the alleged violation'. Fearing that I would be exposed as ignorant of the Law, I nonetheless risked the question, 'Is this not state action?' My superior was not looking as European as he did five minutes earlier. He was angry. 'We do not need much theory here, Krisztina. We have to do the Law and we have enough work with that'. I sent the P8 form letter to the applicant. She never came back. A pity she missed her classes on state action at Harvard Law School and therefore did not know how to argue against the P8.[54]

Until 2001, a case had to be registered before its admissibility could be considered.[55] Two out of three applications did not even pass the registration stage. To stress the incongruity of this situation, Morvai places Article 3 of the Statute of the Council of Europe and a few statistical figures as an epigraph to her article. The Article of the Statute refers to 'the enjoyment by all persons [within the jurisdiction of the members of the Council of Europe] of human rights and fundamental freedoms'. The statistical figures are for 1994: just under 10,000 individual applications were introduced that year; under 3,000 were registered, less than 600 were declared admissible. The discrepancy between the theory (all enjoy human rights) and the practice (a selected few are heard at Strasbourg) is the focus of Morvai's account. She writes:

As I began to work on the cases [assigned to me], I realized that most applications were submitted by poor, uneducated and really desperate people. Their letters were mostly handwritten and the applicants were not represented by lawyers. The first problem I faced followed from the fact that these submissions were not model legal briefs, or even homework done for legal writing assignments, but long, detailed testimonies of suffering, pain or 'just' allegations of injustice. The long description of facts is typically not followed by reference to a particular provision of the Convention, or where there is such a reference, it is hardly 'accurate'. In other words, people often tell their stories without translating them into the language of the Law, or if they do, the translation does not appear faithful to those who speak the Law. For example, many applicants characterize their suffering as 'degrading and inhuman treatment' under Art. 3 of the Convention just because they are treated inhumanely by bureaucrats, judges, husbands or neighbours. If they spoke the Law they would know that there is nothing unLawful in the fact that, for many people, life is a degrading experience and the world is a pretty inhuman place to live in.[56]

The use of the capital L throughout the text to refer to Law is obviously sarcastic. First, the separation of powers supposedly at the core of the notion of the rule of law did not exist in practice: bureaucrats, not judicial decision-makers, dealt with most of the applications (as they still do). Second, these bureaucrats enjoyed almost unrestricted discretionary power at the initial stage of the proceedings.

Morvai suggests that they used that power against the applicants 'who dare[d] to submit an application to the haven of European human rights without the services of a lawyer'.[57]

Morvai points to the construction of the poor applicant as the undeserving-of-attention Other, who fails to be recognized as a human being deserving full human rights:

> [The bureaucrats] tend not to understand why these people are not more educated, coherent or intelligent. Lack of education, lack of style and lack of means make most applicants the Other. Even a rich criminal is less of the Other than a poor applicant with any kind of complaint. The lawyer of the rich criminal (or sometimes the criminal himself) provides coherent submissions, straightforward legal analysis. He is stylish and easy to handle. He and we speak the same language. The whole thing is smooth and elegant. Sort of *European*. The bureaucracy constructs a legal issue of him and a procedural efficiency issue of the Other.[58]

That last sentence is the key to Morvai's conclusion:

> Dozens of applications arrive each week, from poor people, from disabled people, from battered wives . . . If you look at the published decisions of the European Commission and Court of Human Rights you do not see these people. You learn that there are some problems in Europe: civil proceedings are too lengthy, journalists cannot always say what they want, the due process rights of white collar defendants are often not fully observed.
>
> But on the whole, Europe is in good shape. It looks nice, smells nice, feels nice and it is cheerful. Just like Uncle Blaze.[59]

Uncle Blaze appears as an iconographic figure in Morvai's article. He had been a 'tall, good-looking, well-dressed, self-confident' man who had lived in France for fifteen years before returning to Hungary, where he happened to become a neighbour, invariably 'cheerful', to the Morvai family.[60] Morvai had looked up to him as a child; her mother called him 'a real *European*'. When Morvai proudly told him that she had a job at the Council of Europe, however, 'his smile [had been] somehow more mysterious than normally'.[61] Morvai does not explain what she means by this. She seems to intimate that Uncle Blaze was less of a dupe than she was about what was really happening in 'cheerful' Europe and had suspected what she would find behind the varnish of the rule of law and human rights for all.

Gaining procedural efficiency: At the cost of bureaucratic twitching?

Strasbourg judges and Registry lawyers who are aware of Morvai's piece tend to dismiss it as an unscientific account, either bordering on dishonesty or at least the result of an extreme response to an unhappy experience which had sprung from a clash of personalities between her and her superior. The testimony of people who had worked in the Commission contemparaneously with Morvai could indeed easily be gathered to build up the picture of an institution which was committed to handling, in as professional and compassionate a manner as possible, the applications which were arriving before it. This second reality is accurate enough. It does not, however, preclude the possibility that the reality reported by Morvai also existed *at the same time*.

Ignoring Morvai's 'truth', especially in the midst of a plethora of commentaries which praise the unique success of the Convention, is to ignore the basic fact that human rights law is not equipped to deal with human suffering. Whilst it could be retorted that expecting human rights law to be able to respond to human suffering may be asking too much from it, conversely, not expecting it to contribute to the alleviation of human suffering is also problematic, as it seems to throw the baby out with the bathwater.[62] A conundrum arises: the institution cannot function without the establishment of effective procedures which must therefore be regarded as necessary; however, these often appear disturbing from a humanistic point of view. The question becomes: what kind of judicial institution do we want and can it be established?

Many things have changed since Morvai worked at the Registry of the European Commission of Human Rights. Following a truly dramatic increase in individual applications and decisions by the Strasbourg institutions,[63] Protocol 11 came into force in November 1998. It signalled the creation of a new, permanent Court and the disappearance of the Commission after a transitional period of one year. Protocol 11 had been conceived in the 1980s, before the fall of the Berlin Wall was anticipated. The accession to the Council of Europe and the Convention of Central and Eastern European countries in the 1990s meant events had already superseded it by the time it came into force. A new Protocol was immediately discussed. As this new Protocol was negotiated, working methods within the Court were amended so as to 'streamline' procedures.[64] To mention three: warning letters were phased out (though a proposal to eliminate them altogether was defeated under pressure from Registry lawyers); fact-finding missions (previously carried out by the Commission) were apparently being avoided, leaving facts disputed, thus legally non-established, making it in turn more difficult for the Court to find serious violations of human rights in cases of alleged torture, disappearances and the burning of villages where facts are typically disputed;[65] decisions of inadmissibility adopted by committees of threes began to be recorded simply in minutes, with no document setting out the decision and its reasons. Protocol 14, signed in May 2004, is not yet in force. Perhaps its most controversial provision (amongst other welcome changes) is the addition of an 'elastic' condition of inadmissibility, namely, that 'the applicant has not suffered a significant disadvantage'.[66]

All these changes can be expected to make the Strasbourg procedure more efficient from a bureaucratic perspective, but they cannot be said to help make the system more responsive to the suffering expressed by the applicants.

It is commonly stated that the Court has become 'a victim of its own success'. In the run up to Protocol 14, numbers (of applications, decisions, pending cases, judgments) were constantly debated. The image of *Modern Times* where Charlie Chaplin's hands continue mechanically to twist in the gesture which they have repeatedly performed in the previous hours came to my mind as I was told of the 800 letters which arrived daily at Strasbourg. How were all these letters handled? I was shown closets full of documents as well as piles of papers on desks. Could the Strasbourg staff lose their composure and start to twitch as they sorted letters, affixed stamps and turned their attention to the next batch of documents?

The comparison between the Strasbourg Court and *Modern Times* should obviously not be pushed too far. The Court is not the mad machine of Chaplin's factory. Nonetheless, despite some reassuring signs within the Convention system, such as the fact that the Court has recommended, in respect of the initial stage of the proceedings, neither the abolition of the possibility of using any of the national official languages recognized in states belonging to the Council of Europe nor the creation of a requirement of being legally represented,[67] the procedural strains under which the Court functions throw into relief the question of how it can adequately respond to the individual applicants who come calling at its doors. The pertinence of this question is highlighted in the next section through the discussion of a 'lost' case which, given that it was declared inadmissible by a committee of three after 2002, never gave rise to a reasoned decision.[68]

Dragoi and the thousands and thousands of forgotten cases: The indecency of the Strasbourg procedures

Mr and Mrs Dragoi brought an application at Strasbourg on 13 May 2003 alleging that the Romanian government had violated the Convention.[69] Seventeen months later they received a letter consisting of five short paragraphs notifying them that the Court, in a committee of three judges (the French, Czech and San Marinese judges), had found that no violation was apparent from the documents which they had submitted.[70] They were told that this decision was final and that no appeal was possible to any other court; they were asked to understand that the Registry would not be in a position to give them any further information concerning the decision; they were finally informed that their file would be destroyed one year after they had received the said letter. Mr and Mrs Dragoi are far from alone in having received such a letter from Strasbourg. In 2004, just under 20,000 cases were declared inadmissible by committees of threes. These cases, which can only be traced at Strasbourg for a very limited period, will almost never find their way into a legal commentary. Quantitatively, however, they are far more representative of the Strasbourg case law than the comparatively few judgments which are, by contrast, the subject of abundant commentary.

Given that it follows a pro-forma, the letter Mr and Mrs Dragoi received in October 2004 contains no indication as to the circumstances which led them to apply to Strasbourg. To cut a long story short, the Dragois bought a flat in Bucharest in 1967. Five years later Mr Dragoi, then aged 52, came to Belgium and became the first violinist in the Philharmonic Orchestra of Antwerp. His wife, a doctor five years his junior, joined him in Belgium in 1981. They paid off the loan on their flat in 1983. Two years later, they formalized in writing their agreement that Mrs Dragoi's sister could occupy it as they continued to live in Belgium. In 1987, the flat was confiscated by the government following their failure to get the visas on their Romanian passports renewed – an oversight due to the fact that Mr Dragoi was then being treated for prostate cancer. After the fall of the Ceauşescu regime, Mr and Mrs Dragoi tried to regain the ownership of the flat. They turned to various administrative and judicial authorities, up to the Supreme Court; but to no avail. As these proceedings were taking place, Mrs Dragoi's sister acquired, in 1998, the ownership of the flat from a governmental agency. Mr and Mrs Dragoi believe that her success in getting the flat was helped by the fact that the Minister of Finances was the nephew of her husband. They think that corruption stained both the administrative and the judicial proceedings in Romania.

The day they received the letter notifying them of the Strasbourg decision, Mr Dragoi phoned me in despair – having got my number through a mutual friend. There was of course nothing I could do but to listen to his pain, disbelief and incomprehension. The octogenarian explained to me in a frail and indignant voice that this was the home to which he and his wife had always intended to return, that it was not so bad for him because he was an old man but that he was thinking of his wife. He wanted her to be able to finish her days in Bucharest. How could the Court have taken such a decision? Surely there was a mistake somewhere. And why some time in the previous year did it take so long for the reception of a document requested by the Court to be acknowledged? The Romanian member of the Registry who appeared to be in charge of their case could not be trusted. She was acting in the interests of the Romanian government; she must have failed to transmit some documents to the judges. And anyway why was the letter informing them of the decision written in Romanian, while they had specifically requested for the language of the procedure to be French? The person who signed it could not even have understood what he had signed. And why was he not a judge?

Mr and Mrs Dragoi could not explain to me which articles of the Convention they – or rather their lawyer (who preferred, however, not to sign their petition to Strasbourg) – argued had been violated. As it turns out, it was Article 6 of the Convention (fair trial) and Article 1 of Protocol 1 (peaceful enjoyment of possessions). It is easy to say, with the insight of the inadmissibility decision, that their application was misguided: the confiscation of their flat was an instantaneous act which took place when Romania was not party to the Convention, potentially rendering their claim inadmissible *ratione temporis*; their allegation that the Supreme Court had failed to act in an impartial way in proceedings which took place after the Convention came into force in respect of Romania could have appeared to lack substance. However, the lawyer they had consulted in Belgium, a prominent member of the Brussels Bar, had not told them their case was hopeless. He had admittedly informed them that over 90 per cent of applicants have their claims dismissed by the Court, as I saw in the relevant correspondence. But this warning was unlikely to deter the Dragois. They felt their case was now in the hands of an excellent lawyer who was known to get positive results even in difficult cases; they also believed that the European Court of Human Rights was bound to see and correct the injustice of their situation.

This is not the place to enter a debate on the legal or indeed moral merits of the Dragois' claims.[71] What I wish to stress is that, to them, the emotional stakes could hardly have been higher. They turned to the Strasbourg Court after a protracted judicial journey which had taken them all the way to the Romanian Supreme Court. In these circumstances, the letter they received from the Strasbourg Registry in October 2004 is nothing less than disgraceful. The language of the letter (Romanian), its signature by a member of the Registry unlikely to understand it (his name was Early), the fact that the case was clearly handled by Romanian lawyers (those at the Registry), the lack of reference to the facts of their case, the complete absence of legal reasoning – all this makes them wonder whether the judges who are said to have taken the decision really took it and, if so, whether they were given all the relevant details. Paradoxically the Strasbourg Court itself has endorsed, in decisions concerning Article 6, the adage according to which not only must justice be done, but it must also be seen to be done. In their conversation with me, Mr and Mrs Dragoi came back over and over again to a conspiracy theory. I reassured them, as no doubt their lawyer will have done too, that nothing as sordid as what they were imagining explained the outcome of their case. They thought I was naïve and did not understand how justice works in Romania. One must admit that the Strasbourg Court has not done much to try to alleviate their fears.

Does the Court feel justified in expediting cases by the fact that proceedings before it are free? Even if this position was acceptable (which I personally do not think it is) the proposition that proceedings at Strasbourg are free, though formally true, is somewhat risible: the costs of exhausting national remedies and of having an application to Strasbourg prepared are of course often enormous.[72] I saw a bill from the Dragois' Brussels lawyer of 1,950 euros, a large sum when one lives, as they do now, on social benefits; Mr Dragoi sold his two violins to pay some legal expenses. Though it would be ridiculous to expect the Strasbourg Court to manage to eliminate the financial implications of turning either to national or to international justice, it is just as stupid not to recognize that the Court is part of a system. In this context, we may have to ask whether human rights as practised at Strasbourg are for the very rich, the naïve, the intrepid, or those who have nothing to lose.[73]

The case of the Dragois (rather than the *Dragoi* case which, strictly speaking, does not exist) met the usual fate of applications to Strasbourg; namely, that of being declared inadmissible by a committee of three. In 2004 alone, another 19,391 cases ended in the same way.[74] It would not even be right to say that all these cases then sink into oblivion, as they have not made it into the limelight in the first place. The applicants are left without any explanation as to the reasons why their claim – the story of their life to Mr and Mrs Dragoi, and no doubt to other applicants too – is dismissed.

Once we understand the poignancy of inadmissibility decisions, we should not be surprised that applicants sometimes turn to violence. One Monday morning in April 2002, I arrived at the Court and found its door damaged. The shape of the shattering initially made me think bullets had been fired. Gossip in the corridors put me right: stones had been thrown at the door in the quietness of the previous Sunday afternoon by a 'mad woman', furious at the decision of the Court. Suffering and madness are indeed often related.

Must we not ask whether it might have been better for this unnamed woman, the Dragois, and countless other disappointed applicants, if the European Court of Human Rights had not existed? The resounding title of European Court of Human Rights promises much – far more than the Court can deliver. Flashy headlines in the media on magnificent victories and even sober commentaries by distinguished lawyers fail to make the public aware of the inherent limitations of the Convention system.

Would Marx have cared? Especially in its so-called 'scientific' version, Marxism is not renowned for paying attention to the individual. My reporting the plight of summarily dismissed applicants who were – supreme irony – fighting for the recovery of a property which they had started to lose under communism may appear to some very un-Marxist. As Ernest Bloch has noted, however, the fight for human dignity is in the cradle of Marxism; and man in its very centre.[75] I cannot believe that the plight of this octogenarian couple who cannot come to terms with what is, to them, an incomprehensible and irremediable loss, would have left Marx indifferent.

The legally-legal issues which retain the attention of the Court

The question arose during the negotiations which led to Protocol 14 as to whether the Court should exist primarily in order to answer individual applicants or in order to contribute to the creation of a constitutional understanding of human rights law. The debate, which received no unequivocal answer, could appear as a red-herring from a Marxian perspective. Marx insisted that the role fulfilled by an institution must be explored by looking not at what the institution says it does, but at what it actually does, thus deciphering – unmasking – what happens below the surface of ideology. The previous section highlighted the plight of the forgotten individuals who will never make it to the annals of the Court. The present section notes how the majority of cases which successfully clear the first hurdle of being declared admissible concern legal procedural issues, raising the question of what happens to potentially other important human rights issues, such as racism which, as the next section explains, hardly figures in the case law of the Court.

Remember the sarcastic words of Morvai:

> If you look at the published decisions of the European Commission and Court of Human Rights you . . . learn that there are some problems in Europe: civil proceedings are too lengthy, journalists cannot always say what they want, the due process rights of white collar defendants are often not fully observed.
>
> But on the whole, Europe is in good shape.[76]

This passage suggests that the Court is not tackling the real problems which beset Europe. Its underlying thesis could be phrased as follows: the Court is fulfilling its ideological function of appearing to protect the human rights of all within the jurisdiction of the Council of Europe, while in fact concentrating on the protection of the rights of the privileged and forgetting about everyone else (who thus become the 'Other'). The lawyer-backed applicant has a legal issue, which nicely fits the terms of the Convention, constructed out of his case; the poor, legally illiterate applicant is seen as posing a problem of procedural efficiency, of how best to eliminate him from the system.

Ever since the Court has started to function, the bulk of its case law has concerned Article 6 of the Convention, which guarantees a fair trial. Within this case law, most cases concern the failure by national authorities to provide a trial within a reasonable time. The figures are astounding. On the basis of the survey of activities produced by the Registry of the Court for the period between 1959–1990, I have counted that, out of the 272 principal issues which were raised in the 235 cases decided by the Court in these three decades, 143 concerned Article 6. Of these, 58 concerned lengthy proceedings. Ten years later, this trend had not changed.[77] Even if one puts aside the 'lengthy' proceedings cases, Article 6 remains today the provision most often argued before the Court, immediately followed by Article 5, on the legality of detention.[78]

It would be ridiculous to argue that Articles 6 and 5 do not concern crucial rights.[79] Failure by the Court to find these Articles applicable can have dramatic consequences; findings of violation of both Article 6 and Article 5 can be very important. A multitude of examples could be taken to make these two points. *Maaouia* v. *France* will be reviewed to illustrate the former;[80] *Sander* v. *United Kingdom*,[81] which happens to deal with racism, the subject of the next section, to illustrate the latter.

Maaouia was decided on 13 September 2000. The applicant was a Tunisian national who had been ordered to leave the territory of France on his release from prison, where he was serving a sentence for a criminal conviction. He tried to get this order lifted by instigating judicial proceedings. He complained at Strasbourg that these proceedings had been excessively lengthy. The Court, by fifteen votes to two, ruled that Article 6 did not apply. In its opinion, the contentious proceedings were neither of a criminal nor of a civil nature (as mentioned in Article 6), but of an administrative character (not mentioned in Article 6). Fair trial guarantees provided by Article 6 therefore did not apply to the type of 'administrative' proceedings which had been pursued by Mr Maaouia. This conclusion, to which Judge Loucaides and Judge Traja objected,[82] results in 'aliens' enjoying no procedural protection under Article 6 with respect to the way the judiciary deals with administrative orders related to expulsion and probably, by extension, residence permits as well as the granting and revocation of national citizenship.[83] It is open to serious criticism.[84]

Sander, decided on 9 May 2000, concerned the criminal trial by jury of the applicant, an Asian. During the trial, the national judge received a note from a juror to the effect that at least two jurors had made openly racist remarks and jokes. After having discussed the matter with counsel in chambers and hearing submissions in open court, the judge recalled the jury and reminded them of their oath. The jury confirmed in a letter to the judge their intention to reach a verdict without racial bias; in another letter, one juror apologised for the offence he might have caused, adding that he was in no way racially biased. The judge did not dismiss the jury, who proceeded to find the applicant guilty of conspiracy to defraud – while acquitting another co-accused, also of Asian origin.

The Strasbourg Court concluded that a lack of impartiality of the national court had not been established from a subjective point of view. However, the matter was different from an objective point of view. The judge's admonition could not be expected to change overnight the racist views of the juror who had admitted to having made racial comments. In this context the direction given by the judge to the jury could not dispel the reasonable fear of a lack of impartiality. The Court found that the judge should have taken a more robust approach towards ensuring the impartiality of the court. It decided, by a close majority of four votes to three, that there had been a violation of Article 6 (1). This is an important ruling, the more welcome since *Gregory* v. *United Kingdom*, decided on 25 February 1997,[85] the facts of which were similar, had gone in the opposite direction.[86]

Whilst the importance of Articles 5 and 6 cannot be overstated, their preponderance in the case law of the Court is nonetheless disturbing. I am reminded of a friend of mine, neither scholar nor lawyer, who had met a French lawyer during his holidays. The lawyer happened to have represented a number of applicants at Strasbourg. My friend commented: 'He was working on human rights – or rather he said he was working on human rights, but you know it was not really human rights. He was just trying to get clients out of jail.' My view is certainly not that criminals and prisoners do not deserve treatment fully compatible with human rights. However, if it turns out that the system is used by people whose life trajectory has happened to put them in fairly regular contact with lawyers, questions need to be raised about the kind of persons and issues that the system inadvertently – or not so inadvertently – leaves out. There is more to human rights than Article 5 and Article 6 issues.

That human rights go beyond issues of lawful detention and fair trial is borne out by the case law of the Court. Most prominently, the Court has a developed – if not uncontroversial – case law on Article 10 (freedom of expression), Article 8 (respect for private and family life), Article 1 of Protocol 1 (property), Article 3 (the prohibition of torture and inhumane and degrading treatment) and, increasingly, Article 2 (the right to life). However, other issues are conspicuously absent. For example, the Court has almost totally ignored racism – with *Sander* a noteworthy exception, but an exception nonetheless.

The persisting ignorance of racial discrimination by the Court: The false promise of *Nachova*

Racism is a problem which plagues Europe. However, 'leafing through the annals of the Court, an uninformed observer would be justified to conclude that, for over fifty years democratic Europe has been exempted of any suspicion of intolerance and xenophobia'.[87] These are not the words of an embittered former probationary lawyer, but of a judge of the Strasbourg Court who could not follow his colleagues in their refusal to confront racism in a case decided in 2002. It took the Court another two years before it eventually found for the first time that a state had been guilty of racial discrimination – in the case of *Nachova* v. *Bulgaria*, decided on 26 February 2004 by a Chamber.[88] This decision, however, turned out to be a false promise. On 8 June 2005, the Court, sitting in a Grand Chamber,[89] confirmed only part of the decision of the Chamber. The question therefore unfortunately remains: how can we explain the Court continually ignoring the problem of racism? Commentators tend to give technical answers to this question. These answers are reviewed in this section to show that they fail to provide a convincing explanation.

The relevant provision in the Convention is Article 14.[90] It provides: 'The enjoyment of the rights and freedoms set forth in this Convention shall be secured without discrimination on any ground such as sex, race, colour [etc.]'. In legal jargon, Article 14 is said not to be free-standing, which means that it must be used in conjunction with another provision of the Convention. In concrete terms, an applicant who wants to rely on it must claim that he or she has been discriminated against in his or her enjoyment of another right guaranteed by the Convention. While this obviously limits the opportunities for applicants to claim discrimination,[91] one would nonetheless expect that there are plenty of circumstances where people are racially discriminated against in their enjoyment – or lack of enjoyment – of the rights guaranteed by the Convention. The fact that Article 14 is not free-standing must be rejected as a plausible explanation for the paucity of its case law.

The fact that the Convention fails to produce a 'horizontal effect' does not provide a better explanation. It is true that the Convention is not meant to regulate what happens between private parties (horizontal effect), but only what happens between an individual and a state (who are considered to be in a vertical relationship). For example, if an employer is guilty of racial discrimination, the responsibility of the state is normally not engaged under Article 14 of the Convention, even if the complaint can be attached to another provision of the Convention; the only exception is if the behaviour of the state is itself reprehensible, for example because it has made it impossible for the victim of the racial discrimination to seek redress. In conclusion, the absence of horizontal effect limits the use of Article 14; it still does not explain the dearth of relevant case law.

One argument sometimes put forward is to the effect that the absence of case law on Article 14 is due to the fact that applicants themselves do not raise the issue of racial discrimination very often.[92] Admittedly the Court can only adjudicate on issues which are brought to it by – typically – individual applicants. However, the Court has repeatedly been asked, notably by Kurds in cases against Turkey and by Romas in cases against Bulgaria, to find that the abuses of human rights complained of were racially motivated. It took a Chamber decision (*Nachova*, partly overturned by a Grand Chamber) for the Court for the first time not to reject this type of claim.[93] Had an applicant been successful on this issue, it is likely that similar claims would have followed.[94] Presumably, if applicants and their lawyers fail to bring to Strasbourg an issue which is known to affect a substantial part of the population, it is because they feel there is no point in raising it.

Three major obstacles to making a successful claim under Article 14 have been erected by the Court. The first is that the applicant must prove his or her allegation 'beyond reasonable doubt'. In other words, the onus is on the applicant to prove that racial discrimination has occurred; even when he or she has made a prima facie case of discrimination, the burden of proof is not shifted to the state; thus, the state is not asked to satisfy the Court that its action was devoid of racial discrimination. As Judge Bonello explains in his dissenting opinion in *Anguelova* v. *Bulgaria*, decided on 13 June 2002, proof beyond reasonable doubt is typical of a criminal procedure where a person is presumed innocent until the state proves him or her guilty. Whilst such a standard of proof makes sense in the criminal context, it is virtually impossible for a plaintiff who alleges racial discrimination to attain. In the words of Bonello, it is in this matter 'as unreal as it is unrealistic and unrealisable'; it becomes 'a standard that only serves to ensure that human rights harm, however flaunted and forbidding, remains unharmed'.[95] For the Maltese judge, it is the more objectionable since such a standard is not even mandated by the Convention, but imposed by the Court, of its own accord.[96] In *Nachova*, a Chamber of the Court finally took a different approach towards the standard of proof required, but it was overruled on this point by the Grand Chamber.

A second difficulty which can be attributed to the Court concerns the absence of a concept of 'indirect' discrimination in European human rights law. Illegal direct discrimination occurs when a person is directly discriminated against on a prohibited ground – typically race or sex. This is what happened in the *Anguelova* case. Ms Anguelova's son had been pursued and ill-treated by the Bulgarian police, resulting in his death. Presumably, *but for* the fact that he was a Roma, this would not have happened. By contrast, indirect discrimination occurs when prima facie non-discriminatory rules or practices adversely and disproportionately affect members of a particular group. For example, in *Abdulazis, Cabales and Balkandali* v. *United Kingdom*, decided on 28 May 1985,[97] the applicants were women of foreign nationality who could not be joined by their husbands. They argued that the Immigration Rules in force were contrary to Article 14 in that their main effect was to prevent immigration from the New Commonwealth and Pakistan so as to keep the number of coloured immigrants down. They did not convince the Court. The Court remains unlikely to accept this type of reasoning even today, because it relies on statistical or sociological evidence for establishing the discrimination, which does not sit well with the standard of proof beyond reasonable doubt which it favours, as we have seen. As there are many cases of racial discrimination which happen indirectly, this is a serious setback. The refusal to embrace the concept of indirect discrimination is entirely the making of the Court.

The third reason why the case law on Article 14 is underdeveloped is again a matter of policy by the Court. This is that, quite often, the Court declares that having found a violation of a particular provision of the Convention, it is unnecessary for it to examine the merits of a second allegation, related to the violation of another provision. Such a declaration is invariably made when applicants allege a violation of Article 14.[98] The refusal to look at further complaints is justified when it is clear that the applicant has tried every possible line of argument in the hope that at least one would succeed. It is, however, utterly unjustified when the left-unexamined allegation concerns racial discrimination. Having that allegation taken seriously is important for the applicant. Presumably Ms Anguelova wanted it to be recognized both that the Bulgarian authorities were responsible for the death of her son (which the Court did) and that his ill-treatment had been racially motivated (which the Court did not, to Judge Bonello's dismay). From the perspective of a human rights European policy, the limited assessment of the Court is also unsatisfactory: it lets states off the hook on important issues which remain as a result ignored within the Convention system and by the defendant state. Given that this system is supposed to set the prevailing standards in Europe, the failure is unfortunate, to say the least.

Given the past record of the Court on Article 14, the ruling of its First Section in *Nachova and Others* v. *Bulgaria*, decided on 16 February 2004, was extremely welcome.[99] The applicants in this case were relatives of two young men of Roma origin who had been killed by the military police. The two twenty-one-year olds, conscripts in the army, had escaped from a construction site where they had been brought for work. The commanding officer dispatched four military police officers to locate and arrest them. Having found them (which had not been difficult given that they had returned to their home) the officers fired fatal shots in the course of their arrest. The victims were clearly unarmed; they had been standing by a fence which they may have thought of climbing to escape, although one had a bullet in his chest, rather than his back, suggesting he might have decided to surrender. The Court had no difficulty finding that the use of lethal force had not been 'absolutely necessary' as provided by Article 2 of the Convention. This was not the first ruling of this kind. What was new is that the Court went on to find a violation of Article 14.

The Court had received third-party comments from the European Roma Rights Centre; it also referred to reports of international organizations (both governmental and not) on the situation of Roma in Europe and, in particular, Bulgaria. As well as commenting upon the general situation, the applicants remarked that the bullets had been fired in an inhabited compound, involving a risk to life that would probably have not been taken in a non-Roma area;[100] one witness, a bystander who was there as the events were unfolding, had reported that the major in charge had verbally abused him, shouting, 'You damn Gypsies'.[101] The Court first reproved the domestic authorities for having 'failed in their duty under Article 14 of the Convention, taken together with Article 2, to take all possible steps to establish whether or not discriminatory attitudes may have played a role in [the] events'.[102] It then proceeded to examine the allegation of a violation of Article 14 from a substantive – as opposed to procedural – point of view. On this issue, the Court stated:

> [I]t has become an established view in Europe[103] that effective implementation of the prohibition of discrimination requires the use of specific measures that take into account the difficulties involved in proving discrimination . . . [T]he Court considers that in cases where the authorities have not pursued lines of inquiry that were clearly warranted . . . it may, when examining complaints under Article 14 of the Convention, draw negative inferences or shift the burden of proof to the respondent Government.[104]

Having done this, the Court unanimously found yet again a violation of Article 14, taken together with Article 2, of the Convention – this time on its substantive aspect.

The Bulgarian Government successfully requested for the case to be referred to a Grand Chamber. The Court, sitting in a Grand Chamber, confirmed the finding of violation in respect of the two limbs (substantive and procedural) of Article 2. It went on to find that the failure by the authorities to investigate the 'possible racist overtones in the events that led to the death of [Mr Angelov and Mr Petkov]' resulted in a 'violation of Article 14 of the Convention taken together with Article 2 in its procedural aspect'.[105] However, the identification of a duty for the authorities 'to investigate the existence of a *possible* link between racist attitudes and an act of violence'[106] fell short of the reversal in the burden of proof which had been accepted by the Chamber. On this front, the Grand Chamber asserted that it could not 'lose sight of the fact that its sole concern is to ascertain whether *in the case at hand* the killing [of the two men] was motivated by racism'.[107] For the majority of the judges of the Grand Chamber, it was 'not possible to speculate on whether or not [the two men's] Roma origin had any bearing on the officers' perception of them'.[108] According to them, it could not be excluded that the man who had fired the shots 'was simply adhering strictly to the regulations [condemned by the Court under Article 2] and would have acted as he did in any similar context, regardless of the ethnicity of the fugitives'; there was 'nothing to suggest that [he] would not have used his weapon in a non-Roma neighbourhood'.[109] In other words, 'the Court [did] not consider that it [had] been *established* that racist attitudes played a role in Mr Angelov's and Mr Petkov's deaths'.[110] The finding that there had been 'no violation of Article 14 of the Convention taken in conjunction with Article 2 of the Convention in respect of the allegation that the events leading to the death of Mr Angelov and Mr Petkov constituted an act of racial violence' was adopted by eleven votes to six.

Even if the unanimous finding by the Grand Chamber of a violation of Article 14 taken in conjunction with Article 2 in respect of the authorities' failure to *investigate* possible racist motives is welcome,[111] it remains that the approach of the Court in this area lacks vigour. This timidity is congruent with a context where even mentioning the word 'racism' has been, for a long time, beyond the Court. A search in the Court's website[112] indicates that the word made its first appearance in the Strasbourg case law in *Jersild*, a judgment of 1994 which could hardly be said to have adopted a decisive stance against racism, as we have seen.[113] Admittedly, the *Sander* judgment of 2000, reviewed in the previous section, referred to 'the importance attached by all Contracting States to the need to combat racism'. This view was confirmed by the Grand Chamber in *Nachova*.[114] Given the Court's 'surprisingly limited'[115] record on the issue, however, these could sound like rather empty words.

Two decades ago, Peter Fitzpatrick wrote an article which argued that 'racism is compatible with and even integral to law'.[116] He took the example of the British Race Relations Act 1976: while the Act was supposed to combat racism, it did nothing against it – notably because of the applicable rules of evidence. Fitzpatrick argued that 'the very foundational principles of law as liberal legality import racism into law, those principles of equality and universality which stand in their terms opposed to racism'.[117] To rephrase this statement in simple terms: law says it is against racism, in fact it is only too happy to endorse it. Fitzpatrick referred to the Marxist view which finds capitalism and racism 'compatible, even symbiotic'.[118] This perspective expects oppression in society to be legitimized by law. Applying this to the law of the European Convention, the fact that the Court has found ways, technical and thus apparently (but only apparently) neutral, which have ensured that racism in Europe remains the social thread that it has long been, is not surprising.

The capitalist foundation of the ECHR: *Messochoritis* and the whole case law

Examined in a Marxist light, the Convention system suddenly ceases to appear as the beautiful achievement which it is generally heralded as being. It is revealed instead as a legal system which sustains a skewed political system, which itself goes hand in hand with a deeply oppressive economic system. In short, the Convention participates in capitalism, in the worst sense of the term.

The institutions of the state, law and private property are central to capitalism and liberalism – two 'isms' which at least one kind of Marxism regards as hardly dissociable.[119] Marx did not like these institutions; he had hoped that they would have become superfluous in the communist society which he expected to succeed capitalist society. In fact, they are still with us. Every judgment of the Court can be seen as supporting them. *Messochoritis* v. *Greece*, decided on 12 April 2001,[120] is one among many, many cases in point.

The case emerged after the Greek state refused to pay the applicant for works he had carried out in a military airport, on the order of the relevant State department but outside the terms of the contract signed with the State. After a three-year long judicial procedure, a court in Athens recognized the claim of the applicant and ordered the state to pay him. The State appealed, triggering a procedure which lasted for over seven years. The applicant was eventually paid in 1999. He complained at Strasbourg that the judicial resolution of his case had taken too long. The Court found that the overall length of the administrative proceedings indeed constituted a violation of Article 6 (1) of the Convention. *Messochoritis*, involving as it does a contract, money, the military and courts, illustrates the symbiosis which exists between the Court and a social organization which Marx would have abhorred.

The judgment forces us to consider what is meant by 'human rights'. In this case, the Court found that there had been a violation of the Convention. Most people, however, would probably fail to see a violation of human rights in the facts of the case. This is to say that a gap exists between the sense we intuitively attribute to the expression 'human rights violation' and the meaning the term receives once human rights have been judicially institutionalized. Marx would not have been surprised by the discrepancy. On the contrary, he would have seen it as the *raison d'être* of human rights: making people believe they are free while the system they support is alienating.

Human emancipation: Found neither in human rights nor, of course, in the Stalinist gulag

The anthropologist Talal Asad urges us today to 'examine critically the assumption that . . . human rights always lead in an emancipatory direction, that they enable subjects to move beyond controlling power into the realm of freedom'.[121]

Rejecting the idea that human rights are 'simply a persuasive and reasoned language that comes down from a transcendent sphere to protect and redeem individuals', he posits instead that the language of human rights 'articulates inequalities in social life'.[122] This makes Asad doubt that the human rights project, part and parcel of modernity, could bring about 'practical equality and an end to all suffering'.[123] His hardly disguised intimation is that we should look beyond human rights for real emancipation.

Marx, to whom Asad specifically refers,[124] would have concurred with this conclusion. He conceived of the religious state, the political state and human emancipation as three historical stages due to succeed each other in linear progression. In world historical terms, the political state and its concomitant human rights thus represented a step in the right direction;[125] but they were only a step. What Marx wanted was true emancipation. By this he meant the establishment of a society where man would be able to 'take the abstract citizen back into himself and . . . become a species-being', recognizing his own forces as social forces.[126]

History has shown that Marx's belief that the institutions of state, law and property would wither away was ridiculously naïve. His utopia of communal society rested on the assumption that power would cease to be a force to be reckoned with.[127] But power is everywhere, as Michel Foucault has masterfully demonstrated.[128] Not surprisingly, given the utopian character of his project, Marx failed to indicate anywhere in his work how the transformation from bourgeois man to species-being would be achieved. Though he mentioned that there would be 'a political transition period in which the state [could] be nothing but the revolutionary dictatorship of the proletariat',[129] he never explained in detail how communist society would come about and how it would work.

Taken as a political programme, Marx's writings were at best hollow, at worst dangerous. Had they had little impact, this would not have mattered much.[130] But Marx, who died in 1883, inspired revolutions and dictatorships throughout the world, starting in 1917 in what became the Soviet Union. The most appalling acts were committed in the twentieth century in the name of Marxism and communism. Marx would never have condoned them. Even though his liberal detractors concede this, they still tend to blame him for not having seen that human rights were valuable, in their own right.[131] They maintain that Marx was wrong to suggest that rights could be disposed of. As Robert Fine puts it, a standard Marxist view became that '[i]f civil liberties were merely an illusion obscuring the harsh realities of wage slavery, then the only significance of their loss would be to clarify the class struggle'.[132]

I find it disingenuous to criticize Marx for ideas that have been used in a way that he could not have imagined (even if he referred to the dictatorship of the proletariat) and to hold him partly if unwillingly responsible for the Stalinist gulag. It is difficult to think that Marx would not have wanted to be more forthcoming about what the idea of rights offered, had he had the benefit of hindsight. This is indeed what self-declared Marxists have done in the 1970s and

1980s, such as E. P. Thompson in Britain and Claude Lefort in France, when it became clear to them that the abuses of the Stalinist regime had to be denounced in no uncertain terms.

Thompson and Lefort: A valuable rule of law even in the face of objectionable legal rules

In 1975 the British historian E. P. Thompson published *Whigs and Hunters*,[133] a study of the 'Black Act'. This piece of legislation was adopted in 1723 in the wake of the enclosure laws which had started to transform, from the fifteenth century, common lands into private lands, thus depriving peasants from the hunting and foraging rights they had historically enjoyed. The Black Act, named after the rebels who blackened their faces in disguise, criminalized infringements of these enclosures laws. Law had thus turned free-born Englishmen into trespassers and criminals who could be sentenced to death. Thompson showed how the law was used to serve the interests of the propertied class against the peasantry; he referred to the Act as 'a form of state-sponsored Terror'.[134] But he refrained from inferring that 'law is an instrument of brute force by which the ruling class consolidates and reinforces its hegemony'.[135] This would have been the 'conventional Marxian conclusion'.[136] In a famous afterword, Thompson stated instead that the rule of law is an 'unqualified human good'.[137]

Daniel Cole stresses that this afterword was motivated by Thompson's wish to make clear that he rejected, at the end of his study, the pessimistic view that law does not matter.[138] Incidentally, of course, this view would have made the study redundant. As Thompson remarked, '[why spend] three years trying to find out what could, in its essential structures, have been known without any investigation at all?'[139] More importantly the view was not tenable. Thompson, who had resigned his membership of the Communist Party in 1956 following his disturbing experience of the Soviet regime,[140] wrote in the 1975 afterword:

> [T]here is a very large difference, which twentieth-century experience ought to have made clear even to the most exalted thinker, between arbitrary extra-legal power and the rule of law . . . The rhetoric and the rules of a society are something a great deal more than sham. In the same moment they may modify, in profound ways, the behaviour of the powerful, and mystify the powerless. They may disguise the true realities of power, but, at the same time, they may curb that power and check its intrusions.[141]

He continued, in a passage which remains eminently cogent at the beginning of the twenty-first century:

> To deny or belittle [the unqualified good of the rule of law] is, in this dangerous century when the resources and pretentions [sic] of power continue to enlarge, a desperate error of intellectual abstraction. More than this, it is a self-fulfilling error,

which encourages us to give up the struggle against bad laws and class-bound procedures, and to disarm ourselves before power. It is to throw away a whole inheritance of struggle *about* law, and within the forms of law, whose continuity can never be fractured without bringing men and women into immediate danger.[142]

Thompson talked of 'the notion of the regulation and reconciliation of conflicts through the rule of law' as 'a cultural achievement of universal significance'.[143] In a statement that perfectly applies to the handling of the 'War on Terror' by the American and British governments, he exclaimed:

[W]e feel contempt for men whose practice [belies] the resounding rhetoric of the age. But we feel contempt not because we are contemptuous of the notion of a just and equitable law but because this notion has been betrayed by its own professors . . . If I judge the Black Act to be atrocious, this is not only from some standpoint in natural justice, and not only from the standpoint of those whom the Act oppressed, but also according to some ideal notion of the standards to which 'the law', as regulator of human conflicts of interest, ought to attain.[144]

'Ideal notions of what law might be' had developed at a particular 'cultural moment'. This was an achievement which Thompson urged us to cherish.

Thompson's argument was echoed in Lefort's 1979 essay on 'Politics and Human Rights' (which I have already quoted above).[145] The French thinker wanted to understand what distinguished and preserved democracy from totalitarianism. Like Thompson, he had been shocked by what was happening in the Soviet Union.[146] The experience and efforts of dissidents throughout the socialist states made it clear to him that human rights were not merely 'formal, intended to conceal a system of domination' but that they could also 'embody a real struggle against oppression'.[147] It was therefore crucial to grasp the meaning of the 'historical mutation' which assigned limits to power and fully recognized right as existing outside power.[148] In Lefort's view, the separation between power and rights, achieved in the eighteenth century, and the representation of right 'as something which is ineffaceably external to power' constituted an 'unprecedented event'.[149] Like Thompson, he thought that the rule of law was (a) extremely valuable and (b) an achievement that could not be taken for granted.

He made it clear that his observations did not exempt law from criticism:

[T]hese remarks are not intended to call into question the justified criticism brought against the actual application of human rights, or . . . the laws that are supposed to be based on them . . . As long as they are made at the factual level, these criticisms are valid, whether they denounce the vices of legislation . . . or the iniquities in the system of justice . . . or whether they dismantle the mechanisms by which opinion is manipulated or fabricated.[150]

At the same time, 'the symbolic dimension of human rights' had to be acknowledged and the benefit of it having become 'a constitutive element of [democratic] political society' recognized and valued.[151]

Thompson no doubt would have agreed, even though some commentators misunderstood him, 'wrongly supposing that [his] avowal of the Rule of Law [committed] him to defending the existing legal (and economic) order'.[152] Cole persuasively rebuts this interpretation. He summarizes Thompson's conception of the Rule of Law as follows:

> [T]he Rule of Law is an 'unqualified good' to the extent it (actually) limits ruling powers by requiring equal application of the legal rules to rich and poor, the powerful and powerless. The Rule of Law is by no means *sufficient* to ensure just legal rules or a just society in general, but it is a necessary condition in that its opposite – unbridled power – ensures injustice.[153]

Thompson's aim was to combine 'reverence for the Rule of Law and distrust of legal rules'.[154]

Ipek: Law is not just a sham

This section uses one case decided by the Strasbourg Court on 17 February 2004, *Ipek* v. *Turkey*,[155] to illustrate the value of the rule of law. I have laboured the point in this chapter that the privileged person who has access to a lawyer is at an advantage when it comes to accessing the European Convention system. I now want to counterbalance this argument by observing that the fact that the system *is* in principle open to everyone has the practical consequence that even the poor and illiterate sometimes manage to rely upon it.[156]

On the morning of 18 May 1994, armed soldiers arrived at the hamlet of Dalherezi, near the village of Türeli, in the province of Diyarkabir, then the scene of fierce fighting between the PKK and the security forces, in Turkey. The soldiers ordered the inhabitants to leave their homes and took them to the school on the outskirts of the hamlet. They separated the men from the women and children; they set the houses of the hamlet on fire. Once they had finished, they selected at random six young men to carry their gear back to the *rendez-vous* where they were to be picked up. They came back in the afternoon, burning any house which remained standing and threatening the villagers with violence if they extinguished the fires. It appeared later that the six young men had been taken away to a military establishment. The following morning, three were released, unharmed; three were never seen again.

The foregoing is a summary of what the Court established in the *Ipek* judgment.[157] The Court discounted the Turkish Government's suggestion that the PKK could have destroyed the hamlet and abducted the young men as acts of reprisals for refusal to assist them.[158] Rejecting the Government's blunt denial of any responsibility for these events, the Court found, unanimously, that Turkey had violated the following provisions of the Convention: Article 2 (right to life) in both its procedural and substantive strands, Article 3 (prohibition of inhuman treatment),[159] Article 5 (right to freedom), Article 13 (right to a remedy), as well as Article 1 of Protocol 1 (right to the peaceful enjoyment of possessions).

The applicant in this case was the father of two of the young men who disappeared. Anything but an affluent *bourgeois*, he was a shepherd living in humble conditions. Someone who attended the fact-finding mission conducted at Ankara by the Court told me: 'it was as if he had sprung right from the Old Testament'. Mr Ipek, who the Court mentioned came from 'a simple and unsophisticated background',[160] is not the kind of person that Morvai's account would lead us to expect to win anything at Strasbourg. Admittedly, it is unlikely that he would have managed to pursue his case without the involvement of the Kurdish Human Rights Project established in London.[161] This does not detract from the fact that the theoretical opening of the Convention system allows, if the conditions are right, its practical opening.

This is not to suggest that cases like *Ipek* eliminate the need to criticize the law of the Convention or the case law of the Court. Even *Ipek* is not unproblematic. Three areas of concern can be mentioned. First, the application was lodged on 18 November 1994 but it was not declared admissible until 14 May 2002, with the fact-finding mission taking place as late as November 2002. Surely the interval of eight years is not conducive to justice, both because the facts are more and more difficult to establish as time goes by and because the period during which the applicant had to wait to see his case processed was inordinately long, especially in the light of the seriousness of his complaint. Second, the Court disposed of his allegation that he and his sons had been discriminated against on the ground of their Kurdish origin, in violation of Article 14 of the Convention, in just two sentences:

> The Court has examined the applicant's allegation. However, it finds that no violation of this provision can be established on the basis of the evidence before it.[162]

Nachova v. *Bulgaria*, adopted the day before by a Chamber of the Court from a different Section[163] and admittedly overruled by a Grand Chamber as discussed above, indirectly highlights the shortcomings of this reasoning. More generally, it is difficult to think that the refusal by the Court to touch upon the real causes of the violations of the Convention does anything to promote a resolution of the conflict. Third, the way the Court arrives at a sum in terms of pecuniary and non-pecuniary damages, as well as costs and expenses, seems rather arbitrary. While this point is not as important as the previous two, the incapacity of the Court to achieve consistency and transparency in this field can not be ignored, for, in the long term, it is damaging to its reputation and perhaps even to its integrity.

The criticisms I have levied against the *Ipek* judgment in this section, and against various aspects of the Strasbourg system elsewhere, show that law matters. There would be no point in voicing them if there was no hope that the Court might change its practice and/or reasoning. This hope is generated by a belief, however cautious, in the benefits of law. Law is a sham, assuredly, but it is not just a sham.

Conclusion

Marx did not *believe* in human rights. He observed that their emancipatory potential was severely limited by the fact that they reflected the capitalist economy in which they were inscribed. He urged us to be aware of their ideological function. He warned us that not everyone benefited from them and that, in that sense, they were not universal.[164]

In application of this teaching, this chapter has aimed at going below the surface of what is generally said about the European Convention system, paying particular attention to the proposition that the system is open to all who fall within its jurisdiction. This proposition is widely accepted. It is formally true. In practice, however, economic and social barriers exist which make it difficult to take it at face value.

This conclusion has been supported by turning to materials, such as inadmissibility decisions, which are generally ignored in legal commentaries and by highlighting the saliency of issues, such as racism, which hardly figure in the Strasbourg case law. Significantly no resort has been made to judges' separate opinions in order to illustrate the way Marxian insights remain pertinent today. This is in stark contrast with the situation in the previous two chapters where a statist and a consequentialist reasoning were shown to have made some inroad in the reasoning of Judges Costa and Loucaides, respectively.

It would of course have been extremely surprising to find that one of the Strasbourg judges had strong Marxist inclinations. However, Marxism need not be seen as entirely subversive. Marx was ambivalent towards human rights rather than fiercely critical of them. While he put forward the idea that the rights of man were the rights of selfish man, he also held that their recognition in the eighteenth century had marked progress from feudalism. Put in simplistic terms: better have human rights than no rights at all in a society that is not communist – communist in Marx's sense of the word.

This view has found an expression in the argument, put forward in the twentieth century by thinkers who declared themselves to be Marxist, that the rule of law is a creation which must be cherished. Tampering with the rule of law and the idea of human rights in the absence of a more effective emancipatory project is indeed dangerous. At the same time, however, we must have the intellectual and moral honesty to confront the inherent limitations of the human rights concept and the emancipatory model it purports to embody.

Notes

1 This essay has been reproduced in many collections. I have used: Karl Marx, 'On the Jewish Question', in David McLellan, *Karl Marx: Selected Writings* (2nd edn, Oxford: Oxford University Press, 2000) 46–64. The statement put at the head of this chapter appears at 60.

2 The account presented in this paragraph is based on David McLellan, *Marx Before Marxism* (London: Macmillan, 1980), at 1–4 and 24–30.

3 On possible responses to this fact, see Wendy Brown, 'Rights and identity in late modernity: Revisiting the "Jewish Question"', in Austin Sarat and Thomas R. Kearns (eds.), *Identities, Politics and Rights* (Ann Arbor: University of Michigan Press, 1997) 85–130, at 91–2, including note 10.

4 Though Germany was then merely a name used to denote a group of states which shared past membership of the Holy Roman Empire as well as a language, and which suffered from economic underdevelopment compared with France and England.

5 McLellan, *Marx*, at 133.

6 Michael Rosen, 'Karl Marx (1818–83)', *Concise Routledge Encyclopedia of Philosophy* (London: Routledge, 2000) 528–9, at 528.

7 Quoted in Marx, 'Jewish Question', at 56.

8 Ibid.

9 'The German Jews seek emancipation. What sort of emancipation do they want? Civil, political emancipation. Bruno Bauer answers them: No one in Germany is politically emancipated. We ourselves are not free. How then could we liberate you? You Jews are egoists if you demand a special emancipation for yourselves as Jews. You ought to work as Germans for the political emancipation of Germany, and as men for the emancipation of mankind, and consider your particular sort of oppression and ignominy not as an exception to the rule but rather as a confirmation of it': ibid., at 46–7.

10 Ibid., at 51.

11 Marx cites a source reporting that 'people in the U.S. do not believe that a man without religion can be an honest man' and concludes: 'North America is the land of religiosity par excellence': ibid., at 50–1, see also 59.

12 Ibid., at 51.

13 'We say to them [the Jews]: because you can be politically emancipated without completely and consistently abandoning Judaism, this means that political emancipation itself is not human emancipation': ibid., at 58.

14 Ibid., at 53, see also 57.

15 Ibid., at 60.

16 Ibid., at 60–1.

17 Ibid., at 61.

18 Neil Stammers remarks to me that the opposite view, according to which the civil sphere should be at the service of the political sphere, plants the seeds of totalitarianism. While this is a pertinent observation, it distorts in my view the nature of the communal interest which Marx would have wanted to guide humanity.

19 As Costas Douzinas remarks, '[f]or Marx, the "man" of the rights, rather than being an empty vessel without determination, and therefore unreal, non existent, is too full of [white, *bourgeois*] substance': *The End of Human Rights: Critical Legal Thought at the Turn of the Century* (Oxford: Hart, 2000), at 100.

20 Marx, 'Jewish Question', at 61.

21 As noted in Chapter 2.

22 For a critique of the way the judicialization of the rights discourse in the United States – but in an analysis which has a wider resonance – fails to induce responsible and committed citizens, see Mary Ann Glendon, *Rights Talk and the Impoverishment of Political Discourse* (New York: Free Press, 1991).

23 *Casado Coca* v. *Spain*, 24 February 1994, Series A, No. 285-A, (1994) 18 EHRR 1

24 *Janowski* v. *Poland*, 21 January 1999, ECHR 1999-I, (2000) 29 EHRR 705

25 Brown, 'Rights and Identity', at 107. In a less theoretical but not wholly dissimilar vein, Aileen McColgan explains the aim of her book *Women under the Law* as follows: 'to illustrate the perils of entrenched rights by examining their impact upon women [though for] "women" could be substituted any group of relatively disadvantaged people, the degree and type of danger posed by such rights varying with the nature of the disadvantage': Aileen McColgan, *Women under the Law: The False Promise of Human Rights* (Harlow: Longman, 2000), at 2. McColgan specifically warns against the risk that 'the advantaged may use their "rights" further to damage the position of the disadvantaged': ibid., at 6. This and other risks (including the non accountability of the judiciary) lead her 'to challenge the view held by most people of a liberal bent, as well as by many who would consider themselves radical, that "rights" are, in general, a "good thing"': ibid., at 1.

26 My legal training, in Belgium, may explain why I react in the way I do to this case. In Belgium lawyers cannot advertise their services either. On the difficulty of taking an objective view on what ultimately are cultural practices, see Chapter 6.

27 Marie-Bénédicte Dembour and Magda Krzyżanowska-Mierzewska, 'Ten years on: The voluminous and interesting Polish case law' 2004 *European Human Rights Law Review* 517–43, at 534–5.

28 Etienne Balibar, *Masses, Classes, Ideas: Studies on Politics and Philosophy Before and After Marx*, transl. by James Swenson (New York: Routledge, 1994), at 44.

29 Ibid., at 45 and 46, emphasis in the original. This leads Balibar to invent the concept of 'equaliberty' to render his idea that equality is the exact measure of freedom, and vice versa: one is present/absent in society exactly to the extent that the other one is: ibid., at 46–8. Thus, the revolutionaries of 1789 were fighting against two adversaries and two principles *at once*: *absolutism*, which appears as the negation of freedom ("the royal will is law") and *privileges*, which appear as the negation of equality ("might makes right"): ibid., at 47.

30 Claude Lefort, 'Politics and Human Rights', in Claude Lefort, *The Political Forms of Modern Society: Bureaucracy, Democracy, Totalitarianism*, ed. and introd. by John B. Thompson (Cambridge, Mass.: MIT Press, 1986) 239–72, at 248. This is the translation of an essay originally published under the title 'Droits de l'homme et politique', in Claude Lefort, *L'invention démocratique: Les limites de la domination totalitaire* (Paris: Fayard, 1981) 45–83. My references are to Thompson's edition unless otherwise indicated.

31 Ibid., at 250.

32 Ibid., at 251.

33 *Sunday Times* v. *United Kingdom (No. 1)*, 26 April 1979, Series A, No. 30, (1979–1980) 2 EHRR 245.

34 Mark Jordan, *Doing the Rights Thing: The Not So Difficult Guide to the Human Rights Act 1988 and the Law of the European Convention on Human Rights* (Haywards Heath: EOS Education, 2001), at 6.33. Chronologically, this was the twenty-third judgment of the European Court of Human Rights.

35 Examples include *Müller and Others* v. *Switzerland*, 24 May 1988, Series A, No. 133, (1991) 13 EHRR 212; *Otto-Preminger-Institut* v. *Austria*, 20 September 1994, Series A, No. 295-A, (1995) 19 EHRR 34; *Wingrove* v. *United Kingdom*, 25 November 1996, RJD 1996-V, (1997) 24 EHRR 1. For a defence of this approach, see Paul Mahoney,

'Universality versus subsidiarity in the Strasbourg case law on free speech: Explaining some recent judgments' (1997) *European Human Rights Law Review* 364–79. For a critical response, which encompasses the use of the margin of appreciation by the Court and goes to the heart of the Convention system, see Lord Lester of Herne Hill, 'Universality versus subsidiarity: A reply' (1998) *European Human Rights Law Review*, 73–81.

36 So it may not have the courage to run some stories: Herdís Thorgeirsdóttir, 'Self-censorship among journalists: A (moral) wrong or a violation of ECHR law?' (2004) *European Human Rights Law Review* 383–99.

37 Para. 32 of the judgment.

38 Alvin W. Gouldner, *The Two Marxisms: Contradictions and Anomalies in the Development of Theory* (London: Macmillan, 1980).

39 On the merits of the Marxian claim to science, see David M. Walker, *Marx, Methodology and Science: Marx's Science of Politics* (Aldershot: Ashgate, 2001).

40 Rosen, 'Marx', at 529. Walker insists, however, that Marx did not view history's necessary purpose as the attainment of communism, as if a movement towards the goal of socialism was inevitable. Such determinism, according to Walker, has wrongly been imputed to Marxism: Walker, *Marx*, at 66.

41 Ibid., at 8.

42 Ibid. For a similar view, see McLellan, *Marx*, at 214–20; Gerald Allan Cohen, *History, Labour and Freedom: Themes from Marx* (Oxford: Clarendon, 1988); Upendra Baxi, *Marx, Law, and Justice: Indian Perspectives* (Bombay: N.M. Tripathi, 1993).

43 Quoted in Walker, *Marx*, at 34.

44 Ibid., at 72.

45 Ibid., at 40. For a general discussion of the term 'materialism' in philosophical thought: ibid., at 57–9.

46 Marx himself did not use the phrase 'historical materialism'.

47 Walker, *Marx*, at 66–7.

48 Ibid., at 67.

49 For McLellan, alienation is the crucial theme which runs throughout the whole of Marx's writings, even if it has been claimed that Marx had abandoned the concept in his later work: McLellan, *Marx*, at 216–18.

50 '[F]or Marx, human rights were the prime example of ideology of their time': Douzinas, *End of Human Rights*, at 163.

51 'Marx's analysis in the "Jewish Question" is neither a moral critique nor an ontological claim about the "nature of rights". Rather, Marx's characterization of rights as egoistic rests on a reading of the ways in which the historical emergence of the "rights of man" naturalize and thus entrench historically specific, unavowed social powers that set us against each other, preoccupy us with property, security, and freedom of movement, and stratify us economically and socially': Brown, 'Rights and identity', at 106.

52 Erik Fromm, *Marx's Concept of Man* (New York: Ungar, 1961); Norman Geras, *Marx and Human Nature: Refutation of a Legend* (London: NLB, 1983).

53 Krisztina Morvai, 'The construction of the Other in European human rights enterprise: A narrative about democracy, human rights, the rule of law and my neighbour Uncle Blaze', in Peter Fitzpatrick and James Henry Bergeron (eds.), *Europe's Other: European Law Between Modernity and Postmodernity* (Dartmouth: Ashgate, 1998) 245–51.

54 Ibid., at 249.
55 Marie-Bénédicte Dembour, '"Finishing off" cases: The radical solution to the problem of the expanding ECtHR caseload' (2002) *European Human Rights Law Review* 604–23, at 610.
56 Morvai, 'Construction', at 247–8.
57 Ibid., at 248. In the eloquent words of Wendy Brown, 'Who, today, defends their rights without an army of lawyers and reams of complex legal documents? In this regard, rights, rather than being the "popular and available" currency depicted by [some scholars], may subject us to intense forms of bureaucratic domination and regulatory power even at the moment that we assert them in our own defense': Brown, 'Rights and Identity', at 115, note 48.
58 Ibid., at 248–9, emphasis in the original.
59 Ibid., at 251.
60 Ibid., at 246.
61 Ibid.
62 This of course only holds true if one assumes that there is a connection between human rights and the alleviation of human suffering. This is an assumption which pervades the thought of those I name protest scholars. Upendra Baxi is a case in point. Tellingly, the preface of his book *The Future of Human Rights* (New Delhi: Oxford University Press, 2002) starts with a heading entitled 'Human Suffering and Human Rights'. Baxi takes it as 'axiomatic that the historic mission of "contemporary" human rights is to give voice to human suffering, to make it visible, and to ameliorate it': ibid., at 4. See also Upendra Baxi, 'Voices of suffering and the future of human rights' (1998) 8 *Transnational Law and Contemporary Problems* 125. Other human rights approaches are not so concerned with human suffering (see Chapter 8).
63 Tables compiled by the Court for the period between 1988 and 2001 indicate an exponential increase. Thus, for example, there were 4044 provisional files opened in 1988, 5848 in 1992, 10,166 in 1995, 16,201 in 1998 and 31,408 in 2001: *Three Years' Work for the Future: Final Report of the Working Party on Working Methods of the European Court of Human Rights* (Strasbourg: Council of Europe, 2002), at 110 (back cover).
64 Dembour, '"Finishing off"'.
65 See nonetheless three recent cases where verdicts of violation were reached against Russia in respect of events in Chechnya, the facts of which were disputed by the Russian Government: *Khashiyev and Akayeva* v. *Russia* (Applications 57942/00 and 57945/00); *Isayeva, Yusupova and Bazayeva* v. *Russia* (Applications 57947/00, 57948/00 and 57949/00); *Isayeva* v. *Russia* (Application 57950/00), all decided on 24 February 2005.
66 Marie-Aude Beernaert, 'Protocol 14 and new Strasbourg procedures: Towards greater efficiency? And at what price?' (2004) *European Human Rights Law Review* 544–57, at 551–4.
67 These measures have generally been called for by commentators from Western Europe: Beernaert, ibid., at 556–7; Pierre Lambert, 'Quelle réforme pour la Cour européenne des droits de l'homme?' (2002) 52 *Revue trimestrielle des droits de l'homme* 795–805, at 799. Such views fail to take into consideration the reality of Eastern Europe – on which, see e.g.: Marie-Bénédicte Dembour and Magda Krzyżanowska-Mierzewska, 'Ten years on: The popularity of the Convention in Poland' (2004) *European Human Rights Law Review* 400–23, at 415–19.

68 Dembour, '"Finishing Off"', at 610.

69 This application received the following number: 18079/03.

70 The letter bore the following reference: CEDH-LR 11.OR (CD1) [next line] ADD/aro.

71 As to the moral language in which interested parties generally phrase their claims to a property expropriated under communism, see Filippo Zerilli, 'Sentiments and/as property rights: Restitution and conflict in post-socialist Romania', in Maruška Svašek (ed.), *Postsocialism: Politics and Emotions in Central and Eastern Europe* (Oxford: Berghahn, 2006). It is worth noting, however, that in the *Dragoi* case, the new owner is not a former tenant but a family member of the former owners who say their trust and hospitality have been abused.

72 Aileen McColgan reports that the *Rights Brought Home* White Paper published in 1997 about the incorporation into British law of the European Convention on Human Rights spoke of an average of £30,000 for enforcing rights at European level: McColgan, *Women*, at 12. One stark problem denounced by McColgan about entrenched rights is that 'only those who can afford legal action can benefit from them': ibid., at 6.

73 Like for example the two applicants in the so-called *McLibel* case: *Steel and Morris* v. *United Kingdom*, (Application 68416/01) 15 February 2005, (2005) 41 EHRR 22.

74 A further 409 cases were declared inadmissible by Chambers (rather than committees of three) in 2004. In the same year, 841 cases were declared admissible. (These figures are reached by adding up those given in the Annual Activity Report 2004 of the four sections of the Court, available on the Court's website.)

75 Ernest Bloch, *Natural Law and Human Dignity* (Cambridge, Mass.: MIT Press, 1986), at 187.

76 Morvai, 'Construction', at 251.

77 Patrick Mowbray writes: '[B]etween January and August 2000 the Court delivered 248 judgments in respect of Italy (out of a total of 417 judgments). The vast majority of these judgments concerning Italy resulted in a finding of a violation of Article 6 (1)': Patrick Mowbray, *Cases and Materials on the European Convention on Human Rights* (London: Butterworths, 2001), at 307.

The Court itself finds the concentration of resources which this situation entails problematic. It has rightly identified the failure of the national authorities to redress the repeated findings of a violation of Article 6 as one of the causes of the backlog from which it is suffering.

78 This trend manifests itself in particular in the case law of the Court in respect of Poland: Dembour and Mierzewska, 'Polish Case Law', at 518. It is clear, however, that these cases represent only a fraction of the problems which Polish people would wish the Court to address: ibid., at 527. Significantly, the part of Karen Reid's excellent guide to the Convention which deals with the substantive case law of the Court is structured in two parts, related respectively to 'Fair Trial Guarantees' and 'Other [Problem Areas]': Karen Reid, *A Practitioner's Guide to the European Convention on Human Rights* (London: Sweet and Maxwell, 2004).

79 Thus, a commentator was able succinctly to assert that the fact that 'freedom of the person and fair trial should require most attention comes as little surprise; deprivation of liberty and the provision of justice lie at the heart of civil rights': Jim Murdoch, 'Safeguarding the liberty of the person: Recent Strasbourg jurisprudence' (1993) 6 *International and Comparative Law Quarterly* 494–522, at 494.

80 *Maaouia* v. *France*, 5 October 2000, ECHR 2000-X, (2001) 33 EHRR 42.

81 *Sander* v. *United Kingdom*, 9 May 2000, ECHR 2000-V, (2001) 31 EHRR 44.

82 See their dissenting opinion in the case.

83 As confirmed by *Naumov* v. *Albania*, declared inadmissible on 4 January 2005.

84 Hélène Tigroudja, 'L'inapplicabilité de l'article 6, 1 de la Convention à la procédure de relèvement d'une interdiction du territoire' (2002) 50 *Revue trimestrielle des droits de l'homme* 433–62.

85 *Gregory* v. *United Kingdom*, 25 February 1997, RJD 1997-I 296, (1997) 25 EHRR 577.

86 At issue in *Gregory* was the response of the judge who had received a note during the trial for robbery of the applicant, a black British citizen, to the effect that one member of the jury should be discharged due to the racial sentiments he had expressed. Instead of doing this, the judge, after consulting the prosecution and the defence as to what should be done, recalled the jury and directed them to decide the case according to the evidence in the case and nothing else. By eight votes to one, the Court found that Article 6 (1) had not been violated. A third ruling on an allegedly racist jury had been adopted by the Court earlier, in *Remli* v. *France*, 23 April 1996, RJD 1996-II 8, (1996) 22 EHRR 253. Mr Remli was of Algerian origin. He had been sentenced to life imprisonment for intentional homicide. He complained before the Strasbourg Court that the national court had refused to take formal note of the fact that a juror had been overheard saying 'What's more, I'm a racist'. The Court found by a close majority of five votes to four that Article 6 (1) had been violated.

87 Dissenting opinion of Judge Bonello in *Anguelova* v. *Bulgaria*, 13 June 2002, ECHR 2002-IV, (2004) 38 EHRR 31. The year before, Caroline Picheral had observed that the Court had never found a violation of Article 14 of the Convention on grounds of racial discrimination: Caroline Picheral, 'Discrimination raciale et Convention européenne des droits de l'homme (L'apport de la jurisprudence)' (2001) 46 *Revue trimestrielle des droits de l'homme* 517–39, at 518.

88 *Nachova and Others* v. *Bulgaria*, 26 February 2004, (2004) 39 EHRR 37.

89 *Nachova and Others* v. *Bulgaria*, 8 June 2005.

90 It should be noted, however, that Article 3 may also be relevant. The Court found the isolation, based on ethnic origin, race and religion, of the Greek Cypriot community living in the Karpas region of Northern Cyprus a inhuman and degrading treatment imputable to the Turkish authorities and thus in violation of Article 3: *Cyprus* v. *Turkey*, 10 May 2001, ECHR 2001-IV, (2002) 35 EHRR 30. Thirty years before, the Commission had already stated that 'publicly to single out a group of persons for differential treatment on the basis of race might, in certain circumstances, constitute a special form of affront to human dignity' in violation of Article 3: *East African Asians* v. *United Kingdom* (Applications 4403/70-4419/70, 4422/70, 4434/70, 4443/70, 4476/70-4478/70, 4486/70, 4501/70 and 4526/70-4530/70) 14 December 1973, (1981) 3 EHRR 76. The case concerned the change of British nationality law implemented in haste to deprive Asians of their passports and right to abode in the United Kingdom just as they found themselves expelled from East Africa. The case was not referred to the Court. The Committee of Ministers declared itself satisfied with the measures taken by the United Kingdom to deal with the flow of refugees which the crisis produced. On the both promising and unsatisfactory relationship established by the Court between Article 3 and Article 14 of the Convention in the face of racial discrimination, see Dominique Rosenberg, 'Enfin . . . le juge européen sanctionne les violations du principe de non-discrimination raciale en relation avec le droit à

la vie (Arrêt *Nachova et autres c. Bulgarie* du 26 février 2004)' (2005) 61 *Revue trimestrielle des droits de l'homme* 171–201, at 178–82.

91 Protocol 12, once in force, will eliminate this limitation in respect of the states that have ratified it.

92 James A. Goldston, 'Race discrimination in Europe: Problems and prospects' (1999) *European Human Rights Law Review* 462–83, at 464.

93 See also, more recently, *Moldovan and Others (No. 2)* v. *Romania*, 12 July 2005, where the Court found unanimously a violation of Article 14 taken in conjunction with Articles 6 and 8 as well as a violation of Article 3, in a case concerning domestic proceedings brought by Roma villagers following the killing of fellow Roma and the destruction of homes.

94 The case law on the criminalization of homosexuality and on the treatment of Jehovah Witnesses in Greece comes to mind as two examples of a snowball effect developing from successful cases.

95 Points 13 and 10, respectively, of his dissenting opinion.

96 See his points 9 and 10, and for comparative assessment with the practice of the Inter-American Court of Human Rights and the Supreme Court of the United States, his points 11 and 12.

97 *Abdulaziz, Cabales and Balkandali* v. *United Kingdom*, 28 May 1985, Series A, No. 94, (1985) 7 EHRR 471.

98 Goldston, 'Race discrimination', at 466.

99 The case gave rise to celebratory reviews which, in the light of the subsequent Grand Chamber's judgment, unfortunately proved premature: B. Plese, 'The Strasbourg Court finally redresses racial discrimination' (2004) *Roma Rights* 109–18; Rosenberg, 'Enfin . . .'

100 Para. 150 of the judgment.

101 Para. 161 of the judgment.

102 Para. 163 of the judgment.

103 Whether this is a substantive or a rhetorical statement is open to discussion. I am arguing elsewhere that the Court finds either a consensus or a divergence of views in Europe on the one hand and either an evolution in standards or not on the other hand as it sees fit. This is not entirely surprising given that these notions are never thoroughly objective but rather an appreciation of facts open to various interpretations: Marie-Bénédicte Dembour, 'Diversity or commonality: The power to toss the human rights coin' (2005) *Mediterranean Journal of Human Rights* 65–91.

104 Paras. 168 and 169 of the judgment.

105 Paras. 166 and 168 of the judgment.

106 Para. 161 of the judgment, emphasis added.

107 Para. 155 of the judgment, emphasis added.

108 Para. 152 of the judgment.

109 Para. 150 of the judgment.

110 Para. 158 of the judgment, emphasis added.

111 In the Chamber's judgment, Judge Bonello had suggested in a concurring opinion that it would have been preferable for the Court to consider altogether separately the procedural and the substantive violations of Article 14. In the Grand Chamber's judgment, the six partly dissenting judges (Judges Casadevall, Hedigan, Mularoni, Fura-Sandström, Gyulumyan and Spielmann) argue exactly the opposite and conclude that 'the majority of the Court did not give sufficient weight to the sufficiently

strong, clear and concordant unrebutted presumptions which arose out of the factual evidence *in the case taken as a whole* and which leads [them] to conclude that there has been a violation of Article 14 taken together with Article 2 of the Convention': point 7 of their partly dissenting opinion, emphasis added.

112 Consisting in inserting in HUDOC the term 'racism' in the box 'text'.

113 *Jersild* v. *Denmark*, 23 September 1994, Series A, No. 298, (1995) 19 EHRR 1, on which see Chapter 4. In *Unabhängige Initiative Informationsvielfalt* v. *Austria*, decided on 26 February 2002, the Court yet again managed to escape mentioning racism. The applicant in this case was the publisher of a periodical called the 'TATblatt'. In response to an opinion poll against immigration organized by Jörg Haider's Austrian Freedom Party, the Tatblatt had suggested that Haider was inciting people to 'racist agitation'. Haider requested that the Tatblatt be prevented, through an injunction, from repeating this statement. The courts granted the injunction. The applicant argued at Strasbourg that the injunction was in breach of Article 10. The Court unanimously found a violation of the Convention, noting that 'there is little scope under Article 10 Para. 2 of the Convention for restrictions on . . . debates on questions of public interest' and that the 'press plays an essential role in a democratic society', but it did not mention racism.

114 Para. 145 of the judgment.

115 Picheral, 'Discrimination', at 517.

116 Peter Fitzpatrick, 'Racism and the innocence of law' (1987) 14 *Journal of Law and Society* 119–32, at 119.

117 Ibid.

118 Ibid. The words of Lord Justice Waite, in a decision of 18 April 1997 to refuse leave of appeal against a decision of the Employment Appeal Tribunal which had found no racial discrimination, come to mind:

> [Miss Somjee], if I may presume to advise her, should not lose sight of the fact that although race discrimination is a serious evil which the law is rightly astute to prevent, the opportunity to complain of discrimination puts a powerful weapon in the hands of the complainant. Charges of race discrimination are extremely hurtful and are not always easy to resist, at all events, without time, trouble and expense. Those who abuse the right of complaint by over-persistent or unscrupulous use of it must expect to suffer the consequence of having such misuse penalised by adverse costs order.
>
> (Cited in para 24 of *Somjee* v. *United Kingdom*, 15 October 2002, (2003) 36 EHRR 16.)

Fitzpatrick argues the exact opposite of Lord Justice Waite. His view is that law is not at all astute at preventing race discrimination and charges of race discrimination are all too easy to resist. Ms Somjee brought an application to Strasbourg. Her complaint that the British judicial proceedings had been excessively lengthy in contravention of Article 6 of the Convention was declared admissible and upheld in a judgment of 15 October 2002. Her complaint that she had suffered racial discrimination in contravention of Article 14 was declared inadmissible on March 2000. One expects that this was, to her mind, the more important complaint.

119 But, for the view that Marxism is compatible with (or even an extension of) liberalism, see Robert Fine, *Democracy and the Rule of Law: Marx's Critique of the Legal Form* (Caldwell, New Jersey: Blackburn Press, 2002), at 1.

120 *Messochoritis* v *Greece* (Application 41867/98) 12 April 2001

121 Talal Asad, 'What do human rights do? An anthropological enquiry' (2000) 4 *Theory and Event* 27, at para. 40.

122 Ibid., at para. 43.

123 Ibid., at para. 57.

124 Ibid., at para. 43.

125 'Political emancipation is of course a great progress. Although it is not the final form of human emancipation in general, it is nevertheless the final form of human emancipation inside the present world order': Marx, 'Jewish Question', at 54.

126 Ibid., at 64.

127 Claude Lefort says it eloquently: 'La critique de l'individu s'exerce d'emblée dans les horizons d'une théorie de la société où se trouvent abolies *la dimension du pouvoir* et avec celle-ci la dimension de la loi et celle du savoir . . .': Lefort, *L'invention*, at 62, emphasis added. This passage can be translated as follows: '[Marx] criticizes the individual from the perspective of a theory of society where *what is carried out by power* and, in its wake, by law and by knowledge is abolished.'

128 For some remarks on reading Marx after Foucault, see Brown, 'Rights and identity', at 110–12.

129 'Critique of the Gotha Programme' [1875], reproduced in McLellan, *Karl Marx*, 610–16, at 611.

130 In a review of three books about Marx, William Booth asks yet again whether one should 'step back from Marxism's political fate so as to evaluate its ideas': William James Booth, 'Marx After 1989' (1995) 23 *Political Theory* 527–54, quote at 528. Booth rightly calls for Marxism's theoretical and practical crises to be distinguished.

131 See e.g. Norman P. Barry, *An Introduction to Modern Political Theory* (London: Macmillan, 1981), at 195–6.

132 Robert Fine, 'The rule of law and Muggletonian Marxism: The perplexities of Edward Thompson' (1994) 21 *Journal of Law and Society* 193, at 204.

133 E. P. Thompson, *Whigs and Hunters: The Origins of the Black Act* (London: Allen Lane, 1975).

134 Ibid., at 258, as summarized by Daniel H. Cole, '"An Unqualified Human Good": E. P. Thompson and the Rule of Law' (2001) 28 *Journal of Law and Society* 177–203, at 181.

135 Cole, ibid., at 181.

136 Ibid.

137 Thompson, *Whigs*, at 266.

138 Cole, 'Unqualified', at 183.

139 Thompson, *Whigs*, at 260.

140 Cole, 'Unqualified', at 184.

141 Thompson, *Whigs*, at 265.

142 Ibid., at 266.

143 Ibid., at 265.

144 Ibid., at 268.

145 The essay is dated 1979, even though it first appeared in published form in 1981: Lefort, 'Politics'.

146 Ibid., at 240.

147 Ibid., at 240–1.

148 Ibid., at 254.

149 Ibid., at 255 and 256.

150 Ibid., at 259.

151 Ibid.

152 Cole, 'Unqualified', at 189.

153 Ibid.

154 Ibid., at 203.

155 *Ipek* v. *Turkey*, 17 February 2004, ECHR 2004-II.

156 In more theoretical terms, one could say with Wendy Brown that '[b]eing regarded by the state *as if* we were free and equal is an improvement over being treated as if we were naturally subjected and unequal vis-à-vis stratifying social powers'. This is because an analysis 'concerned with the way ideological idealism masks social power [has the potential of sliding] into one that emphasizes the discursive production of political possibility': Brown, 'Rights and identity', at 107, emphasis in the original.

157 See paras. 150–9 of the judgment, as well as para. 117.

158 Para. 134 of the judgment.

159 This violation was found in respect of the applicant who 'bore the weight of having to make numerous futile enquiries in order to find out what happened to his two sons . . . and who was not even informed of the outcome of the investigations pursued in respect of his complaints'. Thus, '[t]he manner in which his complaints [had] been dealt with by the authorities must be considered to constitute inhuman treatment contrary to Article 3': para. 183 of the judgment.

160 Para. 135 of the judgment; see also para. 115.

161 Mr Ipek was initially represented before the Court by Kevin Boyle and Françoise Hampson, who were among the founders of the Kurdish Human Rights Project (KHRP). Later Mr Ipek's representatives included William Bowring, Philip Leach and Anke Stock, who are all connected with the KHRP. The names of the representatives appear, as usual, in the judgment of the Court (at para. 2). Iraqi, Iranian and Turkish Kurds on the one hand and British lawyers on the other hand created the KHRP in London in 1992 after Boyle went to Diyarbakir at the request of local lawyers to explain in a public forum how complaints might be brought to Strasbourg. On his return, the KHRP started to receive from Human Rights Association lawyers in Diyarkabir documents which testified to gross violations of human rights, from torture to village destructions, killings and rape. The London-based lawyers worked at turning these documents into complaints at Strasbourg, which were in turn turned into communications to the Turkish government. Over the next decade, official hearings by the old Commission brought out the Convention physically to the South East of Turkey, while the judgments of the Court produced some accountability on the part of Turkey regarding its ruthless military campaign in the – largely peasant – Kurdish region (Boyle, personal communication). It is unlikely that *Ipek* would have existed without the KHRP.

162 Para. 213 of the judgment.

163 *Nachova* was a judgment of the First Section, *Ipek* of the Second.

164 But Brown remarks that for Marx – especially the early Marx – history was making 'its way towards true, as opposed to strategic, universalism', which is in stark contrast to the view held by most post-Marxist critics that 'universalism is unredeemable insofar as it is always one with the hegemonic aims of the historically dominant': Brown, 'Rights and identity', at 101, note 29.

6

The Convention in a particularist light

How can the proposed Declaration be applicable to all human beings, and not be a statement of rights conceived only in terms of the values prevalent in the countries of Western Europe and America? (Herskovits)

Cultural relativism is widely recognized as the doctrine which stands opposed to the idea, central to the human rights credo, that human rights are universal. It is generally understood as asserting that each culture nurtures its own values and ways of being and doing; is understandable and must be understood within its own terms; and should not be morally assessed by a culture external to it, even in the name of human rights. The doctrine tends to result in a denunciation of human rights as an expression of imperialism.

Discussions about human rights and relativism typically involve references to Asia, Africa and/or the Middle East.[1] This is because the debate between universalism and relativism tends to be conducted as if it were concerned with how the rest of the world should react to something which originated in the West. This chapter springs from the view that this is not the most fruitful way to conceive of it.

The chapter shows that the debate is inescapable even *within* the confines of Europe, i.e. internally to the fairly homogeneous region from which human rights are said to have originated. In concrete terms, it examines the doctrine of the margin of appreciation developed in the Strasbourg case law as an expression of relativism, and it disputes the claim that the prohibition of torture and inhuman and degrading treatment contained in Article 3 of the Convention can meaningfully be said to be absolute when what is being prohibited is in fact culturally shaped. Human rights cannot be said to be 'inherent' to human nature.

The problem of the applicability of human rights in a relativist perspective need not be about the standing of one region of the world as against another. What relativism highlights is that minimal common standards are never entirely *common*: they always stand in the way of more peculiar, or particular, norms. The debate between universalism and particularism thus captures the difficult and always controversial accommodation between unity and diversity in mankind.

The reference to 'particularism' in the last sentence, as well as in the title of this chapter, is not due to an inadvertent slip of the pen, as will become clear by the end of the chapter. The chapter nonetheless discusses and criticizes 'cultural relativism', given the prominence of this expression in the literature.

The AAA Statement of 1947: An outdated view of culture

The 'Statement on Human Rights' (hereafter 'Statement') produced in 1947 by the American Anthropological Association (hereafter 'AAA') constitutes a convenient point from which to start this chapter, as it is often taken to epitomize the cultural relativist position towards human rights.[2]

The Executive Board of the AAA sent the Statement to the UN Commission on Human Rights as the latter was working on the draft of what became, a year later, the Universal Declaration of Human Rights. The Statement expressed the fear that the Declaration might not be universal.[3] Indeed the Declaration proved to spring from a particular conception of the human good. It only makes sense in a certain kind of society and polity: that which its drafters knew. It is replete with concepts, such as legal personality (Article 6), nationality (Article 15), access to public service (Article 21), protection against unemployment (Article 23), and periodic holidays with pay (Article 24), which are simply not known to most human societies which have historically existed on earth. Significantly, it was drafted when a considerable portion of the world remained colonized and had no input into its formulation.[4] Returning to the Statement, it can be observed that the UN Commission on Human Rights never referred to it in its proceedings, nor did it reply to the AAA. This is not surprising given that the Statement merely argued that the Commission was facing a 'problem' but did not include any specific advice on how to overcome it.

The Statement opens by stressing that a human rights Declaration would need to seek respect for the individual *both* as individual and as member of 'his' society (in a disregard, still typical in the 1940s, of any feminist concerns). It hammers home the point about the importance of guaranteeing 'respect for the cultures of differing human groups', clearly having in mind the destruction of cultures which colonialism, imperialism and the very establishment of the United States had heralded.[5] Shifting the emphasis slightly, it asserts that the Declaration must 'take into full account the individual as a member of the social group of which he is a part, whose sanctioned modes of life shape his behavior, and with whose fate his own is thus inextricably bound'. It asks the question posed at the head of this chapter: 'How can the proposed Declaration be applicable to all human beings, and not be a statement of rights conceived only in terms of the values prevalent in the countries of Western Europe and America?'[6]

The Statement identifies three core propositions:

1 The individual realizes his personality through his culture, hence respect for individual differences entails a respect for cultural differences;
2 Respect for differences between cultures is validated by the scientific fact that no technique of qualitatively evaluating cultures has been discovered;

3   Standards and values are relative to the culture from which they derive so that any
     attempt to formulate postulates that grow out of the beliefs or moral codes of one
     culture must to that extent detract from the applicability of any Declaration of
     Human Rights to mankind as a whole.[7]

Interestingly, the great majority of anthropologists would firmly object today to
each of these propositions. To use the current social sciences jargon, the first
proposition 'essentializes' or 'reifies' culture. In other words it treats culture as a
static 'thing', rather than as a dynamic process. It fails to consider that the cultural
group is never a completely homogenous unit, that it brews dissenting voices
within it, that it constantly evolves. Saying that the individual realizes his personality through his culture misses this point, by linking too rigidly individual
development to a respect for (a presumably all-integrated, 'functionally' function-
ing)[8] culture.

The second proposition seems to imply that tolerance of all cultures is warranted on the basis that scientific evaluation of cultures cannot (yet) be conducted. It is now widely accepted, however, that ethics is not a matter of science.
Moreover, as anthropologist Alison Renteln has repeatedly and cogently argued,
the recognition that different societies hold different values need not lead to
tolerance of these differences.[9] For her, it is clear that 'the relativist is not
prevented from offering criticism'.[10] The awareness that a critique is ethnocentric
may weaken the critique, but without necessarily rendering it impotent.[11]

The third proposition embodies a view of cultural organic growth which does
not sit comfortably with the current anthropological view of culture as contested
ground, permeable to all kinds of influences.[12]

In short, the AAA Statement relies on a defective conception of culture. Another
problem is the relativism it preaches, which has left many an anthropologist uneasy,
as discussed in the next section.

Cultural relativism: An embarrassing doctrine but also a valuable legacy

Melville Herskovits is recognized to have been the primary author of the 1947
AAA Statement. Alongside Ruth Benedict, Herskovits was a student of Franz
Boas. Boas, Benedict and Herskovits, three key figures in American anthropology,
successfully challenged the doctrine of cultural evolutionism which had dominated anthropological thinking since the birth of the discipline in the late nineteenth century. Cultural evolutionism sought to rank human societies according
to their stage of development along a progression conceived of as linear. Boas
and his disciples insisted that cultures travel in different directions, propelled both
by different values and by fortuitous circumstances, making the hierarchical
evaluation of cultures invalid. Under the influence of these scholars, cultural
relativism became a core tenet of anthropology in the 1920s and 1930s, especially

in the United States. The doctrine is commonly – though perhaps wrongly – understood as entailing tolerance for all culturally embedded moral systems. After World War II shook the assumption that external value judgments on what a particular culture produces are unwarranted, cultural relativism lost its hold on the discipline of anthropology. Though the AAA Executive Committee endorsed the Statement Herskovits had prepared, the Statement immediately elicited critiques from within the anthropological ranks.[13] By the 1970s, anthropologists avoided any reference to the doctrine, as if they were embarrassed by it.[14]

What is in the doctrine which warrants such embarrassment? The question of what exactly cultural relativism entails is highly disputed. What is not contested is that it derives from the empirical observation that moral systems are embedded in culture and that different cultures produce different moral systems. However, the recording of an uncontested empirical observation hardly warrants the label of doctrine.[15] The important question therefore is: which ethical position does cultural relativism advocate? There is a view, especially among the detractors of the doctrine, that cultural relativism entails tolerance for any culturally embedded moral system on earth – perhaps even any morality, whether or not it is culturally embedded.[16] Those who take cultural relativism to mean this (including many philosophers) oppose it on the ground that it leads to indifference and/or inaction.[17] However, such a position arguably distorts the view of those who, somewhat reluctantly, side with cultural relativism – primarily anthropologists. These have remarked that the observation that cultures produce different moral norms does not say anything about the respective value of these norms.

The American anthropologist Elvin Hatch has recently defended what he tellingly calls the 'good side' of relativism – thus implicitly acknowledging the general discomfort the doctrine inspires.[18] This good side mainly consists in highlighting a double problem: first, the difficulty of 'establishing reasonable and general grounds for making moral judgments about the actions of others' and, second, the 'strong tendency among the more powerful peoples of the world to use their own standards, or standards favourable to them, in their relations with others'.[19] In Hatch's wake, one can say that the doctrine of cultural relativism is best seen as a counterpart to the arrogance and abuse of universalism, rather than as a call for anything and everything to be tolerated.

Where cultural relativism has remained acceptable in anthropology is in its antiracism and denunciation of colonialism.[20] Obviously, such denunciation was a major motivation for Herskovits who repeatedly stressed that the 'values of the ways of life of [peoples under western hegemony had] been consistently misunderstood and decried'.[21] In a remark which could be said to anticipate the Foucauldian concept of discourse, Herskovits observed that 'eternal verities only seem so because we have been taught to regard them as such'.[22]

Returning once more to the 1947 Statement on Human Rights, my own view is that, whatever its shortcomings, it was right to suggest that the formulation of so-called human rights criteria cannot but derive from a particular culture with the consequence that the applicability of any Declaration of Human Rights to humankind is a delusion: the concept of human rights is not incontrovertible in humankind's repertoire.

Handyside: The margin of appreciation as – seemingly – an expression of cultural relativism

We have already seen that *Handyside* v. *United Kingdom*, decided on 4 November 1976,[23] was the first case where the doctrine of the margin of appreciation was used by the Court. The appearance of the doctrine in the ruling was linked to the observation that there is no uniform concept of morals in Europe. Considering that the absence of a universal morality is precisely the premise on which cultural relativism is based, *Handyside* can be expected to be highly relevant to our discussion. It is therefore discussed in some detail in this section. If it is possible to connect the appearance of the doctrine of the margin of appreciation in *Handyside* with cultural relativism, it should nonetheless be said at the outset that such an embodiment of cultural relativism is an abused rather than a genuine form of the doctrine. This will be discussed in the next section.

At the heart of the case was *The Little Red Schoolbook* (hereafter 'Schoolbook'), initially published in Denmark in 1969 and intended for a readership of teenagers. Alongside 'useful' advice, the Schoolbook contained passages on sex and drugs which turned out to be extremely controversial. One for example read:

> Porn is a harmless pleasure if it isn't taken seriously and believed to be real life. Anybody who mistakes it for reality will be greatly disappointed. But it's quite possible that you may get some good ideas from it and you may find something which looks interesting and that you haven't tried before.[24]

Another passage, headed 'Be yourself', stated:

> Maybe you smoke pot or go to bed with your boyfriend or girlfriend – and don't tell your parents or teachers, either because you don't dare to or just because you want to keep it secret.
>
> Don't feel ashamed or guilty about doing things you really want to do and think are right just because your parents or teachers might disapprove. A lot of these things will be more important to you later in life than the things that are 'approved of'.[25]

The Schoolbook had been in circulation in a number of European countries without this causing any problem. In 1971, however, after adverse media coverage in some newspapers and complaints being received by the Director of Public Prosecutions, the publisher of the English version was prosecuted and convicted under the Obscene Publications Act of England and Wales. Along with its standing type, copies of the book were seized (although as many as 90 per cent of the total print-run of 20,000 copies were missed and almost immediately sold, so popular was the book). The English publisher, Mr Handyside, argued at

Strasbourg that the British authorities had violated Article 10 of the Convention, guaranteeing his freedom of expression.

On the face of it, he seemed to have a strong case. How could it be argued that action against the book was 'necessary in a democratic society' when most societies in Europe were happy for the book to be in free circulation? The answer is: by stressing that each society has its own views on what morals require and by letting national authorities determine in great part these moral requirements.

The Court reasoned:

> [I]t is not possible to find in the domestic law of the various Contracting States a uniform European conception of morals. The view taken by their respective laws of the requirements of morals varies from time to time and from place to place, especially in our era which is characterised by a rapid and far-reaching evolution of opinions on the subject. By reason of their direct and continuous contact with the vital forces of their countries, State authorities are in principle in a better position than the international judge to give an opinion on the exact content of these requirements as well as on the 'necessity' of a 'restriction' or 'penalty' intended to meet them . . . Consequently, Article 10 para. 2 . . . leaves to the Contracting States a margin of appreciation.
>
> Nevertheless, Article 10 para. 2 . . . does not give the Contracting States an unlimited power of appreciation. The Court, which . . . is responsible for ensuring the observance of those States' engagements . . . is empowered to give the final ruling on whether a 'restriction' or 'penalty' is reconcilable with freedom of expression as protected by Article 10 . . . The domestic margin of appreciation thus goes hand in hand with a European supervision . . .[26]

The reasoning of the Court holds in four steps, which can be summarized as follows:

1 Europe does not enjoy a uniform concept of morality;
2 The Court may therefore not be in a very good position to assess moral requirements;
3 Hence the Convention must be understood as granting member states a margin of appreciation;
4 Ultimate assessment on whether the Convention has been violated or not nonetheless remains in the hands of the Court.

Cultural relativist insights permeate this reasoning. First, as we have already noted, cultural relativism arises from the recognition that different societies/cultures hold different moralities; the Court's granting of a margin of appreciation to the defendant state is motivated by the absence of any uniform morality in Europe. Second, it is the Court's view that national authorities probably understand better than itself – the international body instituted to implement commonly agreed rules – the requirements of their own local society; cultural relativism likewise insists that moral assessment is informed by cultural understanding, and possibly even depends on enculturation. Third, the implicit reference by the Court to a tension between European-wide standards and national peculiarities mirrors the tension between universalism and relativism. Finally, the Court leans towards the side of universalism by stressing that no one but itself can ultimately decide whether the Convention is respected or not. The dominant position of universalism is a standard feature of the universal versus relativist debate; relativism, when defended, is defended not for its own sake, but just for its 'good side', with great caution.[27]

In the *Handyside* case, relativism nonetheless seemingly won the day. By thirteen votes to one, the Court did not find that the UK had violated the Convention. Although it forcefully asserted that Article 10 is 'applicable not only to "information" or "ideas" that are favourably received or regarded as inoffensive or as a matter of indifference, but also to those that offend, shock or disturb the State or any sector of the population',[28] the Court found that in this case the authorities had not overstepped their margin of appreciation. Attaching particular importance to the intended readership of the Schoolbook, namely children and adolescents aged from twelve to eighteen, it ruled that 'the competent English judges were entitled, in the exercise of their discretion, to think . . . that the Schoolbook would have pernicious effects on the morals of many of the children and adolescents who would read it'.[29]

The Court rejected the argument that the lack of action against the book by other authorities (both in other Member states and in other parts of the UK) indicated that the course adopted in England was not 'necessary in a democratic society'. Like the English, these authorities had acted within the sphere of their margin of appreciation.[30] They had simply come to a different assessment of the requirements of morals in their jurisdiction. One can see why Richard Clayton and Hugh Tomlinson have written that, in one form, the margin of appreciation amounts to 'an interpretative obligation to respect domestic cultural traditions and values when considering the meaning and scope of human rights'.[31]

The reasoning of the Court implicitly suggested that *Handyside* was about the protection of English moral values. This is highly disputable, however. What arguably lay at the heart of the case was the crisis surrounding respect for authority in Europe in the late 1960s (particularly evident in the French May 1968 movement). Interestingly, this was not readily apparent in the judgment, except indirectly when the Court quoted passages from the Schoolbook. In this light, the reference by the Court to the absence of 'a uniform European conception of morals' appears as a strategy which allows it not to identify the issue at the centre of the case. The next section argues that the reference to a doctrine of the margin of appreciation in the ruling is hardly a genuine expression of cultural relativism, though the way the doctrine is presented as being about the respect of local morality (culture) is typical of many arguments that claim to be cultural relativist.

Masquerading as an expression of cultural relativism: The abuse of the cultural argument

In the previous section, I wrote that the Court did not find the UK in *Handyside* in violation of the Convention when the relevant authorities developed their own response to the circulation of the Schoolbook. I did not qualify this statement further, and it could have been taken to suggest the development of a national response. This shortcut was necessary for the sake of brevity but conceptually unfortunate: intimating that there was a 'national' response is highly problematic, considering that the question of the moral requirements entailed by the circulation of the Schoolbook was vigorously contested. The Court indicated that it felt that the state authorities were in a better position than itself to answer this question, given their 'direct and continuous contact with the vital forces of their countries'. The English sensitivity was implicitly respected in *Handyside*. Which English people were we talking about, however? Considering that the Schoolbook continued to sell well after the prosecution of its publisher, was it not the sovereignty of the state, or the respect of figures of authority more generally, rather than the 'morality' prevailing in England and Wales, which the Court was seeking to protect in *Handyside*?

On the face of it, the doctrine of the margin of appreciation makes it possible for a particular 'national' way to be respected against external imposition of 'common' (or alien) standards. Another perspective, however, would have it that the doctrine protects those with the power to say to the 'foreigners' (namely the Strasbourg Court) what the local culture is – either the state or the most vocal and powerful in the country.[32] This observation is directly in line with one of the reasons why cultural relativism has been decried.

Adamantia Pollis has written an article that, in effect, turns around the fact that a state's claims of cultural distinctiveness may be a 'wanton exercise of power by the elites'.[33] She thus perceptively calls for the modern state to be incorporated as a significant player in the dialogue between universalists and cultural relativists.[34] It has long been noted that those in power may be tempted to abuse the concept of culture, for example by objecting to the application of universal human rights norms by reference to cultural motivations which in fact have nothing to do with culture.[35] Jack Donnelly gives a number of examples of such 'cynical manipulation', including the trial of two political opponents of President Banda of Malawi before a 'traditional court' which did not have the 'slightest connection with authentic traditional practices'.[36] But we do not need to go to other continents to grasp the potential for the cultural card to be played in bad faith.[37] Mr Handyside alluded to it before the Strasbourg Court. He argued that the action of the English authorities under the 'protection of morals' was a pretext to muzzle a small-scale publisher who had published works by Che Guevara and Fidel Castro, related to the Congolese Revolution and emerging from the Women's Liberation Movement.[38] He thus obliquely accused the authorities of abusing the concept of the protection of morals to pursue an objective which had nothing to do with morals[39] and all to do with the silencing of a politically unwelcome voice. For the Court, the fact that Mr Handyside was able in 1971 to publish a revised edition of the Schoolbook where the offensive passages had been deleted or amended, without being subjected to prosecution, was hard to reconcile with this theory of political intrigue.[40] The conclusion of the Court on this point is persuasive. It remains the case that culture is often used as a cover for pursuing political objectives which have nothing to do with culture, such as the suppression of opposition or, more mildly in *Handyside*, the wish to see respect for authority restored.

Playing the cultural or the moral card can be done by the authorities in bad or in good faith. In both cases, the fact that the interests and values of all members of society, however bounded the latter appears, are not as homogeneous as the dominant cultural discourse would have it, tends to be neglected. We must be wary of the term 'culture'. If we insist on using it, we must analyse what it stands for and who in concrete terms holds the cultural views attributed to them. Michael Freeman rightly insists on this point. He refers to governments and intellectuals as 'gatekeepers' to the cultures of their peoples and stresses that we must 'interrogate official and/or dominant discourses to determine whether those who are subordinated, excluded and/or marginalized regard their situation as culturally legitimate'.[41]

In summary, in the face of something which resembles a cultural relativist argument, it is crucial to ask whether the argument really refers to a cultural value. The question of whether the supposed cultural value is really shared by the people said to belong to the relevant culture also needs to be asked. If a careful analysis shows that either of these questions must be answered negatively, there is no real cultural relativist argument to speak of. Instead, there is an abuse of the term 'culture' which, strictly speaking, has nothing to do with cultural relativism, and everything to do with a masquerade of cultural relativism. It must be acknowledged that cultural relativism tends to suggest that culture is a thing which is shared, i.e. to use the sociological jargon, to reify culture (i.e. to make it into a thing, from the Latin *res*)[42] and to obliterate the dissent around cultural issues which exists in society. To this extent, it lends itself to be used in a counterfeit rather than a genuine manner.

The real problem with cultural relativism: The tolerance of the intolerable – *T* v. *United Kingdom*

The other thing which cultural relativism fails to do is to highlight the idea that culture as such can be oppressive. In the nineteenth century John Stuart Mill had already talked of the 'despotism of culture'.[43] When culture is abusive, cultural relativism is particularly problematic for it seems to allow for the abandonment of the common rule, and thus, for inaction when action is required. This amounts to what R. J. Vincent has aptly termed 'cowardice of moral abstention'.[44]

One wonders whether the Court could not be said to be guilty of such cowardice when it concludes that there has been no violation of the Convention after having stressed that there is no common standard between the states parties. The example of *T* v. *United Kingdom*, decided on 16 December 1999,[45] comes to mind. The applicant was one of the two children who, aged 10, dragged a toddler - James Bulger – from a shopping mall to an abandoned railway and killed him.[46] The applicant child complained at Strasbourg, among other things, that his trial in England had amounted to inhuman and degrading treatment contrary to Article 3 of the Convention, notably on account of the fact that the United Kingdom set an inordinately low age of criminal responsibility (ten years of age). He contended that 'there was a clear developing trend in international and comparative law towards a higher age of criminal responsibility',[47] as evidenced by the United Nations Standard Minimum Rules for the Administration of Juvenile Justice (known as the Beijing Rules) and a recommendation by the UN Committee on the Rights of the Child that the United Kingdom should raise the age of criminal responsibility.[48]

The Court recalled that the Convention was a 'living instrument', thus making it 'legitimate when deciding whether a certain measure is acceptable under one of its provisions to take account of the standards prevailing amongst the member States of the Council of Europe'.[49] In effect this suggested that the standards to be applied are not necessarily external to what happens to be the received norm. The Court continued: 'In this connection, the Court observes that, at the present time there is not yet a commonly accepted minimum age for the imposition of criminal responsibility in Europe'.[50] The moral cowardice denounced by Vincent seems to show its head, for the Court concluded:

> The Court does not consider that there is at this stage any clear common standard amongst the Member States of the Council of Europe as to the minimum age of criminal responsibility. Even if England and Wales is among the few European jurisdictions to retain a low age of criminal responsibility, the age of ten cannot be said to be so young as to differ disproportionately from the age-limit followed by other European States. The Court concludes that the attribution of criminal responsibility to the applicant does not in itself give rise to a breach of Article 3 of the Convention.[51]

The reasoning of the Court could perhaps be summarized as follows: given the absence of a common age of criminal responsibility in Europe, we accept that virtually anything goes. (Though there would clearly be a limit to this: an age of two could not be acceptable.)

If relativism is understood as entailing tolerance of culturally embedded values and practices, it leads to 'moral neutrality and inaction in situations that are intolerable'.[52] This argument was made by Hatch by reference to gross violations of human rights ('political executions, genocide, genital mutilations, honor killings, and the like'[53]). *T* v. *United Kingdom* presents us with a more benign illustration of the argument, at least if we accept that a low age of responsibility is part of British 'culture'. (The practice is contestable in the eyes of many a British academic and practitioner and, presumably, a part of the general public,[54] but, as said above, it is in the nature of culture to be contested.) The five dissenting judges objected to the verdict of non-violation by saying: 'It seems to us that the authorities' principal reason for bringing these proceedings against children of eleven years of age was retribution . . . However, vengeance is not a form of justice and in particular vengeance against children in a civilised society should be completely excluded'.[55] Obviously there was no justification in the opinion of these judges for the particularism of England and Wales, as it ran counter to 'civilized' standards.

Chris Brown has warned that we must be wary of taking too seriously the position that there 'appears to be no independent reference point which can be brought into play in order to allow us to make judgments which do not reflect and privilege the values and interests of a particular way of life' as 'there is a danger that this position will lead to a version of moral relativism which disables any kind of cross-cultural criticism, with [unacceptable] consequences'.[56] This is persuasive until one takes on board Renteln's observation that the relativist is not prevented from expressing a critique, but is bound only to acknowledge its possible ethnocentrism.[57]

The good side and inescapability of cultural relativism

Even though cultural relativism seems to lead to the intolerable being tolerated, one should be wary of condemning the doctrine at a stroke. This is because it has a good side,[58] namely, the fact that it counteracts universalism, holding at bay its tendency towards arrogance. Instead of saying 'we know best' or 'we know', relativism poses the question 'what do we know?'[59] Universalists too often assume that they are on firm ground in making judgments about others. They can easily end up imposing their ways on others for no other reason than sheer dominant position, without even realizing this, so full are they of their good intentions.

The whole difficulty of the universalism versus relativism debate is therefore to assess which side of the coin one is dealing with: the good or the bad side of cultural relativism – or, conversely, the bad or the good side of universalism. The exercise is not necessarily easy to conduct and it may lead to controversial conclusions, but it cannot be avoided.

For example, some will feel that *T* v. *United Kingdom* is a manifestation of the good side of relativism. Instead of having said 'we know what the treatment of children in a criminal court requires', the Court indicated that it did not feel competent to rule and impose one view as to the relevant requirements: to some extent, the UK was allowed to develop its own response to crimes committed by children. Of course, not everyone will approve of the solution adopted by the

Court. Many will regret, along with the dissenting judges, that the common standards emerging in international law were disregarded.

In any concrete manifestation of the debate between universalism and relativism, what some regard as an expression of the good side of relativism (inaction when no action is required) is regarded by others as an expression of its bad side (inaction when action *is* required). The two sides exactly mirror each other. On the one hand, the so-called common rule may be an undue imposition by the powerful on the less powerful. On the other hand, the particular norm which constitutes an exception to this rule may be oppressive and morally wrong. The central difficulty is to identify which is which. The merit of the debate between cultural relativism and universalism is to point out this difficulty.

Whenever common standards are predicated, the tension between universalism and relativism inevitably arises. Because of this, wishing cultural relativism away will not do. There is no point in dismissing the doctrine as untenable in the face of (universal) human rights, for we cannot live without it, even though it is not clear how to avoid the scepticism which underlies it.[60] In consequence, the Strasbourg Court could not function without something which allows it to bring out the good side of cultural relativism. The tension between the insistence on respect for a common standard embodied in a superior rule (universalism) and respect for national decisions through the application of the margin of appreciation (cultural relativism) cannot be eliminated. The Court must thus be able to take *either* one *or* the other direction. It must be allowed to opt for what would be recognized as a cultural relativist position, even if this seems odd for a judicial institution concerned with enforcing supposedly universal human rights. The doctrine of the margin of appreciation allows it to do so.[61]

In summary, a complete rejection of the doctrine of cultural relativism would amount to throwing the baby (the real difficulty of deciding whether tolerance or intolerance of culture is called for) out with the bathwater (the identification of abusive cultural arguments). One must assuredly be aware of the potential which cultural relativism offers for over-simplified and abusive references to culture. At the same time, one simply cannot neglect the valuable intuition that the excesses of universalism need to be counteracted. Of course cultural relativism will always encompass the risk of leading to inaction when action is required. But then the question of defining when action is required and when it is not can be very problematic. In fact, the whole point of the universalism versus relativism debate is precisely to highlight the difficulty of this question, now explored through further discussion of case law.

Delcourt versus *Borgers*: Inaction versus action, or when is action required?

Considering my training as an anthropologist and my sympathy with the intuition (if not the label) of cultural relativism, I had thought that I would easily have found rulings in the Strasbourg case law where the Court had used the doctrine of the margin of appreciation in a way which could be construed as an expression of cultural relativism of which I approved whole-heartedly. In my admittedly limited knowledge of the case law, I have been able to identify only one. This is the early ruling of the Court in *Delcourt* v. *Belgium*, dating back to 1970.[62]

The case concerned the participation of a member of the Procureur Général's department at the deliberations of the Court of Cassation. In Belgian law, the role of this person was understood to be limited to providing advice of a doctrinal and scientific nature to the Belgian Supreme Court, which explained his presence at the Court's deliberations. Even though he was formally part of the Prosecution Service, he was not considered to be a party to the proceedings. Mr Delcourt argued that his presence violated the principle of equality of arms and was therefore in violation of Article 6 of the Convention. The Court disagreed, stressing both the peculiar and the historically entrenched character of the contested Belgian system.[63]

The Court remarked that the at-first-sight 'unusual' Belgian way of proceeding '[did] not seem to have any equivalent today in the other member States of the Council of Europe, at least in criminal cases'.[64] It was satisfied, however, that 'the Procureur Général's department at the Court of Cassation functions wholly independently of the Minister of Justice', that its members are 'bound to serve the public interest in all objectivity' and are not a real party to the proceedings before the Court of Cassation.[65] In this particular case, the fact that the system had been established for more than a century and a half supported the conclusion that the Convention had not been violated. In all this time, the contested legislation and practice appeared 'never to have been put in question by the legal profession or public opinion in Belgium'.[66] In the words of the Court: 'This wide measure of agreement would be impossible to explain if the independence and impartiality of the men on whose shoulders fell the administration of this institution at the Court of Cassation were doubted in Belgium, if the worth of their contribution to the body of decisions of the highest court were disputed or if their participation at the deliberations of the judges had been thought in a single case to open the door to unfairness or abuse'.[67] The Court unanimously ruled that there had been no breach of the Convention.

Delcourt was decided on 17 January 1970. Over twenty years later, on 30 October 1991, the Court overruled *Delcourt* in *Borgers*.[68] The latter case raised exactly the same issue as the former, except that the Court also considered the fact that the applicant was in a position neither to reply to the submissions of the member of the Procureur Général's department nor to address the Belgian Court of Cassation last. By eighteen votes to four, the Court now found a violation of Article 6 of the Convention. It found that the notion of fair trial, including the rights of the defence and the principle of equality of arms, had 'undergone a considerable evolution in [its] case-law, notably in respect of the importance attached to appearances and to the increased sensitivity of the public to the fair administration of justice'.[69] In its view, 'the opinion of the procureur général's department cannot be regarded as neutral from the point of view of the parties to the cassation proceedings . . . Once the avocat général had made submissions unfavourable to the applicant, the latter had a clear interest in being able to submit his observations on them before argument was closed . . . Further, and above all, the inequality was increased even more by the avocat général's participation, in an advisory capacity, in the Court's deliberations.'[70]

With customary honest vehemence, Judge Martens, dissenting, remarked that 'it is quite something for an international court to hold that the very proceedings . . . before the highest court in one of the member states are "unfair" or (to put it less bluntly) are in violation of . . . Article 6'.[71] With equally characteristic insight, the Dutch judge added: 'The need for caution in this area is all the greater since . . . its members [of the Court] have been schooled in different procedural traditions . . . It may be that those who are completely unfamiliar with a particular procedural institution will be more readily inclined to find it incompatible with the requirements of "fair trial" than those who form part of the same tradition.'[72] Although Martens did not say it in so many words, it is clear that he thought that a particular tradition easily blinds its followers to the merits of another tradition. What he does not specify is that his own socialization may indeed have influenced his opinion. As he remarked, the Belgian tradition was not wholly dissimilar to that existing in the Netherlands – as well as that in France and Italy.

Was the Court right in *Delcourt* or in *Borgers*? My personal inclination is to think that the Belgian system did not amount to unfair justice. But I admittedly studied law in Belgium in the 1980s and, as such, had been indoctrinated into its system. Do I miss something when I think that the Belgium system was adequate – not wonderful or superior, just adequate? Do I suffer from a delusion or from false consciousness? Judging from the Court's judgment in *Borgers*, many may think so.[73] They may have a point. After all false consciousness is a common consequence of 'successful' enculturation.[74] But how are we to dismiss the possibility that my opponents might *not* have a point? How do we know who is right and who is wrong when controversies of the kind we are discussing arise? Both sides may see the other as having been indoctrinated. How do we distinguish between objective standards and subjective ones, which pass for objective ones?[75] It is the strength of cultural relativism to remind us that this question is worth asking.

Johnston: An unfortunate cultural relativist application

In the great majority of cases, scepticism is *de rigueur* – not always, however. The difficulty is to find where one must abandon doubt and embrace certainty. *Johnston and Others* v. *Ireland*, delivered on 18 December 1986, is a case where the Court in my view wrongly adopted what could be called a cultural relativist position.[76]

The applicants in this case were a couple and their daughter. The first applicant, Mr Johnston, had separated from his wife in 1965. A few years later, he started to live with the second applicant. The third applicant, a daughter, was born of this relationship in 1978. The applicants brought two sets of issues before the Court. These related on the one hand to the impossibility of the first two applicants marrying due to the fact that the first applicant was already married and could not obtain a divorce, and, on the other hand, to the status of the third applicant as an illegitimate child. The Court found a violation of the Convention on the latter point, but not on the former.

Only the dispute relating to the impossibility of divorce in Ireland is discussed here. This part of the dispute arose from the provision of the Irish Constitution, Article 41, which recognizes 'the Family as the natural primary and fundamental unit group of Society' and endows it with 'inalienable and imprescriptible rights, antecedent and superior to all positive law'. Until 1996, Article 41 continued: 'No law shall be enacted for the grant of a dissolution of marriage.'[77] Although it was possible under Irish law for spouses to conclude a formal separation agreement (which Mr Johnston and his wife did in 1982),[78] divorce could not be obtained under this regime, with the resultant inability of a separated spouse to remarry. In 1986, a majority of the population voted in a national referendum against amending the Constitution so as to allow divorce in Ireland.[79]

The first and second applicants argued that their inability to marry constituted a violation of various Articles of the Convention.[80] The Court rejected their claim. With its reference to the doctrine of the margin of appreciation, the reasoning of the Court on Article 8 is of particular interest to us. The Court held:

> Although the essential object of Article 8 . . . is to protect the individual against arbitrary interference by the public authorities, there may in addition be positive obligations inherent in an effective 'respect' for family life. However, especially as far as those positive obligations are concerned, the notion of 'respect' is not clear-cut: having regard to the diversity of the practices followed and the situations obtaining in the Contracting States, the notion's requirements will vary considerably from case to case. Accordingly, this is an area in which the Contracting Parties enjoy a wide margin of appreciation . . .
>
> [The Court] is of the opinion that . . . the engagements undertaken by Ireland under Article 8 . . . cannot be regarded as extending to an obligation on its part to introduce measures permitting the divorce and the re-marriage which the applicants seek.[81]

The Court did not speak in *Johnston* of national authorities who were 'closer' to the local situation and therefore better able to appreciate local requirements, as it had done in *Handyside*. Instead it referred to the 'engagements undertaken by Ireland under Article 8 . . . [not] extending to an obligation [to provide what the applicants wanted]'. In so doing it implicitly positioned its reasoning on the terrain of power and sovereignty rather than that of culture and relativism,[82] thus stressing – again without using the word – the subsidiary character of the Convention system of protection. The effect of the *Johnston* ruling is nonetheless to uphold the Irish 'culture', or rather the Irish *dominant* culture. As such it can be approached as a cultural relativist application.

Indeed the good side, the bad side and the defect of cultural relativism, identified in previous sections, can be seen in the ruling. The good side (if one agrees with this perspective) is that the Irish peculiarity of not allowing divorce following the Irish stress on the Family – with a capital F – is respected. Those who do not agree with this view will see the bad side of the ruling immediately, namely that respect for family life, here of the separated spouse and his new partner, fails to be guaranteed. Of course the good and the bad sides of the ruling are in direct opposition to each other, in line with the general discussion of cultural relativism above.

The typical defect of a cultural relativist position, namely, that it fails to take sufficient account of dissent by acting as if a supposedly single culture were homogeneous, is also readily apparent. It was obliquely referred to in the only dissenting opinion to the judgment adopted by a majority of sixteen. Quoting nothing but the terms of a report produced by a Committee of the Irish Parliament in 1967, Judge De Meyer remarked that the constitutional prohibition of divorce is 'coercive in relation to all persons, Catholics and non-Catholics'.[83] In other words the Constitution erases the plurality of views regarding marriage and divorce which exists in Ireland, being content to follow the views of the majority as if the minority did not exist.

Ireland imposed one view, the sanctity of marriage, on all residents in Ireland. The Court did not find any fault with this imposition. Without using the word, it decided to respect Irish 'culture', as expressed in its then Constitution. However, culture can be abusive, especially of the rights of women, and this is what happened here. Of course both men and women may wish to seek divorce, and the first applicant in *Johnston* was indeed a man. However, divorce is also very much linked to women's emancipation, in the sense that it allows them to be independent from men.[84] In this light, *Johnston* must be seen as resulting in an indirect defence of the subjugation of women by men through respect for deeply entrenched constitutional values – 'culture'. In my opinion, *Johnston* constitutes a most unfortunate application of cultural relativism.[85]

The gloss of universalism in the application of Article 3 of the Convention: *Tyrer*

Article 3 of the Convention provides that: 'No one shall be subjected to torture or to inhuman or degrading treatment or punishment.' The prohibition is expressed in absolute terms: there is no second paragraph in Article 3 allowing for the admission of exceptions. While derogation from substantive provisions of the Convention is often permissible under Article 15 in the 'event of a public emergency threatening the life of the nation', such derogation is not possible in respect of Article 3. For many an author, the absolute character of the protected rights tends to exclude any application of the idea of pluralism and of the doctrine of the margin of appreciation to Article 3.[86] Writing about the whole field of human rights, Jack Donnelly asserts that 'it is difficult to imagine cultural arguments against [provisions which protect against] inhuman or degrading treatment'.[87] By contrast, this section argues that Article 3 is always dependent on *cultural* arguments. That this is not readily admitted shows precisely the importance of having a doctrine like cultural relativism.

To anticipate the conclusion of this section, the question of what is human or inhuman treatment can only receive an answer that is culturally entrenched – whether this is recognized or not. It would therefore be surprising if cultural arguments were not to be advanced in response to claims that inhuman and degrading treatment has been inflicted. Admittedly, in a world view which favours universalism, these cultural arguments are likely to be either flatly rejected or, if they are taken on board, not accepted as *cultural* arguments. The impression is thus created that a universal position is held. Too often, however, a universal position is, at bottom, a cultural position in disguise – the strength of cultural relativism is precisely to teach us this.

Tyrer v. *United Kingdom*[88] was the first case in which the issue of the use of corporal punishment for disciplining youngsters came before the Court.[89] By six votes to one, the Court concluded in a judgment delivered on 25 April 1978 that the UK had violated Article 3 of the Convention, thus defeating the cultural arguments which had been advanced by the Government. *Tyrer* illustrates all the points mentioned in the previous paragraph: cultural arguments were invoked to justify treatments or punishments which appear contrary to Article 3 of the Convention; the Court did not like this and responded by casting its ruling in decidedly universal terms; despite its gloss, the ruling referred to nothing but the by-then dominant culture.

Anthony Tyrer, the applicant, was from the Isle of Man. Aged 15, following an unprecedented incident with schoolmates, he was convicted in court of unlawful assault occasioning actual bodily harm. In accordance with the legislation in force on the Isle of Man, he was sentenced to three strokes of the birch. The punishment was administered the day his appeal was dismissed (a few weeks later), on his bare buttocks, at a police station, in the presence of a doctor and his father. He was sore for about a week and a half afterwards.[90] Mr Tyrer lodged an application with the Commission claiming that the punishment contravened Article 3 of the Convention. When he later declared, having attained 'full age', that he wished to withdraw his application, the Commission refused to accede to his request in view of the 'general questions' which the case raised.[91]

> The contested legislation in force on the Isle of Man provided that: Any person who shall –
>
> a   unlawfully assault or beat any other person;

    b   make use of provoking language or behaviour tending to a breach of the peace, shall be liable . . . to a fine . . . or to be imprisoned . . . and in addition to, or instead of, either such punishment, if the offender is a male child or male young person, to be whipped.

Precise provisions specified the nature of the instrument to be used, the number of strokes which could be given, where the punishment could be carried out and the other conditions governing its administration.[92]

The Isle of Man is not part of the United Kingdom; it is a dependency of the Crown with its own government, legislature, courts and administration. The United Kingdom thus tried to rely before the Court on the paragraph of Article 63 of the Convention which read: 'The provisions of this Convention shall be applied in such territories [to which a Government has extended the application of the Convention by specific declaration to this effect] with due regard . . . to local requirements'.[93] The Court refused to consider that there were any specific local requirements to take into consideration in this case. Article 63 had been 'designed to meet the fact that, when the Convention was drafted, there were still certain colonial territories whose state of civilisation did not, it was thought, permit the full application of the Convention'.[94] The Isle of Man was 'an up-to-date society' which 'ha[d] always been included in the European family of nations'.[95] The Court shared the view of the Commission that 'there were no significant social or cultural differences between the Isle of Man and the United Kingdom which could be relevant to the application of Article 3'.[96] To no avail, the Agent of the Government repeatedly requested the Chamber of the Court to carry out an 'investigation on the spot', as it had power to do, so that it should 'become acquainted at first hand with local circumstances and requirements in the Isle of Man'.[97]

The Attorney-General for the Isle of Man was heard by the Court. He cited statistics which indicated that corporal punishment had been inflicted no more than four times a year in the previous decade (and in some years not at all).[98] He explained that a recent petition in favour of the retention of judicial corporal punishment had obtained 31,000 signatures from amongst the approximate total of 45,000 persons entitled to vote on the Island.[99] His main argument, it seems, was that 'the judicial corporal punishment at issue in this case was not in breach of the Convention since it did not outrage public opinion in the Island'.[100] Presented in this form, the argument implied: this is our ways of doing things; there is no need for external interference.

The Court could not have accepted such an argument, which amounts to the worst form of cultural relativism, that which suggests that abuse can – or must – be tolerated because it constitutes locally generated and accepted culture (thus resulting in cultural relativism's bad side to emerge).[101] The Court stated: 'it is never permissible to have recourse to punishments which are contrary to Article 3 . . . whatever their deterrent effect may be'.[102] It is indeed the case that the dominant perspective has it that inhuman or degrading treatment can *never* be acceptable; let us accept it for the moment. Even if Article 3 were absolute in the sense that it permits no exceptions,[103] it remains the case that identifying what is a practice contrary to Article 3 cannot be done in universal terms. Abuse in one society is not necessarily abuse in another (it may be, but it may not be). The Court did not highlight the difficulty there is in identifying what is an abusive practice. Perhaps it did not even perceive this difficulty. This led it to conclude too quickly that a violation of Article 3 had occurred. Such a conclusion would have warranted a more rigorous reasoning.

The Court rightly noted that it was not an appropriate defence to argue that the punishment was not degrading because it was carried out in private and without publication of the name of the offender: 'it may well suffice that the victim is humiliated in his own eyes, even if not in the eye of others'.[104] It welcomed the safeguards provided by prior medical examination and the presence of a doctor, the regulation of the number of strokes and dimensions of the birch, the administration by a police constable in the presence of a more senior colleague, the permission for a parent to attend.[105] In its view, however, these safeguards did not save the punishment from the accusation that it violated Article 3. It reasoned:

> The very nature of judicial corporal punishment is that it involves one human being inflicting physical violence on another human being. Furthermore, it is institutionalised violence, that is in the present case violence permitted by the law, ordered by the judicial authorities of the State and carried out by the police authorities of the State . . . Thus, although the applicant did not suffer any severe or long-lasting physical effects, his punishment – whereby he was treated as an object in the power of the authorities – constituted an assault on precisely that which it is one of the main purposes of Article 3 . . . to protect, namely a person's dignity and physical integrity. Neither can it be excluded that the punishment may have had adverse psychological effects. The institutionalised character of the violence is further compounded by the whole aura of official procedure attending the punishment and by the fact that those inflicting it were total strangers to the offender.[106]

In his dissenting opinion, Judge Sir Gerald Fitzmaurice unravelled the tautological nature of the Court's reasoning. He pointed out that 'all punishment is degrading, at least if it involves imprisonment and the (mostly unpleasant and often humiliating) incidents of prison life and discipline'.[107] For the argument of the Court not to be tautological, the contested punishment should have entailed 'a degree of degradation recognizably greater than that inherently bound-up with any normal punishment that takes the form of coercion or deprivation of liberty'.[108] The Court wrote *as if* it found the punishment of Mr Tyrer to be in violation of Article 3 because of specific circumstances. Its reasoning, however, was not persuasive, for the criteria it set out would have led it to find 'all corporal punishment, in all circumstances, inherently [to involve], as such, an unacceptable level of degradation'. The criticism directed at the institutionalization of the violence shows this. 'To be "institutionalized" is, in an ordered society, insepar-able from any punishment for crime, since non-institutionalized punishment, except such as the law tolerates, must be illegal.'[109] Not without justification Sir Gerald thought that the Court would have found any corporal punishment inflicted within a judicial system to be contrary to Article 3.[110]

The British judge's own defence was purportedly limited. He stressed that the point of his dissenting opinion was not to advocate such punishment but to make it clear that, not being degrading for juvenile offenders, it could not be found to be in violation of Article 3.[111] Sir Gerald expressly linked his dissenting opinion to his socialization:

> I have to admit that my own view may be coloured by the fact that I was brought up and educated under a system according to which the corporal punishment of schoolboys . . . was regarded as the normal sanction for [misbehaviour]. Generally speaking . . . it was often considered by the boy himself as preferable to probable alternative punish-ments such as being kept in on a fine summer's evening to copy out 500 lines or learn several pages of Shakespeare or Virgil by heart . . . [T]hese beatings were carried out without any of the safeguards attendant to Mr Tyrer's: no parents, nurses or doctors were ever present. They also not infrequently took place under conditions of far greater intrinsic humiliation than in his case. Yet I cannot remember that any boy felt degraded or debased. Such an idea would have been thought rather ridiculous . . . [I]ndeed . . . these occasions were often seen as matters of pride and congratulation.[112]

Sir Gerald's experience was of course far from unique in England. The journalist Jeremy Paxman begins a chapter of his book *The English: A Portrait of a People*:

> It is not often you meet someone who has had a bottom transplant. The man in question, jowly, balding, 50ish, in a pinstripe suit and well made shoes, looks the picture of British probity . . . By day, he runs a merchant bank. At night, he likes to be spanked until the blood runs. His obsession has become known as *le vice anglais*.
>
> The surgery on his backside . . . became necessary after a lifetime of corporal punishment . . . His beatings began as a child at the hands of his father. Kissing between father and son had been banned at the age of five, on the grounds that it was effeminate. Corporal punishment was to be 'taken like a man', so when the boy was beaten as a punishment he was expected to show no emotion. If he survived the ordeal without crying, his father congratulated him. Over the next ten years, 'my backside was assaulted by no less than seventeen people, including parents, nanny, teachers, prefects'. He says it with no hint of self-pity, laughing at the recollection. At this stage, the beatings, the common coin of English education at the time, had no sexual connotations [sexual compulsion came later, hence the need for surgery]. They were just part of a schooling system that aimed to achieve Squire Brown's ambition for his son Tom and turn him into a 'brave, helpful, truth-telling Englishman, and a gentleman, and a Christian'.[113]

Discipline, including corporal punishment, long remained a feature of British so-called public schools – in fact private institutions linked to the upper classes. Sir

Gerald's socialization explains his opinion in *Tyrer*, so much so that he himself says he has to admit it. His constant reference to corporal punishment of *juveniles* – as opposed to adults – again reveals where he comes from: a system where a good thrashing was taken to be an essential part of the process of turning a child into a gentleman.

If Sir Gerald's view was undoubtedly coloured by his cultural experience, so was the view of the rest of the Court. The *Tyrer* ruling is best explained by reference to 'modern opinion' concerning supposedly now 'common standards'. The Court stated:

> The Convention is a living instrument which . . . must be interpreted in the light of present-day conditions. In the case now before it the Court cannot but be influenced by the developments and commonly accepted standards in the penal policy of the member states of the Council of Europe in this field.[114]

When *Tyrer* is cited in textbooks on the law of the Convention – and it is often cited – it is because of this passage, which laid down for the first time in explicit terms one of the key general principles of interpretation of the Convention: that of evolutive interpretation.[115] Referring to common standards as the quoted passage does is ultimately hollow, however, for any comparative exercise lends itself to highlight either commonality or diversity.[116]

Had the Court so wished, it could have found that the peculiarity of the Isle of Man's stance did not denote an unacceptable exception to an otherwise firmly established rule in Europe, but partook of a minority perspective which was worth protecting in pluralist Europe. This did not happen for, as Sir Gerald noted, after a long period when 'under all skies, corporal methods [were] seen as the obvious and natural way of dealing with juvenile [but also, it should be pointed out, non-juvenile] misbehaviour . . . modern opinion has come to regard corporal punishment as an undesirable form of punishment'.[117]

'Modern opinion' now holds the view that corporal punishment is an abhorrent form of punishment. This opinion, which is common but not universal – as Sir Gerald's minority opinion clearly shows – is taken to reflect a universal standard. But we all know that this opinion has not always been prevalent (and none of us can predict what will become of it in the future).

By and large, corporal punishment has become unacceptable in the West, especially as a means of judicial punishment. By contrast, imprisonment is not generally held to be problematic. It is therefore not particularly surprising that the Court has not found imprisonment to be, as such, in breach of Article 3. Significantly there nonetheless exists a section of the public opposed to the principle of imprisonment. This minority may grow in the future, and come to represent the general opinion. Robert Legros, Professor of Criminal Law at Brussels in the 1980s, used to teach his students (of whom I was one) that our descendants may come to regard our jails with the same abhorrence as we ourselves regard pre-modern criminal punishment. Will the position that jailing is acceptable one day be regarded as retrograde as Sir Gerald's position on corporal punishment appeared in 1978 or, even more so, a quarter of a century later?

Far from what is generally suggested in the relevant literature, Article 3 of the Convention does not constitute an area outside the bounds of the universalism versus cultural relativism debate. Cultural arguments are regularly advanced in this area. But they are suppressed: they are either rejected outright or disguised and given a universal gloss. While the universal position may be presented as the only tenable one in respect of an issue as fundamental to human dignity as the prohibition of degrading treatment, the truth of the matter is that such a position is universal only in a limited sense of the term. As cultural relativism reminds us, no moral view exists completely outside cultural norms. A 'universal' position, untainted by cultural arguments, is at best an ideal, which needs to be acknowledged as such, at worst an unrecognized utopia or a pretence (or both).

Rethinking the terms of the opposition: Universalism versus particularism

In common parlance, cultural relativism is opposed to universal human rights. The expressions 'cultural relativism' and 'universality' are thus the terms in which the relevant debate is generally conducted. These terms, however, could be said to be mismatched. Let us refer to the dictionary:

- Universal: . . . Of or throughout the universe, the world, or all nature; existing or occurring everywhere or in all things.
- Relative: . . . Constituted, or existing, only by relation to something else; not absolute or independent.[118]

As can readily be seen, the two words do not really go together. Etymologically, one would expect the following oppositions: relativism versus absolutism; universal versus particular. The associations of ideas offered by the thesaurus confirm that these two are the real pairs:

> **Relation - Adj.** *relative*, not absolute.
> **Unrelatedness: absence of relation - Adj.** *unrelated*, absolute; independent; owing nothing to . . .
>
> **Generality - Adj.** *general*, generic, typical, representative, standard; . . . all-embracing, blanket, across-the-board . . . *universal*, . . . international, cosmopolitan, global, worldwide, . . . widespread[;] *extensive*; pervasive, prevalent . . .
> **Speciality - Adj.** *special*, specific, particular; peculiar, singular, unique[;] *one;* individual, idiosyncratic, characteristic, idiomatic, original . . . *characteristic*; distinctive, marked, out of the ordinary[;] *unusual.*[119]

'Absolute' means that which is 'capable of being known or conceived out of relation'. As against cultural relativism, one would expect an absolutist doctrine.

This doctrine would assert that human rights can be known or conceived without being related to culture. Alternatively we could keep the 'universal' root and construct the universalism versus particularism opposition. This is what I recommend we do.

It would be unwise to refer to the debate we have discussed in this chapter as the (out-of-culture) absolutism versus cultural relativism debate. The debate on whether human rights are absolute or relative is assuredly important. Chapter 4 has attempted to address it. The central question of that chapter was whether human rights take priority over, or give way to, other considerations. The question raised in the present chapter is whether human rights are subject to cultural accommodation. This can be seen as a subset of the question addressed in Chapter 4. At the same time, the reference to '(out-of-culture) absolutism' has nothing to do with the denial that exceptions to the rule exist or can exist. Indeed, such an absolutist doctrine could well provide for both definitions of, and exceptions to, human rights: definitions *and* exceptions would both be held to exist independent of culture – to be absolute.[120]

The distinction between the questions tackled in the two chapters can be made more concrete by referring to our discussions about Article 3 of the Convention. Chapter 4 explored whether Article 3 acts in an absolute way or whether its case law is infused with proportionality, so that the prohibition it lays down implicitly allows for exceptions on consequentialist grounds. Let us assume that we had concluded that Article 3 allows no exceptions. Had we concluded so (which we have not), the question of whether Article 3 is absolute in the sense that it is not culturally relative would remain entire. We could rephrase it in the following way: can we determine what is *and* what is *not* prohibited under Article 3 in a universal manner, independent of local references? I propose we refer, following the example of others,[121] to this latter debate as the universalist versus particularist debate.

Human rights are said to be universal. This is generally held to mean that human rights exist everywhere, for every human being. The position that human rights are everywhere the same is doctrinal; it can be named under the term 'universalism'. Its opposite is to be aware of and insist on local specificity, in line with the reflection, commonly made, that local circumstances must be taken into consideration in the application of human rights. This second position can be called 'particularist'.

The doctrine of particularism could appear superfluous: who does not know that human rights cannot receive a blanket application across the board? This is constantly asserted. For example, admittedly using the conditional, Michael Perry nonetheless observes that 'the optimal specification [of the universal norms] might be relative to cultural particularities'.[122] Perry quotes Philip Alston, Jack Donnelly and even John Paul II in support of this contention. In the words of the late Pope: 'Certainly there is a need to seek out and to discover the most adequate formulation for universal and permanent moral norms in the light of different cultural contexts.'[123] I have argued something not entirely dissimilar, though

I shall explain below that I am less ready to start from a universalist position than the people I have just quoted.

The doctrine of cultural relativism is mistrusted. In these circumstances, talking of 'particularism' rather than 'cultural relativism' presents a number of advantages. First, it avoids the unfortunate reifying reference to culture. (It is perfectly possible to substitute 'social', 'socially constructed' or 'social construction' whenever 'culture' or 'cultural' appears in this chapter.) Secondly 'particularism' does not in itself suggest a tendency to moral indifference or inaction. Finally, and most importantly, it leaves intact the major insight of so-called cultural relativism, namely, that local circumstances always inform moral decisions and that 'the universal' is never completely beyond 'the local'.

A brief but crucial point: Universalism is a doctrine too

The term 'universalism' is not part of the lexicon of all human rights scholars. Many simply talk of 'universal human rights'.[124] It is crucial, however, to recognize that holding that human rights are universal is a doctrine, even if universalism is so common that its doctrinal status is generally overlooked, in the light of the created impression that the universality of human rights is a fact. To labour the point: this universality is not a fact; it is as much a doctrine as cultural relativism/particularism.

Oscillating between universalism and particularism

The debate between universalism and particularism expresses a ubiquitous dilemma which arises out of human unity and diversity. It is bound to arise whatever the limits of the constituency (the whole world, a regional system, a nation, a village) in which a supposedly universal (read more simply, common) norm is invoked. Herskovits wrote: 'The problem of drawing up a Declaration of Human Rights was relatively simple in the eighteenth century, because it was not a matter of *human* rights, but of the rights of men [no women yet] within the framework of the sanctions laid by a single society.'[125] The logic underlying this statement could suggest that drawing up rights at European level must have been easier than doing so at world level, but more difficult than at national level. Ease and difficulty are assuredly relative. What needs to be perceived, however, is that establishing common standards is never completely unproblematic, however small the constituency in which these common standards are to apply, because no constituency is ever completely homogeneous.

Something akin to the universalism versus particularism debate is going to surface whenever something akin to human rights is being talked about. This is why the Court was predestined to invent something like the margin of appreciation; obviously it could have invented something else, but it needed to develop something which made it possible for opposition to universalism to surface.

Time and again, it has been asked: as a concept of Western origin, do human rights have any relevance outside the Western world? Cultural relativists are held to give a negative answer to this question, in contrast to universalists who would answer it positively. This is not, however, the pertinent question. The important question is: how do you seek unity while accommodating diversity? There are those who think that opposition to universalism entails a rejection of human rights. But universalism and particularism do not offer us the choice of being either a universalist or a particularist. Even though the debate is too often framed as if it needed to be resolved in favour of either universality or particularity,[126] of necessity, we are *both* universalist and particularist.

Universalism cannot exist independently of particularism. It is in opposition to practices which appear abhorrent that universal norms are being set, and it is by reference to local particularities that these universal norms are implemented. The reverse is also true: particularism does not exist independently of universalism. As moral beings concerned with ethics, we are not just beings of culture; we respond to what could be termed the call of universalism. This is to say that we are always somewhere between the ideal represented by universalism (which should be recognized as an ideal) and the reality of our being embedded in culture (which is inescapable). We oscillate between the two positions in a pendulum-like motion.

Universalism and particularism are thus best conceived as encompassing each other. As human rights law strives to reach the universal, it must accommodate the particular. Failing that, it will inexorably appear rigid, inadequate, unjust. However, we are talking of a tension in the real sense of the term – there is no rest to be had. Controversies as to whether a universalist or a particularist position should be favoured continually surface; they cannot be buried and forgotten.

In the universalism versus particularism debate, the second term is widely apprehended as the minor term of the opposition. Given that the terms are in tension, there is no good reason for this to be so: we need both terms, if not in equal measure (for how could we measure them?), let us just say 'equally'. This is where I depart from those whom I call universalists who give the upper hand to the universal norms, even though they admit that their implementation needs to be subjected to local variation.[127] Chris Brown has talked of the need for dialogues that explore 'the different ways there are to be human' while recognizing that '[e]ngagement must involve the exercise of judgment'.[128] I am attracted to this formulation, for it combines a constant and in my view healthy scepticism towards universality with a rejection of relativity and indifference.

Conclusion

The universality of human rights is commonly asserted. Saying that human rights are *not* universal suggests that one does not believe in human rights. Such agnosticism would be the position of so-called cultural relativists who would tolerate anything and everything in the name of culture, even the intolerable. This position is untenable. But the idea that human rights are universal, full stop, is also untenable. Universalism is a doctrine; it asserts the universality of human rights, something that can never be thoroughly achieved. The fact that such universality is an impossibility cannot be overlooked. This is why we need a doctrine to set against the doctrine of universalism.

However, cultural relativism has been persuasively derided. Even its natural proponents – anthropologists – are reported to have avoided referring to it for the last thirty years. The greatest problem with the doctrine is that it can lead to indifference when condemnation is required. It presents two subsidiary problems. First, its implicit reference to a supposedly homogeneous enduring culture masks the fact that there is always internal dissent and scope for change in society. Second, an appeal to cultural arguments by those in power can be a way to achieve political ends rather than respect for tradition. These two problems can largely be addressed by being aware of the need to identify them when they arise.

The central problem of cultural relativism is more intricate. This is that cultural relativism can lead to tolerance where intolerance is called for. However, it is important to note that universalism leads to the exactly contrary problem: it allows intolerance to surface when tolerance is called for. The danger inherent in the former doctrine is indifference; in the latter, it is arrogance. The bad side and the good side of universalism are unwarranted and warranted action; the bad side and the good side of its opposite are unwarranted and warranted inaction. These strengths and weaknesses mirror each other. The problem of when to impose common standards and when to allow particular norms to subsist will not disappear by wishing cultural relativism away.

We need something like cultural relativism not only because we need a counterpoint to the arrogance of universalism (thus developing a healthy scepticism towards the norms we incorporate through socialization) but also because the debate between universalism and its contrary is inescapable. Given that what is not universal is particular, we can usefully refer to the doctrine which stands against universalism as particularism.

Particularism does not command that we should tolerate all that is going on outside our own frame of reference and be indifferent to the plight of the 'other'. Rather, it brings the question when universalism needs to be imposed and when particularism is justified to the fore. This question will arise time and time again, whenever common norms are asserted. The way the debate is conducted can take various lexical forms. In the Strasbourg Convention system it appears notably, but not only, under the name of the doctrine of the margin of appreciation.

Notes

1 See e.g., in an abundant literature, R. Panikkar, 'Is the notion of human rights a Western concept?' (1982) 120 *Diogenes* 75–102; R. J. Vincent, *Human Rights and International Relations* (Cambridge: Cambridge University Press 1986), at 37–57; Jack Donnelly, *Universal Human Rights in Theory and Practice* (1st edn, Ithaca: Cornell

University Press, 1989), 107–60; (2nd edn, 2003), 71–119; Christina M. Cerna, 'Universality of human rights and cultural diversity: Implementation of human rights in different socio-cultural contexts' (1994) 16 *Human Rights Quarterly* 740–52; Adamantia Pollis, 'Cultural relativism revisited: Through a state prism' (1996) 18 *Human Rights Quarterly* 316–44.

2 [Melville Herskovits], 'Statement on human rights', (1947) 49 *American Anthropologist* 539–43, at 539. The Statement is partly reproduced in Henry J. Steiner and Philip Alston, *International Human Rights in Context: Law, Politics, Morals* (Oxford: Oxford University Press, 2000), at 372–4.

3 Karen Engle rightly points out, however, that Herkovits did 'not argue against the idea of a declaration on human rights. Rather, [he suggested] that any declaration must attend to differences among cultures': Karen Engle, 'From skepticism to embrace: Human rights and the American Anthropological Association from 1947–1999' (2001) 23 *Human Rights Quarterly* 536–59, at 540.

4 Even though the seven principal drafters of the Declaration included a Chinese who professed adherence to Confucianism, the Judeo-Christian tradition was undoubtedly the overwhelming influence: Stephen P. Marks, 'From the "Single Confused Page" to the "Decalogue for Six Billion Persons": The roots of the Universal Declaration of Human Rights in the French Revolution' (1998) 20 *Human Rights Quarterly* 459–514, at 490.

5 [Herskovits], 'Statement', at 540–1.

6 Ibid., at 539.

7 Ibid., at 541–2.

8 On functionalism in anthropology, see Adam Kuper, *Anthropology and Anthropologists: The Modern British School* (3rd edn, London: Routledge, 1996).

9 For one of her earlier pieces, see e.g. Alison Renteln, 'Relativism and the search for human rights' (1988) 90 *American Anthropologist* 56–72. Others have made the same point. For example, the international relations scholar R. J. Vincent succinctly remarked: 'In logic, the doctrine of cultural relativism cannot rank cultures as equal or unequal': Vincent, *Human Rights*, at 54. Unlike Renteln, Vincent did not continue by saying that a relativist, while being aware of the ethnocentric character of his/her critique, *can* be critical.

10 Renteln, 'Relativism', at 64.

11 Ibid.

12 Adam Kuper, *Culture: The Anthropologists' Account* (Cambridge, Mass.: Harvard University Press, 1999); Jane K. Cowan, Marie-Bénédicte Dembour and Richard A. Wilson (eds.), *Culture and Rights: Anthropological Perspectives* (Cambridge: Cambridge University Press, 2001); Richard G. Fox and Barbara J. King (eds.), *Anthropology Beyond Culture* (Oxford: Berg, 2002).

13 See most notably H. G. Barnett, 'On science and human rights' (1948) 50 *American Anthropologist* 352–5.

14 Elvin Hatch, *Culture and Morality: The Relativity of Values in Anthropology* (New York: Columbia University Press, 1983), esp. at 37–9, 46–7 and 103; Engle, 'From skepticism', at 548. Wilcomb E. Washburn wrote in the late 1980s: 'Once argued confidently and aggressively by anthropologists, cultural relativism is now dealt with ambiguously and humorously, even by *the few* willing to grapple directly with the subject': Wilcomb E. Washburn, 'Cultural relativism, human rights, and the AAA', (1987) 89 *American Anthropologist* 939–43, at 939, emphasis added.

15 P. H. Nowell-Smith, 'Cultural relativism' (1971) 1 *Philosophy of the Social Sciences* 1–17.

16 As Herskovits noted in his answer to detractors of cultural relativism: Melville Herskovits, *Cultural Relativism: Perspectives in Cultural Pluralism* (New York: Random House, 1972), at 64.

17 A good example is John J. Tilley, 'Moral arguments for cultural relativism' (1999) 17 *Netherlands Quarterly of Human Rights* 31–41. See also Nowell-Smith, 'Cultural Relativism'.

18 Elvin Hatch, 'The good side of relativism' (1997) 53 *Journal of Anthropological Research* 371–81; see also Clifford Geertz 'Anti anti-relativism' (1984) 86 *American Anthropologist* 263–78.

19 Hatch, 'The good side', at 372.

20 Engle, 'From skepticism', at 551.

21 Herskovits, *Cultural Relativism*, at 541.

22 His relativism was thus also epistemological. He remarked: 'Even the nature of the physical world, the colors we see, the sounds we hear, are conditioned by the language we speak, which is part of the culture into which we are born': ibid., at 542.

23 *Handyside* v. *United Kingdom*, 7 December 1976, Series A, No. 24, (1979–1980) 1 EHRR 737, already discussed in Chapter 3.

24 Quoted in para. 32 of the judgment.

25 Ibid.

26 Paras. 48 and 49 of the judgment.

27 See Marie-Bénédicte Dembour, 'Following the movement of a pendulum: Between universalism and relativism', in Jane Cowan, Marie-Bénédicte Dembour and Richard Wilson (eds.), *Culture and Rights: Anthropological Perspectives* (Cambridge: Cambridge University Press) 56–79, at 73.

28 Para. 49 of the judgment.

29 Para. 52 of the judgment.

30 Para. 54 of the judgment.

31 Richard Clayton and Hugh Tomlinson, *The Law of Human Rights* (Oxford: Oxford University Press, 2000), at 274, n. 6.32. It would be wrong, however, to think that the doctrine of the margin of appreciation always amounts to a form of cultural relativism. Its application in respect to national security matters, for example, does not really lend itself to such an analysis. As we have seen in Chapter 3, there the doctrine serves more to protect sovereignty than culture. For this second form, Clayton and Tomlinson speak of the doctrine as 'a standard of judicial review to be used when enforcing human rights protection' (ibid.). See also Eva Brems, 'The margin of appreciation in the case-Law of the European Court of Human Rights' (1996) *Zeitschrift für ausländisches öffentliches Recht und Völkerrecht* 240–314, at 309 and 294.

32 On this, see also Chapter 3, which discussed how the doctrine of the margin of appreciation allows the interests of the state to be preserved, as a realist perspective would either predict (descriptive realists) or command (normative realists).

33 Pollis, 'Relativism revisited', at 323.

34 Ibid., at 243. To recall, her article is entitled: 'Cultural relativism revisited: Through a state prism'.

35 Pollis talks of 'the state's exploitation of [the cultural] contention': ibid, at 320.

36 Donnelly, *Universal Human Rights*, 1st edn, at 119–20.

37 To paraphrase Chris Brown, 'Cultural diversity and international political theory: From the requirement to "mutual respect"?' (2000) 26 *Review of International Studies* 199–213, at 200.

38 Paras. 52 and 10 of the judgment.

39 For an interesting discussion of what the term 'morals' covers, see Christopher Nowlin, 'The protection of morals under the European Convention for the Protection of Human Rights and Fundamental Freedoms' (2002) 24 *Human Rights Quarterly* 264–86.

40 Para. 52 of the judgment.

41 Michael Freeman, 'Human rights and real cultures: Towards a dialogue on "Asian values"' (1998) 16 *Netherlands Quarterly of Human Rights* 25–39, at 30.

42 Another common term in social sciences is the verb 'to essentialize', which refers to the idea that something is given an essence which it does not really have.

43 Cited in Vincent, *Human Rights*, at 55. Today it is common to refer to the cultural subjugation of women when thinking of this phenomenon. See, e.g., Tracy Higgins, 'Anti-essentialism, relativism and human rights' (1996) 19 *Harvard Women's Law Journal* 89; Susan Moller Okin, Joshua Cohen, Matthew Howard and Martha C. Nussbaum (eds.), *Is Multiculturalism Bad for Women?* (Princeton: Princeton University Press, 1999). *Johnston* v. *Ireland*, 18 December 1986, Series A, No. 112, (1987) 9 EHRR 203, discussed in a subsequent section, demonstrates that this phenomenon is not just a feature of far-away countries.

44 Vincent, *Human Rights*, at 55.

45 *T* v. *United Kingdom*, 16 December 1999, ECHR 1999-IX, (2000) 30 EHRR 121.

46 The Court rendered a similar judgment about the second murderer on the same day. See *V* v. *United Kingdom* (Application 24888/94) 16 November 1999.

47 Para. 62 of the judgment.

48 Para. 62 of the judgment.

49 Para. 70 of the judgment. It had started its reasoning on this complaint by observing, predictably (see Chapter 3), that Article 3 enshrines one of the most fundamental values of democratic society and that the prohibition it lays down is formulated in absolute terms so that the nature of the crime committed by the applicant – which had been very shocking – was immaterial. In line with its previous case law, it then remarked that 'ill-treatment must attain a minimum level of severity if it is to fall within the scope of Article 3' and that the 'assessment of this minimum is, in the nature of things, relative', depending on all the circumstances of the case.

50 Para. 71 of the judgment. Not surprisingly given that the conventional view is that the doctrine of the margin of appreciation has no place in respect of Article 3 of the Convention, the Court did not invoke the doctrine as such; its solution is nonetheless directly in line with what an application of the doctrine would have heralded.

51 Para. 72 of the judgment. The Court held by twelve votes to five that there had been no violation of Article 3 in respect of the applicant's trial. It found by sixteen votes to one that there had been a violation of Article 6 para. 1 in respect of the applicant's trial and unanimously that there had been a violation of Article 6 para. 1 in respect of the setting of the applicant's tariff and of Article 5 para. 4.

52 Hatch, 'Good side', at 372.

53 Ibid., at 372. I have disputed the wisdom of this position in respect of genital mutilations: Dembour, 'Movement of a pendulum'.

54 See e.g. Jane Fortin, *Children's Rights and the Developing Law* (2nd edn, London: Butterworths, 2003), at 550–66.

55 Joint partly dissenting opinion of Judges Pastor Ridruego, Ress, Makarczyk, Tulkens and Butkevych.

56 Brown, 'Cultural diversity', at 207.

57 Above, text to notes 10 and 11. I suspect that Brown would actually agree with this.

58 To borrow Hatch's useful phrase: Hatch, 'Good side'.

59 Raymundo Panikkar is very good at asking this question. As such, he is often taken for a cultural relativist in human rights scholarship. I would say that this is a mistake. Significantly, Panikkar is not against human rights, of which he speaks as 'a sacred duty': Panikkar, 'Western concept?', at 101.

60 Hatch, 'Good side'.

61 Which is not to say that the margin of appreciation is always about the universalist versus cultural relativist tension, as the discussion of *Handyside* in a previous section and Chapter 3 amply demonstrate.

62 *Delcourt* v. *Belgium*, 17 January 1970, Series A, No 11, (1979–80) 1 EHRR 355. This was the eighth judgment of the Court.

63 It did so without having recourse to the doctrine of the margin of appreciation, which is not surprising given that *Delcourt* was decided in 1970 when the doctrine of the margin of appreciation did not occupy the position in the Convention system which it later acquired. As we have seen in Chapter 3, the Commission had first referred to it in *Greece* v. *United Kingdom*, on which it reported in 1958; the Court, in *Handyside*, decided in 1976.

64 Para. 30 of the judgment.

65 Paras. 32 and 33 of the judgment.

66 Para. 36 of the judgment.

67 Para. 36 of the judgment.

68 *Borgers* v. *Belgium*, 30 October 1991, Series A, No. 214, (1993) 15 EHRR 92.

69 Para. 24 of the judgment.

70 Paras. 26 and 27 of the judgment.

71 Para. 4.1 of his dissenting opinion.

72 Ibid., para. 4.5.

73 The more so given that the Court has often found proceedings before Courts of Cassation to be in violation of Article 6 of the Convention, for lack of due respect to the principle of equality of arms, since *Borgers*. For recent cases, see *Chesnay* v. *France* (Application 56588/00), *Casalta* v. *France* (Application 58906/00) and *Lafaysse* v. *France* (Application 63059/00), all decided on 12 October 2004.

74 As the opponents of 'female genital mutilation' say of those who (in their own words) practise 'female circumcision'. For a less dramatic application, one could mention the absence of Strasbourg applications against France by applicants who, on their detention in France, are prevented from making immediate contact with their lawyers. This could be explained by reference to the fact that French lawyers are so used to the system that they do not see what lawyers trained across the Channel would regard as thoroughly unacceptable and a clear violation of Article 5 of the Convention. On the French criminal justice, see e.g. Jacqueline Hodgson, 'Human rights and French criminal justice: Opening the door to pre-Trial Defence', in Simon Halliday and Patrick Schmidt (eds.), *Human Rights Brought Home* (Oxford: Hart, 2004) 185–208, esp. at 197–201; 'The detention and interrogation of suspects in

police custody in France: A Comparative Account' (2004) 1 *European Journal of Criminology* 163–99.

75 Panikkar, 'Western concept?', at 406–7.

76 Cerna also refers to this case in her discussion of the universality versus diversity debate: Cerna, 'Universality', at 750.

77 The Constitution was amended on 17 June 1996 to provide for the dissolution of marriage in certain specified circumstances.

78 Para. 12 of the judgment.

79 Para. 34 of the judgment.

80 Namely Articles 12, 8, 14 (combined with Article 8) and 9.

81 Paras. 55 and 57 of the judgment. For a discussion of the reference by the Court to positive obligations, see Chapter 4.

82 I have already suggested above that the defence of 'national culture' and national sovereignty can be related. See section above on 'Masquerading as an expression of cultural relativism'.

83 Para. 5 of his dissenting opinion. Interestingly, the Belgian judge concluded that the prohibition constituted a violation not only of Article 8 of the Convention, but also of Article 9, on freedom of conscience and religion. Religion, of course, is often regarded as an aspect of culture. The fact that it creeps in here is another indication, if any proof to this effect was required, that *Johnston* is a case about 'culture'.

84 However, divorce has also been identified as 'a key force that drives many women into poverty': Jennifer Mather Saul, *Feminism: Issues and Arguments* (Oxford: Oxford University Press, 2003), at 10.

85 It would be interesting to research whether *Johnston* has a legitimizing effect on other European jurisdictions which continue to withhold the possibility of divorce, such as the Maltese.

86 Mireille Delmas-Marty, 'Pluralisme et traditions nationales (Revendication des droits individuels)', in Paul Tavernier (ed.), *Quelle Europe pour les droits de l'homme?* (Brussels: Bruylant, 1996) 81–92, at 83; [J. G. C. Schokkenbroek], 'The margin of appreciation' in P. van Dijk and G. J. H. van Hoof, *Theory and Practice of the European Convention on Human Rights* (The Hague: Kluwer, 1998), at 86. But for a different view, see Clayton and Tomlinson, *Law of Human Rights*, at 276: 'There is no reason in principle why the doctrine of margin of appreciation could not be applied to *all* of the Articles of the Convention' (emphasis in the original).

87 Donnelly, *Universal Human Rights*, 1st edn, at 122. One wonders whether it would still be possible to be so categorical today, given the policy of the US authorities towards interrogation of suspected terrorists – though this is admittedly a political rather than a cultural argument.

88 *Tyrer* v. *United Kingdom*, 25 April 1978, Series A, No. 26, (1979–1980) 2 EHRR 1. This was the nineteenth judgment of the Court.

89 It did so again in *Campbell and Cosans* v. *United Kingdom*, 25 February 1982, Series A, No. 48, (1982) 4 EHRR 293; *Costello-Roberts* v. *United Kingdom*, 23 February 1993, Series A, No. 247-C, (1995) 19 EHRR 112; and *A* v. *United Kingdom*, 23 September 1998, RJD 1998-VI, (1999) 27 EHRR 611. On these rulings, see note 110 below.

90 Para. 9 of the judgment.

91 Paras. 21 and 24 of the judgment.

92 Paras. 11 and 12 of the judgment.

93 This paragraph appears in Article 56 of the Convention since the entry into force of Protocol 11. For an analysis of its current relevance, see Syméon Karagiannis, 'Le territoire d'application de la Convention européenne des droits de l'homme. *Vaetera et nova*' (2005) 61 *Revue trimestrielle des droits de l'homme* 33–120, at 63–9.

94 Para. 38 of the judgment.

95 Ibid.

96 Para. 37 of the judgment.

97 Paras. 6 and 7 of the judgment.

98 Para. 18 of the judgment.

99 Para. 15 of the judgment.

100 Para. 31 of the judgment.

101 See also para. 29 of *Campbell and Cosans*: 'Corporal punishment is traditional in Scottish schools and, indeed, appears to be favoured by a large majority of parents . . . Of itself, this is not conclusive of the issue before the Court for the threat of a particular measure is not excluded from the category of "degrading" . . . simply because the measure has been in use for a long time or even meets with general approval'.

102 Para. 31 of the judgment.

103 But on the utilitarian response to this argument, see Chapter 4, which asks whether utilitarian considerations can justify inflicting torture or inhuman and degrading treatment, which could lead in effect to exceptions to the blanket prohibition contained in Article 3. While Chapter 4 demonstrated that utilitarian considerations enter the reasoning of the Court, it did not raise directly the question of whether this has led the Court to admit exceptions to Article 3. If this question were to attract a positive answer, one would expect the exceptions to be phrased implicitly rather than explicitly.

104 Para. 32 of the judgment.

105 Para. 32 of the judgment.

106 Para. 33 of the judgment.

107 Para. 6 of his dissenting opinion, emphasis added.

108 Ibid.

109 Para. 9 of Sir Gerald's dissenting opinion.

110 Corporal punishment as school discipline could, and indeed has, been treated differently. In *Campbell and Cosans*, the Court found that the threat of corporal chastisement in Scottish state schools (punishment had not been inflicted) did not constitute a violation of Article 3 (unanimous) but did constitute a violation of the second sentence of Article 2 of Protocol 1 on the right of parents for their philosophical convictions to be respected as their children are educated (by six votes to one, Judge Sir Vincent Evans dissenting). In *Costello-Roberts*, the Court did not find any violation of the Convention following 'three whacks' actually inflicted on a seven-year-old in an independent school (by five votes to four in respect of Article 3 of the Convention). Finally, in *A* v. *United Kingdom*, no one – not even the Government – contested that the failure to secure the criminal conviction of a stepfather who had administered unreasonable corporal punishment was in breach of Article 3 (unanimous).

111 Paras. 13 and 14 of his dissenting opinion. The concurring opinion of Judge Sir John Freeland in *Costello-Roberts* expressed such limits in a more convincing tone. Sir John stressed the passage in the *Costello-Roberts* ruling to the effect that the

finding that Article 3 was not violated in this case should not 'be taken to approve in any way the retention of corporal punishment as part of the disciplinary regime of a school'. These words could be seen as constituting a casebook application of a cultural relativist position, namely: 'we shall not impose our way of doing things to you, even though we do not quite understand your way and certainly do not find it superior to ours; but we do not feel that we are on so much higher ground that we can step in and overrule you'.

112 Para. 12 of his dissenting opinion.

113 Jeremy Paxman, *The English: A Portrait of a People* (Penguin, 1999), at 207–8.

114 Para. 31 of the judgment.

115 As noted in Chapter 2.

116 Marie-Bénédicte Dembour, 'Diversity or commonality: The power to toss the human rights coin', (2005) *Mediterranean Journal of Human Rights* 65–91.

117 Para 11 of Sir Gerald's dissenting opinion.

118 *The Shorter Oxford English Dictionary* (Oxford: Clarendon Press, 1973).

119 *Roget's Thesaurus of English Words and Phrases* (London: Penguin, 1987), at nos. 9, 10, 79 and 80, respectively.

120 Upendra Baxi is thus right to stress that the universality and absoluteness of rights are two different questions: Upendra Baxi, *The Future of Human Rights* (New Delhi: Oxford University Press, 2002), at 104–5.

121 First and foremost G. W. F. Hegel. Human rights scholars versed in political philosophy thus tend to speak of particularism rather than cultural relativism. See e.g. Daniel A. Bell and Joseph H. Carens, 'The ethical dilemmas of international human rights and humanitarian NGOs: Reflections on a dialogue between practitioners and theorists' (2004) 26 *Human Rights Quarterly* 300–29, at 307.

122 Perry, 'Are human rights universal?', at 505.

123 Ibid., at 505–6.

124 E.g. Donnelly, *Universal Human Rights*. I should nonetheless stress that there are scholars defending the universality of human rights who use the term 'universalism'. See e.g. Perry, 'Are human rights universal? at 481 (also at 504, quoting Philip Alston on 'universalist aspirations').

125 Herskovits, *Cultural Relativism*, at 542, emphasis in the original.

126 For example Vincent concludes the chapter of his book on 'Human rights and cultural relativism' by asserting that he has 'presented an argument for the universality of [human rights] application': Vincent, *Human Rights*, at 57.

127 Above at 77.

128 Brown, 'Cultural Diversity', at 213.

7

The Convention in a feminist light

> Women are born free and remain equal to men in rights.   (de Gouges)

The first article of the 'Declaration of the Rights of Man and of the Citizen' adopted by the French National Assembly in 1789 proudly stated: 'Men are born and remain free and equal in rights'. One year later, Olympe de Gouges asserted in a pendant 'Declaration of the Rights of Woman', of her own making: 'Women are born free and remain equal to men in rights.'[1] This stance did not go down well. On 3 November 1793, de Gouges was guillotined – like a man – for having forgotten the virtues of her sex and having inappropriately sought to become a statesman.[2]

In their early formulations, the natural rights of man were not meant to be the rights of every human being. The great majority found compelling rather than repulsive the idea that some categories of people, including women and slaves, fell outside their ambit. This is no longer the case. Today few would dare to deny that human rights are meant to be the rights of every single human being. A feminist critique has nonetheless emerged in the last two decades which argues that human rights have been and remain typically male in their conception.

On the surface, the Strasbourg Court has a good record in terms of women's rights. It has long affirmed that 'the advancement of the equality of the sexes is a major goal' in the Council of Europe, and over 25 per cent of its judges are now women. Stephanie Palmer is nonetheless of the view that 'the vast majority of cases [which have come before the European Court of Human Rights] do not address the experience of women';[3] Susanne Baer sketches the citizen behind the European Convention on Human Rights as 'male, resourceful, orderly, behaved, and serving the general good'.[4]

Can Palmer and Baer be dismissed as ranting feminists in an age when women, especially in the West, have successfully fought for the rights to vote, to be educated, to manage their property, to open a bank account, to exercise a profession, to receive equal pay for equal work, to keep their nationality upon marriage with a foreign man, and so on and so forth; a list which reminds us that what we take for granted today was far from being considered 'natural' even one or two generations ago?[5] The answer is a resounding no.

The affirmation in law of women's entitlement to equal rights is assuredly a momentous achievement. While it must be celebrated, it should not lead to complacency. In a challenge to this part of the human rights credo which would make us believe that human rights are (or have become) gender-neutral, this chapter demonstrates that feminist perspectives are bound to reveal the Convention law as persistently male-oriented. It does so by applying the insights of the liberal, 'woman's voice' (generally known as cultural), radical and post-modern strands of feminist critique to selected case law.

Feminism and feminisms

Virtually all the 'isms' explored in this book have more than one variant: there are distinct ways of being liberal, utilitarian, Marxist, particularist or realist. When it comes to feminism, however, the variants are so pronounced that for someone to refer to herself – and possibly, though more rarely, himself – as a feminist does not say much about her position. It is nonetheless possible to speak of feminism in the singular. Janet Halley has usefully identified the common points of feminisms as follows:

> First, to be feminism, a position must make a distinction between m and f. Different feminisms do this differently: some see men and women; some see male and female; some see masculine and feminine. While 'men' and 'women' will almost always be imagined as distinct human 'groups', the other paired terms can describe many different things: traits, narratives, introjects. However a particular feminism manages these subsidiary questions, it is not 'a feminism' unless it turns in some central or core way on the distinction between m and f.
>
> And secondly, to be a feminism in the United States [or elsewhere[6]] today, a position must posit some kind of subordination as between m and f, in which f is the disadvantaged or subordinated element. At this point feminism is both descriptive and normative; it takes on the quality of a justice project while also becoming a subordination hypothesis. Feminism is feminism because, as between m and f, it carries a brief for f.[7]

Halley goes on to explain that feminisms differ on more than one count: most importantly, they register subordination in different places – for example, sex or ethical reasoning – and they see subordination as being structural (in which case it will stay until the structure is changed) or episodic (in which case it is not necessarily *always* in the present structure).

In short, feminism asks the woman question. It is a way of looking at the world, seeing it as organized along gendered lines which benefit men, and trying to change it so that women are empowered. In the human rights field, a feminist critique has taken a long time to be expressed – or, perhaps more accurately, to be heard. For two centuries, the vibrant and clear message sent by Olympe de Gouges in her Declaration of 1790 remained dormant in human rights scholarship. In the last twenty years, however, feminist critiques of human rights have become inescapable.[8]

This chapter follows a classification which is found in various synthesizing works. It discusses the liberal, woman's voice, radical and post-modern strands of feminism in turn. To put it in the simplest terms, the liberal strand seeks to ensure that men and women be treated equally; the woman's voice strand stresses that women conduct their lives differently from men, follow different modes of thinking and behaving, which results in different aspirations and priorities; the radical strand argues that men dominate women, so that a complete transformation of underlying assumptions is required before a female agenda can be enacted; the post-modern strand emphasizes the infinite variety of women's positions and concerns, thus resisting defining *the* strategy which would address the problems faced by (all) women. This theoretical framework is admittedly simplistic: feminist scholars do not necessarily fit within these four categories. It nonetheless provides the advantage of presenting a (limited) variety of feminist agendas in a didactically clear manner.

The feminist liberal agenda: Working for sex equality

The obvious place to start a review of legal feminist critiques is the liberal agenda which can be said to have animated the 'first wave' feminists of the eighteenth to the mid-twentieth centuries and which remains extremely influential today.[9] In brief, the legal feminist liberal agenda aims to ensure that women enjoy the same rights as men, within what are regarded as the meritorious tenets of liberal law. At its heart lies the assumption that women are equal to men, with the consequence that women must not *in principle* be excluded from rights enjoyed by men – and vice-versa. In other words, the feminist liberal critique does not ask anything else than for liberalism to be true to its fundamental intuition that all must have their rights guaranteed.

Laws which explicitly guarantee, or implicitly endorse, the principle of sex equality constitute the great achievement of liberal feminism.[10] Today, the *principle* of sex equality is for the most part accepted. However, assessing what sex equality means in the practice of actual rights is riddled with difficulties. The controversial question immediately and recurrently arises: which situations are the same – and thus require equal treatment – and which situations are different – and thus justify a difference in treatment? To rephrase the second branch of this question: how should women (or men) be treated when they are *not* in the same position as their counterpart?[11] This of course brings us back to the first branch: how do we establish that women (or men) are or are not in the same position?

The implementation of a feminist liberal agenda is far from a straightforward matter. This in itself explains why debates on the meaning of sex equality remain persistent. A second reason for liberal feminism's continued relevance is that it is concerned not just with the formal allocation of rights but also with the under-representation of women in politically and socially significant positions (including the judiciary), as well as their over-representation among the poor.[12]

The presence of female judges at Strasbourg

On the face of it, the Strasbourg Court has gone a long way towards pursuing the feminist liberal agenda, i.e. in protecting the equality of the sexes. On the institutional front, the Court now includes an impressive percentage of women judges. In terms of the principles it follows, it has repeatedly declared the advancement of the equality of the sexes to be a major goal. The present and the following sections discuss these two aspects in turn.

The European Court of Human Rights has, since its inception, consisted of a number of judges equal to the number of states party to the Convention.[13] Each state presents a list of three candidates to the Parliamentary Assembly of the Council of Europe, which elects one of these candidates.[14] Before Protocol 11 came into force, only three women had been elected as (permanent) judges at the Strasbourg Court: Helga Pedersen, the Danish judge between 1971 and 1980; Denise Bindschedler-Robert, the Swiss judge between 1975 and 1991; and Elisabeth Palm, the Swedish judge from 1988 (who continued to serve in the new Court until 2003). As can readily be seen, the old Court had never counted more than two women at any one time and included only one in its closing years. But in the run-up to the establishment of the new Court in 1998, the Assembly encouraged the presentation of at least one female candidate per national list.[15] While many states failed to comply with this recommendation,[16] enough female candidates were presented and elected to make the presence of female judges at the Strasbourg Court noticeable.

At its inception on 1 November 1998, the new Court included 8 women among its 41 judges.[17] Furthermore, through its rules of procedure, the Court opted to pursue a 'policy aimed at securing a balanced representation of the sexes' within its four sections.[18] The trend of ensuring a female presence on the Strasbourg bench has since been accentuated, with 12 out of 44 judges being women at the time of writing.[19] Each section of the Court included two women in 1998, but now three. Though it remains possible for a chamber of seven judges drawn from a section not to include any woman, the days when an all-male composition was common are gone.

At one level, the presence of female judges at the Strasbourg Court is highly noticeable. Until the election of seven women and eleven men judges to the International Criminal Court created by the Rome Statute of 1998,[20] no international or national supreme court could pride itself on having brought as significant a proportion of women to its benches as the European Court of Human Rights. At another level, however, the female presence at the Strasbourg Court is hardly noticeable. The previous chapters have tentatively identified a judge with statist inclinations,[21] another who reasoned along utilitarian lines,[22] and two who expressed opinions consonant with particularist arguments.[23] Reassuringly for the establishment, I did not come across a judge who conspicuously displayed Marxist inclinations. More disconcertingly, any strikingly feminist line that a woman judge might have taken in a dissenting opinion (a form particularly useful in my analysis as its author is free to express herself outside the constraints of collegiality) has escaped me.[24] I shall comment further on this absence below.

Championing the equality of the sexes since *ABC*

Pre-Protocol 11, the near-absence of women judges at the Court meant that many cases were adopted by all-male benches. Such a male predominance did not prevent the old Court from declaring that it championed a sex equality agenda. A landmark decision in this respect is *Abdulaziz, Cabales and Balkandali v. United Kingdom,* decided on 28 May 1985,[25] which has already been introduced in Chapter 5 and is more commonly known as the *ABC* case.

The applicants in this case were three women, lawfully settled in the United Kingdom, who were respectively of Indian, Asian and Middle Eastern origin. Each was married to a man who had no right of abode in the United Kingdom. The Immigration rules then in force (hereafter 'the Rules') prevented these three men from joining or remaining with their wives in the United Kingdom. While the Rules would have allowed a lawfully settled man to be joined by his non-British patrial wife, the reverse was not true. The applicants alleged a number of violations of the Convention, particularly of Article 14 combined with Article 8.

We have seen above that Article 14, which prohibits discrimination in the enjoyment of the rights guaranteed in the Convention on a number of grounds, including sex, is not a 'free-standing' provision.[26] To be invoked it must be coupled with another Article of the Convention. Here the applicants submitted that they had suffered discrimination in respect of their right to protection of family life, guaranteed by Article 8 of the Convention. The Court accepted that Article 8 was applicable, but it did not consider that the family life provision was violated. In its view, the applicants had not demonstrated that they could not follow their husbands to live with them in their own countries, as the Government had argued.[27] The arguable sexism of this argument escaped the Court . . .

The applicants also alleged discrimination on grounds of sex, contrary to Article 14. The British Government had tried to justify the difference of treatment between men and women made by the Rules by reference to the need to protect the domestic labour market. The Court accepted that protection of this market was indeed the aim of the Rules, but it was 'not convinced that the difference that may exist between the respective impact of men and of women on the domestic labour market [was] sufficiently important to justify the [contested] difference of treatment'.[28] The applicants had argued that the Government's stance 'ignored the modern role of women'.[29] The Commission had furthermore remarked that the 'commitment to the reunification of the families of male immigrants . . . no longer corresponded to modern requirements as to the equal treatment of the sexes'.[30] The Court declared, in a passage which it would repeat in subsequent judgments:

> [I]t can be said that the advancement of the equality of the sexes is today a major goal in the member States of the Council of Europe. This means that very weighty reasons would have to be advanced before a difference of treatment on the ground of sex could be regarded as compatible with the Convention.[31]

The Court unanimously concluded that the applicants had been victims of discrimination on ground of sex.[32] The end result of this judgment was that the British Government subsequently made it equally difficult for men to be joined by their alien wives, thus treating all spouses equally.

What's in a name: *Burghartz*

Since the *ABC* case, the Court has often reiterated that sex equality is a major goal in the Council of Europe and that strong justification has to be advanced for a difference of treatment to be acceptable under Article 14 of the Convention. One case when this happened is *Burghartz* v. *Switzerland*, decided on 22 February 1994.[33]

The two applicants in this case were a Swiss couple. They had married in Germany, where they had chosen the woman's name as their family name (Burghartz). When they came back to Switzerland, the authorities initially insisted that their family name should be the husband's name, although they eventually withdrew this demand in the course of legal proceedings which reached the Federal Court. However, the name issue persisted in so far as the husband wanted to retain his surname (Schnyder) before the family name. Swiss law explicitly allowed a woman to do this. The applicants argued that Mr Burghartz was discriminated against on grounds of sex, in contravention of Article 14 taken in conjunction with Article 8 of the Convention. According to the Swiss Federal Court, there was no support in the Civil Code for Mr Burghartz to be allowed to bear the name 'Schnyder Burghartz'. In its words:

> The Swiss Parliament, out of a concern to preserve family unity and avoid a break with tradition, had never agreed to introduce absolute equality between spouses in the choice of name and had thus deliberately restricted to wives the right to add their own surnames to their husbands.[34]

The all-male Court held that this restriction violated the Convention, but only by five votes to four. Interestingly, the dissenting judges did not refer to equality or gender. Judge Thór Vilhjálmsson found that the prejudicial effect was not such as to bring it within the proper scope of international protection of human rights. The other three dissenters, Judges Pettiti and Valticos and Judge Russo, were of the opinion that rules governing family names were beyond the scope of Article 8 and remained within the state's domain.

From a feminist perspective, these dissenting opinions beg two questions. Firstly, one wonders whether they reflect the dissenters' real motivations or whether, perhaps even unconsciously, the dissenting judges were resisting an equality of the sexes agenda. Secondly, one must ask upon which criteria the degree of importance of a particular claim is to be assessed. Many feminists have suggested that women may well decide this issue in a way different from men.

The shortcomings of the 'Add Women and Stir' liberal approach

This is one of the reasons why many feminists may feel that a liberal approach is unable, by itself, to deliver a feminist agenda. Furthermore, liberalism, when it has taken on board a sex equality agenda, only requires that women have the same rights as men, and men the same rights as women.[35] In the *ABC* case the Court found a violation of Article 14 of the Convention on the ground of sexual discrimination. The British Government eliminated the discrimination by treating the foreign men like the foreign women and denying all aliens the right to be joined by their spouse; the women applicants failed to gain the substantive right they had been hoping for. In the *Burghartz* case the Court also found a violation of Article 14 of the Convention on grounds of sex discrimination, thus opening the way for the first applicant, who was a man, to have the right to insert the name of his wife in his name. This is in line with the trend, noted by Judge Tulkens, that it is often men who contest at Strasbourg differences in treatment based on sex.[36]

In a liberal view of sex equality, *both* men and women suffer from sex discrimination. It therefore does not matter that *ABC* failed to give the female applicants the right they were seeking nor that the first applicant in *Burghartz* was a man. What is important is that both women and men may bring cases before the Court; it is then up to each individual to decide whether he or she wishes to do this.

For a feminist, however, the fact that a judicial battle gives rise to measures which do not improve the position of women or that it is men who seek to take advantage of the provision on the prohibition of sex discrimination is deeply problematic, given that the intended original purpose, to redress women's subordination, is missed. A feminist will typically point out that the achievement of sex equality, when men seek rights which were until then the preserve of women, can perpetuate female oppression, as could be the case if men were gaining equal access to children.[37] Palmer's conclusion that a 'perverse but consistent result of rights-based strategies is the reinforcement of the most privileged groups in society'[38] is pertinent here.

Following an old saying, Eva Brems has characterised the liberal feminist agenda as the 'Add Women and Stir' approach.[39] The slight slur of the label is no doubt intended. It would be wonderful if one could just add women to the political and legal concoction, and everything would be fine in the new melting pot. But things are not so simple. In particular, 'woman's voice' feminists observe that women are not men, and should not have to be like men.

The woman's voice feminist agenda: Calling for women to be recognized as different from men

There is a sense in which liberal feminism understands the fight for sex equality as the fight for women to be treated like men. But why should a woman want to be treated like a man, especially if it is accepted that feminine modes of thought and behaviour do not coincide with masculine ones? What feminists accordingly should strive for is to ensure that female traits receive proper recognition, rather than being dismissed as irrational and unreliable in a world which favours masculine reasoning. The strand of feminism which has put forward this argument most clearly is widely known as cultural feminism. As an anthropologist I find the reference to culture obscure, or at least misleading. Here I thus refer to it as the woman's voice feminist agenda after Carol Gilligan's book *In a Different Voice*,[40] which soon became emblematic of this strand of feminism.[41]

Written by a social psychologist and published in 1982, the book discusses differences in girls' and boys' psychological development by reference to their assessment of moral issues. It documents the logical, abstract, deductive reasoning favoured by boys and contrasts it with the emotional, concrete and contextual reasoning favoured by girls who tend to place the maintenance of relationships and networks at the centre of their preoccupations. The study concludes that it is wrong to regard as universal the masculine model of an 'ethic of rights'. This mistake, commonly made, is heavy with consequences. Having debunked the partiality of the masculine model, *In a Different Voice* calls for the valuing of the feminine model of an 'ethic of care'.

Woman's voice feminists contrast the masculine and the feminine within human nature, in terms of both their biological and ethical components. They recognize that childbearing and lactating female capacities place women in a unique position, such that women may not aspire to become 'like men'. They see this biological position as inextricably linked with an ethical female disposition towards care, whereby the female psychological structure is characterized by a relational orientation. Women may positively want to be 'caring' mothers, partners, friends. In particular this leads them, so the theory goes, to shun confrontational and absolute solutions to their problems and to seek instead accommodations which take everyone into consideration and are less clear-cut in their effects. This has direct implications for the way they use – or do not use – law.

Law tends to look at individuals *qua* individuals and to decontextualize situations, picking up facts deemed legally relevant and omitting others. This is arguably of little help to women who are 'naturally' inclined to look at things in a relational, contextual manner. As Palmer, writing on the Convention, has noted, 'rights are inherently individualistic and competitive and women's experience is not easily translated into this narrowly accepted language of rights'.[42] In its most radical form, woman's voice feminism sees law (especially as we know it in the West) as too abstract, individualistic and confrontational in character to have much to offer women.[43] In its milder form, it calls for the female voice to be heard in law alongside the male one. In institutional terms this requires the physical collocation of women. Substantially this demands the accommodation of rights whose definition comes to reflect an ethic of care. The following two sections offer some reflections on the record of the Strasbourg Court in respect of these two issues.

Is a distinctly female voice heard within the Court? An open question

The days when the Court was unabashedly predominantly male are gone. Does the small but growing female presence within the Court ensure that a 'typically' female voice is now raised and heard in its midst? This question is tricky not least because what a distinctly female voice would consist of (and whether it should be encouraged) is in itself controversial.[44] Let me bypass these difficulties in order to posit that, whatever the merits of these objections, it is clear that a female voice hardly emerges from the midst of the Strasbourg Court.

A postgraduate student from Stanford University, Nina-Louisa Arold, has researched what she calls the inner legal culture of the European Court of Human Rights.[45] One aspect which interested her was the way judges managed their differences but also shared commonalities. Among the latter Arold identified the value of equality, including between the judges. She writes (in language which betrays that she is not a native English speaker): 'I learned from all the four female judges who I interviewed that they never felt treated differently in any way compared to their male colleagues (interviews 2, 7, 8, 11).'[46] The person who let me have a copy of this thesis happened to be one of Arold's female judge interviewees. Interestingly she had crossed off her number in the passage I have quoted, suggesting that she did not find the student's observation reflected her experience at the Court.

Female judges from other jurisdictions have complained of a sexist attitude among their male colleagues. Patricia Wald, who spent two years in The Hague as judge of the International Criminal Tribunal for the former Yugoslavia, wrote when she was a Circuit Judge for a US Court of Appeal:

> For now, the judiciary is still a newly integrated male club, and women judges are expected to be agreeable, charming, bright, incisive, non-threatening, loyal, not irritatingly individualistic, supportive, cheerful, attractive, maybe witty – to a point, but not pushy, insistent, aggressive, sarcastic, unyielding, or any of the other qualities our male colleagues exhibit every day.[47]

When she was a Lord (!) Justice of Appeal, Brenda Hale, who has since become the first woman judge to sit in the British House of Lords, referred to Erika Rackley's image of the female judge as mermaid:[48]

> In order to become a judge a woman has to give up her own voice and adopt that of a man - like the little mermaid who had to give up her voice to be near her prince. I hope that Stackley [sic] is wrong but do acknowledge how difficult it is to get it

right – to forge a new picture of a judge who does not fit the traditional model but is still recognisably a judge.[49]

It is a fairly common experience that women who have achieved success on men's ground have come in the course of their career to adopt 'masculine' mores – becoming more male than a male in the same way as the newly converted often become, according to the French saying, more Catholic than the Pope. It can never be assumed that a woman will display 'typical' female characteristics – whatever these are – but this may be especially true of women who have had to compete on male grounds.

To me, it is a great puzzle that I have not encountered a dissenting opinion which I would have recognized as being resolutely (or even half-resolutely) feminist in its inspiration. A number of possible explanations come to mind. Perhaps women judges are careful, consciously or not, not to display their female, all-too-female, view of the law, making it impossible for an external observer like me to discern their *f* (female/feminine/feminist) voice in the bench. Perhaps they are waiting for the Court to be ready to hear them before they speak out. Or perhaps they have simply internalized the hegemonic male norms. What will not do is to say that the absence of an overtly feminist agenda (by female *or* by male judges) is due to feminism having become so mainstream that it is now unnecessary for a distinctive *f* voice to be raised. The case law discussed in the rest of this chapter amply demonstrates this point.

Buckley and *Chapman*: Applicants who are mothers

The aim of this section is to ask whether the Strasbourg Court has been able to accommodate a perspective which reflects the 'ethic of care' associated by woman's voice feminism with women. From what I can see there is very little trace of such an ethic in the Strasbourg case law, a conclusion which is not particularly startling if an 'ethic of rights' is accepted to be at the basis of the Court.[50] This section reviews two cases where women applicants were arguably trying to make their 'caring' voice heard, but without success: *Buckley* v. *United Kingdom*, decided on 25 September 1996,[51] and *Chapman* v. *United Kingdom*, decided on 18 January 2001.[52] These cases are best known among human rights experts for raising minority issues, especially regarding the lifestyle of the gypsy community in the UK.[53] Here, however, I shall read them in a woman's voice feminist light.

In *Buckley*, the applicant was a gypsy woman who submitted that the British Government had violated Article 8 of the Convention guaranteeing the right to respect for home, private and family life (as well as Article 14 taken together with Article 8), by legally preventing her from living with her family in a caravan which she had placed on a piece of land she owned. The Government submitted that any interference which could have arisen with the applicant's rights under the

Convention resulted from planning regulations intended to preserve the rural character of the countryside, thus implicitly adopted for everyone's benefit. The Court accepted the applicant's claim that there was an issue of home protection.[54] Article 8 therefore applied. However, the Court felt that it could not 'substitute its own view of what would be the best policy in the planning sphere or the most appropriate individual measure in planning cases' for that of the Government.[55] This was an area where 'the national authorities in principle enjoy[ed] a wide margin of appreciation'.[56] For the Court the national authorities 'arrived at the contested decision after weighing in the balance the various competing interests at issue'.[57] By six votes to three the (all-male) Court ruled that there was no violation of Article 8.[58]

Such a summary, as might be found in legal textbooks,[59] omits the fact that Ms Buckley was a woman, facing a typically (if not exclusively) female predicament of bringing up three children alone. Her arguments, as summarized by the Court, highlight that part of the story:

> The applicant accepted that gypsies should not be immune from planning controls but argued that the burden placed on her was disproportionate. She stated that, seeking to act within the law, she had purchased the site *to provide a safe and stable environment for her children and to be near the school they were attending.*[60] She drew attention to the fact that, at the time of the events complained of, the official site further down Meadow Drove [where the Government argued she could have gone to live] had not yet opened. In any event, the official site had since proved *unsuitable for a single woman with children.* There had been reports of crime and violence there and the Inspector's report of May 1995 had noted that the site was bleak and exposed. In the circumstances, therefore, the official site could not be considered an acceptable alternative for the applicant's own site.[61]

The Court referred only once to the familial situation of the applicant when it observed, in cursory fashion, that her rights regarding her 'home' were 'pertinent to her and her children's personal security and well-being'.[62]

By contrast the importance of the applicant's familial situation was not lost on the dissenting judges, especially Judge Repik. The Slovakian judge remarked in his dissenting opinion:

> There was never any mention [in the domestic proceedings] of the applicant's rights to respect for her home or of the importance of that right to her, given her financial and family situation. Nor was any account taken of the possible consequences for the applicant and her children were she to be evicted from her land.

In the words of Repik:

> The Court underestimates the cogency of arguments advanced by the Commission, which reported in detail on the condition of the Meadow Drove site and the numerous incidents which have occurred there. The safety of the applicant's family is not guaranteed there and it is an unsuitable place for bringing up her children.

Judge Repik concluded this part of his argument with the words: 'The applicant did not, therefore, refuse to move there out of sheer capriciousness.' This may have been offered as a response to the widespread view that an 'ethic of rights' allows an individual applicant to pursue a right in a selfish manner. It would not have been general social considerations which Judge Repik would then have had in mind. Rather the image of the applicant conveyed by his dissenting opinion is that of a struggling mother who is trying to take care of three children as best she can.

The facts in *Chapman* were very similar to *Buckley*. The applicant was again a gypsy woman who 'due to harassment while she led a travelling life, which was detrimental to the health of the family and the education of [her four] children, [had] bought a piece of land . . . with the intention of living on it in a mobile home'.[63] Planning permission to do so was refused and enforcement notices served. The applicant argued that this constituted a violation of Article 8 (as well as other articles) of the Convention. This time, the Court sat as a Grand Chamber. It made it clear that it did not need to follow *Buckley* in *Chapman* if circumstances in the contracting states had changed in the four-year interval.[64] The developing international legislation on minority rights seemed to indicate some kind of change. The Court found that what was at stake in *Chapman* was not the right to respect for the home of the applicant but the ability for her to maintain her identity as a gypsy and to lead her private and family life in accordance with that tradition.[65] In terms of minority rights this could have constituted a promising departure from *Buckley*. Unfortunately the Court relied on a static, and as such unconvincing, concept of tradition.[66] This led it to suggest that the applicant's lifestyle could have been worthy of protection only if she had stuck to a tradition of itinerancy.[67] Leaving this point aside, as far as the Court was concerned, the contested 'decisions were reached by the [responsible planning] authorities after weighing in the balance the various competing interests'.[68] By a narrow majority of ten votes to eight the Court found that there had been no violation of Article 8 of the Convention.

As in *Buckley*, the majority (which included two women judges) failed to consider the applicant as a woman who was the principal carer for some members of her family (no longer her children by the time the case was heard by the Court, but her 90-year-old father who required constant care). To quote one paragraph of the judgement:

> The seriousness of what is at stake for this applicant is demonstrated by the facts of the case. The applicant followed an itinerant lifestyle for many years, stopping on temporary or unofficial sites. She took up residence on her own land by way of finding a long-term and secure place to station her caravans. Planning permission was however refused for this and she was required to leave. The applicant was fined twice. She left her land but returned as she had been moved on constantly from place to place. It would appear that the applicant does not in fact wish to pursue an itinerant lifestyle. She was resident on the site from 1986 to 1990 and between 1992

and those proceedings. Thus the present case is not concerned as such with traditional itinerant gypsy lifestyles.[69]

The dissenting judges (who included two women) borrowed heavily from this paragraph in their dissenting opinion. They did so while alluding to the familial position of the applicant:

> In the present case, the seriousness of what is at stake for this applicant is readily apparent. The applicant *and her family* followed an itinerant lifestyle for many years, stopping on temporary or unofficial sites and being increasingly moved on by police and local authority officials. *Due to considerations of family health and the education of the children*, the applicant took the step of buying land on which to station her caravans with security. Planning permission was however refused for this and they were required to leave. The applicant was fined twice and left her land. She returned though, as they had again been moved on constantly from place to place. She *and her family* remain on their land subject to the threat of further enforcement measures. Her situation is insecure and vulnerable.[70]

As legal convention requires the focus in this passage is still on the individual applicant. However the applicant is no longer regarded as a single individual, and the emphasis subtly shifts to highlight how she acts out of consideration for her family rather than for strictly personal purposes.[71]

From a feminist perspective, *Chapman* is interesting on a second front. It has been argued that women's position as carers means that they are not primarily interested in civil and political rights, because what tends to matter first and foremost is the well-being of the people in their care; social and economic rights would thus arguably suit their needs better.[72] If women want human rights to enable them to provide shelter, food, education or health to their loved ones, then *Chapman* is a clear reminder that European human rights law, as currently interpreted and practised at the Strasbourg Court, has little to deliver in this respect:

> Article 8 does not in terms give a right to be provided with a home . . . While it is clearly desirable that every human being has a place where he or she can live in dignity and which he or she can call home, there are unfortunately in the Contracting States many persons who have no home. Whether the State provides funds to enable everyone to have a home is a matter for political not judicial decision.[73]

The Court repeats the idea: 'If the applicant's problem arises through lack of money, then she is in the same unfortunate position as many others who are not able to afford to continue to reside on sites or in houses attractive to them.'[74] In practice Mrs Chapman (who did not ask for the state to provide her with a material home but for planning laws to be conceived differently) is in an impossible situation: she cannot go to an 'authorized site' as no place is available there, but she cannot put a caravan on the land she owns either. The Court makes it clear that where the applicant should go and live in these circumstances is not a question it feels it should address.

The radical feminist agenda: Getting rid of patriarchy

The section above suggested that one might wish the Court to become more attuned and responsive to women's position as carers.[75] However, radical feminists have argued that '[c]ultural feminism is conservative of the status quo . . . insofar as it supports an exaggerated notion of the differences between men and women'.[76] For the leading radical feminist Catharine MacKinnon,[77] getting women to think of themselves as carers is a male trick. She writes: '*Why* do women become these people, more than men . . . For me, the answer is clear: the answer is the subordination of women'.[78] From her perspective, if women adopt a caring role, it is because this is the role traditionally assigned to them; to men's obvious convenience, this role contributes through its emphasis on relationships and responsibilities to the perpetuation of women's subordination.

The starting point of MacKinnon's feminism was her dissatisfaction with both the liberal and the woman's voice feminist strands. Both these approaches, she observed, use a male yardstick: the former to profess 'we're the same, we're the same, we're the same'; the latter to stress 'we're different, we're different, we're different'.[79] According to her, however, the real problem is not whether men and women are the same or different, it is that men subordinate women. For radical feminism, the key issue is patriarchy, and the aim is the empowerment of women.

Radical feminism locates the basis of women's oppression in sex. It rests on the idea that men reduce women to their sexuality and use them as sexual objects. In MacKinnon's phrase, 'Man fucks woman: subject, verb, object'.[80] As a result, radical feminism pays particular attention to sexual (or sexually-charged) issues: pornography, prostitution, rape, sexual harassment, female genital mutilation, abortion, sterilization, anorexia and other issues related to the sexed body. The radical feminist perspective makes it possible, and indeed imperative, for the personal to become political. The theory admits that not all women are aware of the continual sexual oppression to which men subject them, but explains this away through 'false consciousness'. The primary task is accordingly to raise women's consciousness and to make it possible for them to become women on their own terms – feminism 'unmodified'.

Radical feminists show that law, far from being neutral as it claims, is on the whole made by men for men, and excludes women. They question the neutrality of legal concepts which lawyers generally take for granted.[81] In particular they urge a reconceptualization of the public-private dichotomy - *the* feminist issue according to Carole Pateman.[82] To give an example, sexual abuse typically occurs in the home; traditional liberal theory would classify it as belonging to the private, i.e. non-political and/or unregulated,[83] sphere. This conceptualization is unacceptable to radical feminists; sexual abuse must be understood as 'an urgent, public, political issue concerning power and powerlessness, dominance and subordination'.[84]

A disappointing record on rape: *X and Y*, *SW*, *Aydin* and *Stubbings*

Rape is one of the issues which has been of central concern to radical feminists. In this section, I try to imagine what a radical feminist might say about the Court's treatment of rape cases. I review four cases: *X and Y* v. *Netherlands*, delivered on 16 March 1985;[85] *SW* v. *United Kingdom*, decided on 22 November 1995;[86] *Stubbings and Others* v. *United Kingdom*, decided on 22 October 1996;[87] and *Aydin* v. *Turkey*, decided on 25 September 1997.[88] While I cannot rule out that a radical feminist might find my analysis simplistic and overlooking important aspects of male domination, I feel safe in saying that she would accept my conclusion that the record of the Strasbourg Court is disappointing from a radical feminist perspective. Radical feminism seeks a complete transformation of the overarching patriarchal structure. Accordingly, even when a battle is apparently won, you can only realize that it has not really been won if you look at a deeper level.[89]

In three of the four cases listed above the Court reached decisions which may be considered to have delivered a blow to the traditional public-private dichotomy, but without knocking it out. I shall give a brief account of each case before turning to a discussion of the way, *ex hypothesi* disappointing, the Court has approached the public-private dichotomy.

In the first case, the applicant Y was a mentally handicapped girl who had been raped, aged sixteen, by a family member of the directress of the institution where she lived. X, the father of the girl and the first applicant before the Court, had attempted to institute criminal legal proceedings against the rapist in the Netherlands, but to no avail. His daughter, who was still mentally a child, could not lodge a complaint with the police.[90] Her father could not do this either, for the complaint legally had to be signed by the victim herself.[91] X and Y alleged a violation of (inter alia) Article 8 of the Convention before the Strasbourg institutions. The Court accepted that the civil law remedies which would have been available to the victim were insufficient in the case of wrongdoing of the kind she had suffered.[92] Although it recognized that the gap in Dutch law could have been unintentional,[93] this did not justify the absence of an adequate legal action. The (all-male) Court unanimously ruled that Y was a victim of a violation of Article 8 of the Convention.[94]

SW v. *United Kingdom* concerned the conviction of a man for the rape of his wife. The applicant argued that his conviction, one of the first in Britain for marital rape, violated Article 7 of the Convention guaranteeing the non-retroactivity of criminal offences. The Court was not convinced by this argument. It spoke of the 'essentially debasing character of rape' which is 'so manifest' that the national judicial decisions could not be found to contravene Article 7, the aim of which it identified as ensuring that no one is subjected to arbitrary prosecution or conviction.[95] The Court continued: '[T]he abandonment of the unacceptable idea of a husband being immune against prosecution for rape of his wife [is] in conformity not only with a civilised concept of marriage but also, and above all, with the fundamental objectives of the Convention, the very essence of which is respect for human dignity and human freedom.'[96] The Court (again an all-male bench) unanimously ruled that there had been no violation of the Convention.

The *Aydin* case was brought by a Turkish woman of Kurdish origin. She reported that, in the context of Turkish operations against PKK members, she had been taken one morning to gendarme headquarters with her father and sister-in-law, separated from the latter, and maltreated and raped in the course of a detention which lasted over a period of three days. She was seventeen at the time of the alleged facts. The Strasbourg Commission went on a fact-finding mission and found her account credible, despite some inconsistencies and inconclusive medical reports.[97] The Court accepted, by fourteen votes to seven, the facts as established by the Commission.[98] (The one woman on the bench, Judge Palm, voted with the majority.) The Court proceeded to find that the 'especially cruel act of rape to which [the applicant] was subjected amounted to torture in breach of Article 3 of the Convention'.[99] To reach this conclusion, the Court reasoned:

> Rape of a detainee by an official of the State must be considered to be an especially grave and abhorrent form of ill-treatment given the ease with which the offender can exploit the vulnerability and weakened resistance of his victim. Furthermore, rape leaves deep psychological scars on the victim which do not respond to the passage of time as quickly as other forms of physical and mental violence. The applicant also experienced the acute physical pain of forced penetration, which must have left her feeling debased and violated both physically and emotionally.[100]

I shall now attempt a radical feminist reading of these cases. The judgment in *X and Y* was firmly based on the ground of the public-private dichotomy. The Court first recalled that 'although the object of Article 8 is essentially that or protecting the individual against arbitrary interference by the public authorities . . . there may be positive obligations inherent in an effective respect for private or family life'.[101] It went on to observe 'that the choice of the means calculated to secure compliance with Article 8 in the sphere of the relations of individuals between themselves is in principle a matter that falls within the Contracting States' margin of appreciation'.[102] In this respect, the Government presented an argument which consisted of a straightforward application of the liberal public-private distinction. It referred to 'the difficulty encountered by the legislature in laying down criminal law provisions calculated to afford the best possible protection of the physical integrity of the mentally handicapped', and continued: 'to go too far in this direction might lead to unacceptable paternalism and occasion an inadmissible interference by the State with the individual's right to respect for his or her sexual life'.[103] Far-fetched, this argument reveals the absurdity to which the distinction between the public and the private 'spheres' can lead. The Court flatly rejected it.[104] Considering the facts of the cases, this is the least we could expect, making this victory, in the grand scheme of things, rather hollow. Not surprisingly, the verdict was unanimous.

The central issue debated before the Court in *SW* was the foreseeable character of the offence of marital rape: was the applicant convicted of a conduct which constituted a criminal offence when it took place? The Government and the Commission answered in the affirmative: '[G]iven the recognition of women's equality of status with men in marriage and outside it and of their autonomy over their own bodies, the adaptation of the ingredients of the offence of rape was reasonably foreseeable.'[105] The Court unanimously followed this. The judgment contains no direct criticism of the public-private distinction. However the decision clearly bypasses, even if does not overtly challenge, the traditional view according to which sexual relationships within marriage belong to the private sphere and are not a proper site for the state to intervene. Since much of the violence directed against women occurs in the home, the collapse of the distinction in this case is to be welcomed. Nonetheless a feminist could be expected to note that a purely legal step such as the formal criminalization of marital rape cannot be expected to give rise to sexual equality in marriage.[106] Moreover, radical feminists might laugh at the Court's reference to a 'civilised concept of marriage',[107] given their tendency to regard marriage as a male-constructed institution.[108]

For the Court to have been able to equate, in *Aydin,* rape with torture could hardly be considered a revolutionary step in the late 1990s. The Court was following the lead of those other international courts which had recognized rape as a war crime.[109] What is noteworthy about *Aydin* is that the Court accepted that the applicant had actually been raped, despite arguably poor evidence. We have already seen in Chapter 5 how rules of evidence can easily work against those who are not in a position of power. This is, in particular, true when rape is alleged. In *Aydin,* however, the Commission was ready to say that it had found 'strong, clear and concordant evidence' supporting the applicant's allegations.[110] Two-thirds of the Court were ready to follow the Commission on this point; fourteen judges found it unlikely that the applicant would have fabricated her allegations.[111] The complete denial by the Turkish authorities that any operation had taken place in the applicant's village may have helped in this respect. The seven dissenting judges, however, did not think the allegation of rape had been proved beyond all reasonable doubt. They pointed out that the applicant had married her cousin a few days after the contested events, a fact which they said was 'surprising in the cultural context of the region' (without giving more details), and that she appeared to have had her first child shortly after the marriage (which seems irrelevant). While the majority did not follow this opinion, a radical feminist might nevertheless object to the words of the Court, including when it considered rape of a detainee *by an official of the State* 'especially grave and abhorrent',[112] thus remaining enclosed in a public-private dichotomy and implicitly downgrading the suffering of the woman who is raped by someone she knows and loves. The subsequent ruling in *Selmouni*,[113] where the Court unanimously rejected the allegation of rape by the male applicant, also throws up many questions as to the feminist status of *Aydin*. A radical feminist could argue that the difference in findings between *Aydin* and *Selmouni* points to the readiness by the Court to cast women, as opposed to men, in the role of victim.[114]

However one chooses to look at *Aydin*, one case which puts the final nail in the coffin of the reception by the Court of a radical feminist agenda is surely *Stubbings and Others* v. *United Kingdom*, decided less than a year before *Aydin*. *Stubbings* concerned four women who alleged that they had been sexually abused, and in two cases raped, in their childhoods, respectively by their adoptive father and brother, their natural fathers (in two cases) and by a school staff member. All four women had a history of depression. All said that they had only understood in the course of therapy the connection between their ongoing psychological problems and the sexual abuse they had suffered. By that time more than six years had elapsed since they had reached their eighteenth birthdays. In the case brought by Ms Stubbings against her adoptive father and brother, the House of Lords decided in 1993 that her action for civil compensation was time-barred under the Limitation Act 1980. As a result of this ruling the other applicants were also barred from starting or continuing civil proceedings. Criminal proceedings remained an available option, but required more stringent proof. The four women claimed at Strasbourg that these circumstances violated their right of access to court, guaranteed by Article 6 of the Convention. They also claimed that they had been discriminated against in comparison with other categories of victims, in violation of Article 14 taken together with Article 6 and/or Article 8.[115] The Court (an all-male bench) was not persuaded by this argument. It ruled by seven votes to two that there had been no violation of Article 6 and by eight votes to one that there had been no violation of Article 14.

The Court recalled that contracting states enjoy a certain margin of appreciation over the question of how to regulate access to court.[116] In the instant case, the Court found that '[t]he time-limit in question was not unduly short; indeed it was longer than the extinction periods for personal injury claims set by some international treaties'.[117] This referred to an argument presented by the British Government, according to which the six-year limitation period was 'proportionate and generous' and 'longer than that included in many international conventions concerned with personal injury in transport . . . which allowed two years from the date of disembarkation in which to bring a claim for personal injury sustained during international carriage by air and sea respectively'.[118] The Court further remarked that 'the United Kingdom legislature [had] devoted a substantial amount of time and study to the consideration of [limitation]'.[119] Since the mid-1930s there had been six official bodies reviewing the English law of limitation and reporting to Parliament, four legislative reforms and one consolidating statute (the Limitation Act 1980). The Court did not question the relevance of the international conventions and successive legislative reforms to the case before it.[120]

The Court's observation that '[t]here has been a developing awareness in recent years of the range of problems caused by child abuse and its psychological effects on victims, and it is possible that the rules on limitation of actions applying in member States of the Council of Europe may have to be amended to make special provision for this group of claimants in the near future'[121] is of little consolation. The two dissenters each stressed that many years could elapse before the victim became aware of the causal link between her suffering and the abuse.[122] They both found the English law to violate the Convention – one in two respects. Neither of them apparently agreed with the following assertion: 'I have the greatest difficulty in accepting that a woman who has been raped does not know that she has suffered a significant injury.' This remark had been made by a member of the House of Lords in the *Stubbings* case and was quoted in the Strasbourg Court's judgment.[123] It shows a complete disregard for what psychological experts and victims of sexual abuse report.

Confronted with such reasoning, one cannot help sharing the logic and anger evident in the famous essay MacKinnon wrote on human rights, admittedly with another context in mind:

> What most often happens to women escapes the human rights net. Abuses of women as women rarely seem to fit what these laws [human rights conventions] and their enforcing bodies have in mind; the more abuses there are, the more they do not fit . . . Male reality has become human rights principle, or at least the principle governing human rights practice . . . The violations of the human rights of men better fit the paradigm of human rights violations because that paradigm has been based on the experiences of men.[124]

The right to have an abortion: Neither in the Convention nor in *Open Door, Bowman, Tokarczyk* or *Odièvre*

When it comes to illustrating the way in which human rights law at Strasbourg fails to address women's predicament in a male-dominated society, abortion is an excellent case in point. It is to be noted from the outset that it is generally wrong to say of any feminist that she is *pro*-abortion. What happens is that most feminists reject the anti-abortion stance on the ground that many women feel they want, or rather need, an abortion in the course of their fertile life.[125] They are therefore likely to ask for abortion not to be criminal, to be effectively available, and to be respectful and empowering rather than punishing of women.[126] These three points can easily be seen as human rights issues. The European Court of Human Rights has not addressed them, though not for lack of opportunity. In cases such as *Open Door Counselling and Dublin Well Woman v. Ireland*, delivered on 29 October 1992,[127] *Bowman* v. *United Kingdom*, decided on 19 February 1998,[128] or *Tokarczyk* v. *Poland*, declared inadmissible on 31 January 2002,[129] the Court could have argued that abortion cannot be made criminal and must be available.[130] Instead, it refrained from making any direct statement on these issues.[131] Interestingly, in *Odièvre* v. *France*, decided on 13 February 2003,[132] it expressed unease at the fact that abortions do happen.

The Constitution of Ireland 'acknowledges the right to life of the unborn'.[133] By contrast, abortion is legal in the United Kingdom provided some conditions are met. In *Open Door*, the main applicants were two organizations[134] which had given precise information to pregnant women in Ireland on clinics which were performing abortions in Britain; had booked appointments for these women; and had sometimes prepared their travel arrangements. Open Door and Dublin Well Woman came under a judicial injunction to refrain from all these activities, considered to be contrary to the Constitution of Ireland, in the late 1980s. The applicants complained at Strasbourg of a violation of Article 10 of the Convention, guaranteeing freedom of expression, on the grounds that imparting information on specific, reputable, clinics performing abortion in the United Kingdom constituted an essential service.

The Court was satisfied that there had been an interference with Article 10, which was prescribed by law and which pursued a legitimate aim – that of protecting morals. It did not find, however, the interference to be proportionate. While the Government enjoyed a wide margin of appreciation, especially in a matter concerning the nature of human life in respect of which it is impossible to find a uniform European conception of morals, this power of appreciation was not unlimited.[135] The Court observed that 'the injunction limited the freedom to receive and impart information with respect to services which are lawful in other Convention countries and may be crucial to a woman's health and well-being'.[136] The Court was 'struck by the absolute nature of the Supreme Court injunction which imposed a "perpetual" restraint on the provision of information to pregnant women concerning abortion facilities abroad, regardless of age or state of health or their reasons for seeking counselling on the termination of pregnancy [as subsequently] highlighted by the case of . . . X'.[137] X was the fourteen-year-old girl whose case received widespread media coverage at the time: the Irish authorities had prevented her from travelling to the UK to seek the termination of a pregnancy which had resulted from rape, triggering a decision in her favour from the Irish Supreme Court, based on the EC principle of free movement of services. The Strasbourg Court also had regard to the evidence, which had not been disputed by the Government, suggesting that

> [T]he injunction has created a risk to the health of those women who are now seeking abortions at a later stage in their pregnancy . . . and who are not availing themselves of customary medical supervision after the abortion has taken place . . . Moreover, the injunction may have had more adverse effects on women who were not sufficiently

resourceful or had not the necessary level of education to have access to alternative sources of information [such as English telephone directories].[138]

By fifteen votes to eight, the Court found a violation of Article 10.

One breathes a sigh of relief at the verdict of violation. However, the judgment is disappointing on more than one count. First the question is only addressed from the perspective of freedom of expression. This may make sense in terms of internal Convention legal reasoning, but it does nothing to dispel the impression that Convention law has been phrased by men to answer men's concerns: if these concerns happen to coincide with women's concerns, fine; if they do not, never mind. Second, to the extent that women are considered, it is almost in terms of poor souls who need protection. For example, the Court refers to information available elsewhere 'although in a manner which was not supervised by qualified personnel and thus less protective of women's health'.[139] It would of course be counterproductive to reject protective measures when individuals are vulnerable, but too often protection of women in fact means control. Third, there is very little indication that the Court took on board the significance of the abortion issue in women's lives. Its reference to services that 'may be crucial to a woman's health and well-being' appears an unfortunate understatement. Judge Morenilla must be applauded for his use of stronger words in a concurring opinion where he refers to 'an area of information so important for a large sector of Irish women'.[140] Finally, the issue before the Court hardly touched the core of the issue. Even so, eight of the twenty-three judges managed to find no violation of the Convention, referring in one phrase or another to the 'paramount place accorded to the protection of unborn life in the whole fabric of Irish public policy'.[141] For a feminist, this poor score can only be extremely worrying, indicating how entrenched the patriarchal structure of society remains.[142]

This conclusion is unfortunately supported by the other decisions I have mentioned, which I shall now briefly review. In *Bowman*, the applicant was the executive director of the Society for the Protection of the Unborn Child who, prior to a general election, had distributed leaflets in Halifax on the three local candidates' views on abortion. This action led to her prosecution for infringement of the Representation of the People Act, which prevented unauthorized persons from spending more than £5 on publishing materials with a view to influencing the election of particular candidates. Mrs Bowman complained of a violation of Article 10. The Court observed that the contested restriction constituted 'one of the many detailed checks and balances which [made] up United Kingdom electoral law'.[143] For the majority of the (male) judges, this restriction, while provided by law and pursuing a legitimate aim, was disproportionate. Though applying only during the four to six weeks which preceded the election, the restriction was placed at such a low level that the Court was not 'satisfied that, in practice, [the applicant] had access to any other effective channels of communication'.[144] By fourteen votes to six, the Court found a violation of the Convention.

The dissenters focused on the way British electoral law aimed at maintaining equality of arms as between candidates. Interestingly, neither the judgment nor the dissenting opinions mentioned abortion. The word only surfaced in the account of the facts, which described the content of the leaflets which Mrs Bowman had distributed: in these leaflets the – female – Labour candidate was (objectionably) presented as a leading 'pro-abortionist'.[145]

Tokarczyk arose out of the conviction of the applicant to eighteen months' imprisonment for having aided and abetted abortion. In return for payment, Mr Tokarczyk, who lived in Lublin near the eastern Polish border, had been driving women who wanted to have an abortion to Ukraine after abortion became illegal in Poland in 1993. The Court accepted that the motives of the applicant were not exclusively commercial but also inspired by his belief that abortion should not have been made unlawful. The applicant argued his conviction had been politically motivated; he stated that his activities harmed the financial interests of local gynaecologists who practised clandestine abortion for high fees and irritated 'fanatical' Catholic circles opposed to the idea that abortion is a woman's choice. Mr Tokarczyk complained inter alia of a violation of Article 10, guaranteeing freedom of expression. The relevant Chamber, which included two women, failed to address any of the arguments he had specifically raised about abortion. Wording its decision as if the applicant's offence was like any other ordinary criminal offence,[146] the Court unanimously found the application manifestly ill-founded.

The three cases which have just been reviewed were examined by the Court in the light of Article 10 of the Convention. Such a focus conveniently made it possible for it to ignore debates on the meaning of abortion.[147] Of course, the Court can be expected to be as divided as the rest of society on the issue of abortion. Some may therefore find it wise that it has managed to avoid a direct debate on the merits of abortion. From a feminist perspective, however, this approach is extremely disappointing, the more so since the Court has not always refrained from expressing a principled disapproval of abortion.

In *Odièvre* v. *France*, decided on 13 February 2003, the applicant complained that, having been abandoned at birth, she was unable to trace her natural mother who had given birth anonymously as is possible under French law (in a practice known as *accouchement sous X*). Ms Odièvre complained that she had been prevented from finding out her personal history in contravention of Article 8 of the Convention.[148] By ten votes to seven, the Court did not find a violation of the Convention, reasoning that the French legislation had sought 'to ensure sufficient proportion between the competing interests'[149] of the child 'in its personal development' and the mother 'in remaining anonymous [while] giving birth in appropriate medical conditions'.[150] The case was not as such about abortion. Nevertheless the contentious law 'sought . . . to avoid abortions, in particular illegal abortions'.[151] In his concurring opinion, Judge Ress, joined by Judge Kuris, was very clear on this connection: 'It is clearly in the general interest for appropriate measures to be taken . . . to protect children's lives by reducing so far as possible the number of abortions, whether legal or illegal.'[152] Also concurring, Judge Greve – a woman – argued that 'no society should in the name of the promotion of human rights be forced to leave a woman with abortion as the only apparent safe option'.[153]

The seven dissenting judges, among whom one woman (Judge Tulkens), objected to the verdict of non-violation to the extent that, far from balancing interests, 'French law accepted that the mother's decision constituted an *absolute* defence to any requests for information by the applicant, irrespective of the reasons for or legitimacy of that decision [with the result that] the rights of the child . . . are entirely neglected and forgotten.'[154] Responding to the argument about the 'need to avoid illegal abortions', the dissenters observed that 'at present there is no reliable data to support the notion that there would be a risk of an increase in abortions . . . if the system of anonymous births was abolished'.[155] This is a sound argument. Jennifer Saul has observed: 'Many women know that if they carry a pregnancy to term and give birth, they will be psychologically incapable of putting the child up for adoption', with their decision therefore not really being 'between abortion, adoption, and keeping the child, but rather . . . between abortion and keeping the child'.[156] The dissenters also refused the proposition, implicit in the Court's judgment, that 'the French system [was] the only one that ensures respect for the right to life' within the countries of the Council of Europe.[157] All this appears to me very sensible, but only a minority of judges – who included only one woman while two female judges voted with the majority – took this view.

Women's 'non-feminist' choices: False consciousness or essentialism?

In the case law reviewed above, women judges failed to articulate an instantly recognizable feminist perspective. If anything, it is men (Judge Repik in *Buckley*, Judge Morenilla in *Open Door*) who seemed to be one small step ahead on the feminist path. Radical feminists might tend to dismiss the views of women – judges or otherwise – who do not adopt what they recognize as a clear feminist agenda. In the view of the former, the latter suffer from false consciousness; they have not seen the light yet; they are mistaken in thinking they know what they think, who they are and what they believe; they would become feminists were they more aware of their conditions and conditioning. I personally do not find this line of argument utterly convincing. While I completely support some of the radical feminist agendas (especially on abortion), I tend to agree with those who criticize the radical strand of feminism for being 'deterministic' and 'essentialist'.

The first term refers to the readiness of the theory to posit as a given that the keys to understanding social life and women's position are respectively sex and sexual oppression/patriarchy. The opening words of MacKinnon's 1989 seminal book declare: 'Sexuality is to [radical] feminism what work is to marxism: that which is most one's own, yet most taken away'.[158] In the same way that Marxism can be criticized for reducing everything to economics, radical feminism can be criticized for reducing everything to sex. It is doubtful that sex determines the whole of social life.

The second term refers to the fact that radical feminism assumes that all women and, for that matter, also men, 'tick' in the same way; that what is true of one woman (or man) is also true of any other woman (or man), thus essentializing them. In other words, radical feminism is a 'grand theory' which fails to account for, and take account of, the complexity of social life. This has been particularly well pointed out by post-modern feminists.

The post-modern feminist critique: Recognizing women as different from one another

Post-modern feminism developed in the late 1980s.[159] It accepts the major insights of other strands of feminism, including the fact that women tend to be different from men and that male power exerts a crucial influence in a fundamentally gendered world. Nonetheless it seeks to problematize these assumptions. In the wake of the late French philosopher Michel Foucault, post-modern feminism has been interested in uncovering the ways in which power and knowledge, which it sees as intertwined, are constructed within particular discourses. The focus is on how we come to understand the world, including ourselves. The aim is to deconstruct the 'naturalness' of the certainties we learn. Meta-narratives are distrusted, myths debunked, basic concepts questioned.

This results in a sceptical attitude and a drive to go beyond appearances; nothing can ever be taken at face value. In turn this leads to fragmentation, as no grand theory is possible. Ironically, perhaps, this theoretical position offers greater inclusiveness. A grand theory, by reducing reality to one key factor, ignores factors which do not fit. For example radical feminism cannot talk about women who feel oppressed first and foremost by reason of class, race or religion. By contrast, post-modern feminists recognize that for any woman to assume that because she is a woman, she can speak for all women, smacks of arrogance and naïvety. It is wrong for a white middle-class educated woman, however well-intentioned, to think that she understands the reality of women she has never met.

Part of the post-modern critique is therefore to deconstruct the categories of 'woman' and 'gender', which other strands of feminisms tend to essentialize. The emphasis is on listening to the 'other'. Post-modernists typically explore rather than explain, as their theoretical perspective makes them wary of conceptual generalization. As a result, they avoid suggesting how the world could be put right. They do not have an agenda as such. Rather they offer a critique which does not take one definite direction.

By stressing that one woman is not another woman, so that no definite solution to the problem of subordination can be found, post-modern feminism admittedly undermines other forms of feminism.[160] But the fact that the post-modern turn has left many feminists in disarray need not concern us here.[161] Suffice it to stress that under post-modernism, everything is constantly thrown into question. Problems are repeatedly identified, solutions rarely offered.

When the Other is ignored: *Karaduman* and *Dahlab*

A post-modern institution is a contradiction in terms. It would therefore be impossible to ask the Strasbourg Court to become post-modern. The Court could not even follow a post-modern feminist agenda, which does not exist as such. Where post-modernism – an attitude rather than a recipe – could nonetheless be reflected is in a readiness by individual judges to explore a situation in unconventional ways rather than being satisfied with reasoning along established principles. The Court could show awareness that the reality of one woman is not the reality of another. This section reviews two cases which concern what is often called, in a homogenizing shorthand, 'the Muslim veil'.[162]

In *Karaduman* v. *Turkey*,[163] the applicant was a graduate of the University of Ankara. Having successfully completed her studies, she was refused her certificate by the University on the grounds that she had provided a photograph where she appeared with a headscarf, in contradiction with the University's regulations on student dress. When the case arrived at Strasbourg, the Turkish government argued that the headscarf could not be reconciled with the secular principle enshrined in the national Constitution. The Commission declared the case manifestly ill-founded on 3 May 1993. In *Dahlab* v. *Switzerland*,[164] the applicant was a teacher in an infant school in Geneva. When she was in her mid-twenties and already teaching, she converted to Islam and married an Algerian national. Mrs Dahlab continued to teach, now wearing a Muslim headscarf. No staff or parent commented. Four years later, however, her head-cover was found objectionable by an inspector. The applicant was told she had to stop wearing the veil at school. She eventually brought the case to Strasbourg. On 15 February 2001, the Court (which included two women)[165] declared, by undisclosed majority, the case manifestly ill-founded.

In *Karaduman*, the Commission seems to have assumed, as is commonly done in the West, the existence of a link between the wearing of a headscarf and fundamentalist religious groups of an extreme political persuasion. In *Dahlab*, the Court stated that the provision of the Koran which some Muslims interpret as imposing the veil on women is 'not easily reconcilable with the principle of equality of the sexes'. 'Thus', the Court continued, 'it appears difficult to reconcile the wearing of the Muslim veil with the message of tolerance, of respect for others and especially of equality and non-discrimination which all teachers must transmit to their pupils in a democracy.'[166]

These are gratuitous assertions: neither demonstrated nor even argued. It was neither established nor even suggested that Ms Karaduman belonged to a fundamentalist movement. Sociologists have demonstrated that there is no necessary link between the veil and fundamentalism. Moreover, they have pointed out that different women wear the veil – or rather, different kinds of veil – for different reasons: to affirm cultural or religious identity; to express resistance to Westernization; to ensure for themselves a passage in public places (such as Western schools or offices) which would otherwise be closed to them by parents or husbands who would be wary of seeing them get 'lost'; to avoid sexual objectification; as beautification, etc.[167] In both cases, the Strasbourg organs displayed a complete ignorance of the various meanings of the veil. They relied on the liberal principle of formal equality, but this was, from a post-modern feminist perspective, thoroughly inadequate: treating women equally does not necessarily mean treating them alike. In *Dahlab*, the Court referred to grand concepts – tolerance, equality and non-discrimination, democracy. It did not explore, however, what these entailed in practice.

Admittedly many feminists would welcome the *Karaduman* and *Dahlab* decisions. Many would applaud the Court for having 'reiterate[d] that the advancement of the equality of the sexes is today a major goal in the member States of the Council of Europe'. However, the post-modern critique alerts us to the hollowness of this formula. Not only does it fail to encompass strategies to alleviate the predicament of all women, but it also contributes to the obfuscation created by a complex of power and 'knowledge' which, in this case, puts the West on a pedestal and demonizes Islam. Elsewhere I have noted that the Court has so far failed to protect religious interests which fall outside Christianity.[168] The entire mode of thought which leads to such a failure has to be challenged. It has to do with what Foucault calls 'discourse', i.e. the way we naturalize our system of knowledge and power, and our resulting inability to comprehend 'the other'.

I am not saying that violations of the Convention *should* have been found in the *Karaduman* and *Dhalab* cases. Instead, what I am suggesting is that the Strasbourg institutions should have approached the Muslim veil as a complex reality of which they were generally ignorant rather than as a symbol of oppression of which they had understood the premises and the consequences. In other words, they needed to be ready to learn more about it rather than dismissing it at the stage of admissibility as raising no valid issue of rights for the women who were wearing it.[169] Such a summary approach, which led to the cases being declared manifestly unfounded without any effort having been made to understand the viewpoint of the female applicant, seems to have been somewhat abandoned in *Leyla Sahlin* v. *Turkey*, decided by a Chamber on 29 June 2004 and which was pending before a Grand Chamber at time of writing.[170]

What is not in a name: The simply and shockingly inadmissible *Halimi*

Under post-modernism, the Other (often written with a capital O) is anyone, including you and me. It is nonetheless easy to fall into the trap of associating her with the exotic, as the previous section has arguably done. Nothing justifies this tendency. This section focuses on a case, *Gisèle Taïeb dite Halimi* v. *France*,[171] which need not be associated with exoticism. Unfortunately for my present purposes, it nonetheless so happens that the applicant in this case was of Tunisian origin. While this identity would probably need to be taken into consideration if the various layers of Halimi's predicament and of its meaning to her were to be understood, it is irrelevant to the legal case – as a personal experience of mine will confirm.

The applicant in the case was a lawyer whose involvement in the defence of the Algerian cause in the 1960s and in feminist causes has assured her a wide notoriety in France.[172] She is known as Gisèle Halimi. Her official name, however, is Gisèle Taïeb. She became Halimi after she married a man of this name in 1951, whom she divorced in 1959. She continued to use the name of Halimi in her professional life without any opposition on the part of her ex-husband. But when she sought to reconcile her private and public names by changing her last name to Halimi or Gisèle-Halimi, Mr Halimi objected. Following these objections, the French administration refused to accede to her request of having her name changed. Gisèle Halimi (for how could we name her otherwise?) alleged at Strasbourg a violation of Article 8 of the Convention.

In the wake of the *Burghartz* case, which also concerned the use of name after marriage and which was discussed earlier in this chapter, one might have thought that the applicant would not have found it difficult to persuade the Court that a violation of the Convention had occurred. Not so. The Court could not see how the impossibility for the applicant of using the name of Halimi in her private life was damaging to her personality. As for the use of the name in her public life, it had never been problematic. The Chamber ruled unanimously on 20 March 2001 that the case was manifestly ill-founded.

It is a lawyer who works at the Registry of the Court who directed me to this decision. She found it absolutely appalling. To her, it just showed how the judges fail to understand the position of women. The Court – which in this case included two women – was impervious to the fact that the applicant's predicament was the result of the tradition under which women use the name of their husband, making it unlikely that a man would ever be in the position of Gisèle Halimi. Moreover, the Court was unwilling to contemplate the possibility that the situation complained of by the applicant was important to women. In its decision, the Court expressed 'serious doubts as to whether the inconveniences reported by the applicant can be considered to constitute a substantial infringement of the exercise of her right to respect for her private life'.[173]

As for me, I vividly recollect my mother's puzzlement, anger, and sense of loss when, as a teenager, I brought back the authorization she had signed for me to have a passport. The signature on the document read: M. F. Dembour. This last name was legally my father's, not hers. The administration had refused to proceed with my request for a passport. My mother said: 'But I always sign Dembour. It has been my name for twenty-five years.' To her, the idea that she should use her maiden name simply did not correspond to the person she was. It was wrong – though she complied and duly signed another form using, for my sake, a signature which was not hers.

I personally would not choose to use the name of my husband if I were married. I find the practice far too enmeshed in patriarchism. This is irrelevant, however, to the merits of my mother's experience or Gisèle Halimi's case. It seems clear to me that the society in which they live, which has induced them to be known by the name of their husband, should recognize the new identity they have forged for themselves. And, here, one cannot help returning to the question of whether it was completely coincidental that the successful first applicant in *Burghartz* was a man.

Burghartz is widely remembered for having reiterated that where there is a differential treatment between men and women, very weighty reasons are required to justify the differential treatment.[174] In *Halimi*, there was of course no difference of treatment between men and women as such; it is only that women happen to be in a different position. One would have thought that the Court would nonetheless have been able to make links between the two cases and offer Gisèle Halimi what she was requesting.

Airey: An amazingly progressive judgment

I have been criticizing the Court throughout this chapter in order to demonstrate that, yes, the feminist critique has a point when it suggests that human rights law is constructed on gender lines which bypass or at least work to the disadvantage of women. In fairness, the Court has also been good to women. For a beautiful example of a case where the Court used its legal imagination in order to relieve the predicament of a woman, one can turn to *Airey* v. *Ireland*, decided more than a quarter of a century ago, on 11 September 1979.[175] This was the twenty-fifth judgment of the Court. It is generally quoted because for the first time it identified effectiveness as one of the major principles of interpretation of the Convention. This section shows that there is more to the ruling than this – assuredly crucial – point.

Let me first present the facts of the case, as established by the Court:

Mrs. Joanna Airey, an Irish national born in 1932 . . . comes from a humble family background and went to work at a young age as a shop assistant. She married in 1953 and has four children, the youngest of whom is still dependent on her. At the time of the adoption of the Commission's report, Mrs. Airey was in receipt of unemployment benefit from the State but, since July 1978, she has been employed. Her net weekly wage in December 1978 was £39.99. In 1974, she obtained a court order against her husband for payment of maintenance of £20 per week, which was increased in 1977 to £27 and in 1978 to £32. However, Mr. Airey, who had previously been working as a lorry driver but was subsequently unemployed, ceased paying such maintenance in May 1978.

Mrs. Airey alleges that her husband is an alcoholic and that, before 1972, he frequently threatened her with, and occasionally subjected her to, physical violence. In January 1972 . . . Mr Airey was convicted . . . of assaulting her and fined. In the following June he left the matrimonial home; he has never returned there to live, although Mrs. Airey now fears that he may seek to do so.

. . . For about eight years prior to 1972, Mrs Airey tried in vain to conclude a separation agreement with her husband . . . Since June 1972, she has been endeavouring to obtain a decree of judicial separation on the grounds of Mr. Airey's alleged physical and mental cruelty to her and their children, and has consulted several solicitors in this connection. However, she has been unable, in the absence of legal aid and not being in a financial position to meet herself the costs involved, to find a solicitor willing to act for her.[176]

As we have already seen, the Irish Constitution was changed in order to make it possible for a marriage to be dissolved only in 1996. Before that, spouses could be relieved from the duty of cohabiting either if they concluded a deed of separation or if they obtained from the High Court a decree of judicial separation, to be granted only on the ground of either adultery, cruelty or unnatural practices.[177]

Mrs Airey alleged at Strasbourg that the prohibitive cost of hiring a solicitor to represent her before the High Court left her unable to obtain a judicial separation. She argued that this was in contravention of Articles 6 para 1 (fair trial), 8 (private and family life), 13 (effective national remedy) and 14 (non-discrimination) of the Convention. The Court ruled, by a majority, that Mrs. Airey had indeed, in effect, been denied access to a court in violation of Article 6 – as well as Article 8.

Before examining the reasoning of the Court, it is worth reporting why Judge Thór Vilhjálmsson failed to find any violation of the Convention in this case. To quote him:

It is not in dispute that the applicant has access to the High Court in the formal sense . . . Thus, the difficulties which, according to the applicant, bar her from the remedy formally open to her under Irish law are factual in their nature. These difficulties [mainly] concern payments which she would have to make . . . to such lawyers as would represent her before the High Court. Bearing this in mind I have, without much hesitation but admittedly with regret, come to the conclusion that the applicant does not have a case under Article 6 para.1 of the Convention . . . An individual's ability or inability to claim his or her rights under the Convention may stem from several reasons, one of them being his or her financial position. It is, of course, deplorable that this should be so. [But] the war on poverty cannot be won through broad interpretation of the Convention . . .

As regard the alleged violation of Article 8 of the Convention, [it is] in my opinion . . . a far-fetched interpretation of Article 8 to come to the conclusion that the duty to respect Mrs. Airey's private and family life includes the duty to help her to seek judicial separation in the High Court . . .

[As for Article 14 of the Convention, the alleged difficulties] concern her dealings with the legal profession rather than with the Irish Government . . . I find no violation of Article 14 in this case.

Three propositions underlie this dissenting opinion: (1) there is nothing a judge can do when an individual has no case under the law; (2) the Convention is not there to alleviate the problems arising out of poverty; (3) the Convention system is there to counteract arbitrariness by national authorities. If all the judges on the Bench had been convinced by their validity and/or applicability to the case, Mrs Airey would not have been successful in her application. Instead the (all-male) Court held by five votes to two that there had been a breach of Article 6 para. 1 of the Convention.

The Court reasoned, in a way that dealt a serious blow to proposition (1):

> The Convention is intended to guarantee not rights that are theoretical or illusory but rights that are practical and effective . . . This is particularly [true] of the right of access to the courts in view of the prominent place held in a democratic society by the right to a fair trial . . . It must therefore be ascertained whether Mrs. Airey's appearance before the High Court without the assistance of a lawyer would be effective, in the sense of whether she would be able to present her case properly and satisfactorily . . . [T]he Court considers it most improbable that a person in Mrs. Airey's position . . . can effectively present his or her own case . . . The Court concludes from the foregoing that the possibility to appear in person before the High Court does not provide the applicant with an effective right of access . . .[178]

The Court went on to respond to the objection by the Government that there had been 'no positive obstacle emanating from the State' and that 'the alleged lack of access to court [stemmed] solely from Mrs. Airey's personal circumstances, a matter for which Ireland cannot be held responsible under the Convention.'[179] It said, in a way that substantially qualified proposition (3):

> [F]ulfilment of a duty under the Convention on occasion necessitates some positive action on the part of the State; in such circumstances, the State cannot simply remain passive and 'there is . . . no room to distinguish between acts and omissions'. . .[180]

The Court concluded the part of its judgment on Article 6 by circumscribing the scope of its ruling:

> In certain eventualities, the possibility of appearing before a court in person, even without a lawyer's assistance, will meet the requirements of Article 6 para. 1; there may be occasions when such a possibility secures adequate access even to the High Court. Indeed, much must depend on the particular circumstances.
>
> In addition, [Article 6 para. 1] leaves to the State a free choice of the means to be used towards [guaranteeing an effective right of access to the courts]. The institution of a legal aid scheme . . . constitutes one of those means but there are others such as, for example, a simplification of procedure.[181]

In other words, the Court managed to circumvent proposition (2) by making it clear that either some people would need to be helped or a system would need to be invented which made it possible for their rights to be secured. (One wishes that the judges who, in *Chapman*, argued that it was not the business of the Convention to provide individuals with homes had taken this point on board.)

I find *Airey* an astonishing and wonderful judgment. Astonishing because my inherent scepticism towards law and human rights would have led me to expect that the unrefined liberal views of Thór Vilhjálmsson would have prevailed. But five judges found a violation of Article 6 of the Convention.[182] Moreover, in response to the applicant's argument that she had been discriminated against on the ground of property in that judicial separation was more easily available to those who could afford to pay than to those without financial resources,[183] three of the seven judges who constituted the Bench objected to the finding by the other four that it was not necessary to examine the case under Article 14 taken in conjunction with Article 6 para. 1 of the Convention. For those who only know the line subsequently adopted by the Court on Article 14 (reviewed above in Chapter 5), this is nothing short of extraordinary.[184]

Airey is a wonderful judgment. There was a female applicant who had been abused by her husband – whatever Judge O'Donoghue, the second dissenting judge, said[185] – and who was struggling economically. She was not in the best position to win before the Court, but she did. Of course this does not mean that everything was happy ever after for her or for other women. *Airey* is nonetheless a comforting ruling which shows that it can pay off to bring issues which can be characterized as feminist into the terrain of human rights law.

Conclusion

On the face of it, the Strasbourg Court has a good record in terms of women's rights. For many years now, it has 'reiterated that the advancement of the equality of the sexes is today a major goal' in the Council of Europe. Also noticeable is the composition of the so-called 'new Court', established in 1998, which includes proportionately more and more women. The feminist critique nonetheless invites us to scratch below the surface of this apparently women-friendly institution to uncover male patriarchy, or at least male bias.

Françoise Tulkens, a member of the new Court since its inception, thinks that fewer applications originate from women than from men.[186] Is it because women are to some extent prevented from accessing the judicial system, due to their comparatively disadvantaged social and economic position? Is it because they are not interested in a win–lose settlement of their disputes? Is it because the Convention fails to address the root causes of their subordination, and thus, their real problems and concerns? Is it because the judiciary is unable to comprehend the aspirations and claims of women who do not fit the white, middle-class, able-bodied, heterosexual model? Asking these questions shows that the insights of the various strands of the feminist critique which have been discussed in this chapter as though they existed apart from and perhaps even in opposition to each other are best conceived as complementing each other.

Of course most of the factors which are invoked in the previous paragraph operate beyond the Strasbourg Court. They permeate the entire legal order. It would therefore be disingenuous to single out the European Court of Human Rights for its failure to have fully taken on board a feminist agenda. The Court certainly should not be made to bear sole responsibility for realities that lie beyond its competence and control. At the same time, the reiterated claim by the Court that 'the very essence of [the Convention] is respect for human dignity and human freedom'[187] and the emancipatory appeal of human rights, not to mention the claim of neutrality by liberalism, make it important to assess whether the practice matches the theory.

The cases which have been discussed in this chapter indicate that the record of the Court in terms of its openness to women is not as good as is generally assumed and as the Court itself probably likes to think. Admittedly, the Court has pursued the liberal agenda of sex equality. This agenda alone, however, cannot ensure women's equality in dignity and attention.[188] While the concept of human rights is supposed to be universal, it has traditionally neglected one half of humanity. It continues to do so.

This conclusion is one with which virtually all human rights feminist scholars would concur. Interestingly, however, it does not tend to affect their determination in seeing human rights deliver its promises. Most accept the liberal framework and believe in human rights – what they want is the infuriating gap between human rights theory and practice to disappear or at least be reduced. My position is slightly different, as explained in the next chapter.

Notes

1 De Gouges's Declaration is reproduced amongst other sources in: Micheline R. Ishay (ed.) *The Human Rights Reader: Major Political Writings, Essays, Speeches and Documents. Fom the Bible to the Present* (New York: Routledge, 1997), at 140–7. My translation of Article 1 is slightly different from that of Ishay, who offers: 'Woman is born free and lives equal to man in her rights.' For the context in which de Gouges produced her Declaration, see Linda Kelly, *Women of the French Revolution* (London: Hamish Hamilton, 1987); Anne Soprani, *La révolution et les femmes. 1789–1796* (Paris: MA Editions, 1988).

2 In an ironic twist of de Gouges' famous line, 'If woman has the right to mount to the scaffold, she ought equally to have the right to mount to the tribune': quoted in Joan W. Scott, 'The imagination of Olympe de Gouges', in Eileen Janes Yeo (ed.), *Mary Wollstonecraft and 200 Years of Feminisms* (London: Rivers Oram Press, 1997) 36–45, at 38.

3 Stephanie Palmer, 'Feminism and the promise of human rights: Possibilities and paradoxes', in Susan James and Stephanie Palmer (eds.), *Visible Women: Essays on*

Feminist Legal Theory and Political Philosophy (Oxford: Hart, 2002) 91–115, at 114. See also her earlier essay: 'Critical perspectives on women's rights: The European Convention on Human Rights and Fundamental Freedoms', in Ann Bottomley (ed.), *Feminist Perspectives on the Foundational Subjects of Law* (London: Cavendish, 1996) 223–42.

4 Susanne Baer, 'Citizenship in Europe and the construction of gender by law in the European Charter of Fundamental Rights', in Karen Knop (ed.), *Gender and Human Rights* (Oxford: Oxford University Press, 2004) 83–112, at 106.

5 For the situation in the UK during the nineteenth and twentieth centuries, see e.g. Sandra Fredman, *Women and the Law* (Oxford: Oxford University Press, 1997), Chapter 2. Mary Wollstonecraft's writings remain one of the most powerful descriptions of the historical legal subjection of women in the West.

6 Halley's cautionary reference to the United States, as if she warned that she only wishes to talk about what she knows, is both welcome and irritating: welcome to the extent that it acknowledges the limits of the speaker's knowledge, irritating to the extent that it legitimizes not getting to know what happens beyond the speaker's borders.

7 Janet Halley, 'Take a break from feminism?', in Knop (ed.), *Gender*, 57–81, at 61.

8 Karen Knop notes: 'A working bibliography on women's international human rights published in 1989 contained 142 publications, ten cases, and a list of 15 international governmental and non-governmental organizations and other sources of information. By 2003, it had grown into a website that includes approximately 700 articles, over 766 treaties, cases, and other legal documents, and 246 links to other websites': Karen Knop, 'Introduction', in Knop (ed.), *Gender*, 1–12, at 1. These figures are interesting even though a bibliography on women's international human rights is not a bibliography on a feminist critique of human rights.

Particularly useful in putting feminist approaches to human rights on the scholarly map have been: Hilary Charlesworth, Christine Chinkin and Shelley Wright, 'Feminist approaches to international law' (1991) 85 *American Journal of International Law* 613–45; Rebecca J. Cook (ed.), *Human Rights of Women: National and International Perspectives* (Philadelphia: University of Pennsylvania Press, 1994); Julie Peters and Andrea Wolper (eds.), *Women's Rights, Human Rights* (New York: Routledge, 1995); Kelly D. Askin and Dorean Koenig (eds.), *Women and International Human Rights Law* (New York: Transnational Publishers Inc., 1999): Vol. 1 *Introduction to Women's Human Rights Issues*; Vol. 2 *International Courts, Instruments and Organizations and Select Regional Systems*; Vol. 3 *Toward Employment*.

9 It would be wrong, however, to reduce all the arguments found in first wave feminism to liberal feminism. Consider for example Article XI of de Gouges' Declaration: 'The free communication of thoughts and opinions is one of the most precious rights of woman, since that liberty assures the recognition of children by their fathers. Any female citizen thus may say freely, I am the mother of a child which belongs to you, without being forced by a barbarous prejudice to hide the truth; [an exception may be made] to respond to the abuse of this liberty in cases determined by the law.' De Gouges' formulation bears little correspondence to Article XI of the official French Declaration, which reads: 'Free communication of ideas and opinions is one of the most precious of the rights of man. Consequently, every citizen may speak, write, and print freely, subject to responsibility for the abuse of such liberty in the cases determined by law.'

10 The concept of gender may be more appropriate here, but it is not the one used in law, and I have not used it either.

11 One example, which might be considered far-fetched today: given that only women give birth, why should they be entitled to maternity leave on the principle of equality? See on this issue, L. Vogel, 'Debating difference: Feminism, pregnancy, and the workplace' (1990) 16 *Feminist Studies* 1, 9–32.

12 See e.g. Nicola Lacey, *Unspeakable Subjects: Feminist Essays in Legal and Social Theory* (Oxford: Hart, 1998), at 61.

13 Current Article 21 of the Convention. As we have seen in Chapter 2, the reason normally given for this is to ensure that all legal systems are represented at the Court. A critical commentator has nonetheless qualified this system as 'timid' ('*peu audacieux*') and compared it disfavourably to that of the Inter-American Court of Human Rights and the future African Court of Human and Peoples' Rights where not all member states are/will be represented: Syméon Karagiannis, 'Le territoire d'application de la Convention européenne des droits de l'homme. *Vaetera et nova*' (2005) 61 *Revue trimestrielle des droits de l'homme* 33–120, at 41, note 20.

14 Current Article 22 of the Convention. For a less than flattering account of this election process, see Jean-François Flauss, 'Brèves observations sur le second renouvellement triennal de la Cour européenne des droits de l'homme' (2005) *Revue trimestrielle des droits de l'homme* 5–32.

15 Order no. 519 (1996) 1 on the Procedure for examining candidatures for the election of judges to the European Court of Human Rights.

16 For an analysis of the presentation of female candidates to the new Court in 1998, see Jean-François Flauss, 'Radioscopie de l'élection de la nouvelle Cour européenne des droits de l'homme' (1998) *Revue trimestrielle des droits de l'homme* 435–64, at 439–40. The European Assembly has since marked its dissatisfaction with the lack of compliance by a number of states with the request to include the name of at least one woman in candidates' lists. See points 18 and 19 of Recommendation 1649 (2004) 1 and point 3 of Resolution 1366 (2004) – Candidates for the European Court of Human Rights. In its reply of 20 April 2005, the Committee of Ministers has asked the Assembly to show more flexibility it its approach, i.e. to drop its refusal to consider lists which do not include at least one woman: see points 6–9 of CM/AS Rec 1649 final (Doc. 10506).

17 For the list of the judges of the Court at 17 January 2001, see Philip Leach, *Taking a Case to the European Court of Human Rights* (1st edn, London: Blackstone, 2001), at 329–30. Perhaps not insignificantly, the eight female judges came from Sweden, Belgium, Slovakia, Croatia, the Netherlands, 'the Former Yugoslav Republic of Macedonia', Norway and Bulgaria.

18 Article 14 of the Rules of Procedure of the European Court of Human Rights. Judge Tulkens has noted that the adoption of this rule was secured with a minimal majority: Françoise Tulkens, 'Droits des hommes, droits des femmes', Lecture notes of 31 March 2000, ms.

19 The Court's website contains the current list of judges. It is to be noted that the judges' current term of office is of six years (but will be increased to nine when Protocol 14 comes into force); half the bench is elected every three years.

20 On the International Criminal Court, see e.g. Dominic McGoldrick, Peter Rowe and Eric Donnelly (eds), *The Permanent International Criminal Court: Legal and Policy Issues* (Oxford: Hart, 2004).

21 Namely, Judge Costa. See Chapter 3.

22 Namely, Judge Loucaides. See Chapter 4.

23 Namely, Judge Fitzmaurice and Judge Martens – who are incidentally as far apart as one could expect judges to be on the conservative-progressive political spectrum. See Chapter 6.

24 Admittedly the material presented in this chapter is limited. The table presented in Appendix 2, which records the voting pattern of the judges who participated in the 14 decisions discussed in this chapter, graphically demonstrates the limitation of my sample: only 5 women (but as many as 59 men) were judges in these decisions; these women account for only 14 votes (out of a total of 177 votes recorded in the table). Nonetheless I have obviously read far more decisions than are discussed in this chapter. Moreover, and perhaps more significantly, none of my contacts at Strasbourg were able to direct me towards a dissenting opinion which struck them as being feminist in outlook.

25 *Abdulaziz, Cabales and Balkandali* v. *United Kingdom,* 28 May 1985, Series A, No. 94, (1985) 7 EHRR 471. Chronologically, this was the seventy-fourth judgment of the Court.

26 See Chapter 2 and Chapter 5.

27 Para. 68 of the judgment.

28 Para. 79 of the judgment.

29 Para. 75 of the judgment.

30 Para. 77 of the judgment.

31 Para. 78 of the judgment.

32 Para. 84 of the judgment. Let us recall that the Court unanimously rejected the plea of the applicants that they had been discriminated against on grounds of race. Only a minority of the Commission had thought that the effect of the Rules, namely the prevention of immigration from the New Commonwealth and Pakistan, was not coincidental. On nationality rules as race discrimination, see Marie-Bénédicte Dembour, 'Human rights law and national sovereignty in collusion: The plight of quasi-nationals at Strasbourg' (2003) *Netherlands Quarterly of Human Rights* 63–98, at 91–4.

33 *Burghartz* v. *Switzerland,* 22 February 1994, Series A No. 280-B, (1994) 18 EHHR 101.

34 Para. 9 of the judgment.

35 Except if differences in treatment are legitimate. Whether situations are different or the same is always a potentially controversial question. To give two examples drawn from the Court's case law: In *Van Raalte* v. *Netherlands,* 21 February 1997, RJD 1997-I, (1997) 24 EHRR 503, the (male) applicant complained that only *male* workers of single status had to contribute to a social security scheme benefiting families in the Netherlands; in *Petrovic* v. *Austria,* 27 March 1998, RJD 1998-II 67, (2001) 33 EHRR 14, the (male) applicant complained that only *mothers* could be granted benefits during parental leave in Austria. The Court rejected both claims that a violation of Article 14 of the Convention (taken together with Article 1 of Protocol 1 on property) had occurred.

36 Tulkens, 'Droit des femmes'.

37 Palmer observes that fathers have often resorted to Article 14 taken together with Article 8 to gain access to their children born out of wedlock or from whom they were separated after divorce: Palmer, 'Critical Perspectives', at 233. These male

applicants have not always been successful, far from it. For recent cases illustrating this trend, see *Sahin* v. *Germany,* 11 October 2001, ECHR 2003-VII, (2003) 36 EHRR 43, *Sommerfeld* v. *Germany* 11 October 2001, ECHR 2003-VIII, (2004) 38 EHRR 35 and *Hoffmann* v. *Germany,* also decided on 11 October 2001. For an early example of a male applicant, unsuccessfully, claiming a violation of Article 14 on ground of sex, see *Rasmussen* v. *Denmark* 28 November 1984, Series A, No. 87, (1985) 7 EHRR 371. The case concerned the time-limit imposed on a husband to contest the paternity of a child born during marriage.

38 Palmer, 'Critical Perspectives', at 225.

39 Eva Brems, 'Enemies or allies: Feminism and cultural relativism as dissident voices in human rights discourse' (1997) *Human Rights Quarterly* 136–64 at 138.

40 Carol Gilligan, *In a Different Voice: Psychologist Theory and Women's Development* (Cambridge, Mass.: Harvard University Press, 1982).

41 On the reasons why this particular work became emblematic but also the impasse to which it led, see Maria Drakopoulou, 'The ethic of care, female subjectivity and feminist legal scholarship' (2000) 8 *Feminist Legal Studies* 199–226, at 208.

42 Palmer, 'Critical perspectives', at 225. It has therefore been suggested that 'women lawyers are faced with the choice of being good feminists and bad lawyers, or the converse': Carol Smart, *Feminism and the Power of Law* (London: Routledge, 1989), at 22 (referring to Mary Jane Mossman).

43 John Hardwig, 'Should women think in terms of rights?' (1984) 94 *Ethics* 441.

44 Gilligan has often been criticized for the essentialism that would characterize her approach. However, Jo Bridgeman and Susan Millns note that the most sophisticated accounts of woman's voice difference, including Gilligan's, speak of tendencies, not essences: Jo Bridgeman and Susan Millns, *Feminist Perspectives on Law: Law's Engagement with the Female Body* (London: Sweet and Maxwell, 1998), at 61.

45 Nina-Louisa Arold, 'Do germ-cells of a global human rights culture exist? A case study of the inner legal culture of the European Court of Human Rights', A thesis submitted to the Stanford Program in International Legal Studies at the Stanford Law School, Stanford University, in partial fulfilment of the requirements for the degree of Master of the Science of Law (May 2001), 96 pp.

46 Ibid., at 71.

47 Quoted in the Rt. Hon. Dame Brenda Hale, 'Equality and the judiciary: Why should we want more women judges?' (2001) *Public Law* 489–504, at 498.

48 Erika Rackley, 'Representations of the (woman) judge: Hercules, the little mermaid and the vain and naked Emperor' (2002) 22 *Legal Studies* 602–24.

49 Hale, 'Equality', at 498.

50 This is not to deny that there have been endeavours to reconcile the two with the aim of producing a caring, as opposed to an 'uncaring', legal system. This has been attempted within both feminist and humanist projects. See e.g. Joan C. Tronto, *Caring for Democracy: A Feminist Vision* (Utrecht: Universiteit voor Humanistiek, 1995); Selma Sevenhuisen, *Citizenship and the Ethics of Care* (London: Routledge, 1998).

51 *Buckley* v. *United Kingdom,* 25 September 1996, RJD 1996-IV 1271, (1997) 23 EHRR 101.

52 *Chapman* v. *United Kingdom,* 18 January 2001, ECHR 2001-I, (2001) 33 EHRR 18.

53 For commentaries on *Chapman* which focus on this aspect while reaching opposite conclusions: Florence Benoît-Rohmer, 'La Cour de Strasbourg et la protection

de l'intérêt minoritaire: Une avancée décisive sur le plan des principes?' and Dominique Rosenberg, 'L'indifférence du juge européen aux discriminations subies par les Roms', both in (2001) *Revue trimestrielle des droits de l'homme*, at 999–1015 and 1016–1033 respectively. Since *Chapman* (and the other cases raising similar issues decided on the same day), the Court has again ruled on a case brought forward by a gypsy applicant against the British government: *Connors* v. *United Kingdom* (Application 66746/01) 27 May 2004, (2005) 40 EHRR 9. *Connors* was different from the previous cases in that it concerned the summary eviction of a gypsy family from a public site where they were legally resident.

54 Para. 46 of the judgment.

55 Para. 75 of the judgment.

56 Ibid.

57 Para. 84 of the judgment.

58 See Appendix 2 for the pattern of voting on this issue. By eight votes to one (Judge Pettiti dissenting), the Court also ruled that there was no violation of Article 14 taken together with Article 8.

59 See e.g. Clare Ovey and Robin C. A. White, *Jacobs and White European Convention on Human Rights* (3rd edn, Oxford: Oxford University Press, 2002) at 252.

60 Para. 64 of the judgment, emphasis added.

61 Para. 65 of the judgment, emphasis added.

62 Para. 76 of the judgment.

63 Para. 12 of the judgment.

64 Para. 70 of the judgment.

65 Para. 73 of the judgment.

66 The arguments developed in Chapter 6 about the need not to essentialize culture are applicable here. Culture must be recognized as always being in flux. The same applies to the concept of tradition. On the difficulties that a legal concept of tradition as unchanging creates for the protection of minority – and in these particular case studies, native – rights, see James Clifford, *The Predicament of Culture: Twentieth-Century Ethnography, Literature, and Art* (Cambridge, Mass.: Harvard University Press, 1988), Chapter 12; Jean Jackson, 'Culture, genuine and spurious: The politics of Indianness in the Vaupes, Colombia' (1995) 22 *American Ethnologist* 3–28; Elizabeth Povinelli, 'The sense of shame: Australian multiculturalism and the crisis of indigenous citizenship' (1998) 24 *Critical Inquiry* 575–611.

67 The Court, however, adopted a different approach in *Connors* as it recognized an 'apparent shift in habit in the gypsy population which remains nomadic in spirit if not in actual or constant practice': para. 93 of the judgment.

68 Para. 114 of the judgment.

69 Para. 105 of the judgment.

70 Para. 4 of the dissenting opinion, emphases added.

71 It should be noted that a similar shift is noticeable in *Connors*. In this case, the Court noted the seriousness of what was at stake for the male applicant and his family who were made homeless 'with consequent difficulties in finding a lawful alternative location for their caravans, in coping with health problems and young children and in ensuring continuation in the children's education' (para. 85 of the judgment). The Court (which included three dissenters from *Chapman*, i.e. Judges Lorenzen, Bonello and Tulkens, as well as Judges Rozakis, Bratza, Botoucharova and Steiner) unanimously found a violation of Article 8. It is interesting that the applicant was

male. Noting this fact acts as a reminder that a sophisticated feminist critique need not be just about women. In particular not all those who display an 'ethic of care' are women; inversely, not all women display an 'ethic of care'.

72 See e.g. Shelley Wright, 'Human rights and women's rights: An analysis of the United Nations Convention on the Elimination of All Forms of Discrimination against Women', in Kathleen E. Mahoney and Paul Mahoney (eds.), *Human Rights in the Twenty-First Century*, (Dordrecht: Nijhoff) 75–88, at 87; Ursula O'Hare, 'Realizing human rights for women' (1999) *Human Rights Quarterly* 364–402, at 367; Charlesworth, Chinkin and Wright, 'Feminist approaches', at 635. It is striking that Section B ('Women's rights and CEDAW') of Chapter 3 ('Civil and political rights') of a widely used collection of materials on human rights contains recurrent references to the socio-economic situation of women and the 'feminization' of poverty: Henry Steiner and Philip Alston, *International Human Rights in Context: Law, Politics, Morals* (Oxford: Oxford University Press, 2000), at 158–224.

73 Para. 99 of the judgment. Somewhat by contrast, the Court indirectly castigated the national authorities for having made the applicant and his family homeless in *Connors*: see esp. para. 85 of the judgment.

74 Para. 113 of the judgment. The Court also said that the authorities do not have to provide enough authorized sites to offer all gypsies a place: para. 98 of the judgment. This suggests that the Court did not consider the claim of the applicant to be related to her gypsy identity. The dissenting judges disagreed. To them it was 'disproportionate to take steps to evict a gypsy family from their home on their own land in circumstances where there has not been shown to be any other lawful, alternative site reasonably open to them': para. 5 of the dissenting opinion.

75 Though the argument can be extended to male applicants as suggested by the discussion of *Connors* above.

76 Frances Olsen, 'Children's rights: Some feminist approaches to the United Nations Convention on the Rights of the Child', in Philip Alston, Stephen Parker and John Seymour (eds.), *Children, Rights and the Law* (Oxford: Clarendon, 1992) 192–220, at 203.

77 See her two seminal books: Catharine MacKinnon, *Feminism Unmodified: Discourses on Life and Law* (Cambridge, Mass.: Harvard University Press, 1987); *Toward a Feminist Theory of the State* (Cambridge, Mass.: Harvard University Press, 1989).

78 MacKinnon, *Feminism Unmodified*, at 38.

79 As explained by Hilaire Barnett, *Introduction to Feminist Jurisprudence* (London: Cavendish, 1998), at 165.

80 MacKinnon, *Feminism Unmodified*, at 71.

81 For a beautiful demonstration of such blindness (by feminists who are not especially radical): Hilary Charlesworth and Christine Chinkin, 'The gender of *jus cogens*', (1993) *Human Rights Quarterly* 63.

82 Carole Pateman, 'Feminist critiques of the public/private dichotomy', in A. Phillips (ed.), *Feminism and Equality* (Oxford: Blackwell, 1987) 103.

83 Making something into a public issue does not necessarily entail calling for its regulation by the state, so that the issues of regulation and politicization must be kept distinguished: Lacey, *Unspeakable Subjects*, esp. Chapter 3.

84 Barnett, *Feminist Jurisprudence*, 171.

85 *X and Y* v. *Netherlands*, 16 March 1985, Series A, No. 91, (1986) 8 EHRR 235.

86 *SW* v. *United Kingdom*, 22 November 1995, Series A, No. 355-B, (1996) 21 EHRR 363. See also *CR* v. *United Kingdom*, decided on the same day.

87 *Stubbings and Others* v. *United Kingdom*, 22 October 1996, RJD 1996-IV, (1997) 23 EHRR 213.

88 *Aydin* v. *Turkey*, 25 September 1997, RJD 1997-VI, (1998) 25 EHRR 251.

89 Halley refers to the 'feminist paranoid structuralism' which posits that when 'things in the world seem to be organized in a way that does not invoke $m > f$ or require us to carry a brief for f, this perception is probably a deep error and profoundly counter-intuitive investigation will eventually reveal that, yep, it's $m > f$ all over again': Halley, 'Take a break', at 62. Ralph Sandland echoes this when he writes, admittedly of Carol Smart who led the post-modern strand of feminist legal critique in the United Kingdom, but in a remark which could be extended to a radical feminist: 'From her point of view . . . all cases are wrongly decided, and they would still be wrongly decided if the substantive outcome [had] been different, since all cases must fall to be decided within a given (legal) framework which fails to challenge the deployment of sex(uality)/gender-as-identity, on the one hand, and which legitimises Law on the other': Ralph Sandland, 'Between "Truth" and "Difference": Poststructuralism, law and the power of feminism' (1995) 3 *Feminist Legal Studies* 3–47, at 16.

90 Para. 9 of the judgment.

91 Para. 12 of the judgment.

92 Para. 27 of the judgment.

93 Ibid.

94 Para. 31 of the judgment. The Court ruled that it was not necessary to give a ruling on whether her father had also been a victim: para. 37 of the judgment.

95 Para. 44 of the judgment.

96 Ibid.

97 Para. 40 of the judgment.

98 Para. 73 of the judgment.

99 Para. 86 of the judgment.

100 Para. 83 of the judgment.

101 Para. 23 of the judgment.

102 Para. 24 of the judgment.

103 Para. 25 of the judgment.

104 Para. 27 of the judgment. In so doing, it placed itself firmly within the movement which led, eight years later, to the adoption by the UN of the Declaration on the Elimination of Violence Against Women. Article 4 (c) of this Declaration requests States to '[e]xercise due diligence to prevent, investigate and . . . punish acts of violence against women'.

105 Para. 40 of the judgment.

106 One need not be a radical feminist to make this point: Lacey, *Unspeakable Subjects*, at 241.

107 Para. 44 of the judgment.

108 For a presentation of MacKinnon's views on the abolition of the marital rape exemption and a response to it, see Sandland, 'Poststructuralism', at 31–3.

109 Rape was prosecuted as a war crime in the Tokyo, but not in the Nuremberg, trials: Fiona Beveridge and Siobhán Mullaly, 'International human rights and body politics', in Jo Bridgeman and Susan Millns (eds.), *Law and Body Politics: Regulating the Female Body* (Aldershot: Dartmouth, 1995) 240–72, at 256. The first conviction was delivered by the International Criminal Tribunal for Rwanda, although this has

been lost on commentators generally disinclined to recognize any African lead in the human rights field: Rachel Murray, 'The perception of Africa by the West: Impact on the promotion and protection of human rights', 2001, ms. The International Criminal Tribunal for the Former Yugoslavia has followed suit. In 1993 Theodore Meron suggested that the recognition of rape as a war crime would lead to its recognition as torture or inhuman treatment: Beveridge and Mullally, ibid. This has indeed happened: Patricia Viseur Sellers, 'Individual(s') liability for collective sexual violence', in Knop (ed.), *Gender and Human Rights*, 153–94.

110 Para. 63 of the judgment.

111 Para. 72 of the judgment.

112 Para. 83 of the judgment.

113 *Selmouni* v. *France*, 28 July 1999, ECHR 1999-V, (2000) 29 EHRR 403. The case, in which the Court unanimously found that the treatment of the male applicant by the French police constituted torture, was introduced in Chapter 3.

114 The question of the reason(s) for the apparent inconsistency between *Aydin* and *Selmouni*, both decided by Grand Chambers two years apart, is not easily resolved. It may be that the applicant in *Aydin* was simply more convincing than in *Selmouni*. However, a gender theorist may wonder whether the Court found it difficult to accept the practice of homosexual rape, thus questioning the advance represented by *Aydin*. A realist could surmise that the identity of, and overall situation existing within, the defendant states (respectively Turkey and France) played a role. Finally it cannot be ruled out that the composition of the benches was a contributory factor. This last question is difficult to explore. Only Judges Wildhaber and Jungwiert sat in both cases. Interestingly they both voted with the majority in *Aydin*.

115 Three of them also claimed that there had been a violation of Article 8.

116 Para. 50 of the judgment.

117 Para. 53 of the judgment.

118 Para. 48 of the judgment.

119 Para. 54 of the judgment.

120 Anticipating the next chapter, it could be said that the Court displays here a conception of human rights as ensuring a level playing field where the rule of law and procedural guarantees agreed in as close to an ideal-speech situation as possible are respected, with the substantive result which is thus achieved of little consequence. This conception is characteristic of what I call the deliberative school. The problem then is not so much that the Court has not checked the relevance of the legislative process, but rather that it has not checked its democratic credentials (or the reality of the ideal-speech situation). See in this connection Amy Bartholomew, 'Toward a deliberative legitimation of human rights', *Papers in Social Theory 6: Rights, Movements, Recognition* (Warwick Social Theory Centre/Sussex Centre for Critical Social Theory, 2001) 5–31; Conor Gearty, 'Democracy and human rights in the European Court of Human Rights: A critical appraisal' (2000) 51 *Northern Ireland Legal Quarterly* 381–96.

121 Para. 56 of the judgment.

122 Para. 6 of partly dissenting opinion of Judge Foighel; para. 2 of partly dissenting opinion of Judge Macdonald.

123 Para. 15 of the judgment.

124 Catharine A. MacKinnon, 'Crimes of war, crimes of peace', in Stephen Shute and Susan Hurley (eds.), *On Human Rights: Amnesty International Lectures* (New York: Basic Books, 1993) 83–109, respectively at 85, 92 and 93.

125 They need not be radical feminists. Jennifer Saul reports that 'many women [who seek abortion say they] are concerned not so much with a *right* not to be pregnant as with a *responsibility* not to bring life into the world for which they cannot adequately care': Jennifer Mather Saul, *Feminism: Issues and Arguments* (Oxford: Oxford University Press, 2003), at 120, emphases in the original. This is an observation which easily fits a woman's voice feminist model. A defence of abortion on 'care' and 'rights' ethical grounds is of course entirely possible, as in the following reaction to the screening of images of aborted foetuses aimed at shocking through a simplistic message: 'The other side of the argument is about the life chances of those who are alive, children as well as mothers and fathers too. It is about the awesome hypocrisy of pretending that this story ends happily with a newly born infant, and simply not mentioning the grindingly hard decades to come. It is about liberty – allowing individuals the freedom to make up their own minds about their own lives': Jackie Ashley, 'We already know the truth about abortion', *The Guardian*, 20 April 2004, at 23.

126 On the first two points, see Saul, *Feminism*, Chapter 4. On the third, see, for the situation obtaining in the United Kingdom, Sally Shaldon, *Beyond Control: Medical Power and Abortion Law* (London: Pluto, 1997).

127 *Open Door Counselling and Dublin Well Woman* v. *Ireland*, 29 October 1992, Series A, No. 246, (1993) 15 EHRR 244.

128 *Bowman* v. *United Kingdom*, 19 February 1998, RJD 1998 I-175, (1998) 26 EHRR 1.

129 *Tokarczyk* v. *Poland* (Application 51792/99), decision of 31 January 2002.

130 It may be that the Court will not be able to avoid directly confronting abortion much longer. At the time of writing, *Tysiac* v. *Poland* (Application 5410/03) is pending before the Court. The case concerns a woman who was refused a therapeutic abortion and became nearly blind after having given birth to her child, raising issues under Articles 8, 13 and 14 of the Convention. Another case, *D* v. *Ireland* (Application 26499/02), should likewise, if declared admissible, force the Court squarely to face the issue of abortion.

131 The Commission was slightly more forthcoming. See e.g. *H* v. *Norway* (Application 17004/90) decision of 19 May 1992: '[T]he Commission finds that any interpretation of the potential father's right under these provisions in connection with an abortion which the mother intends to have performed on her, must first of all take into account her rights, she being the person primarily concerned by the pregnancy and its continuation or termination.' Saul's view is consonant with this decision: 'There are relationships even now in which men's lives would be affected as much as women's by the birth of a child. In these relationships . . . it seems to me that men should be seen as having a moral right to a say in the abortion decision. However, it is so overwhelmingly the case that child-rearing is left to women that abortion decisions must – as things currently stand – be legally those of women alone. In a more equitable society, things might be different': Saul, *Feminism*, at 124.

132 *Odièvre* v. *France*, 13 February 2003, ECHR 2003-III, (2004) 38 EHRR 43.

133 Article 40. 3. 30 of the Irish Constitution. This provision came into force in 1983 following a referendum where 67 per cent of the voters expressed their opposition

to abortion: dissenting opinion of Judges Pettiti, Russo and Lopes Rocha, approved by Judge Bigi, in the *Open Door* case.

134 The other applicants were four individuals: two trained counsellors who worked for Dublin Well Woman Centre Ltd and two women of child-bearing age.

135 Para. 68 of the judgment.

136 Para. 72 of the judgment.

137 Para. 73 of the judgment.

138 Para. 77 of the judgment. The consequentialism of the reasoning (see Chapter 4) is striking, as is the recognition that some individuals are more equal than others (see Chapter 5).

139 Para 76 of the judgment.

140 Point 8 of his dissenting opinion.

141 This particular phrase is from Judge Cremona's dissenting opinion.

142 In a wider and insightful analysis, Siobhán Mullaly places *Open Door* in the context of an Irish history where the nation is constructed around Catholicism and in opposition to its neighbour: Siobhán Mullaly, 'Debating reproductive rights in Ireland' (2005) 27 *Human Rights Quarterly* 78–104.

143 Para. 41 of the judgment.

144 Para. 46 of the judgment.

145 Para. 12 of the judgment, emphasis added.

146 In *Open Door*, four dissenting judges similarly argued: 'It is our opinion that the effect of the criminal provisions in question should have been examined as if it were a typical problem of criminal law.' They went on to consider 'what would be the position if Ireland's neighbouring States were to adopt legislation decriminalising drugs, whilst in Ireland itself they remained prohibited under the criminal law': Dissenting opinion of Judges Pettiti, Russo and Lopes Rocha, approved by Judge Bigi.

147 As pointed out by Susan Millns and Sally Sheldon: 'Delivering democracy to abortion politics: *Bowman* v. *United Kingdom* (1999) 7 *Feminist Legal Studies* 63–73, at 68.

148 Para. 24 of the judgment.

149 Para. 49 of the judgment.

150 Para. 44 of the judgment.

151 Para. 45 of the judgment.

152 Para. 2 of concurring opinion of Judge Ress, joined by Judge Kuris.

153 Concurring opinion of Judge Greve, no paragraphs given.

154 Para. 7 of the joint dissenting opinion of Judges Wildhaber, Bratza, Bonello, Loucaides, Cabral Barreto, Tulkens and Pellonpää, emphasis added. The dissenting opinion highlights the fact that the applicant in *Odièvre* lost because the social interest was deemed absolute by the majority, as in *A* v. *United Kingdom* 17 December 2002, ECHR 2002-X, (2002) 36 EHRR 917, discussed in Chapter 4.

155 Para. 9 of their dissenting opinion.

156 Saul, *Feminism*, at 121.

157 Para. 9 of their dissenting opinion.

158 This is also the opening statement of MacKinnon's article: 'Feminism, Marxism, method and the state: An agenda for theory' (1982) 7 *Signs* 515–44.

159 For an introduction, see e.g. Judith G. Greenberg, 'Introduction to postmodern legal feminism', in Mary Joe Frug (ed.), *Postmodern Legal Feminism* (New York: Routledge,

1992) ix-xxxv. In the United Kingdom, Carol Smart's *Feminism and the Power of Law* is an important landmark.

160 'Post-modernism throws into question the bases underlying judgments about what is progressive': Frances Olsen, 'Children's rights', at 215. For Olsen, the post-modern 'tendency to dissolve the category of women altogether' has the unfortunate effect of 'rendering problematic feminist politics': ibid. See also Drakopoulou, 'Ethic of care'.

161 Except to add that the dominant mood today is a yearning for a move beyond post-modernism, where theory and action would again unite. See e.g. Vanessa E. Munro, 'Legal feminism and Foucault – A critique of the expulsion of law' (2001) *Journal of Law and Society* 546–67.

162 For a recent case involving a man and raising issues which are in some aspects parallel, see *Phull* v. *France* (Application 35753/03), declared inadmissible on 11 January 2005. The applicant was a practicing Sikh who had been required to remove his turban while going through a security scanner at an airport.

163 *Karaduman* v. *Turkey* (Application 16278/90), decision of 3 May 1993. See also *Lamiye Bulut* v. *Turkey* (Application 18783/91), which was decided on the same day in the same way.

164 *Dahlab* v. *Switzerland* (Application 42393/98), decision of 15 February 2001.

165 Judges Stráznická and Tsatsa-Nikolovska. The other judges were Judges Rozakis, Baka, Wildhaber, Bonello and Fischbach.

166 My translation of the decision which exists only in French.

167 See especially, Nancy J. Hirschmann, 'Western feminism, Eastern veiling, and the question of free agency' (1988) 5 *Constellations* 345–68; Leila Ahmed, *Women and Gender in Islam* (New Haven, Conn.: Yale University Press, 1992); Homa Hoodfar, 'The veil in their minds and on our heads: The persistence of colonial images of Muslim women' (1993) 22 *Review of Feminist Research* 5–18; Françoise Gaspard and Fahrad Khosrokhavar, *Le foulard et la République* (Paris: La Découverte, 1995); Fadwa El Guindi, *Veil: Modesty, Privacy and Resistance* (Oxford: Berg, 1999).

168 Marie-Bénédicte Dembour, 'The cases that were not to be: Explaining the dearth of case-law on religious freedom at Strasbourg', in Italo Pardo (ed.), *Morals of Legitimacy: Between Agency and System* (Oxford: Berghahn, 2000) 205–28.

169 Also in this sense: Carolyn Evans, *Freedom of Religion under the European Convention on Human Rights* (Oxford: Oxford University Press, 2001), at 206.

170 *Leyla Sahin* v. *Turkey* (Application 44774/98) Fourth Section judgment of 29 June 2004, (2005) 4 EHRR 8; Grand Chamber judgment of 10 November 2005, with a remarkable dissenting opinion by Judge Tulkens.

171 *Gisèle Taïeb dite Halimi* v. *France* (Application 50614/99), decision of 20 March 2001.

172 For an autobiography: Gisèle Halimi, *Le lait de l'oranger* (Gallimard, 1988).

173 My translation.

174 See e.g. Clare Ovey and Robin C. A. White, *Jacobs and White: European Convention on Human Rights* (Oxford: Oxford University Press, 2002), at 355–6.

175 *Airey* v. *Ireland*, 9 October 1979, Series A, No. 32, (1979–1980) 2 EHRR 305.

176 Paras. 8 and 9 of the judgment.

177 Paras. 10 and 11 of the judgment.

178 Para. 24 of the judgment.

179 Para. 25 of the judgment.

180 Ibid.

181 Para. 26 of the judgment.

182 To do this, they incorporated in their reasoning insights from critiques of the dominant liberal conception of human rights which have been discussed earlier in the book. The ruling relies on the concept of positive obligation and adopts an 'it-all-depends' approach, two features which Chapter 4 has argued are in line with a consequentialist logic. Furthermore, the majority was obviously sensitive to the plight of those who find themselves at the disadvantaged end of society. This does not make them Marxists, but it nonetheless makes them progressive. Fortunately the cultural relativist argument displayed by Judge O'Donoghue in his dissenting opinion did not sway his colleagues. To quote: 'It is quite understandable that the rigid position at the moment in Ireland owing to the Constitutional prohibition is somewhat hard to be fully understood and appreciated by those from countries where divorce can be obtained with great facility and expedition'; 'I would again refer to my general observations as to the uniqueness of marriage law in Ireland and the difficulty experienced by those not familiar with its history and features.'

183 Para. 13 of the judgment.

184 See especially the dissenting opinion of Judge Evrigenis.

185 'It is understandable that Timothy Airey should be described by his wife's counsel as a violent and drunken husband from whom his wife shrinks in constant terror. What are the facts? On one occasion only did Mrs. Airey proceed in court against her husband for assault': dissenting opinion of Judge O'Donoghue.

186 Françoise Tulkens, 'Droit des femmes'.

187 *Aydin*, para. 44.

188 Lacey observes that liberal theory is traditionally blind to the way the world is structured along gender lines, so that it has little to offer to women whose position in society places them at structural disadvantage: Lacey, *Unspeakable Subjects*, esp. Chapter 3. Speaking about the Strasbourg Court more specifically, Palmer concurs: 'the "sameness" model adopted by [the Court] renders systemic disadvantage invisible and is unlikely to bring to the forefront women's particular concerns': Palmer, 'Critical perspectives', at 241–2.

8

The human rights creed in four schools

> [T]he strength of the thread does not reside in the fact that some one fibre runs
> through its whole length, but in the overlapping of many fibres. (Wittgenstein)

Finally, we come to the question: what are human rights? There is no single
answer to this question because it depends whom you ask. In support of this
admittedly controversial contention, this chapter seeks to map out the various
concepts of human rights which are encountered in human rights scholarship. Its
primary aim is therefore descriptive rather than normative: documenting and
making sense of the way the expression 'human rights' is used rather than
propounding a particular theory as to how the concept *should be* understood.
I suggest that there are four main concepts of human rights which are in
competition with each other. To present them in the briefest manner, those
I call 'natural scholars' conceive of human rights as *given*; 'deliberative scholars'
as *agreed*; 'protest scholars' as *fought for*; and 'discourse scholars' as *talked about*.

I attach these four concepts to four 'schools'. The term 'school' came to me as
I was writing about various 'scholars'. It is admittedly misleading. The scholars
I bracket together do not necessarily know each other and may not wish to
recognize themselves in the groupings I have created. Moreover, I believe that
the concepts I have identified are not peculiar to the scholarly world but are also
found in the way 'lay' people conceive of human rights. However, a term needs to
be used. Despite its disadvantages and however irritating it may be to post-
moderns committed to the moral imperatives of 'de-schooling', I have settled
on the word 'school' which renders at least part of what I am looking for by
connoting explicit or implicit adherence to a number of precepts.

When I first presented in public the ideas contained in this chapter,[1] I had
detected three schools. I now have four, but do not wish to rule out that
additional ones might usefully be identified. Nonetheless, at the time of writing,
the schema I have constructed appears to me to be reasonably useful, in the sense
that I have always found it possible, so far, to classify a particular human rights
scholar in one of 'my' four schools, though not always squarely.[2] Even if my schema
were to prove in need of serious refinement, I hope that the elements I have
identified will nonetheless spur human rights scholars to recognize explicitly that

we do not always talk about the same thing when we talk about human rights, and will encourage further clarification of the various, competing, understandings of human rights which exist.

Wittgenstein's concept of 'family resemblance'

I started my exploration of the possible meanings of the term 'human rights' open to the idea that human rights might be a 'family resemblance' concept in the Wittgensteinian sense of the term. This section accordingly introduces Wittgenstein's doctrine of family resemblance; the following one offers a tentative application of the doctrine to the concept of human rights.

As an analytical philosopher, Ludwig Wittgenstein (1889–1951) was interested in language and meaning.[3] He departed from the tendency prevalent in philosophy to seek to identify the meaning or the 'essence' of a concept through the identification of key elements, the establishment of conceptual distinctions and the search for conceptual foundations.[4] In his view, a concept should not be defined by what we *think* it means but by what it means in practice – how it is used in everyday life. Wittgenstein's motto was thus to look (to observe) rather than to think. This led him to develop the doctrine of 'family resemblance' to make sense of the fact that some concepts have no core – no common thread running through them.

The two passages most frequently quoted in this respect are the following extracts from his (posthumously published) *Philosophical Investigations*:

> I am saying that these phenomena have no one thing in common which makes us use the same word for all,–but that they are *related* to one another in many different ways.[5]
>
> [I]n spinning a thread we twist fibre on fibre. And the strength of the thread does not reside in the fact that some one fibre runs through its whole length, but in the overlapping of many fibres.[6]

Making sense of Wittgenstein's cryptic prose is a challenge for even the most expert philosopher.[7] It may therefore be useful to turn to a commentary for an explanation of the doctrine. Dallas High writes:

> If, for example, we should examine games – 'board-games, card-games, Olympic games,' etc. – Wittgenstein warns, 'Don't say: "There *must* be something common, or they would not be called 'games.'" Rather, if we '*look*', instead of trying to speculate in advance, we shall not see a feature that is common to *all* games, but a complete series of similarities and relationships where 'common' features, in comparing the games, constantly crop up as well as disappear. If, for example, we look at ball games, we see they have a common feature of being played with balls. But then some are played on courts, others on fields. Then we discover that ball games played on courts have some similarities with other court games – e.g. badminton, shuffleboard, which are not played with balls. Now, new members of the family crop up and others – ball games not played on courts – disappear. The point of all this, as an analogy with the various

topographies of language, is that 'we see a complicated network of similarities overlapping and criss-crossing' – sometimes broad similarities, sometimes detailed similarities – in the family unity of the various functions of speech.[8]

An easy way to grasp the idea of family resemblance is through a matrix. A family resemblance concept X could schematically be presented in the following way (where each horizontal line represents one of the forms in which the concept is encountered in social life, and each letter a distinctive element or characteristic of the concept):

a b c
   b c d
      c d e
         d e f

To convey the use of a particular concept Y in everyday life, it is more likely that the emerging matrix would take a less tidy form, however; for example, something like:

$a\ b\ d$
$b\ e\ f$
$c\ d\ e$
$c\ e\ f$

These two matrices point to the central feature of the doctrine of family resemblance, by showing how the doctrine applies to a concept that lacks a 'common thread' but is replete with partial overlaps. Philosophers typically strive to define a concept by identifying its 'necessary and sufficient' conditions; in the case of a family resemblance concept, however, no such conditions can be found.

Charles Travis notes that there are strong and weak versions of the family resemblance thesis.[9] By definition, if the family resemblance doctrine applies to a concept Z, no common thread runs through all the cases to which Z applies. What does this mean? On a strong version of the thesis, it means that the different combinations making up the matrix representing Z could not contain any common letter. (In other words, Z is defined neither by sufficient nor by necessary conditions.) On a weaker and more persuasive version of the thesis, a common additional letter – call it 'l' – can be found throughout all the combinations making up the matrix, but l does not help to distinguish Z from other concepts. ('l' does not represent a sufficient condition for Z to apply, although this condition is necessary for Z to apply.)

Human rights approached through a family resemblance matrix

Trying to design a matrix which could grasp different uses of the concept of human rights, one could propose that human rights:

a: are moral rights[10]
b: exist irrespective of social recognition

c: are something that every human being has
d: check the arbitrariness of the state
e: result from political and social struggles
f: serve the bourgeois class
l: are used in political discourse

More letters could be identified, e.g.:

g: are based on human nature
h: rest on a socio-legal consensus
i: are transformable into legal rights

The overwhelmingly dominant conception of human rights is that which defines them by reference to what I shall call the '*a b c*' combination, as those 'rights which all persons have insofar as they are human'. Some may say that *b* and *c* imply *g*; others may disagree, for example because they take the view that human rights rest on a strictly religious/metaphysical basis. Similarly it cannot be assumed that *d* and *e* imply *h*: they may or may not.

Personally, I have always been reluctant to understand human rights as encompassing *b* and *c*, for I think that human rights have come into existence by force of language use. While I am ready to accept that human rights have become a fact by being repeatedly invoked in politics, law and common discourse, I do not believe that they would continue to exist were we to cease to talk about them. My tendency is thus to rely on a conception of human rights which combines *d*, *e* and *h* (as well as the insignificant *l*). Others may favour a conception of human rights which combines *c d e* (+ *l*) and which regards human rights primarily as political claims against those in power. No doubt still other variations exist. Marxists, for example, might understand and use the term to cover *d e f* (+ *l*) where the meaning of *d* might be slightly altered to designate rights which are falsely believed to check the arbitrariness of the state. The point is that there exist different conceptions of human rights, which combine a variety of elements in different ways.

Interestingly, few letters in the matrix I have tentatively designed could serve solely to characterize the concept of human rights (as opposed to other concepts). The quality of being moral rights, for example, is not a feature which is specific to the concept of human rights. The only letters which are potential candidates for an exclusive definition of human rights, it seems to me, are *b* (if one excludes the possibility that animals may have rights which exist outside of social recognition) and *c*. I have already said that I am convinced neither by *b* nor by *c*. Given the appeal that human rights in its '*a b c*' combination has in our society, it is likely that many will say that I use the term wrongly if I use it to refer to something other than '*a b c*'; in other words, they will say that I have misunderstood the essence of the concept 'human rights'.

This suggests that 'human rights' is not a family resemblance concept. While the expression is used to refer to different things (*a b c*; *c d e*; *d e f*; etc.) by different people, these different combinations tend not be used concomitantly by the same people. By contrast, people would readily recognize that they use the concept 'game'–Wittgenstein's prototype example of family resemblance – slightly differently in different contexts (e.g. when they refer to board-games, card-games, Olympic games, political games, etc.). The situation with human rights is altogether different: people will typically fight for their own understanding of the term, dismiss other understandings, and thus declare their own understanding as the only one which is valid.

At first sight, therefore, human rights is not a family resemblance concept. What happens instead is that there are competing concepts of human rights around. The next section explores this fact by comparing what two scholars make of the universality of human rights.

The soothing or unsettling effect of the universality of human rights: Donnelly versus Haarscher

Jack Donnelly's *Universal Human Rights in Theory and Practice* has become a classic text in human rights scholarship. The book rests on the dominant definition of human rights as those rights one has simply because one is a human being, which it reproduces in the opening page.[11] For Donnelly, this definition means (1) that human rights are held 'universally' by all human beings and (2) that they hold 'universally' against all other persons and institutions.[12] The inverted commas are in the original, presumably to draw attention to the assertion of universality. Donnelly's position seems encouraging for all of us, almost upbeat. Even if some readers may find the inferences he draws politically or intellectually wanting, they are unlikely to feel that their own moral integrity is being questioned. There is no reason for them to feel personally implicated in the universality of human rights, except for the satisfying promise of being included in the humanity which benefits from human rights. Such a promise can only be soothing. My guess is that, having read the opening page, Donnelly's readers continue their reading, undisturbed.

By contrast, reading Belgian philosopher Guy Haarscher's book on the philosophy of human rights is deeply unsettling.[13] Haarscher also starts from the premise that human rights are everybody's rights. This premise of universality, however, leads him to an altogether different inference. For Haarscher, the human rights imperative demands that the dignity of every single individual should be considered. What human rights require, therefore, is not that the individual be free without limits (or at least without too many limits),[14] but that respect for the *other* individual be the ever-present political norm.[15] Thus, when my rights are secured, I must ensure that the rights of my neighbour are secured, and then those of the neighbour of my neighbour, and so on indefinitely.[16] There always remains yet another fight to be had, or rather fights, in the plural (leading to difficult choices as to where to act first and for whom).[17] I never do quite enough. I must keep intervening.[18] There is no rest. Because human rights cannot be reserved to a few, uninterested in the fate of others,[19] it follows that nothing could be more demanding than to attempt to follow the human rights inspiration. Haarscher's book makes for disturbing reading. It drives the reader to think that human rights are his or her personal responsibility and thus to question his or her moral integrity.[20] Has he, has she done enough for their protection? Logically, but also almost absurdly,[21] the only possible answer is no.

Haarscher's human rights vision: Asceticism or evangelism?

Haarscher refers to this logic as the 'ascetic' dimension of human rights. According to Philip Quinn, asceticism may be characterized as 'a voluntary, sustained and systematic programme of self-discipline and self-denial in which immediate sensual gratifications are renounced in order to attain some valued spiritual or mental state'.[22] The choice of the term by Haarscher, upon which he does not comment, is highly revealing. It may suggest that the Belgian philosopher considers human rights as a religion and, certainly, that he wishes to call for purity in its exercise.

Ascetic practices are found in all the major religious traditions of the world.[23] If human rights is indeed the new 'religion' in the secular world,[24] the term 'ascetic' may seem particularly apposite to qualify its logic, though I personally would say that it misses out the interventionist and, in my term, 'evangelical' living out of human rights recommended by Haarscher. Far from being inward-looking, the ascetic practice of human rights which Haarscher calls for leads to continual intervention. Regrettably Haarscher does not problematize this 'evangelical' intervention. He fails to address ethical objections to intervention, whether they be derived from cultural particularism or linked to the impossibility of political neutrality. Furthermore, it seems to me that Haarscher assumes that one can easily identify and distinguish between human rights victim, violator and professional, presumably respectively innocent, deviant and heroic. David Kennedy has pointed towards the fallacy of such a triangle, which excludes contradictions and ambivalence and assumes that justice can be found or imported rather than having to be 'made' continually.[25]

Haarscher's analysis is nonetheless extremely useful. In particular, Haarscher notes that human rights have entered our contemporary common discourse to the point where everybody agrees with them, thereby creating the impression that adopting a human rights ethic is 'easy',[26] while this ethic is extremely difficult to practise.[27] In his view, the overall enjoyment of human rights in Western societies puts us Westerners in a situation where we understand less and less what they require.[28] Full of our fundamental freedoms, we forget that these freedoms needed to be acquired.[29] Basically contented, we call for the respect of human rights on an imaginary plane: not really fighting for them but invoking them in empty, ineffective declarations.[30] The more protected we are, the less we know what 'to protect' means.[31] The rights for which our forebears fought[32] have thus become the 'hedonist' guarantee of our happiness.[33]

Beside asceticism, hedonism is thus the second dimension in the human rights experience identified by Haarscher. Strictly speaking, hedonism refers to the doctrine in which 'pleasure is regarded as the chief good, or the proper end of action'.[34] An equation between hedonism and selfishness is not necessarily theoretically warranted. It is often made, however: many find immoral the claim that pleasure is to be maximized.[35] The link between hedonism and immorality is one which Haarscher implicitly makes in the (admittedly short) sections where he talks of human rights 'hedonism'.[36] For the purpose of this chapter, I shall follow him in this use of the term 'hedonism' and thus accept the disputable assumption that a 'hedonistic' use of human rights is one which is immoral and/or which is driven by selfishness.[37]

Haarscher identifies a third human rights dimension: the Machiavellian one.[38] He observes that our governments can calculate that leaving us with rights is in their interest in order to pacify us, i.e. to maintain their power.[39] Assuming that everything political depends on a particular balance of forces, human rights is a force to be reckoned with.[40] If the governed manage to convince the government that they are a threat to its power, the government may be inclined to please them, including – today – by giving them rights.[41] Obviously, in this scheme, only those who are in a position to make a difference, either because their predecessors had sufficient weight in the prevalent balance of forces or because they now themselves are strong enough to fight for their own interests, can benefit from human rights.[42]

In conclusion, Haarscher's analysis highlights how the defence of human rights on hedonistic (selfish) grounds and their protection on a Machiavellian (self-interested) calculation result in those most in need of human rights, i.e. the most unprivileged and powerless, being left outside the human rights *acquis*.[43] 'Human rights' suddenly appears a very hollow phrase, with little pretension to universality. And yet, is not universality all that matters in the human rights ethic, properly understood?

The foundational case law on transsexualism

It is not a big step from reading Haarscher to wondering whether human rights instruments and/or institutions are really about human rights. Could the European Court of Human Rights be a misnomer – not really about human rights? Haarscher's analysis of the various dimensions of human rights alerts us to the possibility that the Court might be nothing but a Machiavellian edifice put in place by governments to ensure power, or that it may do no more than preserve the hedonistic (selfish) interests of a selected few, rather than embodying the ascetic, 'true' human rights ethic. Where does one dimension start and the other finish? Are they all present concomitantly? Does this matter, anyway? Donnelly's conception of human rights, for example, would not throw up the same questions. Is Haarscher's view of human rights the one we wish to follow? Those I call protest scholars may do; natural scholars do not. To continue to introduce their differences, I present their likely reaction to the Strasbourg case law on transsexualism.[44]

Some individuals grow up with the certainty, developed from an early age, that they belong to the sex opposite to that to which they have been assigned at birth on anatomical grounds. The split between physical appearance and personal sense of gender identity from which they suffer typically leads to severe depression. The condition is now medically recognized and designated by the term 'transsexualism' – which refers to a move that can either be male-to-female or, less commonly, female-to-male.[45] If transsexualism is diagnosed, hormonal treatment is available to help alleviate the discrepancy between sexual appearance and deep-felt identity. This treatment suppresses or encourages the development of so-called secondary sexual features, related to body and facial hair, breasts and voice tone. Some transsexual people seek an even greater reconciliation between their two contradictory identities and subject themselves to what is today referred to as gender reassignment surgery. This operation, or rather series of operations, involves the removal of the existing sexual organs and the construction of either a vagina-like cavity or of a phallus-like apparatus. Successful hormonal treatment brings about changes such that the transsexual person now appears as the person s/he[46] always felt she was. Surgery more completely reconciles external appearance and inner sense of gender identity, though chromosomes remain of the 'wrong' sex. For the transsexual person determined to follow the operative route, surgery generally leads to improved mental well-being. It does not necessarily signal, however, the end of all her social problems. In some countries, she still encounters problems with regard to her legal identity. This has led a number of post-operative transsexual people to bring cases to Strasbourg.

Their claims, put forward in what I call the foundational Strasbourg case law on transsexualism,[47] involved crucial issues of identity. In the first six cases decided by the Court on their merits,[48] the applicant sought the recognition of her 'new' identity. With one exception (B v. France), these cases were directed against the United Kingdom. British applicants complained about the refusal by the British authorities to make it possible for them to have the original mention of sex on their birth certificate changed, even after gender reassignment surgery. This forced them to reveal their past to people with no direct interest in their history, for example when they applied for a mortgage or a job, opened a bank account, or testified in court. This was embarrassing and painful. The refusal to correct the birth certificate, they contended, violated their right to private life as enshrined in Article 8. Some of them also pointed out that such refusal made it impossible for them to marry a person of their 'now' opposite sex in violation of Article 12.[49] One applicant complained about the impossibility of achieving legal recognition of his social status of father.

Four times running between 1986 and 1998,[50] the Court ruled that the British authorities had not violated the Convention. Its reasoning on Article 8 contained four steps:

1   Article 8 not only protects the individual against interference by the state, but also entails positive obligations inherent in an effective respect for private life. In this case, the refusal by the authorities to *alter* the register of births is not an interference: the applicant wishes them to do – rather than refrain from doing – something.
2   The notion of 'respect' found in Article 8 is not clear-cut, especially as far as positive obligations are concerned.
3   The diversity of practices followed and situations obtained in the Contracting States – with some giving transsexuals the option of changing their personal status and others not – mean that the 'respect' due to transsexuals under Article 8 is bound to vary from case to case. This is therefore an area where the Contracting Parties enjoy a wide margin of appreciation.
4   In determining whether or not a positive obligation exists, regard must be had to the fair balance which has to be struck between the general interests of the community and the interests of the individual. This balance, according to the Court, was respected by the United Kingdom.

The finding of non-violation of Article 8 led the Court either not to find it necessary to discuss the applicant's claim under Article 12 or to find that this provision had not been violated.

While the British applicants were repeatedly losing before the Court, a transsexual applicant, known as B, won her case against France in 1992. The Court was moved by the particularly severe predicament of transsexual people in France. French law made it barely possible to change forenames. The applicant B explained that all her identity documents (identity card, passport, voting card), chequebooks and official correspondence (telephone accounts, tax demands, etc.) referred to her by a male forename.[51] Moreover, as an increasing number of official documents indicated sex, the applicant could not cross a frontier, undergo an identity check or carry out one of the many transactions of daily life without disclosing the discrepancy between her legal and her apparent sex.[52] The Court accepted that in such circumstances, 'even having regard to the State's margin of appreciation, the fair balance between the general interest and the interests of the individual [had] not been attained' in France.[53]

As for the situation in the United Kingdom, even in its first ruling on *Rees* the Court had inserted a paragraph at the end of its reasoning on Article 8 to the effect that:

> [T]he Court is conscious of the seriousness of the problems affecting [transsexuals] and the distress they suffer. The Convention [must] be interpreted and applied in the light of current circumstances . . . The need for appropriate legal measures should therefore be kept under review having regard particularly to scientific and societal developments.[54]

This was an early recognition that the Court might come to restrict the margin of appreciation granted the United Kingdom in subsequent cases. This finally happened in *Goodwin*, decided on 11 July 2002,[55] when the Court found the United Kingdom in violation of both Articles 8 and 12 of the Convention for not allowing the mention of sex to be changed in the birth certificates of the applicants. Sixteen years had passed since *Rees*; evidence, if this were needed, that the natural tendency of the Court is to be conservative, in the lexical sense of the word, viz. to display a 'tendency to preserve or keep intact or unchanged'.[56] Eventually, however, even this conservative Court forced the United Kingdom to move on from a complacent status quo. Now something would have to be done. The law had to be changed – to the benefit of all transsexual people.[57]

A picture of Mr Rees appeared in the *Guardian* on the day following the *Goodwin* verdict. The accompanying text reported that children were still sometimes taunting him. All the suffering this taunting implied reminded me of the remark by Judge Martens, in his powerful dissenting opinion in *Cossey*, to the effect that transsexual people are 'tragic' individuals. Even though the transsexual condition only affects a statistically limited number of individuals, not necessarily economically underprivileged, this does not remove anything from the importance of the treatment of transsexual people as a truly human rights issue. Thus, it is arguably apposite that Judge Martens started his opinion in *Cossey* by referring to the *raison d'être* of human rights, where he stressed the respect for human dignity and human freedom as the principle underlying human rights, including the rights provided in the Convention. Also going to the heart of the *raison d'être* of human rights, Judge Foighel dissenting in *X, Y and Z* claimed: 'It is part of our common European heritage that governments are under a duty to take special care of individuals who are disadvantaged in any way.'

Van Kück's 'normalization' from the perspective of the natural and the protest schools

The latest case brought by a transsexual person, *Van Kück* v *Germany*, decided on 12 June 2003, seems to move away from cutting-edge issues to a certain normalization of the case law on transsexualism. It concerned the refusal by the male-to-female transsexual applicant's health insurance company to reimburse her for the (hormonal and surgical) medical treatment she had undertaken to treat her transsexual condition. Ms Van Kück had brought the dispute before her national courts, and lost. In the opinion of the German courts, her treatment had not been necessary. Ms Van Kück alleged before the Strasbourg Court that her case had not been decided in a way which was compatible with Article 6, which guarantees individuals a fair trial by a tribunal in the determination of their civil rights and obligations. She contended that the interpretation of 'necessary medical treatment' adopted by the German courts was arbitrary and that private information had been misused (thus also leading to a violation of Article 8).

As we have seen in Chapter 5, Article 6 is the most debated provision before the European Court of Human Rights. In this context, *Van Kück* can be viewed as signalling a 'normalization' of the Strasbourg case law on transsexualism. With it, the Court left aside the sensitive and core issue of the personal status of the transsexual person to concentrate on the more pedantic and familiar issue of the requirements of a fair trial. Without dismissing the importance of having gender reassignment surgery recognized as necessary, the issue brought by Ms Van Kück does not seem to have the same fundamental ring as those brought by the previous transsexual applicants.

What would someone like Haarscher make of this? As we have seen, he suggests that all too often claiming *my* human rights is nothing but a banal form of (selfish) hedonism.[58] This is an idea which we have encountered above, in a slightly different form, in our examination of the Convention in a Marxist light in Chapter 5. There we discussed cases where applicants seemed to pursue claims for individual, selfish interests which fit the worst image of a capitalist, materialistic society. Here I am interested in pursuing the slightly different though not completely unrelated idea that the more we become used to having human rights granted to us, the more we take them as our due and start to act on hedonistic (selfish) impulses, leaving behind altruistic ethical ideals.

It is doubtful, I think, that the applicants in what I have called the foundational case law on transsexualism pursued simply selfish interests. Even if Mr Rees noted of the *Goodwin* victory that 'it comes too late for me', which suggests personal disappointment (or resignation?), I suspect that Mr Rees's motives in pursuing the case at Strasbourg were not entirely for his personal gain. Of course he was directly concerned – after all, only a victim can bring a case to Strasbourg. Of course a finding of violation by the Court would have benefited him.[59] Nonetheless his fight was on an issue of principle. It seems likely that the first wave of transsexual applicants were hoping that their action might make the world a better place to live, not just for themselves, but in general. It is less clear that altruistic motives remain central in *Van Kück*, however, as the applicant there was seeking to have the costs of her gender reassignment operation refunded to her by her medical insurance company, potentially – though not necessarily – suggesting a materialistic motive.[60] If this is right, then *Van Kück* may be read as indicating a move away from protest against injustice towards greater hedonism. At the same time, it seems clear that the aim of the applications by past transsexual persons was at least in part to make *Van Kück* possible by having secured the principle of transsexual people's legal recognition.

There will inevitably be applicants at Strasbourg who pursue cases for purely selfish reasons. Probably many of those I call protest scholars – among whom I include Haarscher – find this disturbing; if not an abuse, at least a regrettable consequence of human rights law.[61] By contrast I expect that those I call natural scholars – among whom I include Donnelly – would see no problem with this. Natural scholars do not accept there is anything wrong with taking human rights as our due, for what else are they, if not our due? From the perspective of natural scholars, altruism has nothing to do with human rights logic, which they conceive as providing entitlements, *not* imposing an obligation to fight for the other. To them, the motives underlying the pursuit of having human rights recognized are irrelevant to its moral legitimacy. Above I wrote: 'the more we become used to having human rights granted to us, the more we take them as our due and start to act on hedonistic impulses, leaving behind altruistic ethical ideals'. This is an argument which could be put forward by a protest scholar; a natural scholar would not perceive this as being problematic.

Can we *have* human rights? The responses of the natural and protest scholars

Donnelly has highlighted what he calls the 'possession paradox' of human rights: 'One claims a human right in the hope of ultimately creating a society in [which] such claims will no longer be necessary. Where human rights are effectively protected, we continue to *have* human rights, but there is no need or occasion to *use* them.'[62] In such circumstances lower-level rights are sufficient: we can turn to national law rather than invoking higher rights. Presented in such a way, Donnelly's argument appears logical – and soothing.[63] However, it would fail to convince protest scholars.

In a way only apparently similar to Donnelly, Haarscher stresses that we lose sense of the obligation to fight for human rights as we enjoy them. The inference he draws from this observation is not the one drawn by Donnelly. In Haarscher's view, when human rights are granted to us, we too often come to use them for a hedonistic purpose rather than for the purpose for which they were recognized. A protest scholar like Haarscher is unlikely to think that a specific embodiment of the ideal of human rights into law marks any kind of end to the struggle for the recognition of human rights. However hard-won and however important its positive consequences, a legal or judicial victory is a small victory, which does not amount to Victory with a capital V. The fight must go on.[64]

Donnelly is ready to envisage conditions 'where human rights are effectively protected'.[65] This is not surprising given his alignment with what I call the natural school. Natural scholars believe that some societies do respect human rights, at least by and large. They envisage human rights *law* to be a continuation of the human rights *ideal* and typically speak of the development of international human rights law in the last half-century as progress.

By contrast, it would be surprising for Haarscher, as a protest scholar, to celebrate the existence of a society where human rights are effectively protected. It is in the nature of protest scholars not to be satisfied with the state of the world and always to ask for more, by which I mean that they continually see injustice (human rights abuses) and want to fight it. This is the more so since they are inclined to consider human society globally, taking into account North-South relations, and typically denounce the evils of post-colonialism, capitalism and neo-liberalism. But even at the level of a national and overall democratic society, they are likely to stress the disagreements which arise as to what 'effective protection' of human rights means in practice and to insist on the politically always-contestable nature of the specific meaning of human rights.

Donnelly says that we need human rights most when we do not have (in the sense of enjoy) them. Turning this proposition on its head, we do not need human rights when we have them, since 'the "having" [a right is] particularly important when one does not "have" it'.[66] This possession paradox is not one which interests Haarscher. Haarscher suggests something different, namely, that we lose human rights when we mistakenly think we have them. Douzinas, another protest scholar according to my classification, goes one step further. In *The End of Human Rights*, Douzinas argues that we have come to a point in history where we have actually lost human rights. He traces this loss to the transformation of the language of human rights from a language of rebellion and dissent to 'a criterion of state legitimacy and a new type of positive law'.[67] The sense of insignificance in the grand scheme of things that a legal embodiment of human rights entails appears recurrently in the book. In Douzinas's view, human rights have been 'hijacked' by governments and bureaucrats. Having lost their transcendent character through their instrumentalization, they have lost their *raison d'être*. Douzinas believes that we live in a period that is marked not by the triumph, but by the demise, of human rights. The main aim of his book is to convey the urgency of retrieving the transcendental aspect of the human rights project.

Haarscher's view is less extreme. He sees contemporary human rights as presenting ascetic, hedonistic and Machiavellian dimensions. In his view, like ideal-types in the Weberian sense of the term, these three dimensions are found in practice in different degrees and in various combinations. If we follow either Douzinas or Haarscher, we cannot but think that there is a crucial fault in Donnelly's argument, and this is to think that we can have human rights. What Haarscher's and Douzinas's arguments suggest is that we cannot *have* human rights. This, of course, is in direct opposition to the standard definition of human rights as those rights which every human being *has*.

Can human rights law embody human rights? The responses of the natural and protest scholars

Let me summarize what I have said so far. Those I call natural scholars hold that it is possible for human beings actually to have human rights. Protest scholars hold that human rights can never be had: as a language of protest, human rights are always out of reach, they are 'the negative principle at the heart of the social imaginary';[68] they serve to 'denounce the intolerable';[69] they are 'the promise of the "not yet"'.[70] The natural scholars feel that having human rights (through positive legal rights) is a success. By contrast, at their most extreme, protest scholars believe that this feeling of success actually signals the end (destruction) of human rights.

The ways in which these two schools of thought approach human rights as a legal concept are diametrically opposite. For the natural scholars, there can be a congruence between human rights as a philosophical concept and human rights as a legal concept. The congruence is not necessary – so presented human rights practice can admittedly be an abuse of the human rights ideal. Nonetheless, and this is the important point, congruence *is* possible, even likely. In other words, human rights law normally embodies the philosophical concept of human rights; the former exists in direct continuation of the latter.[71] For natural scholars, there is a link between human rights law and the philosophical concept of human rights – a 'common thread' (to return to an expression we encountered above in our discussion of Wittgensteinian family resemblance).

By contrast, for the protest scholars, human rights represent a perpetual calling, an ideal that can never fully be achieved. Human rights is not about entitlements, but about claims and aspirations.[72] Protest scholars firmly believe that human rights (a) are moral, (b) must be raised when they are not socially recognized, and (c) should concern every human being, especially those who are 'forgotten'. In one sense, they are thus close to adopting a definition of human rights which corresponds to the dominant '*a b c*' combination identified above. In another sense, however, the way protest scholars approach human rights has little to do with the dominant, natural conception. This is because they reject (or at least are not primarily interested in) the premise that human rights are given entitlements.

To try to capture the conception of human rights the protest scholars hold, the matrix which was presented above therefore needs to be redesigned. In particular the word 'rights' needs to be substituted by 'aspirations' or 'claims'. The new matrix could read:

Human rights are

a: moral claims/aspirations
b: which contest the status quo
c: which chiefly concern the oppressed

Further letters could be added, including for example:

d: which are geared towards a more egalitarian and free polity
e: which evolve historically

In conclusion, protest scholars do not share the natural conception of human rights. For them, human rights law can never be truly faithful to the philosophical concept of human rights: there is a real danger that there is a lack of continuity between human rights as a philosophical concept and human rights as a legal concept. Putting it in an extreme form, from their perspective, human rights is drifting to such an extent that no core element possibly subsists between the utterances of the term 'human rights' in the philosophical and in the legal contexts. To the protest scholars, human rights may well constitute a family resemblance concept or, probably more accurately, the legal utterances of the term may constitute an unacceptable abuse of the true human rights concept. In particular, protest scholars are unlikely to think that the European Court of Human Rights (or any other institution) can realize the human rights sought for in the philosophical conception – hence Douzinas's diatribe against human rights professionals whose experience of human rights violations is confined to being served a bad bottle of wine, quoted in the introduction.[73]

Both natural and protest scholars believe in human rights

Natural scholars *believe* that human rights exist, as it were, 'full stop', by which I mean independently of social recognition. They conceive of human rights as entitlements which are based on 'nature', a short-cut which can stand for God, the universe, reason or another transcendental source. Protest scholars also believe in human rights, though in a different way: for them, human rights is a language not so much of entitlement as of protest. Haarscher suggests that there is a good dimension of human rights, the ascetic one. He views the other two dimensions, the hedonistic and the Machiavellian, as travesties of the first. Douzinas similarly bemoans the instrumentalization of human rights by governments and by individuals and despairs of the failure of human rights to achieve anything in practice. He nonetheless remains attached to the idea of human rights. One could even say that he has faith in them, which is why he seeks their transcendental basis, presumably in order to make it possible to invent a practice which would respect this basis. The point I wish to make is that protest scholars also *believe* in human rights, though in a different way from the natural scholars.

What is the basis of human rights? The response of the natural scholars

When it comes to identifying the basis of human rights, natural scholars seem to oscillate between nature and consensus. Donnelly is a good example. He presents human rights *both* as having their source in human nature[74] *and* as constituting 'a social choice of a particular moral vision of human potentiality' directly linked to the historical 'rise and consolidation of liberalism in the modern West'.[75] For a long time I have found this double account contradictory: it seems to me that human rights cannot both have always existed and have arisen historically. However, many natural scholars do not see the contradiction I perceive. For them, human rights are universal even if they have come to receive a particular articulation.

It is not uncommon for natural scholars to rely on the concrete manifestation of human rights in international law in order to dismiss the need to find a metaphysical basis for human rights. Typical of this approach is the position which the French and Catholic philosopher Jacques Maritain proposed in order to allow progress to be made on the actual discussion of what the Universal Declaration of Human Rights would contain. To paraphrase, his advice was: 'forget the basis upon which you believe in human rights, focus on identifying what these human rights are'.[76] This is indeed the approach which was adopted by the Commission of Human Rights of the United Nations (of which he was a member), with the result that the Declaration was ready for signature in 1948.

This approach makes it possible for natural scholars to evade the fact that it is problematic to found human rights on 'nature' (or God, or reason, or the universe) when some people believe in God but others do not, and those who believe in God do not all believe in the same God. The strategy may be useful, but it ignores the fact that natural scholars who rely on it would still believe in human rights in the absence of the so-called consensus which has emerged since World War II. In their logic, the consensus has to be the *proof* of the existence of human rights, not its basis.[77] If pushed, natural scholars would presumably admit that they personally believe that God, nature or reason[78] provides a basis for human rights but that they are willing to sidestep such a grand basis in order to work with others who do not share their belief.

Some natural scholars refuse to rely on consensus to found human rights. For example, Michael Freeman takes issue with Donnelly for appearing to base human rights on consensus so as to avoid controversial philosophical theories of human nature. In Freeman's words, this strategy is unconvincing 'not only because it is not clear that a *sincere* consensus exists, but also because consensus is factual not moral, and therefore, in itself, justifies nothing'.[79] Not surprisingly the search for an ontological basis for human rights has continued to occupy some key natural scholars, most prominently the philosopher Alan Gewirth.[80]

What is the basis of human rights? The response of the protest scholars

The protest scholars encounter the same problem as the natural scholars when it comes to identify the ground on which they base their belief in human rights. Correctly in my view, Haarscher notes that the two main contenders which have historically been proposed to found human rights, namely God and reason, must be dismissed: the former because he is 'dead'; the latter because it is grounded in nothing else than itself, with no real possibility of transcendence.[81] As protest scholars are naturally suspicious of human rights law, the route adopted by some natural scholars of relying on the legal consensus which is represented by the so-called international bill of rights is barred to them. What they do instead is to rely on something less specific, which has to do with social consciousness.

Haarscher, for example, talks of '*dressage*'.[82] The word, which connotes training, is normally used in French with respect to animals. Haarscher does not
explain why he uses the term. While I do not know the extent to which he would
wish to condone its overtones of conditioning, I personally find the term useful
precisely because it provocatively suggests an internalization by the individual of a
logic which may not be natural to him or her,[83] thus pointing out that human
rights emerge from a particular discourse which is devised rather than natural. In
a vein which is not wholly dissimilar, Douzinas states: '[Human] rights are
grounded on human *discourse* and nothing more solid, like nature or humanity.'[84]
'Tradition' is another word which could adequately capture the basis on which
protest scholars found human rights since it implies in-the-long-run continuity
rather than once-and-for-all fixed norms, and presents the further advantage of
being able to accommodate both minor disagreements and positive change.[85] Not
surprisingly, human rights education figures high among the preoccupations of
protest scholars.[86]

Even though a 'tradition' offers more permanence than the mere legal consensus
of a particular historical moment, it is not completely safe from assaults denying
the existence of human rights. It is ultimately as dissatisfying for protest scholars to
shun completely a metaphysical foundation on which to base human rights as it is
for natural scholars. Not surprisingly some protest scholars have wanted to ground
human rights on a more metaphysical basis than social discourse. Significantly,
Douzinas, despite arguing that human rights is founded on nothing more solid
than discourse, also says and repeats in *The End of Human Rights* that the whole aim
of his book is to retrieve the transcendental dimension of human rights.

In conclusion, both natural and protest scholars, who believe in human rights,
face the difficulty that founding human rights on something akin to nature is
unlikely to be universally compelling. In the face of this difficulty, natural scholars
tend to fall back on the legal consensus; protest scholars, on social consciousness.
Neither, however, have been able completely to bypass the search for a more
metaphysical basis.

Those who do not believe in, but are committed to, human rights: The deliberative scholars

Natural and protest scholars believe in human rights. Deliberative scholars are
committed to human rights without *believing* in them. They conceive of human
rights neither as entitlements nor as claims against injustice, but as procedural
principles which should be followed for a democratic polity to function. In their
view, human rights are thus no more than legal and political standards; they are
not moral, and certainly not religious, standards. This perspective leads them to
insist on the limited scope of human rights. For the deliberative scholars, human
rights are there to govern the polity and nothing else. They should not be
conceived as a means through which to shape man's whole life (as religion would).

Human rights are principles of deliberation and/or adjudication. They do not dictate how things should be substantively, but should act as processual guides.

Michael Ignatieff, a typical representative of the deliberative school, writes:

> Human rights [would do well to become] more political, that is, if it were understood as a language, not for the proclamation and enactment of eternal verities, but as a discourse for the adjudication of conflict. [Given that rights are not trumps] what is their use? At best, rights create a common framework, a common set of reference points that can assist parties in conflict to deliberate together.[87]

Conor Gearty is another representative of the school. In the review of the Strasbourg case law he published in 1993, he already expressed the idea that human rights is not about getting the right moral solution, but is about due process. His view was that the Convention was at its best when it operated as a charter for procedural fairness.[88] His most recent book, on the United Kingdom's Human Rights Act, similarly declares itself in opposition to any view of human rights as natural, absolute, universal and inalienable.[89] It is significantly entitled *Principles of Human Rights Adjudication*: both the words 'principles' and 'adjudication' are crucial. Gearty writes: 'If the Human Rights Act does ultimately succeed, it will be because of – not in spite of – the weak version of "rights", riddled with exceptions, that it seeks to guarantee.'[90] He thus echoes Ignatieff's rejection of the Dworkinian idea of rights as trumps: rights are not trumps which give something to somebody; they are principles which allow democratic decisions to be made.

For a deliberative scholar, there are no human rights beyond human rights law: the law, especially as it is embodied in constitutional principles of deliberation, is all there is to human rights. Deliberative scholars are entirely committed to human rights, but their vision of human rights is avowedly secular, by which I mean that they do not approach human rights as a religion. Indeed, they are angered at the quasi-religious awe in which human rights are held, which Ignatieff significantly denounces as idolatry.

In their view, human rights do not and should not dictate content. They should not be expected to provide anything more than 'thin' principles of procedures. It is much, of course, but far less than natural or protest scholars would expect. There is nothing remotely religious in their approach: human rights are solely a matter of agreement. They typically associate human rights and liberalism; they are committed to both.

Those who are sceptical of human rights: The discourse scholars

Makau Mutua begins the preface of his book *Human Rights: A Political and Cultural Critique* with the following words:

I have always found human suffering unacceptable. But I did not name my struggles against deprivation, dehumanisation, and oppression a fight for human rights. For me it was the injunction for persons and groups with a conscience.[91]

Though Mutua shares with the protest scholars a commitment to notice and alleviate suffering, he is deeply sceptical about the claim that human rights would necessarily provide the best means to do something about this suffering. He writes:

Attempts to construct universalist creeds and doctrines – or to present a particular creed or doctrine as universal – run the risk of destroying or decimating dissimilar [cultural] universes. The claim of a universalist warrant is an extremely tricky proposition, if not altogether impossible.[92]

He continues:

I wrote this book [because] I wanted to explain why I believe that the human rights corpus should be treated as an experimental paradigm, a work in progress, and not a final inflexible truth. It is important that the human rights movement be fully exposed so that its underbelly can be critically examined. I know that many in the human rights movement mistakenly claim to have seen a glimpse of eternity, and think of the human rights corpus as a summit of human civilization, a sort of an end to human history. This view is so self-righteous and lacking in humility that it of necessity must invite probing critiques from scholars of all stripes.[93]

Although a protest and a deliberative scholar might sympathize with the ideas contained in the last paragraph, it seems to me that Mutua goes one step further by finding the idea of human rights potentially dangerous. What he finds most shocking is the claim that human rights are universal. He recalls having been born 'in a part of colonial Africa that the British had named Kenya'[94] and how colonialism stripped him of his identity, forcing him to take a 'Christian' name to enter the Church, in a process which is akin to today's human rights 'crusade' (his word). To quote him again:

There was a basic assumption that Christianity was *superior* to, and better than, any African spirituality. It was presented as a cultural package. What is interesting are the parallels between Christianity's violent conquest of Africa and the modern human rights crusade. The same methods are at work and similar cultural dispossessions are taking place, without dialogue or conversation. The official human corpus, which issues from European predicates, seeks to supplant all other traditions, while rejecting them. It claims to be the only genius of the good society.[95]

In a slightly different vein from Mutua, Wendy Brown asks: 'What are the implications of human rights assuming centre stage as an international justice project, or as *the* progressive international justice project?'[96] Urging us to 'take account of that which rights discourse does not avow about itself', she concludes:

It [the rights discourse] is a politics and it organizes political space, often with the aim of monopolizing it. It also stands as a critique of dissonant political projects, converges neatly with the requisites of liberal imperialism and global free trade, and legitimates both as well. If the global problem today is defined as terrible human suffering consequent to limited individual rights against abusive state powers, then human rights may be the best tactic against this problem. But if it is diagnosed as the relatively unchecked globalization of capital, postcolonial political deformations, and superpower imperialism combining to disenfranchise peoples in many parts of the first, second and third worlds from the prospect of self-governance to a degree historically unparalleled in modernity, other kinds of political projects, including other international justice projects, may offer a more appropriate and far-reaching remedy for injustice defined as suffering *and* as systematic disenfranchisement from collaborative self-governance.[97]

Awareness of human rights' social construction and deep scepticism about their supposed benefits is the defining characteristic of those I call discourse scholars. Discourse scholars not only insist that there is nothing natural about human rights – they would say that 'human rights only exist because they are talked about';[98] they also question the fact that human rights are naturally good. This is why they want to examine its underbelly and why they believe that more effective emancipatory projects need to be imagined.

While discourse scholars are very good at exposing the defects of the human rights discourse, they do not really explain what they propose in its stead. The emancipatory project(s) to which they refer are typically vague. This vagueness may strike many as a weakness. Discourse scholars might retort, however, that this uncertainty is the best antidote against arrogance, and should therefore be welcomed in a world which is defined by power.

Interestingly not all discourse scholars take the step, which would be logical from their perspective, of entirely dismissing the human rights discourse. Mutua, for one, is ambiguous. He asks the 'many movement activists and scholars [who] will be disturbed by [his] book' to join him in a 'dialogue about the re-thinking of the entire human rights project so that we can reconstruct it'.[99] The question arises as to why Mutua, so dismissive of human rights, nonetheless keeps referring to them. Is it because he feels that this is the best strategy available to him to convince his interlocutors or could it be that, despite his ire against human rights, there is something in them which he finds attractive?

Martti Koskenniemi, whom I would also classify as a discourse scholar, would probably not be impressed by the course adopted by Mutua. He recognizes that

you may be compelled . . . to choose a purely strategic attitude towards rights. Even as you know that rights defer to policy [by which Koskenniemi means political conceptions of the common good which are neither apolitical nor foundational], you cannot disclose this, as you would then seem to undermine what others (mistakenly) believe is one of your most beneficial gifts to humanity (a non-political and universal rights rhetoric).[100]

But Koskenniemi does not approve of such a strategy. He immediately continues:

It is hard to think of such an attitude as a beneficial basis from which to engage other cultures or to inaugurate a transcultural sphere of politics.[101]

Now allow me to quote myself. I am of course a discourse scholar – had I believed in or at least been committed to human rights, it is unlikely that I would have wished to pursue the critiques of human rights as systematically as I have tried to do in this book. In my 1996 article on 'Human rights talk and anthropological ambivalence', I tried to grapple with the paradox that I did not believe in human rights but could not let go of them. I wrote:

Being engaged with one's world requires an engagement with the debates arising in this world; it may then also require adopting its vocabulary. Ironically, encouraging my readers to use the language of human rights is probably also inviting them to reify the concept. Political claims are at their [most effective] when they are essentialized. It is then that they appear to be unchallengeable, that they can hope to receive a legitimacy which is not contestable. How powerful would a demand to extend the human rights of credit to the poor be [an example I had used earlier on], if the malleable nature of 'human rights' were put to the fore? To be persuasive, the demand needs to invoke something bigger and more permanent than social accident.[102]

I concluded:

I have argued . . . that human rights only exist because they are talked about. I also have noted that such language has become unavoidable on the political scene . . . As for the question of political engagement, it is for [each one of us] to decide whether [we] wish to use such language, which certainly can be beneficial. If [we] decide to do so, [we] should [nonetheless] be aware of the limitations of the concept.[103]

Almost ten years on, my position has not changed. I remain convinced (1) that one should be deeply sceptical of the human rights language and (2) that there is nonetheless no point in shunning this language altogether. I do not think this is just a matter of strategy, however. Much to my intellectual discomfort, if I am completely honest, I have to admit that if I feel for the most part a discourse scholar, there is nonetheless a little part of me which also feels like a natural scholar – as well as a protest and a deliberative scholar, but this is less uncomfortable. It is not impossible that Mutua finds himself in a similar situation.[104] Below I shall try to elaborate on how the tenets of the four schools can come to mingle in the consciousness of a given scholar. For the moment, let me try to recap how the four schools I have identified compare, while already stressing that they should be approached as Weberian ideal-types rather than fixed categories which neatly and perfectly describe single-tracked thought processes.

Mapping the schools

Table 1 should be more or less self-explanatory as it uses terms and refers to elements which have all been introduced in the previous sections. It can be read vertically and horizontally. Thus it can be seen, vertically, that natural scholars conceive of human rights as entitlements, which are for anyone, which can be had, etc; horizontally, that natural scholars conceive of human rights as entitlements, deliberative scholars as principles, etc.

Although Table 2 introduces some new elements, it should not be particularly difficult to comprehend. The first row will speak for itself for those who are acquainted with philosophy; those who are not can ignore it. The second row summarizes extensive discussions held in the previous sections about who *believes* in human rights. The third row refers to a question raised in the introduction, and its answer is now straightforward: both natural and deliberative scholars are committed to liberalism, while neither protest nor discourse scholars are. The fourth row on whether to regard human rights law as signifying progress directly parallels the previous one.

As for the last row, it uses labels which appear to me potentially useful if it is accepted that human rights act somewhat like a religion – at least for some - in our partly secular world. As repeatedly said in the book, the natural scholars represent the orthodoxy. Referring to the deliberative scholars as atheist seems appropriate given their rejection of any religious dimension in the human rights concept. The drive towards both intervention and purity which appears to characterize the protest scholars may justify their label of human rights 'evangelists' though they may prefer to refer to themselves as 'ascetics'.[105] As for the nihilist label, which I attach to the discourse scholars, this is discussed further in the next and concluding chapter of the book.

Table 3 is a diagram. It seeks to position the schools in relation to each other. For the sake of representation, it consists in four blocks which correspond to the 'schools' which I have identified so far. In reality, as the final two sections of this chapter should make clear, positions are encountered on a continuum and slide between extremes – from the most liberal to the most non-liberal and from the most foundational to the most non-foundational. That such sliding occurs acts as a reminder that the heuristically useful term 'school' does not fully capture the way human rights are conceived in academic, judicial[106] and indeed everyday discourse.

Who's who: Naming some representatives of each school

If the schema presented in the above section is truly useful, it should be possible to locate anyone who has a view about what human rights are somewhere in it. Time will tell whether this is indeed the case. In the meanwhile, this section attaches the names of some prominent scholars to each 'school' (which I put here

Table 1. *How the four schools approach human rights*

Human rights (HR)	Schools of thought			
	Natural	**Deliberative**	**Protest**	**Discourse**
Consist in	entitlements	principles	claims/aspirations	what you put into them
Are for	everyone	running the polity fairly	first and foremost those who suffer	should be, but are not, for those who suffer
Can be attained/ had?	yes	not as such (inform a process)	no, for power and suffering carry on	it depends how you look at them
Can be embodied in law?	definitely – this is the aim	definitely – HR come to life through the rule of law	not as such, for law eventually betrays the HR idea	well – HR are referred to in law, but with what implications?
Have a core?	yes – and proliferation of HR is dangerous/ counter-productive	in a sense – HR do not govern all aspects of society	in a sense – though new responses to new injustices will always be needed	no – you can use the phrase in all kinds of ways
Are universal?	yes – definitely, they are part of the structure of the universe	potentially – if the consensus broadens	at source, yes, though they have historically been 'hijacked'	no – universality is a pretence of the powerful
Are based on	Nature/God/ Universe/ Reason (with legal consensus acting as a fallback)	a consensus as to how the polity should be run (with reason in the background)	a tradition of social struggles (with possibly a yearning for the transcendental)	language
Conceived, in summary, as	given	agreed	fought for	talked about

Table 2. *The four schools' broad characteristics*

Characteristics	Schools of thought			
	Natural	**Deliberative**	**Protest**	**Discourse**
Find inspiration in the philosophy of e.g.	Kant	Habermas	Levinas	Derrida
***Believe* in HR, almost as in a faith?**	yes	no – not like that	yes	no
Are liberals?	yes	yes	no	no
See HR law since 1948 as progress?	yes	yes	no	no
Could be labelled, in a religious metaphor, as	orthodox	atheist	ascetic/ evangelical	nihilist

Table 3. *The relative position of the schools in the human rights field*

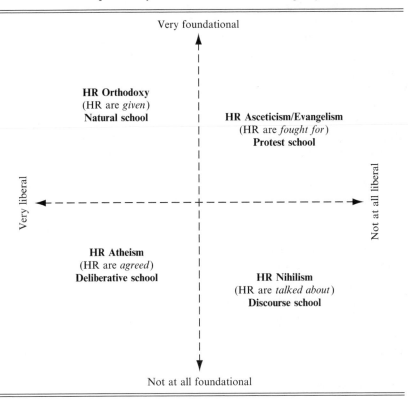

in inverted commas to insist one last time on the limitations of the term). By its very nature, the exercise will result in putting together in the same school scholars who are very different from each other and indeed may have bitter disagreements with each other. It is nonetheless warranted by the fact that they appear to display the hallmarks of the school I associate them with.

The hallmarks of the natural school are that human rights are conceived as entitlements and that human rights law is regarded favourably (at least overall; some of its aspects can be fiercely criticized). (A third hallmark is a character-istically Kantian approach, but this need not detain us here.) Anyone who endorses the fact that human rights are inalienable entitlements is certain to be a natural scholar. When Alan Gewirth writes: 'We may assume, as true by definition, that human rights are rights that all persons have simply insofar as they are human', there can be no doubt as to the school to which he belongs. Michael Perry's book *The Idea of Human Rights* addresses the major critiques which have been levied against human rights (and which have been reviewed in this book). Perry responds to each of them in a tight text, the logic of which is typical of the natural school. The first sentence of the first chapter starts: 'The idea of human rights – the idea that has emerged in international law in the period since the Second World War – is complex':[107] only a natural scholar would be happy to equate in such a way, especially from the very outset, the idea of human rights with human rights law. Later on, Perry makes it clear that his view is that human rights are claims which are ultimately related to 'a norm concerning what anyone and everyone is due simply as a human being'.[108] Human rights talk is 'a way of talking . . . about those things that every state may not do to any human being or must do for every human being'.[109] 'It provides a way of talking about "what is just" from a special angle: the viewpoint of the "other(s)" to whom something (including, inter alia, freedom of choice) is owed or due.'[110] The emphasis on entitlements could not be clearer. Michael Freeman, who has written an important and very clear book *Human Rights: An Interdisciplinary Approach*, is another natural scholar. For him, '[r]ights are . . . *just claims* or *entitlements* that derive from moral and/or legal rules'.[111] His recognition of a number of signifi-cant landmarks in '[t]he progress of human rights since 1948'[112] chimes with the fact that natural scholars conceive of human rights law as a direct continuation of human rights.

It has been said that the lawyers are 'the high priests' of the human rights discourse.[113] The dominance of human rights law in human rights scholarship has been bemoaned by protest scholars.[114] What needs to be seen is that the lawyers' dominance is not so much a cause as a consequence of the orthodox tendency to equate human rights with human rights law. This tendency is not specific to Law. Thus the natural scholars I have identified come from a variety of disciplines: Politics (Donnelly and Freeman), Philosophy (Gewirth) and Law (Perry). It would not be difficult to find scholars of other disciplines who also belong to the natural school.[115]

I have already mentioned that Michael Ignatieff, a historian by training but better known in both the academic and the public spheres for his political commentaries, and Conor Gearty, an academic and practising lawyer who is the director of the Centre for the Study of Human Rights at the London School of Economics, are deliberative scholars. For a deliberative scholar from a different academic discipline, we can turn to the anthropologist Richard Wilson. One hallmark of the deliberative school is the insistence that human rights, which it conceives as principles of deliberation and/or adjudication, have a limited role to play rather than laying down a quasi-religious morality. To quote Wilson: 'human rights are most effective when conceived of as narrow legal instruments designed to defend individuals from political institutions . . . Turning human rights talk into a moral-theological treatise . . . destroys the most important promise of human rights; that is, its possible contribution to . . . the construction of real and lasting democratic legitimacy'.[116] These are the final words of his insightful monograph on *The Politics of Truth and Reconciliation in South Africa*. The fact that the book began by acknowledging the contribution of Habermas and Ignatieff to human rights theory turned out to be a reliable indication as to the school in which to place Wilson.[117] For him, human rights should be a 'language of principle and accountability'.[118] As could be expected, he discusses constitutionalism and the rule of law at length – in an anthropological way which makes a lot of room for legal pluralism, local courts and popular legal consciousness.

Protest scholars have in common that they make it their duty to protest at the injustice of the world; that they choose to do so in the language of human rights; that they conceive of human rights not so much as something tangible as a utopia or a project always in the making (and reversible); that they distinguish between 'bad' and 'good' human rights (though not in such crude terms); and, finally, that they believe in good human rights. I have already placed Guy Haarscher and Costas Douzinas, two legal theorists, in the protest school. A third legal theorist who also belongs to this school is Upendra Baxi who makes a distinction between objectionable 'politics *of* human rights' and emancipatory 'politics *for* human rights'. For him, the passage from the latter to the former occurs through an 'order of progress which makes the state more ethical, governance progressively just, and power increasingly accountable'.[119] There is hope in these words, though Baxi makes it clear that human rights cannot be expected simply to happen. To quote him again: 'In their most creative moment, the labour of politics *for* human rights emerge as Herculean; in more stressed moments, these resemble the ordeals of a Sisyphus.'[120] There is no triumphalism in this account, the less so since 'the future of human rights must forever remain deeply insecure'.[121] In line with what one would expect from a protest scholar, Baxi is clear that '[t]he politics . . . that result in . . . law enunciations of human rights is not the . . . primary . . . source of origin of human rights'.[122] Moreover these enunciations cannot be taken at face value: 'While [epistemic human rights communities] find in every human rights enunciation a signature for a better human future, the rightless peoples, all too often, find these enunciatory moves rather callous.'[123] Despite this, politics *for* human rights leave Baxi in no doubt that 'contemporary human rights movements [are] precious'.[124] This is because they 'deny all cosmological, as well as terrestrial, justifications for the imposition of unjustified human suffering'.[125] In Baxi's view, 'human rights languages are perhaps *all that we have* to interrogate the barbarism of power'; they present 'an inestimable potential [which was] not readily available in the previous centuries'.[126] The IR scholar Ken Booth also belongs to the protest school. He says that he wants 'to argue that we should have human rights not because we are human, but to make us human [given] that humans are not essentially born, they are socially made, and that human rights are part of what might make them at this stage of world history'[127] – a reference, put differently, to training, discourse and/ or education. For him, 'the desirability of dynamic rather than static conceptions of the future' must be emphasised.[128] 'Instead of blueprints (a worked-out model of world government for the twenty-first century, for example) when history would come to an end, the argument is that politics is about travelling hope-fully.'[129] Booth is wary of too solid and eternal a basis for human rights. In his words, '"grounding" implies very demanding requirements. [His] preference is for anchorages'.[130] It is nonetheless his view that '[w]e have no better language [than human rights] at present to set us free',[131] in line with the fact that the protest school has faith in human rights.

Finally there are the human rights nihilists or discourse scholars. For obvious reasons, their voice is the least prominent in human rights scholarship. Beside the lawyer Makau Mutua, the feminist theorist Wendy Brown,[132] the philosopher Alasdair McIntyre and myself, they include the anthropologist Talal Asad, already cited in Chapter 5. Asad observes that human rights discourse is not only about good things but 'also about undermining styles of life by means of the law as well as by means of a wider culture that sustains and motivates the law'.[133] As far as he is concerned, it cannot be assumed that 'universal capital or universal human right will bring with it practical equality and an end to all suffering'.[134] The question must therefore be asked: 'Is human rights discourse the only language [in which] to talk about justice?'[135]

Moving within the liberal and the non-liberal schools

In the section above, I have confidently assigned particular scholars to my four schools, as if these were clear-cut and tight entities. In this section, I want to stress that things in practice are not necessarily as simple as the model implies and that both multiple and ambiguous affiliations are possible.

Let me take the example of Wilson, whom I have identified as a deliberative scholar. While such a classification is in my view pertinent, it is nonetheless worth noting that a number of remarks by Wilson could result in classifying him in the natural school. Most relevant in this respect is his affirmation, repeated many times in his book, that 'there is a strong moral argument that [an] amnesty arrangement [such as emerged from the 1993 South African interim Constitution] can only be entered into by victims themselves . . . and not by others on their behalf'.[136] Alluded to here is nothing but an inalienable entitlement. Later Wilson explicitly refers to positive law as an expression of human rights: 'the redefinition (and some would say deformation) of human rights during democratic transitions to mean amnesty and reconciliation [conflicts] with a state's duty to punish human rights offenders as established in international criminal law'.[137] Wilson believes there is an 'individual right to retributive justice and to pursue perpetrators through the courts' which should not be trumped for the sake of social stability.[138] (This is the more so, according to Wilson, since such an attempt at ensuring social stability is doomed to failure – precisely because of its neglect of the individual right which it negates.) In all this, Wilson presents himself more like a natural than a deliberative scholar.

Let me now introduce Balakrishnan Rajagopal, author of *International Law from Below*, a book which may be said to have consecrated the importance of Third World Resistance in legal scholarship. I have not mentioned Rajagopal in the previous section for the simple reason that I could not decide finally where to classify him. Rajagopal writes that he wants 'to investigate and expose the risks of relying entirely on human rights as the next grand discourse of emancipation and liberation'.[139] Does this make him a protest scholar or a discourse scholar? His denunciation of the way in which 'the present human-rights corpus . . . perpetuates . . . fear, contempt, and loathing of the masses'[140] might incline one to put him in the protest school. But his insistence that 'there are some basic problems in constituting the human-rights discourse as the sole discourse of resistance in the Third World, because it remains caught up in the discursive formations of colonialism that makes it blind to many types of violence'[141] may tilt the balance in favour of the discourse school. The question of whether Rajagopal is a protest or a discourse scholar is not necessarily an important one, however. What matters is the very articulate way in which he demonstrates the interrelationship between the human rights discourse and colonialism and post-colonialism.

For, on the one hand, a liberal scholar like Wilson to oscillate between the deliberative and the natural schools and for, on the other hand, a scholar critical of liberalism like Rajagopal to be somewhere in between the protest and the discourse schools may not seem completely out of order given that these multiple or ambiguous associations respect the fault-line between the two liberal and the two non-liberal schools. The natural and the deliberative schools on the one hand and the protest and discourse schools on the other hand could be seen as two – respectively liberal and non-liberal – camps within which various shades of opinion are encountered.[142] However, things are even more complicated than that: scholars (as well as other people) will often move between the four schools, as the next section intimates.

The concept of human rights: Spun by the four schools

Booth, a protest scholar in my classification, refers approvingly to Donnelly, a natural scholar, in order to endorse the point that 'the critique of universality ignores the degree of actually existing universality in terms of human rights'.[143] This 'cross-over' is interesting and, in a sense, peculiar to Booth: one expects that many protest scholars would reject the point.

For a cross-over occurring between the liberal and non-liberal 'camps' in the opposite direction, one can turn to Gewirth when he assumes the interventionist stance which is more typical of the protest school than the natural school to which he belongs.[144] Gewirth writes that 'under certain circumstances every person ought to assist other persons to have freedom and well-being when they cannot have these by their own efforts and he can give them such assistance without comparable cost'.[145] Significantly, the first-class philosopher does not address the question of when 'comparable costs' are and are not incurred; he can hardly be said to have pursued the interventionist line very far, but at least he has mentioned it. To give a second, perhaps stronger, example of another cross-over, Donnelly argues: '*All* human rights require *both* positive action and restraint on the part of the state.'[146] As we have seen in Chapter 3, this is an insight which can be accommodated within, but is unlikely to have sprung from, the logic of the human rights orthodoxy.

In a first draft of this chapter, I had squarely placed my Sussex political theorist colleague Neil Stammers in the protest school. Stammers is best known in human rights theory for having put social movements on the map of human rights scholarship.[147] He has recently contributed the entry on 'Social Movements and Human Rights' in an excellent anthology on *The Essentials of Human Rights.*[148] The entry is short (1000 words) but mentioned in it are: the ambivalence towards, if not mistrust of, institutionalization;[149] the multifaceted and evolving nature of human rights claims;[150] the endorsement of human rights universality only 'in so far as it points to the ubiquity of oppressive power in the world';[151] the warning that 'human rights and/or struggles for human rights can [not] be simply or easily assessed as being either "good" or "bad"';[152] the awareness that particular instantiations of human rights in positive law are often exclusionary.[153] To me, all these elements emanated from a protest-school perspective. Much to my surprise, Stammers objected to this classification. He then referred me to a paper by Amy Bartholomew entitled 'Toward a Deliberative Legitimation of Human Rights' which he found very insightful.[154] On my reading, the paper proceeds in two steps: (1) it accepts the criticism that human rights as articulated in international law or even as conceptualized in much scholarship is exclusionary – a criticism which I associate with the protest school; (2) it seeks to map out a path from a Habermasian approach which would make it possible for human rights not to succumb to the defect identified in (1) by ensuring that human rights would, as much as possible, really have been agreed upon – an approach which

I associate with the deliberative school.[155] This does not make Stammers a liberal deliberative scholar, but it indicates the limits of my scheme or at least the possibility of permutations within it.

I suspect that all scholars integrate elements of different schools in the conception of human rights they come to propound. Once they come to be struck by the pertinence of an argument put forward in an approach which is fundamentally different from their own, they somehow manage to assimilate it. Certainly I recognize that much integration, not always very neat or clear, has been at work in my own approach. As I have said, I am predominantly a discourse scholar. When it comes to the rights of migrants, however, I tend to rely on a natural conception of human rights, such is my outrage at the destitution of foreigners both in law and in public discourse. Moreover, I have long been attracted by deliberative scholars' insistence that human rights is a concept with limited scope, as generations of students of mine who have had to study Heiner Bielefeldt's definition of human rights can testify.[156] Finally, and perhaps needless to say, I often find myself in complete agreement with the arguments put forward by protest scholars; the only thing which puzzles me in their approach is what I see as their unassailable faith in human rights, despite the fact that they are so good at identifying its shortcomings.

Many arguments about human rights are bound to resonate from school to school. The result must be that human rights scholars from (in my scheme) different schools come to say things which are perhaps not understood in the same way but which are nonetheless not completely different. In conclusion, the schools overlap in different ways and could be said to be family-resemblant siblings. The concept of human rights which has been spun (as spin?) in our society could be the thread of Wittgenstein's quotation:

> [I]n spinning a thread we twist fibre on fibre. And the strength of the thread does not reside in the fact that some one fibre runs through its whole length, but in the overlapping of many fibres.[157]

If human rights has become such a potent phrase in contemporary politics, it is probably because it does not mean one thing, but many things; and what we mean by it when we use it is not very clear to us, let alone to others, who can receive what we say in a different way from what we had intended, which moreover changes according to the context. We can therefore all seem to agree, or at least partly to agree, when in fact we disagree.

Notes

1 In a paper entitled 'Losing its core: Human rights as a drifting concept', presented to a conference held on 25–26 April 2003 at University College London, which has given rise to the following volume: Saladin Meckled-Garcia and Basak Cali (eds.), *Legalisation of Human Rights: Multi-disciplinary Perspectives* (London: Routledge, 2005).

2 It has been remarked to me that it might have been preferable for me to classify ideas rather than people (whose ideas change). To some extent, this is true. However, revising my text so that it refers to ideas rather than scholars might make my classification less directly perceptible. To take my own experience, the schools certainly emerged in my mind as I was trying to make sense of my disagreements with colleagues I deeply respect, and can quote on many things, although I have long sensed that we are not exactly on the same wavelength. This being said, I accept that most of us will be attracted by, and express, a variety of ideas which defy the classification proposed in this chapter.

3 On the significance of this interest, see Dallas M. High, *Language, Persons and Belief: Studies in Wittgenstein's Philosophical Investigations and Religious Uses of Language* (New York: Oxford University Press, 1967), Chapter 1 ('Introduction: "The Sickness of Language"').

4 Thus Wittgenstein argued against the 'craving for generality': Ludwig Wittgenstein, *Blue Book* (Blackwell, Oxford, 1978), at 17–19.

5 Ludwig Wittgenstein, *Philosophical Investigations*, transl. by G. E. M. Anscombe (Oxford: Basil Blackwell, 1958), at 31, para. 65, emphasis in the original.

6 Ibid., at 32, para. 67.

7 J. F. M. Hunter, *Understanding Wittgenstein: Studies of Philosophical Investigations* (Edinburgh: Edinburgh University Press, 1985), at vii.

8 High, *Language*, at 93, emphasis in the original, notes omitted.

9 Charles Travis, *The Uses of Sense: Wittgenstein's Philosophy of Language* (Oxford: Clarendon Press, 1989), at 190.

10 As William Twining remarked to me, this in turn presupposes a concept of rights. An inspiring starting point for such an exploration must be Wesley Hohfeld's four-fold classification of right as privilege, claim, power and immunity: Wesley N. Hohfeld, *Fundamental Legal Conceptions as Applied in Judicial Reasoning* (New Haven: Yale University Press, 1919). I have yet to think about the implications of this observation.

11 Jack Donnelly, *Universal Human Rights in Theory and Practice* (1st edn, Ithaca: Cornell University Press, 1989), at 1. A second edition appeared in 2003 which accommodates and responds to critics. Although it pays far more attention to praxis and struggles, it does not display a fundamentally different approach on human rights. In particular it opens with the same definition: Jack Donnelly, *Universal Human Rights in Theory and Practice* (2nd edn, Ithaca: Cornell University Press, 2003), at 7.

12 Ibid.

13 Guy Haarscher, *Philosophie des droits de l'homme* (4th edn, Brussels: Editions de l'Université Libre de Bruxelles, 1993).

14 Freedom is a common starting point for human rights scholars belonging to the orthodoxy. For example, Alan Gewirth sees human rights as the rights to freedom and well-being of all agents, a generalization that implies, because of the correlation of rights and 'oughts' that 'every person ought to refrain from interfering with the freedom and well-being of all other persons': Alan Gewirth, 'The Basis and Content of Human Rights', in Pennock and Chapman (eds.), *Human Rights* (New York: New York University Press, 1981) 119–47, at 131.

15 Haarscher, *Philosophie*, at 113. See also Upendra Baxi, *The Future of Human Rights* (New Delhi: Oxford University Press, 2002), at 7.

16 Ibid., at 119 and 123.

17 Ibid., at 124.

18 Ibid., at 123.

19 Ibid.

20 Douzinas echoes this stance: 'There is a poetry in human rights that defies the rationalism of law: when a burnt child runs from the scene of an atrocity in Vietnam, when a young man stands in front of a tank in Beijing, when an emaciated body and dulled eyes face the camera from behind the barbed wire of a concentration camp in Bosnia, a tragic sense erupts and places me, the onlooker, face to face with my responsibility, a responsibility that does not come from codes, conventions or rules but from a sense of personal guilt for the suffering in the world, of obligation to save humanity in the face of the victim': Costas Douzinas, *The End of Human Rights: Critical Legal Thought at the Turn of the Century* (Oxford: Hart, 2000), at 245.

21 Haarscher, *Philosophie*, at 124. Baxi refers to 'the ordeals of Sisyphus': *Future of Human Rights*, at viii.

22 Philip L. Quinn, 'Asceticism', *Concise Routledge Encyclopedia of Philosophy* (London: Routledge, 2000) 61. The *Petit Robert* French dictionary offers the following definition of '*ascétisme*': 1. Genre de vie religieuse des ascètes, ensemble des pratiques ascétiques. . . . Doctrine de perfectionnement moral fondée sur la lutte contre les exigences du corps. 2. Par ext. Vie austère, continente, frugale, rigoriste . . .': *Le Petit Robert 1 par Paul Robert: Dictionnaire alphabétique et analogique de la langue française* (Paris, 1982).

23 Quinn, 'Asceticism'.

24 Elie Wiesel, 'A tribute to human rights', in Yael Danieli, Elsa Stamatopoulou and Clarence Dias (eds.), *The Universal Declaration of Human Rights: Fifty Years and Beyond* (Amityville, N.Y.: Baywood, 1999), at 3. Upendra Baxi similarly refers to human rights as the 'new global civic religion': Upendra Baxi, 'The globalization of fatwas: Legal pluralism, violence, and terror', presented at the Anthropology of Law Conference, Edinburgh, 17 June 2004, ms, at 4. See also Luc de Heusch, 'Les droits de l'homme comme objet de réflexion anthropologique', in *Laïcité et droits de l'homme. Deux siècles de conquête* (Brussels: Université Libre de Bruxelles, 1989) 83–95, at 91. Conor Gearty acknowledges the 'quasi-religious concept of respect for human dignity' which human rights entails: Conor Gearty, 'Civil liberties and human rights', in Nicholas Bamforth and Peter Leyland (eds.), *Public Law in a Multi-Layered Constitution* (Oxford: Hart, 2003) 371–90, at 372. It is striking that religious metaphors regularly appear in human rights debates. For one example, see Julie Mertus, 'The impact of intervention on local human rights culture: A Kosovo case study' (2001) 1 *The Global Review of Ethnopolitics* 21–36: 'In Kosovo as in many post-agreement societies, international human rights workers tend to conduct their operations in a *messianic* fashion': ibid., at 29, emphasis added. Not insignificantly, Francesca Klug's study of the Human Rights Act is entitled *Values for a Godless Age*. On a different note, Michael Perry has convincingly argued that the idea of human rights is inescapably religious because there is no intelligible secular version of the conviction that every human being is sacred: Michael J. Perry, *The Idea of Human Rights: Four Inquiries* (Oxford: Oxford University Press, 1998), Chapter 1.

25 David Kennedy, 'The international human rights movement: Part of the problem?' (2001) *European Human Rights Law Review* 245–67, at 254 and 258.

26 Haarscher, *Philosophie*, at 119.

27 Ibid., at 124. Mary Midgley starts her argument 'Towards an ethic of global respon-
    sibility' with the same paradox: in Tim Dunne and Nicholas J. Wheeler (eds.),
    Human Rights in Global Politics (Cambridge: Cambridge University Press, 1999)
    160–74, at 160.
28 Haarscher, *Philosophie*, at 122.
29 Ibid., at 120.
30 Ibid., at 125.
31 Ibid., at 120.
32 Ibid., at 122.
33 Ibid., at 120.
34 *The Shorter Oxford English Dictionary on Historical Principles* (3rd edn, Clarendon
    Press: Oxford, 1973).
35 Justin Gosling, 'Hedonism', in *Concise Routledge Encyclopedia of Philosophy*, at 336.
36 Haarscher, *Philosophie*, at 120–5, 130–2.
37 This assumption is made clear in the following passage: 'Nous sommes tous "pour"
    les droits de l'homme parce qu'il ne viendrait à l'idée d'aucun d'entre nous de les
    refuser, de nous livrer à l'arbitraire et à la violence du cours des choses; et nous
    proclamons également notre foi en la *morale* des droits de l'homme parce qu'autrui
    doit, par définition, en bénéficier. *Mes* droits de l'homme : c'est l'hédonisme au sens
    le plus courant du terme (laissez chacun tel qu'il est, ne lui demandez pas de se
    dépasser, de se transformer, ne le critiquez pas ; demandez-lui simplement ce qu'il
    veut *pour lui* : s'il a quelque bon sens, il demandera d'abord qu' "on" lui assure les
    droits fondamentaux) ; les droits de l'homme *pour tous* : c'est l'ascétisme le plus
    exigeant, la requête d'un combat toujours recommencé, une écoute qu'il s'agit de
    consentir à toutes ces "voix sous les décombres" qui n'en ont jamais fini de
    brouiller la belle musique de nos harmonies humanistes' : ibid., at 121, emphases
    in the original. The equation Haarscher makes between hedonism and lack of
    morality and/or selfishness also appears very clearly in a passage which refers to
    the third, Machiavellian, human rights dimension he identifies and which sum-
    marizes what has been discussed beforehand: 'Bref, ou bien (ce sont les deux
    premières possibilités) les droits de l'homme sont posés *sans recours véritable à
    un commandement moral* (intérêt machiavélien, duplicité hédoniste), ou bien la
    référence éthique est patente et affective, mais fondée sur une *croyance*': ibid., at
    132, first emphasis added, second emphasis in the original. Anticipating on what
    I shall develop below, it is interesting that Haarscher asserts that 'true' human
    rights can only be based on belief. As I said in the introductory chapter, many
    approach human rights as an article of faith. What this chapter suggests is that one
    can identify those who do so – i.e. those who *believe* in human rights – as natural
    and protest scholars.
38 The last two dimensions also appear in Douzinas's analysis, although not in these
    terms: '[T]he radical energy, symbolic value and apparently endless expansive
    potential of rights has led to their adoption both by governments wishing to justify
    their policies on moral grounds and by individuals fighting for the public recogni-
    tion of private desires' (back flap of *End of Human Rights*).
39 Haarscher, *Philosophie*, at 116.
40 Ibid., at 116.
41 Ibid., at 124.
42 Ibid., at 125.

43 Haarscher, *Philosophie*, at 125.

44 For a more detailed review of this case law, see Marie-Bénédicte Dembour, 'Why should biological sex be decisive? Transsexualism before the European Court of Human Rights', in Alison Shaw and Shirley Ardener (eds.), *Changing Sex and Bending Gender* (Oxford: Berghahn, 2005) 39–59.

45 British Medical Association, *Complete Family Health Encyclopedia* (London: Dorling Kindersley, 1995), at 1011.

46 I have inverted the order in which the two possessive adjectives are generally listed, as male-to-female transsexualism is more common than its reverse. For the same reason I thereafter use the feminine form to refer to the 'generic' transsexual person.

47 *Rees* v. *United Kingdom*, 17 October 1986, Series A, No. 106, (1987) 9 EHRR 56; *Cossey* v. *United Kingdom*, 27 September 1990, Series A, No. 184, (1991) 13 EHRR 622; *B* v. *France*, 25 March 1992, Series A, No. 232-C, (1993) 16 EHRR 1; *X, Y and Z* v. *United Kingdom*, 22 April 1997, RJD 1997-II 619, (1997) 24 EHRR 143; *Sheffield and Horsham* v. *United Kingdom*, 30 July 1998, RJD 1998-V 2011, (1999) 27 EHRR 163; *Goodwin* v. *United Kingdom*, 11 July 2002, ECHR 2002-VI, (2002) 35 EHRR 18 (as well as *I* v. *United Kingdom*, decided on the same day as *Goodwin*). Also relevant are the cases brought by transsexual people declared inadmissible by the Court (*Van Oosterwijck* v. *Belgium*, 6 November 1980, Series A, No. 40, (1981) 3 EHRR 357) and by the Commission (*Eriksson and Goldschmidt* v. *Sweden*, Application 14573/89, decision of 9 November 1989; *LF* v *Ireland*, Application 28154/95, decision of 2 July 1997; *Roetjheim* v. *Germany*, Application 31177/96, decision of 23 October 1997). *Van Kück* v. *Germany*, 12 June 2003, ECHR 2003-VII, (2003) 37 EHRR 51, is discussed in the next section as I do not classify it in the *foundational* case law on transsexualism.

48 Seven if *I* v. *United Kingdom*, decided on the same day and in the same way as *Goodwin* is included.

49 Incidentally it is unlikely that they would be more successful in claiming a right to marry someone of their new sex. See *Eriksson and Goldschmidt*.

50 *Rees*; *Cossey*; *X, Y, and Z*; *Sheffield and Horsham*.

51 Para. 56 of the judgment.

52 Para. 59 of the judgment.

53 Para. 63 of the judgment.

54 Para. 47 of the judgment.

55 See also *I* v. *United Kingdom*, decided on the same day.

56 *The Shorter Oxford English Dictionary*,

57 See the Gender Recognition Act 2004.

58 Haarscher, *Philosophie*, at 121.

59 Provided execution included individual measures which satisfy him, which is not necessarily the case.

60 I cannot be dogmatic, however, as admittedly I know nothing about the circumstances of the applicant. It is possible, for example, that Ms Van Kück was financially well-off and did not care at all about the costs of the operation but was seriously concerned about transsexual people who cannot afford to pay for the operation themselves, persuading her to take the case to court for the benefit of others.

61 Though this assertion may need some refinement. Upendra Baxi, whom I classify as a protest scholar in a subsequent section, did me the favour of reading a draft of this chapter. One of his comments reads: 'At the level of positive norms, human rights are

supposed to be *enjoyed* and *exercised*; in other words *consumed*. In different ways the law and economic school (who regard human rights as factor or production like land, capital and labour) and now the corpus of Amartya Sen and further the UNDP public goods approach to understanding and deploying rights-languages, render human rights hedonism almost theoretically unproblematic. There lurks in this genre often an implicit argument that pursuit of self-interest is an unqualified moral good (the sacrosanctity of property and contract) because it maximizes societal resources and wealth and eventually leads to perceptions of enlightened self-interest (one becomes a good hedonist, and contributes to the enjoyment of rights by others etc.)': personal communication.

62 Donnelly, *Universal Human Rights* (1st edn), at 14, emphasis in the original.

63 'Human rights are at once a utopian ideal and a *realistic practice for implementing that ideal* . . . Human rights thus can be seen as a *self-fulfilling moral prophecy* . . . If the underlying vision of human nature is within the limits of "natural" possibility, and if the derivation of a list of rights is sound, then implementing those rights will make "real" that previously "ideal" nature': Donnelly, *Universal Human Rights* (2nd edn), at 15, emphasis added.

64 'The victims know that protection of their human rights under the auspices of the politics *of* [hijacked] human rights is a contingent feat; and they join, if at all, with great and grave caution, the heralding of rare triumphs as historic events for the politics *for* [true] human rights': Baxi, *Future of Human Rights*, at 56, emphasis in the original.

65 See text to note 62.

66 Donnelly, *Universal Human Rights* (2nd edn), at 9. This quotation incidentally leads me to observe that natural scholars are happy to talk about human right in the singular – as Donnelly implicitly does when he speaks of *a* right – while protest scholars tend to speak of human rights in the plural, giving the impression that they consist in a general idea rather than in specific, individual, entitlements.

67 To borrow the words, which I paraphrase heavily in this paragraph, of Martin Loughlin in his review of Douzinas' book: (2001) *Modern Law Review* 151.

68 Douzinas, *End of Human Rights*, at 380.

69 Marie-Bénédicte Dembour, 'Human rights talk and anthropological ambivalence: Universal claims in particular contexts', in Olivia Harris (ed.), *Inside and Outside the Law: Anthropological Studies of Authority and Ambiguity* (London: Routledge, 1996) 19–40, at 34.

70 Douzinas, *End of Human Rights*, at 380.

71 Accordingly, from the perspective of the natural school, judges of the European Court of Human Rights who invoke in their dissenting opinions, as they sometimes do, features of the philosophical essence of human rights, do so legitimately. For an example, see the dissenting opinion of Judge Martens in *Cossey*, quoted above.

72 This is the best formulation I can find. Let me try to expand: protest scholars would not deny that human rights are entitlements, but they nonetheless focus primarily on the claims and aspirations to which these entitlements give rise. They are primarily concerned with *violations* of human rights. Thus Baxi continually stresses that 'the originary authors of human rights are people in struggle and communities of resistance'. This particular quotation comes from *Future of Human Rights* at vi, but the idea is expressed repeatedly in his work.

73 However, some protest scholars are less extreme. Neil Stammers, who offered to me the image of human rights law as a sandbag (see Chapter 3), is an example. Upendra Baxi, who has been involved in long judicial proceedings, most notably related to the Bhopal tragedy, is another. *Pace* Boaventura de Sousa Santos, Baxi recognizes that the human rights 'pillar of emancipation' can of course become the 'pillar of regulation'. He remarks, however, in an observation which ends with a rhetorical question that obviously needs to be answered affirmatively: 'Were this [turning] the only moment of human rights, every triumphal attainment would also be its funerary oration. But does not a regulatory discourse at one moment also become at times an arena of struggle?': Baxi, *Future of Human Rights*, at 86. It may not be insignificant in this respect that Stammers and Baxi are both primarily interested in praxis. They both insist that the real authors of human rights are actual people in struggles. By contrast, Haarscher and Douzinas are philosophers and more interested in founding the idea of human rights, including – in the case of Douzinas – through a return to natural rights.

74 Donnelly, *Universal Human Rights* (1st edn), at 16. In the second edition, he asserts: 'The source of human rights is man's moral nature': at 14.

75 Ibid., (1st edn), respectively at 17 and at 2, inverted commas omitted. See also Chapters 4–5. '"Human nature" is a social project more than a presocial given': ibid., (2nd edn), at 15.

76 Jacques Maritain, 'Introduction' in UNESCO (ed.), *Human Rights: Comments and Interpretation* (Greenwood Press, 1949) 9–17. Liberals generally find that not worrying about human rights foundation is a wise, and unproblematic, approach. See e.g. Michael Ignatieff, *Human Rights as Politics and Idolatry* (Princeton: Princeton University Press, 2001), at 54; Donnelly, *Universal Human Rights* (1st edn), at 22–3. But compare Michael Freeman, 'The problem of secularism in human rights theory' (2004) 26 *Human Rights Quarterly* 375–400.

77 As Michael Perry notes, 'the force of a claim about what ought to be done to or about what ought to be done for human beings does not depend on whether the claim is expressed in the language of rights': Michael J. Perry, *Idea of Human Rights*, at 55.

78 Reason, when conceived as the exercise of a universal faculty which leads to 'discovering' *truths*, would be a basis favoured by natural philosophers. But reason can also be conceived as giving rise to open-ended discussions which lead to non-eternal and always questionable, but so far most convincing arguments.

79 Michael Freeman, *Human Rights: An Interdisciplinary Approach* (Cambridge: Polity, 2002), at 64, emphasis in the original. Elsewhere, Freeman quotes Richard Wilson (a deliberative scholar in my classification) approvingly in the assertion that: 'Rights without a metanarrative are like a car without seat-belts; on hitting the first moral bump with ontological implications, the passenger's safety is jeopardised': Richard A. Wilson, 'Human rights, culture and context: An introduction', in Richard A. Wilson (ed.), *Human Rights, Culture and Context* (London: Pluto, 1997) 1–27, at 9.

80 Alan Gewirth specifically says he is interested in 'arguments that try to prove or justify that persons have rights other than those grounded in positive law': 'Basis and content', at 119.

81 Haarscher, *Philosophie*, at 109–10.

82 Ibid., at 124 and 130.

83 Though Neil Stammers observes to me that animal training often seeks to follow a logic which is within the animal and which is as it were waiting to be activated.

84 Douzinas, *End of Human Rights*, at 371, emphasis added.

85 See the very useful discussion of tradition offered by H. Patrick Glenn in *Legal Traditions of the World: Sustainable Diversity in Law* (Oxford: Oxford University Press, 2000).

86 See e.g. Haarscher, *Philosophie*, at 130 as well as the very last paragraph of his book at 138–9; Upendra Baxi, 'Human rights education', in Rhona K. M. Smith and Christien van den Anker (eds.), *The Essentials of Human Rights* (London: Hodder Arnold, 2005) 159–62; Ken Booth and Tim Dunne, 'Learning beyond frontiers', in Dunne and Wheeler (eds.), *Human Rights*, 303–28.

87 Michael Ignatieff, *Human Rights as Politics and Idolatry* (Princeton: Princeton University Press, 2001), at 20.

88 Conor Gearty, 'The European Court of Human Rights and the protection of civil liberties: An overview' (1993) 52 *Cambridge Law Journal* 89–127, at 98.

89 '[The Human Rights Act is not about human rights] at all, if that phrase is meant to convey the existence of certain inalienable and fundamental entitlements that inhere in us all as human beings': Conor Gearty, *Principles of Human Rights Adjudication* (Oxford: Oxford University Press, 2004), at 8. Presumably the Human Rights Act may be about human rights if human rights are conceived differently. Needless to say, the definition of human rights given and opposed by Gearty in the quoted sentence exactly fits the way the natural school or orthodoxy conceives of human rights.

90 Ibid., at 14.

91 Makau Mutua, *Human Rights: A Political and Cultural Critique* (Philadelphia: University of Pennsylvania Press, 2000), at ix.

92 Ibid at ix.

93 Ibid., at ix-x.

94 Ibid., at x.

95 Ibid., at xi, emphasis in the original. For a powerful response to this line of argument by a protest scholar, see Baxi, *Future of Human Rights*, at xi and 24–7.

96 Wendy Brown, '"The Most We Can Hope For . . .": Human rights and the politics of fatalism' (2004) 103 *South Atlantic Quarterly* 451–63, at 453, emphasis in the original.

97 Ibid., at 461–2, emphasis in the original.

98 As I have done in my 1996 article: Dembour, 'Human rights talk', at 34–5. Compare the famous saying by the philosopher Alasdair MacIntyre: 'the truth is plain: there are no such [natural or human] rights, and belief in them is one with belief in witches and unicorns': Alasdair MacIntyre, *After Virtue* (London: Duckworth, 1985), at 69.

99 Mutua, *Human Rights*, at x.

100 Martti Koskenniemi, 'The effect of rights on political culture', in Philip Alston (ed.), *The EU and Human Rights* (Oxford: Oxford University Press, 1999) 99–116, at 116.

101 Ibid.

102 Dembour, 'Human rights talk', at 35.

103 Ibid., at 36.

104 Jane Cowan is another discourse scholar who acknowledges the paradox of the position she advocates for the scholar engaged, as she is, in minority struggles – in

her case, in the 'Macedonian' part of Greece: 'to support the demands for recognition of the Macedonian minority . . . yet at the same time, to problematize, rather
than celebrate, its project, and to query its emancipatory aura, examining the
exclusions and cultural disenfranchisements it creates from within': Jane
K. Cowan, 'Ambiguities of an emancipatory discourse: The making of a Macedonian minority in Greece', in Jane K. Cowan, Marie-Bénédicte Dembour and Richard
A. Wilson (eds.), *Culture and Rights: Anthropological Perspectives* (Cambridge:
Cambridge University Press, 2001) 152–76, at 171. Wendy Brown acknowledges
that the rights discourse will be used as long as rights are the dominant political
'currency' but that this recognition does not amount to an 'assessment of how they
operate politically nor of the political culture they create': Wendy Brown, 'Rights
and identity in late modernity: Revisiting the "Jewish Question"', in Austin Sarat
and Thomas R. Kearns (eds.), *Identities, Politics and Rights* (Ann Arbor: University
of Michigan Press, 1997) 85–130, at 119.

105 The concern for the oppressed and those who suffer is very prominent amongst
protest scholars. While especially those who insist that the analysis should start with
praxis do it with humility, others seem to me to write as if they were occupying the
moral high ground.

106 Judge De Meyer, whose natural inclinations have been remarked upon at various
points in the book, would appear at the top left corner of the diagram, given his
extreme (in comparative terms) liberalism and foundationalism. I expect that the
other judges of the European Court of Human Rights would have to be placed in
the left hand-side of the diagram, but not necessarily at its top and, for some,
towards the middle of the horizontal axis.

107 Perry, *Idea of Human Rights*, at 11.

108 Ibid., at 47.

109 Ibid., at 45–6. Perry specifically recognizes that these obligations may be conditional
rather than absolute.

110 Ibid., at 46.

111 Freeman, *Human Rights*, at 6.

112 Ibid., at 170.

113 Balakrishnan Rajagopal, *International Law from Below: Development, Social Movements and Third World Resistance* (Cambridge: Cambridge University Press, 2003),
at 216.

114 See e.g. Meckled-Garcia and Cali, *Legalisation*; Tony Evans, 'Disciplining global
society: Human rights as power and knowledge' (2005) 27 *Human Rights Quarterly*
1046–68; Kirsten Hastrup, 'Representing the common good: The limits of legal
language', in Richard Ashby Wilson and Jon P. Mitchell (eds.), *Human Rights in
Global Perspective: Anthropological Studies of Rights, Claims and Entitlements*
(London: Routledge, 2003) 16–32.

115 Lisette Josephides comes to mind as an anthropologist. See her 'The rights of being
human', in Wilson and Mitchell (eds.), *Human Rights* 229–50.

116 Richard A. Wilson, *The Politics of Truth and Reconciliation in South Africa: Legitimizing the Post-Apartheid State* (Cambridge: Cambridge University Press, 2001), at
230.

117 Ibid., at 1–2, see also 17.

118 Ibid., at 228.

119 Baxi, *Future of Human Rights*, at 41, italics omitted.

120 Ibid., at viii, emphasis in the original, to distinguish the politics *for* human rights from the politics *of* human rights.

121 Ibid., at 23.

122 Ibid., at v. For him, 'the originary authors of human rights are people in struggle and communities of resistance': ibid., at vi.

123 Ibid., at vii.

124 Ibid., at xiv.

125 Ibid at xiv.

126 Ibid., at 2–3, emphasis in the original.

127 Ken Booth, 'Three Tyrannies', in Dunne and Wheeler (eds.), *Human Rights* 31–70, at 51–2.

128 Ibid., at 44.

129 Ibid at 44.

130 Ibid., at 43.

131 Ibid., at 65. In an equally upbeat tone, he writes with Dunne: 'We support both education as a human right and an education *in* human rights: both must be part of a politics of common humanity appropriate for the first truly global age': Booth and Dunne, 'Learning', at 325.

132 Chapter 7 should have made it abundantly clear that there are many different feminisms. Feminists will adopt various conceptions of human rights and fall in different schools – or indeed straddle them in various ways. To give some examples, it seems to me that Christine Chinkin could be said to be a natural scholar, Sally Engle Merry a deliberative scholar and Diane Otto a protest scholar.

133 Talal Asad, 'What do human rights do? An anthropological enquiry' (2000) 4 *Theory and Event*, at para. 49.

134 Ibid., at para. 57.

135 Ibid., at para 17.

136 Wilson, *Truth and Reconciliation*, at 8.

137 Ibid., at 25.

138 Ibid., at 26.

139 Ibid., at 173.

140 Ibid., at 182.

141 Ibid., at 186.

142 This recognition that there are different shades within the two camps may be a spur to the identification of further schools, including perhaps a sentiment school, the prototype of which would be Richard Rorty. This fifth school would lie between the protest school and the discourse school. It could be said to be the equivalent in the non-liberal camp to the deliberative school of the liberal camp. Both the sentiment and the deliberative schools could be regarded for the purpose of this classification as the non-foundational schools of the respectively non-liberal and liberal camps. These five schools could be represented in a diagram comprising two columns (the liberal and the non-liberal camps) divided into three levels. At the first level would be those schools which have faith in human rights: the natural school in the liberal camp and the protest school in the non-liberal camp; at the second level would be those who refuse to approach human rights as a faith: the deliberative school in the liberal camp and the sentiment school in the non-liberal camp; and finally at the third level would be those who reject human rights altogether: there would be no such school in the liberal camp

given the 'necessary' association liberals make between liberalism and human rights, but this position would be represented by the discourse school in the non-liberal camp. I suspect, however, that deliberative scholars could usefully be divided into more groupings.

143 Booth, 'Three tyrannies', at 58.

144 This is a matter of degree, however. One could argue that the interventionist stance falls squarely within the logic of the two 1966 UN Covenants which stipulate in their respective preamble: 'Realizing that the individual, having duties to other individuals and to the community to which he [sic] belongs, is under a responsibility to strive for the promotion and the observance of the rights recognised in the present Covenant'.

145 Gewirth, 'Basis and content', at 131.

146 Donnelly, *Universal Human Rights* (1989), at 33, emphasis in the original.

147 See particulary Neil Stammers, 'Social movements and the social construction of human rights' (1999) 21 *Human Rights Quarterly* 980–1008.

148 Neil Stammers, 'Social movements and human rights', in Smith and van den Anker (eds.), *Essentials*, 321–4.

149 Ibid., at 322.

150 Ibid.

151 Ibid at 322.

152 Ibid., at 323.

153 Ibid.

154 Amy Bartholomew, 'Toward a deliberative legitimation of human rights', *Papers in Social Theory* 6 (Warwick Social Theory Centre/Sussex Centre for Critical Social Theory, 2001) 5–31.

155 A note on my own response to this argument: ideally, of course, I would greatly prefer human rights to be the result of open deliberation under fair procedural conditions. My problem with Bartholomew's approach is that it does not concretely evaluate human rights projects by reference to the one test which should count in her perspective: whether these projects have in practice emerged in such ideal or near-ideal conditions. The result is that Bartholomew (and others) invite us to be 'pro-human rights' without having demonstrated that the conditions which would have been required for human rights to be legitimate are in practice fulfilled.

156 To quote: 'Human rights constitute political and legal standards. That is, they require political and legal implementation through national, regional, and international institutions including, if possible, effective monitoring mechanisms. I would like to emphasize this political and legal aspect of human rights, in order to make sure that their scope is *limited*. Unlike Islam and other religions, which claim to shape the whole lives of their adherents, human rights do not represent an all-encompassing "weltanschauung" or way of life, nor do they provide a yardstick by which to evaluate cultures and religions in general. Human rights are not necessarily the highest manifestation of ethical spirit in human history either, because they are not intended to replace, for instance, Christian demands of love, Islamic solidarity, or the Buddhist ethic of compassion. Rather, they concentrate on political justice by setting up some basic normative standards': Heiner Bielefeldt, 'Muslim voices in the human rights debate' (1995) 17 *Human Rights Quarterly* 587–617, at 588, emphasis in the original.

157 Wittgenstein, *Philosophical Investigations*, at para. 67.

9

Conclusion: In praise of human rights nihilism

[T]he highest values are losing their value. (Nietzsche)

I started this book because I found the idea of human rights *both* attractive *and* unconvincing, if not positively dangerous. This ambivalence drove me to ask: can we/should we believe in human rights?

The last chapter has contended that different people will answer this question differently. Natural scholars, who regard human rights as inherent and inalienable entitlements, will respond: of course, we must believe in human rights! Protest scholars will give the same answer, but for a different reason: to them, human rights is the best language we have to set human beings free of oppression. Deliberative scholars do not think the issue is a matter of faith: they look at human rights as good political principles which have been agreed in some circles and hopefully will command greater and greater commitment. Finally, discourse scholars are sceptical: in their view the hype which surrounds human rights talk is misplaced; intellectually untenable and possibly morally counterproductive in inhibiting the imagination of more emancipatory projects.

I have come to the conclusion that I am mostly a discourse scholar. At the end of this book, my personal ambivalence towards human rights has not subsided. I am clearer, however, as to why I am not as enthused by the concept as others are, as well as to the logic of my position.

The appeal of the critique(s) of human rights

As far as I am concerned, a realist, utilitarian, Marxian, particularist and feminist critique of human rights is not only legitimate but also called for. To restrict these critiques to the (admittedly reductive) understandings which this book has given them, I have shown how human rights remain enmeshed in state interests; allow us to evade important moral dilemmas which must be confronted; fail to include in their ambit everyone irrespective of social position; trumpet universal truths which do not hold in the face of social diversity but nonetheless stand because of the prevalent balance of power; and ignore women's concerns without even realizing it.

These critiques are intimately linked, even if their presentation in different chapters and their one-line summary in the previous paragraph could suggest otherwise. From my perspective, the critiques overlap so much that they are virtually the same thing.[1] This is so even though I recognize that each critique can be seen as different from any other and that there are many different ways of being a realist, a utilitarian, a Marxist, a particularist or a feminist. What I am saying is that it is possible to feel one is a realist *because one is also* a utilitarian, a Marxist, a particularlist and a feminist – and *mutatis mutandis* for each of the other four terms.[2]

I am not the first one to allude to the idea that these individual critiques feed off each other. For example, in *The Twenty Years' Crisis* (already quoted in Chapter 3),[3] E. H. Carr chiefly presented himself as a 'realist', a label which stuck as he later became recognized as a precursor of the realist movement which developed in international relations after World War II. For him, '[t]he outstanding achievement of modern realism . . . ha[d] been to reveal . . . the *relative* and pragmatic character of thought itself'.[4] Such 'relativism' or 'particularism' regularly surfaced in the book, for example in the assertion that '"impartiality" is a meaningless concept where there is no common ground at all between . . . contending [worlds]'.[5] Carr also repeatedly acknowledged his debt to Marxism.[6] While he violently disagreed with Bentham[7] and simply did not think about feminism, his work nonetheless shows how the five critiques reviewed in this book could be seen to spring from the same source. To me, they represent different ways of getting at the same thing.

Challenging the orthodoxy: In Nietzsche's footsteps

What unites these critiques, at least in those variants of them which I find most interesting, is a rejection of the human rights credo. They can all be used to take issue with the Kantian affirmation, on which the human rights orthodoxy is based, that 'practical reason' can guide us in moral matters. By accepting that such a possibility is a delusion, they display what could be characterized as a Nietzschean perspective.[8]

Long shunned in courses on ethics, Friedrich Nietzsche (1844–1900) is now regarded as an essential figure in the history of Western philosophy.[9] He is popularly known for having attacked 'almost everything that [was] considered sacred: . . . God, truth, morality, equality, democracy, and most other modern values'.[10] His name is forever associated with 'nihilism', a word which he himself used in many different ways,[11] but which has at its core a reference to 'the devaluation of the uppermost values'. In Nietzsche's words:

> What does Nihilism mean? – *That the highest values devaluate themselves.* There is no bourne. The aim is lacking; 'why?' finds no answer.[12]

Why this devaluation? Johan Goudsblom explains its occurence through the following two questions: 'Have we not learned, as members of a civilized society [inverted commas omitted in the original!], that we must be prepared to discuss and examine the reason why we act the way we do? And yet do we not find, time and time again, that not a single argument with which we may wish to justify our judgments and decisions can withstand critical analysis?'[13] This is the dilemma from which nihilism emerges. According to Nietzsche, Alan White remarks, 'thoughtful human beings [would] of necessity be nihilists – and the thoughtless as well, although they [would be] less likely to know it'.[14]

Nihilism is often misunderstood as entailing a rejection of morality. This is not the best way of understanding Nietzsche's philosophy. To quote Goudsblom again:

> [Nietzsche] felt summoned to a task which no one had yet dared to undertake: the investigation of morality as a problem. He writes that the real moralist can be distinguished from the puritan in that the former dares to make a problem of morality . . . If we do not wish to lapse into new moral prejudices, then we have to take up a position *outside* morality, somewhere *beyond good and evil* . . . [A] right-minded philosopher does not subject himself to the dictates of morality. He plunges the vivisectionist's knife into the virtues of his time. The moral distinction between lies and sacrosanct lies is alien to him; he discriminates between truth and lies – and he goes for the truth.[15]

In fact, Nietzsche, especially towards the end of his life, was calling for new values to be created, especially through the interpretation of old values in a life-affirming way. Many approach him today as an 'impassioned and dedicated moralist'.[16] In the words of Simon May, for example, 'Nietzsche is a thinker who not only repudiates traditional conceptions of god, guilt, asceticism, pity, and truthfulness, but also retains a severe ethic of discipline, conscience, "self-creation", generosity, and honesty.'[17]

Having said this, Nietzsche obviously does not provide any philosophical, moral or intellectual recipe which could be followed step by step. This is in line with the fact that he 'argues for a plurality of perspectives, a plurality of "truths" . . . with none of them the "true" one'.[18] As Robert Solomon usefully remarks, this is not that such 'perspectivism [amounts to] the view that an opinion is as good as every other but rather that an opinion is only as good as its author, as meaningful as the thought that goes into it and the energy and sincerity that motivate it'.[19]

Why be afraid of human rights nihilism?

'Nihilistic thought seeks to show that metaphysical "truths" simply express the subjective values of a given individual or social group, not the immutable, unchanging essence of either the divine, human or natural world.'[20] This, of course, is exactly what I have tried to show in respect of human rights orthodoxy. Human rights are most commonly represented as given – inherent and inalienable. Against this stance, I have intimated that human rights is a 'system of persuasion', a 'kind of rhetoric', an 'expression of the will to power – even to domination – of those making the [human rights] truth-claims over those who are being addressed by them'.[21] While I am not the only one to take this stance, I am in a minority.

My view is that human rights nihilism is healthy and necessary – even if it seems to open an abyss. It is true that it immediately gives rise to the question: what will happen and what should you do if you let go of human rights?[22] Can you even let go of the concept? I certainly have not dared to, and continue to defend human rights as 'strategically useful'. What would Nietzsche have said? I am not sure, but I am clear that he would have looked for a re-evaluation of the devalued values.

In a different but ultimately similar way, Carr the realist called for a 'combination of utopia and reality'.[23] He noted that realism is liable to result in 'the sterilization of thought and the negation of action' when it assumes a purely 'critical and . . . cynical aspect'.[24] In his view, realism's barrenness needs to be corrected by its contrary, utopianism.[25] In his words,

> [T]he realist, in denying any *a priori* quality to political [values], and in proving them to be rooted in practice, falls easily into a determinism . . . [He] runs the risk of treating purpose merely as the mechanical product of other facts. If we recognize that this mechanization . . . is untenable and intolerable, then we must recognize that theory, as it develops out of practice and develops into practice, plays its own transforming role in the process.[26]

At the end of this book, I have no programmatic statement to make about human rights, the political process, justice or human life. I do not see this as a weakness. I feel the more justified in my 'nihilist' critique as I am writing these lines in July 2005, days after four bombs exploded in London. 'Our values and our way of life' are being celebrated by Prime Minister Tony Blair and others as if what these notions entail were clear and 'we' were unequivocally on the side of 'good' against 'evil'. But what 'we hold dear', to quote another phrase used by Blair, cannot be simplified to a glorified mantra of inherent, universal and inalienable human rights – which fall so short, in practice, of what they proclaim. Needless to say, this is said with no sympathy either towards terrorism – from whichever direction it emanates, with or without the seal of state approval – or towards the erosion of civil liberties.

I was privileged to teach for a few years at the Vrije Universiteit Brussel LLM students who came from the four corners of the world. The course aimed at making them think about what place was left to non-Western legal perspectives in a global world dominated by 'the West'. The students reported they found the course intellectually challenging and emotionally intense. I used to tell them that

I was hoping that they would remember our class discussions when, in the future, they might be in a position to make decisions which matter. In the same way, this study does not aim at revolutionizing the world. If it can influence readers, especially but not only those in the orthodoxy, to think twice before they assert their confidence in human rights, it will have achieved its political aim.

Notes

1 Let me repeat that other critiques of human rights which have not been explicitly discussed in this book, for example inspired by communitarianism and critical race theory, could easily have been added to this study. In a sense, they also amount to 'the same thing'.

2 Thus one feels a utilitarian because one is also a realist, a Marxist, a particularist and a feminist, etc. For a challenging utilitarian morality which goes against the grain of our moral 'intuitions', see Jonathan Glover, *Causing Death and Saving Lives* (London: Penguin, 1990), esp. Chapter 20.

3 E. H. Carr, *The Twenty Years' Crisis, 1919–1939: An Introduction to the Study of International Relations* (Basingstoke: Palgrave, 2001).

4 Ibid., at 65, emphasis added.

5 Ibid., at 181. This passage refers to the impossibility of finding a 'single impartial judge in the whole world [when, in the words of a representative of the Soviet Government in 1922,] there was not one world, but two, a Soviet world and a non-Soviet world': ibid.

6 'Marx' or 'Marxism' appear no less than 24 times in the index of *Twenty Years*.

7 Ibid., at 26 and 28. For the way in which Carr's life came to represent 'the unmaking of a liberal', see the introduction by Michael Cox to the 2001 re-edition of *Twenty Years*, at xiv-xix.

8 Admittedly, the debate as to whether Nietzsche's work is antagonistic to the Western philosophical tradition or is in direct continuation with it is not closed: Robert C. Solomon, 'Introduction: Reading Nietzsche', in Robert C. Solomon and Kathleen M. Higgins (eds.), *Reading Nietzsche* (New York: Oxford University Press, 1988) 3–12, at 11.

9 Solomon, 'Introduction', at 3.

10 Maudemarie Clark, 'Nietzsche, Friedrich (1844–1900)', *Concise Routledge Encyclopedia of Philosophy* (London: Routledge, 2000) 630–1, at 630.

11 Thus, he distinguished between 'active' and 'passive', 'theoretical' and 'practical' and 'complete' and 'incomplete' nihilism. For other forms of nihilism to which Nietzsche referred in his work, see Alan White, *Within Nietzsche's Labyrinth* (New York: Routledge, 1990), at 15.

12 Friedrich Nietzsche, *The Will to Power*, transl. by Walter Kaufmann and R. J. Hollingdale (London: Weidenfeld and Nicolson, 1967), at 9.

13 Johan Goudsblom, *Nihilism and Culture* (Oxford: Blackwell, 1980), at x.

14 White, *Nietzsche's Labyrinth*, at 15.

15 Goudsblom, *Nihilism*, at 24, emphasis in the original, references omitted.

16 Solomon, 'Introduction', at 5.

17 Simon May, *Nietzsche's Ethics and his War on 'Morality'* (Oxford: Clarendon, 1999), at v. For an assessment which some would find more balanced, see Lester H. Hunt,

Nietzsche and the Origin of Virtue (London: Routledge, 1991): 'It is clear to me that there are certain Nietzschean ideas which I am . . . committed to denying. These include his devaluation of the intellect, his attempt to formulate an ethic which is *entirely* based on a conception of character, and his denial (at least in certain moods) of the value of spontaneous order. But there are other ideas of his – including his relativism, his experimentalism, and his emphasis on the role the passions play in virtue – which seem to me valuable and important': ibid. at xvii.

18 Solomon, 'Introduction', at 9.

19 Solomon, 'Introduction', at 10.

20 Jon R. Snyder, 'Translator's Introduction', in Gianni Vattimo, *The End of Modernity: Nihilism and Hermeneutics in Post-Modern Culture* (Cambridge: Polity Press, 1988) vi-lviii, at xii.

21 Ibid.

22 But conversely, one could ask: what happens if we keep holding onto human rights. Wendy Brown remarks that 'what rights promise may be as elusive, as otherworldly, as unattainable as that offered by any other political myth' though we tend not to see this by mistakenly thinking of rights as 'concrete, immediate, and available': Wendy Brown, 'Rights and identity in late modernity: Revisiting the "Jewish Question"', in Austin Sarat and Thomas R. Kearns (eds.), *Identities, Politics and Rights* (Ann Arbor: University of Michigan Press, 1997) 85–130, at 123.

23 Carr, *Twenty Years*, at 14.

24 Ibid., at 10.

25 Ibid., at 10.

26 Ibid., at 13–14.

Appendix 1: The Convention: Selected Provisions

The European Convention for the Protection of Human Rights and Fundamental Freedoms

Article 1 (obligation to respect human rights)

The High Contracting Parties shall secure to everyone within their jurisdiction the rights and freedoms defined in Section I of this Convention.

Section I (rights and freedoms)

Article 2 (right to life)

1 Everyone's right to life shall be protected by law. No one shall be deprived of his life intentionally save in the execution of a sentence of a court following his conviction of a crime for which this penalty is provided by law.
2 Deprivation of life shall not be regarded as inflicted in contravention of this article when it results from the use of force which is no more than absolutely necessary:
   a in defence of any person from unlawful violence;
   b in order to effect a lawful arrest or to prevent the escape of a person lawfully detained;
   c in action lawfully taken for the purpose of quelling a riot or insurrection.

Article 3 (prohibition of torture)

No one shall be subjected to torture or to inhuman or degrading treatment or punishment.

Article 4 (prohibition of slavery)

1 No one shall be held in slavery or servitude.
2 No one shall be required to perform forced or compulsory labour.
3 For the purpose of this article the term 'forced or compulsory labour' shall not include:
   a any work required to be done in the ordinary course of detention imposed according to the provisions of Article 5 of this Convention or during conditional release from such detention;

b   any service of a military character or, in case of conscientious objectors in countries where they are recognised, service exacted instead of compulsory military service;

c   any service exacted in case of an emergency or calamity threatening the life or well-being of the community;

d   any work or service which forms part of normal civic obligations.

Article 5 (right to liberty and security)

1   Everyone has the right to liberty and security of person. No one shall be deprived of his liberty save in the following cases and in accordance with a procedure prescribed by law:

a   the lawful detention of a person after conviction by a competent court;

b   the lawful arrest or detention of a person for non-compliance with the lawful order of a court or in order to secure the fulfilment of any obligation prescribed by law;

c   the lawful arrest or detention of a person effected for the purpose of bringing him before the competent legal authority on reasonable suspicion of having committed an offence or when it is reasonably considered necessary to prevent his committing an offence or fleeing after having done so;

d   the detention of a minor by lawful order for the purpose of educational supervision or his lawful detention for the purpose of bringing him before the competent legal authority;

e   the lawful detention of persons for the prevention of the spreading of infectious diseases, of persons of unsound mind, alcoholics or drug addicts or vagrants;

f   the lawful arrest or detention of a person to prevent his effecting an unauthorised entry into the country or of a person against whom action is being taken with a view to deportation or extradition.

2   Everyone who is arrested shall be informed promptly, in a language which he understands, of the reasons for his arrest and of any charge against him.

3   Everyone arrested or detained in accordance with the provisions of paragraph 1(c) of this article shall be brought promptly before a judge or other officer authorised by law to exercise judicial power and shall be entitled to trial within a reasonable time or to release pending trial. Release may be conditioned by guarantees to appear for trial.

4   Everyone who is deprived of his liberty by arrest or detention shall be entitled to take proceedings by which the lawfulness of his detention shall be decided speedily by a court and his release ordered if the detention is not lawful.

5   Everyone who has been the victim of arrest or detention in contravention of the provisions of this article shall have an enforceable right to compensation.

Article 6 (fair trial)

1   In the determination of his civil rights and obligations or of any criminal charge against him, everyone is entitled to a fair and public hearing within a reasonable time by an independent and impartial tribunal established by law. Judgment shall be

pronounced publicly but the press and public may be excluded from all or part of the trial in the interests of morals, public order or national security in a democratic society, where the interests of juveniles or the protection of the private life of the parties so require, or to the extent strictly necessary in the opinion of the court in special circumstances where publicity would prejudice the interests of justice.

2   Everyone charged with a criminal offence shall be presumed innocent until proved guilty according to law.

3   Everyone charged with a criminal offence has the following minimum rights:

   a   to be informed promptly, in a language which he understands and in detail, of the nature and cause of the accusation against him;

   b   to have adequate time and facilities for the preparation of his defence;

   c   to defend himself in person or through legal assistance of his own choosing or, if he has not sufficient means to pay for legal assistance, to be given it free when the interests of justice so require;

   d   to examine or have examined witnesses against him and to obtain the attendance and examination of witnesses on his behalf under the same conditions as witnesses against him;

   e   to have the free assistance of an interpreter if he cannot understand or speak the language used in court.

Article 7 (no punishment without law)

1   No one shall be held guilty of any criminal offence on account of any act or omission which did not constitute a criminal offence under national or international law at the time when it was committed. Nor shall a heavier penalty be imposed than the one that was applicable at the time the criminal offence was committed.

2   This article shall not prejudice the trial and punishment of any person for any act or omission which, at the time when it was committed, was criminal according to the general principles of law recognised by civilised nations.

Article 8 (privacy and family life)

1   Everyone has the right to respect for his private and family life, his home and his correspondence.

2   There shall be no interference by a public authority with the exercise of this right except such as is in accordance with the law and is necessary in a democratic society in the interests of national security, public safety or the economic well-being of the country, for the prevention of disorder or crime, for the protection of health or morals, or for the protection of the rights and freedoms of others.

Article 9 (freedom of thought, conscience and religion)

1   Everyone has the right to freedom of thought, conscience and religion; this right includes freedom to change his religion or belief and freedom, either alone or in community with others and in public or private, to manifest his religion or belief, in worship, teaching, practice and observance.

2   Freedom to manifest one's religion or beliefs shall be subject only to such limitations as are prescribed by law and are necessary in a democratic society in the interests of public safety, for the protection of public order, health or morals, or for the protection of the rights and freedoms of others.

Article 10 (freedom of expression)

1   Everyone has the right to freedom of expression. This right shall include freedom to hold opinions and to receive and impart information and ideas without interference by public authority and regardless of frontiers. This article shall not prevent States from requiring the licensing of broadcasting, television or cinema enterprises.
2   The exercise of these freedoms, since it carries with it duties and responsibilities, may be subject to such formalities, conditions, restrictions or penalties as are prescribed by law and are necessary in a democratic society, in the interests of national security, territorial integrity or public safety, for the prevention of disorder or crime, for the protection of health or morals, for the protection of the reputation or rights of others, for preventing the disclosure of information received in confidence, or for maintaining the authority and impartiality of the judiciary.

Article 11 (freedom of assembly and association)

1   Everyone has the right to freedom of peaceful assembly and to freedom of association with others, including the right to form and to join trade unions for the protection of his interests.
2   No restrictions shall be placed on the exercise of these rights other than such as are prescribed by law and are necessary in a democratic society in the interests of national security or public safety, for the prevention of disorder or crime, for the protection of health or morals or for the protection of the rights and freedoms of others. This article shall not prevent the imposition of lawful restrictions on the exercise of these rights by members of the armed forces, of the police or of the administration of the State.

Article 12 (right to marry)

Men and women of marriageable age have the right to marry and to found a family, according to the national laws governing the exercise of this right.

Article 13 (right to an effective remedy)

Everyone whose rights and freedoms as set forth in this Convention are violated shall have an effective remedy before a national authority notwithstanding that the violation has been committed by persons acting in an official capacity.

Article 14 (prohibition of discrimination)

The enjoyment of the rights and freedoms set forth in this Convention shall be secured without discrimination on any ground such as sex, race, colour, language, religion, political or other opinion, national or social origin, association with a national minority, property, birth or other status.

Article 15 (derogation in time of national emergency)

1 In time of war or other public emergency threatening the life of the nation any High Contracting Party may take measures derogating from its obligations under this Convention to the extent strictly required by the exigencies of the situation, provided that such measures are not inconsistent with its other obligations under international law.

2 No derogation from Article 2, except in respect of deaths resulting from lawful acts of war, or from Articles 3, 4 (paragraph 1) and 7 shall be made under this provision.

3 Any High Contracting Party availing itself of this right of derogation shall keep the Secretary General of the Council of Europe fully informed of the measures which it has taken and the reasons therefor. It shall also inform the Secretary General of the Council of Europe when such measures have ceased to operate and the provisions of the Convention are again being fully executed.

Protocol No. 1 to the European Convention for the Protection of Human Rights and Fundamental Freedoms

Article 1 (Protection of property)

Every natural or legal person is entitled to the peaceful enjoyment of his possessions. No one shall be deprived of his possessions except in the public interest and subject to the conditions provided for by law and by the general principles of international law.

The preceding provisions shall not, however, in any way impair the right of a State to enforce such laws as it deems necessary to control the use of property in accordance with the general interest or to secure the payment of taxes or other contributions or penalties.

Appendix 2: Voting pattern of individual judges in cases discussed in Chapter 7

Chapter 7 discusses selected Strasbourg case law from a feminist perspective. As the text makes clear, the reasoning followed either by the Court or by individual judges in these cases often has nothing to do with feminist concerns. It would therefore be unwarranted to assume that there exists a direct connection between a vote of violation and a vote in favour of women, let alone a feminist vote. Nonetheless, with the exception of the *SW* and *Bowman* cases, which appear in intermediate grey shading in Table 4 below, a vote of violation ('V' in the table) is generally closer to a feminist position than a vote of non-violation ('NV'). 'I' stands for inadmissible. The four individual votes which appear in darkly shaded boxes are those quoted in Chapter 7 either especially approvingly (V) or disapprovingly (NV). In an earlier draft of the table, names of male judges appeared in blue, those of women in pink. This was with a nod to a well-entrenched tradition of dressing the two sexes in different colours and with the view of emphasizing that male judges should not be considered the norm and are no more neutral than women judges. Reluctantly, but with consideration to publication costs, the names of female judges are now simply followed by an (F); corresponding (M)s have been omitted so as not to overburden the table. The table omits two cases discussed at some length in the text: *Karaduman*, declared inadmissible by the Commission, and *Dahlab*, declared inadmissible by the Court by an undisclosed majority.

Table 4. *Voting pattern of judges*

Judges \ Cases	Airey (1979)	XY (1985)	ABC (1985)	Open Door (1992)	Burghartz (1994)	Buckley (1996)	Stubbings (1996)	SW (1996)	Aydin (1997)	Bowman (1998)	Chapman (2001)	Halimi (2001)	Tokarczyk (2002)	Odièvre (2003)
Baka				NV	V				V	NV	NV			
Bernhardt		V	V	V		NV	NV		V	V				
Bigi				NV				NV						
Blayney				NV										
Bonello											V		I	V
Botoucharova (F)											NV		I	NV
Bratza														V
Butkevych											NV			
Cabral Barreto														V
Casadevall									V	V				
Costa											NV	I		NV
Cremona			V	NV										
De Meyer				V					NV	NV				
Evans		V	V											
Evrigenis	V		V											
Fischbach											V			
Foighel				V			V							
Freeland				V		NV	NV	NV	V	NV				
Ganshof vdM	V		V											
Garlicki														NV
Gersing		V	V											
Gölcüklü	V		V	V	V			NV	NV	NV				
Jambrek								NV		NV				
Jungwiert						NV			V			I		NV
Gotchev								NV	V					
Greve (F)											NV	I		NV
Kuris									V		NV	I		NV
Levits										NV			I	
Liesch	V													
Loizou				V		NV			V	NV				
Löhmus						V		NV		V				
Lopes Rocha				NV						NV				
Lorenzen											V		I	
Loucaides												I		V
Macdonald				V			V			V				
Makarczyk							NV		NV				I	
Martens				V				NV						
Matscher			V	NV						NV				
Morenilla				V	V	NV	NV							
O'Donoghue	NV													
Palm (F)				V					V	V				
PastorRidruego											V			
Pavlovschi														NV
Pekkanen				V			NV		V					
Pellonpää														V
Pettiti			V	NV	NV	V				NV	V			
Repik						V		NV						
Ress														NV
Rozakis													I	NV
Russo		V	V	NV	NV				V	V				
Ryssdal	V	V	V	V				NV	V					
Schiel											NV			
Schiemann											NV			
Spielmann				V						V				
Stráznická (F)											V			
Tulkens (F)											V	I	I	V
Türmen											NV			
Ugrekhelidze											NV	I		NV
Valticos				V	NV			NV	V	NV				
Van Dijk										V				
Vilhjálmsson	NV		V	V	NV	NV			V	V	NV			
Walsh		V	V						V	V				
Wiarda	V	V	V											
Wildhaber					V				V	V	NV			V

Select Bibliography

Aldana-Pindell, Raquel. 'An emerging universality of justiciable victims' rights in the criminal process to curtail impunity for state-sponsored crimes' (2004) 26 *Human Rights Quarterly* 605–86

Allison, Lincoln. 'The utilitarian ethics of punishment and torture', in Lincoln Allison (ed.), *The Utilitarian Response: The Contemporary Viability of Utilitarian Political Philosophy* (London: Sage, 1990) 9–29

Allison, Lincoln (ed.). *The Utilitarian Response: The Contemporary Viability of Utilitarian Political Philosophy* (London: Sage, 1990)

Allott, Philip. *Eunomia: New Order for a New World* (Oxford: Oxford University Press, 2001)

Aral, Berdal. 'The idea of human rights as perceived in the Ottoman Empire' (2004) 26 *Human Rights Quarterly* 454–82

Arold, Nina-Louisa. 'Do germ-cells of a global human rights culture exist? A case study of the inner legal culture of the European Court of Human Rights', Thesis submitted to the Stanford Program in International Legal Studies at the Stanford Law School, Stanford University, in partial fulfilment of the requirements for the degree of Master of the Science of Law (May 2001), 96 pp

Asad, Talal. 'What do human rights do? An anthropological enquiry' (2000) 4 *Theory and Event*, 27 pp

Baer, Susanne. 'Citizenship in Europe and the construction of gender by law in the European Charter of Fundamental Rights', in Karen Knop (ed.), *Gender and Human Rights* (Oxford: Oxford University Press, 2004) 83–112

Balibar, Etienne. *Masses, Classes, Ideas: Studies on Politics and Philosophy Before and After Marx*, transl. by James Swenson (New York: Routledge, 1994)

Barnett, Hilaire. *Introduction to Feminist Jurisprudence* (London: Cavendish, 1998)

Barry, Norman P. *An Introduction to Modern Political Theory* (London: Macmillan, 1981)

Baxi, Upendra. 'Voices of suffering and the future of human rights' (1998) 8 *Transnational Law and Contemporary Problems* 125–70

The Future of Human Rights (New Delhi: Oxford University Press, 2002)

Beernaert, Marie-Aude. 'Protocol 14 and new Strasbourg procedures: Towards greater efficiency? And at what price?' (2004) *European Human Rights Law Review* 544–57

Bell, Daniel A. and Joseph H. Carens. 'The ethical dilemmas of international human rights and humanitarian NGOs: Reflections on a dialogue between practitioners and theorists' (2004) 26 *Human Rights Quarterly* 300–29

Bentham, Jeremy. 'Anarchical Fallacies. An examination of the Declaration of the Rights of the Man and the Citizen decreed by the Constituent Assembly in France', in Jeremy Bentham, *Selected Writings on Utilitarianism*, with an introduction by Ross Harrisson (Ware, Hertfordshire: Wordsworth, 2000) 381–459

Bielefeldt, Heiner. 'Muslim voices in the human rights debate' (1995) 17 *Human Rights Quarterly* 587–617

Bloch, Ernest. *Natural Law and Human Dignity* (Cambridge, Mass.: MIT Press, 1986)

Booth, Ken. 'Three tyrannies', in Tim Dunne and Nicholas J. Wheeler (eds.), *Human Rights in Global Politics* (Cambridge: Cambridge University Press, 1999) 31–70

Booth, Ken and Tim Dunne. 'Learning beyond frontiers', in Tim Dunne and Nicholas J. Wheeler (eds.), *Human Rights in Global Politics* (Cambridge: Cambridge University Press, 1999) 303–28

Brems, Eva. 'The margin of appreciation in the case-law of the European Court of Human Rights' (1996) *Zeitschrift für ausländisches öffentliches Recht und Völkerrecht* 240–314

'Enemies or allies: Feminism and cultural relativism as dissident voices in human rights discourse' (1997) 19 *Human Rights Quarterly* 136–64

Bridgeman, Jo and Susan Millns, *Feminist Perspectives on Law: Law's Engagement with the Female Body* (London: Sweet and Maxwell, 1998)

Brown, Chris. 'Cultural diversity and international political theory: From the requirement to "Mutual Respect"?' (2000) 26 *Review of International Studies* 199–213

Brown, Wendy. 'Rights and identity in late modernity: Revisiting the "Jewish Question"', in Austin Sarat and Thomas R. Kearns (eds.), *Identities, Politics and Rights* (Ann Arbor: University of Michigan Press, 1997) 85–130

'"The most we can hope for . . .": Human rights and the politics of fatalism' (2004) 103 *South Atlantic Quarterly* 451–63

Bruinsma, Fred J. and Matthijs de Blois, 'Rules of law from Westport to Wladiwostok: Separate opinions in the European Court of Human Rights' (1997) 15 *Netherlands Quarterly of Human Rights* 175–86

Carens, Joseph. 'Realistic and idealistic approaches to migration' (1996) 30 *International Migration Review* 156–69

Carr, E. H. *The Twenty Years' Crisis, 1919–1939: An Introduction to the Study of International Relations*, with a new introduction by Michael Cox (Basingstoke: Palgrave, 2001)

Cerna, Christina M. 'Universality of human rights and cultural diversity: Implementation of human rights in different socio-cultural contexts' (1994) 16 *Human Rights Quarterly* 740–52

Clayton, Richard and Hugh Tomlinson. *The Law of Human Rights* (Oxford: Oxford University Press, 2000)

Cole, Daniel H. '"An unqualified human good": E. P. Thompson and the Rule of Law' (2001) 28 *Journal of Law and Society* 177–203

Concise Routledge Encyclopedia of Philosophy (London: Routledge, 2000)

Cowan, Jane K. 'Ambiguities of an emancipatory discourse: The making of a Macedonian minority in Greece', in Jane K. Cowan, Marie-Bénédicte Dembour and Richard A. Wilson (eds.), *Culture and Rights: Anthropological Perspectives* (Cambridge: Cambridge University Press, 2001) 152–76

Cowan, Jane K., Marie-Bénédicte Dembour and Richard A. Wilson (eds.), *Culture and Rights: Anthropological Perspectives* (Cambridge: Cambridge University Press, 2001)

Cranston, Maurice. *What are Human Rights?* (New York: Basic Books, 1962)

de Gouges, Olympe. 'Declaration of the Rights of Woman', in Micheline R. Ishay (ed.), *The Human Rights Reader: Major Political Writings, Essays, Speeches and Documents. Fom the Bible to the Present* (New York: Routledge, 1997) 140–7

Delmas-Marty, Mireille. 'Pluralisme et traditions nationales (Revendication des droits individuels)', in Paul Tavernier (ed.), *Quelle Europe pour les droits de l'homme?* (Brussels: Bruylant, 1996) 81–92

Delmas-Marty, Mireille (ed.). *The European Convention for the Protection of Human Rights: International Protection Versus National Restrictions* (Dordrecht: Nijhoff, 1992)

Dembour, Marie-Bénédicte. 'Human rights talk and anthropological ambivalence: The particular contexts of universal claims', in Olivia Harris (ed.), *Inside and Outside the Law: Anthropological Studies of Authority and Ambiguity* (London: Routledge, 1996) 19–40

'Following the movement of a pendulum: Between universalism and relativism', in Jane K. Cowan, Marie-Bénédicte Dembour and Richard A. Wilson (eds.), *Culture and Rights: Anthropological Perspectives* (Cambridge: Cambridge University Press, 2001) 56–79

'"Finishing off" cases: The radical solution to the problem of the expanding ECtHR Caseload' (2002) *European Human Rights Law Review* 604–23

'Human rights law and national sovereignty in collusion: The plight of quasi-nationals at Strasbourg' (2003) 21 *Netherlands Quarterly of Human Rights* 63–98

'Diversity or commonality: The power to toss the human rights coin' (2005) *Mediterranean Journal of Human Rights* 65–91

Dembour, Marie-Bénédicte and Magda Krzyżanowska-Mierzewska. 'Ten years on: The voluminous and interesting Polish case law' (2004) *European Human Rights Law Review* 517–43

Donnelly, Jack. *Universal Human Rights in Theory and Practice* (1st edn, Ithaca: Cornell University Press, 1989)

Universal Human Rights in Theory and Practice (2nd edn, Ithaca: Cornell University Press, 2003)

Douzinas, Costas. *The End of Human Rights: Critical Legal Thought at the Turn of the Century* (Oxford: Hart, 2000)

Drakopoulou, Maria. 'The ethic of care, female subjectivity and feminist legal scholarship' (2000) 8 *Feminist Legal Studies* 199–226

Dunne, Tim and Brian C. Schmidt. 'Realism', in John Baylis and Steve Smith (eds.), *The Globalization of World Politics: An Introduction to International Relations* (Oxford: Oxford University Press, 2001) 141–61

Dunne, Tim and Nicholas J. Wheeler. (eds.), *Human Rights in Global Politics* (Cambridge: Cambridge University Press, 1999)

Dworkin, Ronald. *Taking Rights Seriously* (London: Duckworth, 1978)

'Rights as trumps', in Jeremy Waldron (ed.), *Theories of Rights* (Oxford: Oxford University Press, 1984) 152–67

Engle, Karen. 'From skepticism to embrace: Human rights and the American Anthropological Association from 1947–1999' (2001) 23 *Human Rights Quarterly* 536–59

Evans, Carolyn. *Freedom of Religion under the European Convention on Human Rights* (Oxford: Oxford University Press, 2001)

Evans, Tony. 'Disciplining global society: Human rights as power and knowledge' (2005) 27 *Human Rights Quarterly* 1046–68

Fagan, Andrew. 'Paradoxical bedfellows: Nihilism and Human rights' (2005) 6 *Human Rights Review* 80–101

Fine, Robert. *Democracy and the Rule of Law: Marx's Critique of the Legal Form* (2nd edn, Caldwell, New Jersey: Blackburn Press, 2002)

Fitzpatrick, Peter. 'Racism and the innocence of law' (1987) 14 *Journal of Law and Society* 119–32

Flauss, Jean-François. 'Radioscopie de l'élection de la nouvelle Cour européenne des droits de l'homme' (1998) *Revue trimestrielle des droits de l'homme* 435–64

'Brèves observations sur le second renouvellement triennal de la Cour européenne des droits de l'homme' (2005) *Revue trimestrielle des droits de l'homme* 5–32

Fordham, Michael and Thomas de la Mare. 'Identifying the principles of proportionality', in Jeffrey Jowell and Jonathan Cooper (eds.), *Understanding Human Rights Principles* (Oxford: Hart, 2001) 27–90

Forsythe, David. *Human Rights in International Relations* (Cambridge: Cambridge University Press, 2000)

Freeman, Michael. 'Human rights and real cultures: Towards a dialogue on "Asian Values"' (1998) 16 *Netherlands Quarterly of Human Rights* 25–39

Human Rights: An Interdisciplinary Approach (Cambridge: Polity, 2002)

'The problem of secularism in human rights theory' (2004) 26 *Human Rights Quarterly* 375–400

Fromm, Erik. *Marx's Concept of Man* (New York: Ungar, 1961)

Gearty, Conor. 'The European Court of Human Rights and the protection of civil liberties: An overview' (1993) 52 *Cambridge Law Journal* 89–127

'Democracy and human rights in the European Court of Human Rights: A critical appraisal' (2000) 51 *Northern Ireland Legal Quarterly* 381–96

'Civil Liberties and Human Rights', in Nicholas Bamforth and Peter Leyland (eds.), *Public Law in a Multi-Layered Constitution* (Oxford: Hart, 2003) 371–90

Principles of Human Rights Adjudication (Oxford: Oxford University Press, 2004)

Gearty, Conor and Adam Tomkins (eds.). *Understanding Human Rights* (London: Pinter, 1996)

Geertz, Clifford. 'Anti anti-relativism' (1984) 86 *American Anthropologist* 263–78

Gewirth, Alan. 'The basis and content of human rights', in Pennock and Chapman (eds.), *Human Rights* (New York: New York University Press, 1981) 119–47

Gibbard, Allan. 'Utilitarianism and human rights', in Ellen Frankel Paul, Fred D. Miller Jr. and Jeffrey Paul (eds.), *Human Rights* (Oxford: Blackwell, 1984) 92–102

Gilligan, Carol. *In a Different Voice: Psychologist Theory and Women's Development* (Cambridge, Mass.: Harvard University Press, 1982)

Glover, Jonathan. *Causing Death and Saving Lives* (London: Penguin, 1990)

Goldston, James A. 'Race discrimination in Europe: Problems and prospects' (1999) *European Human Rights Law Review* 462–83

Goudsblom, Johan. *Nihilism and Culture* (Oxford: Blackwell, 1980)

Greer, Steven. 'Constitutionalizing adjudication under the European Convention on Human Rights' (2003) 23 *Oxford Journal of Legal Studies* 405–33, at 416

Griffin, James. *Well-Being. Its Meaning, Measurement, and Moral Importance* (Oxford: Clarendon Press, 1986)

Gross, Oren and Fionnuala Ní Aoláin.'From discretion to scrutiny: Revisiting the application of the margin of appreciation doctrine in the context of Article 15 of the European Convention on Human Rights' (2001) 23 *Human Rights Quarterly* 625–49

Gutman, Amy and Dennis Thompson.*Democracy and Disagreement* (Cambridge, Mass.: Harvard University Press, 1996)

Haarscher, Guy. *Philosophie des droits de l'homme* (4th edn, Brussels: Editions de l'Université Libre de Bruxelles, 1993)

Hale, Rt. Hon. Dame Brenda. 'Equality and the judiciary: Why should we want more women judges?' (2001) *Public Law* 489–504

Halley, Janet. 'Take a break from feminism?', in Karen Knop (ed.), *Gender and Human Rights* (Oxford: Oxford University Press, 2004) 57–81

Harris, D. J., M. O'Boyle and C. Warbrick. *Law of the European Convention on Human Rights* (London: Butterworths, 1995)

Hastrup, Kirsten. 'Representing the common good: The limits of legal language', in Richard Ashby Wilson and Jon P. Mitchell (eds.), *Human Rights in Global Perspective: Anthropological Studies of Rights, Claims and Entitlements* (London: Routledge, 2003) 16–32

Hatch, Elvin. *Culture and Morality: The Relativity of Values in Anthropology* (New York: Columbia University Press, 1983)

'The Good Side of Relativism' (1997) 53 *Journal of Anthropological Research* 371–81

Häyri, Matti. *Liberal Utilitarianism and Applied Ethics* (London: Routledge, 1994)

Henkin, Louis. *The Age of Rights* (New York: Columbia University Press, 1990)

[Herskovits, Melville]. 'Statement on human rights', (1947) 49 *American Anthropologist* 539–43

Herskovits, Melville. *Cultural Relativism: Perspectives in Cultural Pluralism* (New York: Random House, 1972)

Higgins, Tracy. 'Anti-essentialism, relativism and human rights' (1996) 19 *Harvard Women's Law Journal* 89

High, Dallas M. *Language, Persons and Belief: Studies in Wittgenstein's Philosophical Investigations and Religious Uses of Language* (New York: Oxford University Press, 1967)

Ignatieff, Michael. *Human Rights as Politics and Idolatry* (Princeton: Princeton University Press, 2001)

Imbert, Pierre-Henri. 'L'utilisation des droits de l'homme dans les relations internationales', in Société française pour le droit international, *La protection des droits de l'homme et l'évolution du droit international* (Paris: Pedone, 1998) 282–5

Ishay, Micheline R. (ed.). *The Human Rights Reader: Major Political Writings, Essays, Speeches and Documents. Fom the Bible to the Present* (New York: Routledge, 1997)

Jackson, Robert and Georg Sørensen. *Introduction to International Relations* (Oxford: Oxford University Press, 1999)

Janis, Mark, Richard Kay and Anthony Bradley. *European Human Rights Law: Text and Materials* (2nd edn, Oxford: Oxford University Press, 2000)

Jordan, Mark. *Doing the Rights Thing: The Not So Difficult Guide to the Human Rights Act 1988 and the Law of the European Convention on Human Rights* (EOS Education, 2001)

Karagiannis, Syméon. 'Le territoire d'application de la Convention européenne des droits de l'homme. *Vaetera et nova*' (2005) 61 *Revue trimestrielle des droits de l'homme* 33–120

Kennedy, David. 'The international human rights movement: Part of the Problem?' (2001) *European Human Rights Law Review* 245–67

Knop, Karen. 'Introduction', in Karen Knop (ed.), *Gender and Human Rights* (Oxford: Oxford University Press, 2004) 1–12

Knop, Karen (ed.). *Gender and Human Rights* (Oxford: Oxford University Press, 2004)

Koskenniemi, Martti. 'The effect of rights on political culture', in Philip Alston (ed.), *The EU and Human Rights* (Oxford: Oxford University Press, 1999) 99–116

Lacey, Nicola. *Unspeakable Subjects: Feminist Essays in Legal and Social Theory* (Oxford: Hart, 1998)

Leach, Philip. *Taking a Case to the European Court of Human Rights* (2nd edn, Oxford: Oxford University Press, 2004)

Lefort, Claude. *L'invention démocratique: Les limites de la domination totalitaire* (Paris: Fayard, 1981)

   'Politics and human rights', in Claude Lefort, *The Political Forms of Modern Society: Bureaucracy, Democracy, Totalitarianism*, ed. and introd. by John B. Thompson (Cambridge, Mass.: MIT Press, 1986) 239–72

Lester of Herne Hill, Lord. 'Universality versus subsidiarity: A reply' (1998) *European Human Rights Law Review* 73–81

Lindholm, Tore. 'The plurality of normative traditions and the need for cross-cultural legitimacy of universal human rights' (1998) 1 *Human Rights: Universal or Cultural Specific. North-South Coalition Information Bulletin* 10–46

Lochak, Danièle. *Les droits de l'homme* (Paris: La Découverte, 2002)

Luban, David. 'Eight fallacies about liberty and security', in Richard A. Wilson (ed.), *Human Rights in the 'War on Terror'* (Cambridge: Cambridge University Press, 2005) 242–57

McColgan, Aileen. *Women under the Law: The False Promise of Human Rights* (Harlow: Longman, 2000)

McHarg, Aileen. 'Reconciling human rights and the public interest: Conceptual problems and doctrinal uncertainty in the jurisprudence of the European Court of Human Rights' (1999) 62 *Modern Law Review* 671–96

MacIntyre, Alasdair. *After Virtue* (London: Duckworth, 1985)

Mackay of Clashfern, Lord. 'The margin of appreciation and the need for balance', in Paul Mahoney, Franz Matscher, Herbert Petzold and Luzius Wildhaber (eds.), *Protection des droits de l'homme: La perspective européenne/Protecting Human Rights: The European Perspective. Mélanges à la mémoire de/Studies in memory of Rolv Ryssdal* (Köln : Carl Heymans Verlag, 2000) 837–43

MacKinnon, Catharine. *Feminism Unmodified: Discourses on Life and Law* (Cambridge, Mass.: Harvard University Press, 1987)

'Crimes of War, Crimes of Peace', in Stephen Shute and Susan Hurley (eds.), *On Human Rights: Amnesty International Lectures* (New York: Basic Books, 1993) 83–109

McLellan, David. *Marx Before Marxism* (London: Macmillan, 1980)

Karl Marx: Selected Writings (2nd edn, Oxford: Oxford University Press, 2000)

Mahoney, Paul. 'Universality versus subsdiarity in the Strasbourg case law on free speech: Explaining some recent judgments' (1997) *European Human Rights Law Review* 364–79

Mahoney, Paul, Franz Matscher, Herbert Petzold and Luzius Wildhaber (eds.). *Protection des droits de l'homme: La perspective européenne/Protecting Human Rights: The European Perspective. Mélanges à la mémoire de/Studies in memory of Rolv Ryssdal* (Köln: Carl Heymanns Verlag, 2000)

Maier-Katkin, Birgit and Daniel Maier-Katkin. 'At the heart of darkness: Crimes against humanity and the banality of evil' (2004) 26 *Human Rights Quarterly* 584–604

Marks, Stephen P. 'From the "Single Confused Page" to the "Decalogue for Six Billion Persons": The roots of the Universal Declaration of Human Rights in the French Revolution' (1998) 20 *Human Rights Quarterly* 459–514

Marks, Susan. 'Civil liberties at the margin: The UK derogation and the European Court of Human Rights' (1995) 15 *Oxford Journal of Legal Studies* 69–95

Marx, Karl. 'On the Jewish Question', in David McLellan (ed.), *Karl Marx: Selected Writings* (2nd edn, Oxford: Oxford University Press, 2000) 46–64

Meckled-Garcia, Saladin and Basak Cali (eds.). *Legalisation of Human Rights: Multidisciplinary Perspectives* (London: Routledge, 2005)

Mitchell, Wesley C. 'Bentham's Felicific Calculus', in Bhikhu Parekh (ed.), *Jeremy Bentham: Ten Critical Essays* (London: Frank Cass, 1974) 168–86

Morris, Dan. 'Assisted suicide under the European Convention on Human Rights: a critique' (2003) *European Human Rights Law Review* 65–91

Morvai, Krisztina. 'The construction of the Other in European human rights enterprise: A narrative about democracy, human rights, the rule of law and my neighbour Uncle Blaze', in Peter Fitzpatrick and James Henry Bergeron (eds.), *Europe's Other:*

European Law Between Modernity and Postmodernity (Dartmouth: Ashgate, 1998) 245–51

Mowbray, Alastair. *Cases and Materials on the European Convention on Human Rights* (London: Butterworths, 2001)

Mullaly, Siobhán. 'Debating reproductive rights in Ireland' (2005) 27 *Human Rights Quarterly* 78–104

Munro, Vanessa E. 'Legal feminism and Foucault – A critique of the Expulsion of Law' (2001) *Journal of Law and Society* 546–67

Mutua, Makau. *Human Rights: A Political and Cultural Critique* (Philadelphia: University of Pennsylvania Press, 2000)

Nagel, Thomas. 'War and Massacre', in Samuel Scheffler (ed.), *Consequentialism and its Critics* (Oxford: Oxford University Press, 1988) 51–73

Nietzsche, Friedrich. *The Will to Power*, transl. by Walter Kaufmann and R. J. Hollingdale (London: Weidenfeld and Nicolson, 1967)

Nowell-Smith, P. H. 'Cultural relativism' (1971) 1 *Philosophy of the Social Sciences* 1–17

Nowlin, Christopher. 'The protection of morals under the European Convention for the Protection of Human Rights and Fundamental Freedoms' (2002) 24 *Human Rights Quarterly* 264–86

Olsen, Frances. 'Children's rights: Some feminist approaches to the United Nations Convention on the Rights of the Child', in Philip Alston, Stephen Parker and John Seymour (eds.), *Children, Rights and the Law* (Oxford: Clarendon, 1992) 192–220

Orakhelashvili, Alexander. 'Restrictive interpretation of human rights treaties in the recent jurisprudence of the European Court of Human Rights' (2003) *European Journal of International Law* 529–68

Ovey, Clare and Robin C. A. White. *Jacobs and White: European Convention on Human Rights* (Oxford: Oxford University Press, 2002)

'Critical perspectives on women's rights: The European Convention on Human Rights and Fundamental Freedoms', in Ann Bottomley (ed.), *Feminist Perspectives on the Foundational Subjects of Law* (London: Cavendish, 1996) 223–42

Palmer, Stephanie. 'Feminism and the promise of human rights: Possibilities and paradoxes', in Susan James and Stephanie Palmer (eds.), *Visible Women: Essays on Feminist Legal Theory and Political Philosophy* (Oxford: Hart, 2002) 91–115

Panikkar, R. 'Is the notion of human rights a Western concept?', (1982) 120 *Diogenes* 75–102

Perry, Michael J. *The Idea of Human Rights: Four Inquiries* (Oxford: Oxford University Press, 1998)

Pettiti, Louis-Edmond, Emmanuel Decaux and Pierre-Henri Imbert (eds). *La Convention européenne des droits de l'homme: Commentaire article par article* (2nd edn, Paris: Economica, 1999)

Picheral, Caroline. 'Discrimination raciale et Convention européenne des droits de l'homme (L'apport de la jurisprudence)' (2001) 46 *Revue trimestrielle des droits de l'homme* 517–39

Pollis, Adamantia. 'Cultural relativism revisited: Through a state prism' (1996) 18 *Human Rights Quarterly* 316–44

Prebensen, Søren C. 'Inter-state complaints under treaty provisions – The experience under the European Convention on Human Rights' (1999) 20 *Human Rights Law Journal* 446–55

Rackley, Erika. 'Representations of the (woman) judge: Hercules, the little mermaid and the vain and naked Emperor' (2002) 22 *Legal Studies* 602–24

Rajagopal, Balakrishnan. *International Law from Below: Development, Social Movements and Third World Resistance* (Cambridge: Cambridge University Press, 2003)

Rawls, John. 'Classical utilitarianism', in Samuel Scheffler (ed.), *Consequentialism and its Critics* (Oxford: Oxford University Press, 1988) 14–119

Reid, Karen. *A Practitioner's Guide to the European Convention on Human Rights* (2nd edn, London: Sweet and Maxwell, 2004)

Renteln, Alison. 'Relativism and the search for human rights' (1988) 90 *American Anthropologist* 56–72

Rorty, Richard. 'Human rights, rationality, and sentimentality', in Stephen Shute and Susan Hurley (eds.), *On Human Rights: The Oxford Amnesty International Lectures 1993* (New York: Basic Books, 1993) 111–34

Rosen, Michael. 'Karl Marx (1818–83)' *Concise Routledge Encyclopedia of Philosophy* (London: Routledge, 2000) 528–9

Rosenberg, Dominique. 'Enfin . . . le juge européen sanctionne les violations du principe de non-discrimination raciale en relation avec le droit à la vie (Arrêt *Nachova et autres c. Bulgarie* du 26 février 2004)' (2005) 61 *Revue trimestrielle des droits de l'homme* 171–201

Sandland, Ralph. 'Between "Truth" and "Difference": Poststructuralism, law and the power of feminism' (1995) 3 *Feminist Legal Studies* 3–47

Saul, Jennifer Mather. *Feminism: Issues and Arguments* (Oxford: Oxford University Press, 2003)

Scheffler, Samuel. 'Introduction', in Samuel Scheffler (ed.), *Consequentialism and its Critics* (Oxford: Oxford University Press, 1988) 1–13

Scheffler, Samuel (ed.) *Consequentialism and its Critics.* (Oxford: Oxford University Press, 1988)

Simpson, A. W. Brian. *Human Rights and the End of Empire: Britain and the Genesis of the European Convention* (Oxford: Oxford University Press, 2001)

Smart, Carol. *Feminism and the Power of Law* (London: Routledge, 1989)

Smith, Rhona K. M. and Christien van den Anker (eds.). *The Essentials of Human Rights* (London: Hodder Arnold, 2005)

Stammers, Neil. 'A critique of social approaches to human rights' (1995) 17 *Human Rights Quarterly* 488–508

'Social movements and the social construction of human rights' (1999) 21 *Human Rights Quarterly* 980–1008

'The emergence of human rights in the North: Towards historical re-evaluation', in N. Kabeer (ed.), *Inclusive Citizenship: Meanings and Expressions* (London: Zed Books, 2005) 50–68

'Social movements and human rights', in Rhona K. M. Smith and Christien van den Anker (eds.), *The Essentials of Human Rights* (London: Hodder Arnold, 2005) 321–4

Steiner, Henry J. and Philip Alston. *International Human Rights in Context: Law, Politics, Morals* (2nd edn, Oxford: Oxford University Press, 2000)

Sutch, Peter. 'Global civil society and international ethics: Mervyn Frost's restatement of constitutive theory' (2000) *Review of International Studies* 485–9

Taylor, Charles. 'The politics of recognition', in Amy Gutmann (ed.), *Multiculturalism: Examining the Politics of Recognition* (Princeton: Princeton University Press, 1994) 25–74

Thompson, E. P. *Whigs and Hunters: The Origins of the Black Act* (London: Allen Lane, 1975)

Tigroudja, Hélène. 'L'inapplicabilité de l'article 6, 1 de la Convention à la procédure de relèvement d'une interdiction du territoire' (2002) 50 *Revue trimestrielle des droits de l'homme* 433–62

Tulkens, Françoise. 'Droits des hommes, droits des femmes', Lecture notes of 31 March 2000, ms.

Twining, William. 'The contemporary significance of Bentham's *Anarchical Fallacies*' (1975) XLI *Archiv fur Rechts- und Sozialphilosophie* 315

Uniacke, Suzanne. 'Double effect, principle of' in *Concise Routledge Encyclopedia of Philosophy* (London: Routledge, 2000) 216

Van Dijk, P. and G. J. H. van Hoof. *Theory and Practice of the European Convention on Human Rights* (2nd edn, The Hague: Kluwer, 1998)

Van Drooghenbroeck, Sébastien. *La proportionnalité dans le droit de la Convention européenne des droits de l'homme. Prendre l'idée simple au sérieux* (Bruxelles: Bruylant, 2001)

Vincent, R. J. *Human Rights and International Relations* (Cambridge: Cambridge University Press,1986)

Wadham, John. 'What price the right of individual petition? Report of the Evaluation Group to the Committee of Ministers on the European Court of Human Rights' 7 (2002) *European Human Rights Law Review* 169–74

Waldron, Jeremy (ed.). *Theories of Rights* (Oxford: Oxford University Press, 1984)

Walker, David M. *Marx, Methodology and Science: Marx's Science of Politics* (Aldershot: Ashgate, 2001)

White, Alan. *Within Nietzsche's Labyrinth* (New York: Routledge, 1990)

White, Robin. 'Tackling political disputes through individual applications' (1998) 3 *European Human Rights Law Review* 61–74

Whitty, Noel, Thérèse Murphy and Stephen Livingstone. *Civil Liberties Law: The Human Rights Act Era* (London: Butterworths, 2001)

Wiesel, Elie. 'A tribute to human rights', in Yael Danieli, Elsa Stamatopoulou and Clarence Dias (eds.), *The Universal Declaration of Human Rights: Fifty Years and Beyond* (Amityville, N.Y.: Baywood, 1999)

Wilson, Richard A. *The Politics of Truth and Reconciliation in South Africa: Legitimizing the Post-Apartheid State* (Cambridge: Cambridge University Press, 2001)

Wilson, Richard A. (ed.). *Human Rights in the 'War on Terror'* (Cambridge: Cambridge University Press, 2005)

Wilson, Richard Ashby and Jon P. Mitchell (eds.). *Human Rights in Global Perspective: Anthropological Studies of Rights, Claims and Entitlements* (London: Routledge, 2003)

Wittgenstein, Ludwig. *Philosophical Investigations*, tr. G. E. M. Anscombe (Oxford: Basil Blackwell, 1958)

Wolcher, Louis E. 'A meditation on Wittgenstein's Lecture on Ethics' (1998) 9 *Law and Critique* 3–35

Index